QUANTUM GLORY

THE SCIENCE OF HEAVEN INVADING EARTH

PHIL MASON

Quantum Glory: The Science of Heaven Invading Earth
© 2010 by Phil Mason. All rights reserved.

Unless otherwise identified, all Scripture citations are from the NEW KING JAMES VERSION © 1982 Thomas Nelson Inc. Used by permission.

Scripture quotations identified as (KJV) are taken from the Holy Bible, King James Version Public Domain.

Scripture quotations marked (NIV) are taken from the Holy Bible, New International Version®, NIV®. Copyright © 1973, 1978, 1984 by Biblica, Inc.™ Used by permission of Zondervan. All rights reserved worldwide. www.zondervan.com

Scripture quotations marked (NLT) are taken from the Holy Bible, New Living Translation, copyright 1996. Used by permission of Tyndale House Publishers, Inc., Wheaton, Illinois 60189. All rights reserved.

Scripture quotations marked (NASB) taken from the New American Standard Bible®, Copyright © 1960, 1962, 1963, 1968, 1971, 1972, 1973, 1975, 1977, 1995 by The Lockman Foundation. Used by permission. www.Lockman.org

Scripture quotations marked (AMP) are taken from the Amplified® Bible, Copyright © 1954, 1958, 1962, 1964, 1965, 1987 by The Lockman Foundation Used by permission. www.Lockman.org

Scripture quotations identified (Moffatt) are from *The New Testament: A New Translation*, copyright © 1964 by James Moffatt, published by Harper & Row, Inc. Used by permission.

Scripture quotations identified (J.B. Phillips) are from *The New Testament in Modern English*, translated by J.B. Phillips. © J.B. Phillips, 1958, 1960, 1972. Used by permission of Macmillan Publishing Co., Inc.

Scripture quotations identified as (MSG): Peterson, Eugene H. *The Message: The Bible in Contemporary Language*. Colorado Springs: NavPress, 2002. Used by permission. www.biblegateway.com

All emphasis in Scripture quotations is the author's.

Cover Design: Artwork by Rosie Moulton. Dust and Helix Nebula image from NASA Planetary Photo Journal Collection. Courtesy NASA/JPL-Caltech/University of Arizona. Produced by California Institute of Technology. Used by Permission. www.nasaimages.org

©New Earth Tribe Publications [Copyright]

U.S.A. Edition - (Authorized by author Phil Mason)
Published by XP Publishing, a department of XP Ministries
PO Box 1017, Maricopa, AZ 85139
XPpublishing.com

ISBN: 978-1-936101-59-7

ENDORSEMENTS

We are in the midst of a worldwide move of God with signs and wonders breaking out all over the world. In *Quantum Glory*, Phil Mason combines his passion for the science of quantum physics with his personal wealth of experience in supernatural ministry and sound biblical theology. The result is an explosive mix of revelation that has the potential to powerfully envision and activate you to alter the very fabric of the physical world around you through the healing ministry of Christ. This book fills a vital gap in the literature that is emerging in this present wave of revival.

DR. CHE AHN
President, Harvest International Ministry
International Chancellor, Wagner Leadership Institute

Phil Mason is one of the most exciting thinkers, speakers and trainers in the area of Christian spirituality with regard to the New Age movement and the new sciences. Only someone steeped in the Spirit of God could write about something so complex and make it seem thoroughly natural, normal, and readable.

God is still creating ways for His people to respond to His overtures. All creation speaks of Him, and the language and principles of quantum physics are a vital part of His heavenly discourse with humanity. From quantum non-locality through sound waves, string theory, the mathematical order of nature, quantum geometry and the golden ratio, to the alignment between quantum physics and the supernatural, the glory of God, and the key to miracles, you will understand more about the radiant nature of God in this book than in any other tome that is specifically non-specific. I heartily recommend Phil Mason to you as a leader in the field of modern day spirituality, the new sciences and the supernatural gospel of the Lord Jesus Christ.

GRAHAM COOKE
Author, Speaker and Owner of BrilliantBookHouse.com

Phil's book stirs me every time I pick it up. It should leave us all thinking, "How great is our God and Creator!" Genesis 1:31 says; "Then God saw everything that He had made, and indeed it was very good." There is a world that we can't even see with our eyes but it holds together the world we can see. *Quantum Glory* will bring us to realize that all things move and breathe and have their being in God's glory. This book should make us marvel at the amazing God we love and serve!

PASTOR BENI JOHNSON
Bethel Church, Redding, California
Author of *The Happy Intercessor*

Phil Mason is a gifted communicator with a passion for the miraculous presence of God. *Quantum Glory* dives deep into the wonders and weirdness of quantum tunnelling, quantum superposition and endless waves of energy. It takes you on a journey *through the looking glass* into the possibilities and realities of all that exists, bringing you back to earth with awe and worship. Phil delightfully unpacks the dance of science and spirit for the general reader, debunking the myths and revealing the glory of God in the fabric of creation. With a rare breadth of biblical and scientific scholarship this book produces an expectation for miracles today and more to come tomorrow!

PASTOR CHARLES STOCK
Life Centre, Harrisburg, Pennsylvania
Harvest International Ministries National Director (USA)

Phil Mason's book, *Quantum Glory*, puts difficult scientific theories within the grasp of the ordinary person. It gives reasonable intellectual language to spiritual concepts of faith through the exploration of the science of quantum physics. This book is a brilliant read with obvious years of research and great depths of understanding.

DAN MCCOLLAM
Sounds of the Nations, Director of the IWAR
(Institute for Worship Arts Resources), Vacaville, California

Phil's book absolutely resonates with the musician, psalmist and God-lover in me! There is such a depth of rich insight into both the natural laws surrounding the quantum realm and the spiritual principles surrounding the glory realm! Prepare to have your circuits blown!

SEAN FEUCHT
Director of Burn 24/7 Prayer Movement
Co-Author, *Fire and Fragrance:
From the Great Commandment to the Great Commission*

What if heaven is *right here* instead of just *up there*? The theory of quantum non-locality gives cogency to the notion that the spiritual world, the other world, is real and within arm's reach. Perhaps even closer! This book is not a recreational read for those looking for easy devotional material, though it does stimulate awe-inspiring worship. Phil Mason does an extremely creditable job in distilling the essence of a subject that is still in the realm of intense research, and he turns it into a fascinating, faith-building experience.

The science of quantum physics is not for the intellectually fainthearted. However, and this is the fun part, this is the one area of science that comes the closest to describing the "mechanics" of the Kingdom of the Spirit. It is this aspect that makes **Quantum Glory** an exciting, stretching, and stimulating read. While not the last word on the subject, this book is an important catalyst to the discussion about the reality of God's Presence being so close within this "quantum veil." For many, heaven has seemed so far away, but the revelation of quantum non-locality brings it so incredibly near! Brilliant!

DAVID CRABTREE
Senior Leader
DaySpring Church, Castle Hill, NSW, Australia

For decades Phil Mason has pioneered new frontiers in the moves of God. He is an innovative leader, who explores culturally relevant topics that relate to modern seekers. Phil is more than qualified to speak on the relationship between New Age spirituality and quantum physics. As a follower of Christ he has been building a bridge into the New Age community for three decades and has led some extraordinary breakthroughs in supernatural ministry amongst this community. In **Quantum Glory**, Phil distils complex scientific issues into a book that is engaging and accessible for the average reader. His explanation of the interaction between the glory realm of Heaven and the physical world at a quantum level is highly revelatory and it provides a powerful insight into the reality of Heaven invading earth.

WESLEY CAMPBELL
Revivalist and Author, *Be a Hero: The Battle for Mercy and Social Justice* and
Welcoming a Visitation of the Holy Spirit
Kelowna, British Columbia, Canada

Phil Mason's book, **Quantum Glory**, provides a foundation in which every Christian will be equipped to bring the supernatural spiritual realm of Heaven into every quantum particle of earth. Phil does a masterful job describing the way the material and spiritual worlds operate at the quantum level, and how the believer can partner with God's Spirit in releasing the miraculous wherever it is needed. **Quantum Glory** will take you on a journey into the wonder of how God created the world with all of its intricacies, revealing God's glory in each scientific discovery of the quantum realm of matter. Moreover, you will also learn vital biblical truths corresponding to these discoveries, enabling you to better steward the glory realm of Heaven through a demonstration of the supernatural that transforms the quantum world of nature in which you live.

After reading **Quantum Glory**, I feel more empowered and confident that the non-local glory realm of Heaven, where I co-exist with Christ, can affect the local realm of matter in which I also live. I believe I have been given more keys to unlock more of the realities of Heaven, so that the glory of God can shine through me as a light of hope to those who need healing, miraculous intervention, and life purpose. **Quantum Glory** is a must for every student of the supernatural. This book will open up a whole new world of potential in going to the next level of God's will being done on earth as it is in Heaven. Buy it! Read it! Do it!

KEVIN DEDMON
Author, *Unlocking Heaven: Keys to Living Naturally Supernatural* and
*The Ultimate Treasure Hunt: Supernatural Evangelism
through Supernatural Encounters*

A number of years ago, I kept hearing the word "quantum." I did not have a clue what it was, but it seemed to be a buzzword in our stream, so I thought I should explore it a bit more and gain some understanding. I love the supernatural and believe that God is accelerating manifestations of the invisible Kingdom realm in this hour in unprecedented ways. There are quantum realities and possibilities that make the miraculous and the invisible realm understandable to the natural mind. Science is confirming the supernatural, invisible kingdom of God.

So, what is "quantum"? Wikipedia states: In physics, a *quantum* (plural: quanta) is the minimum amount of any physical entity involved in an inter- action. In addition, many scientists have shared with me that the quantum world refers to the operation and function of subatomic energy fields, life, and particles. It might still all sound a bit nebulous, but in my very limited journey I have discovered that the "quantum" world is an invisible subatomic (smaller than or occurring within atoms) world and has a lot to do with "light" and "sound" frequencies. Oh my, does it ever get exciting when you start delving into it!

Scientists do not create new scientific laws, they simply discover what God has already created. For example, we have lightbulbs today because Newton discovered scientific laws that were created by God and put into motion at the beginning of time. He did not create anything new, he simply discovered and applied what was already created. Through his understanding of God's scientific laws regarding light, he was able to make a valuable contribution that we enjoy and depend on today. Every scientific invention have come as a result of discovering laws that God had already created.

Quantum physics is opening up a whole new realm of scientific enlightenment and understanding. That means, in this next era, we will be enjoying many new inventions, insights, and discoveries. Everything is going to grow at a rapid pace, so hold onto your seat belts.

"It is the glory of God to conceal a matter, but the glory of kings is to search out a matter." (Proverbs 25:2) If you are of a "kingly" nature that loves searching out hidden things, you are going to love **Quantum Glory**. It is not a book that you can read quickly, because some of it will "blow your mind" and you will need to read parts of it over and over! It is not a book that everyone will want to pick up for their casual reading entertainment. It is, however, a book for the serious seeker and it needs to be in your reference library, as it contains a wealth of information not only concerning scientific insights but into faith itself. You are being invited to actively live and function in the "God-realm." His Kingdom awaits further discovery. Take the leap…a "quantum" leap, and discover depths of God in fresh realms of revelation and understanding.

PATRICIA KING
Founder of XP Ministries
Author, *The Glory School* (and other resources)

ACKNOWLEDGEMENTS

To my wonderful wife, Maria. You are totally awesome and you have shown such tremendous patience in the countless hours I have spent writing this book in the midst of what is already a hectic schedule of pastoring, lecturing and travelling. You have supported and encouraged me all the way to continue this journey of writing to leave a legacy of our ministry together. Thank you so much for your enduring love and prophetic wisdom.

To my four kids: Simon, Peter, Phoebe and Toby. You guys have also been so tremendously encouraging in my journey as a pastor, public speaker and author. Thanks for showing so much interest in the musings of a father who is captivated by Heaven. I love you all dearly! Simon, thank you for your editorial input and your willingness to read the manuscript as it was taking shape. I have greatly valued your input!

To my spiritual community, New Earth Tribe of Byron Bay. Wow! How did I end up being so blessed to be a part of such a crazy, creative bunch of wild worshippers who love the supernatural ministry of Christ? I love each and every one of you who make up this glorious community and thank you a million times over for your constant love, support and encouragement.

To Bill and Beni Johnson. Words fail to capture or contain the gratitude I have in my heart for you both. You have been so generous toward my wife and I and it has been one of our greatest joys in getting to know you and to be the beneficiaries of your pioneering ministry. Thanks for all the encouragement and interest you have shown in this book and for encouraging me to finish the project. Your passion for this subject has kept me fired up!

To Graham Cooke. You have been such an amazing prophetic mentor and father to Maria and me. You have encouraged us and called out the treasure you saw in us when we were going through the darkest hours of our spiritual journey. Thank you for believing in us and for always being there to prophesy our success and call us into our destiny.

To Professor Raymond Chiao. Your visionary insights as a quantum physicist and as a Christian have been a guiding light on my own journey of discovery. I have gleaned so much from your writings, and meeting you was one of the great highlights of this journey. May your future scientific breakthroughs in the field of gravitational radiation be even greater than your previous breakthroughs in the field of quantum optics!

To my editorial team. I would like to make special mention of Michelle Ricciardello who is a trained physicist. Thank you for reading through all the technical material in this book and offering me your insights and suggestions. Thanks also to Megan Bennett for all your effort in editing the manuscript. Thanks also to Kevin Dedmon, Simon Mason and Charles Stock for your editorial comments and advice.

To all who wrote such generous endorsements. Thank you to Bill and Beni Johnson, Che Ahn, Charles Stock, Rolland Baker, Wesley Campbell, Graham Cooke, David Crabtree, Kevin Dedmon, Sean Feucht, Dan McCollam and Patricia King. It has meant so much to me to have so many wonderful people writing such glowing endorsements.

Finally and most importantly, I would like to acknowledge Jesus. You are my best friend and You speak to me continually of Your unfathomable love and power. As I have been on this crazy journey of revelatory discovery into the remarkable convergence between quantum physics and biblical theology I have been brought to a place of deep awe, reverence and wonder. My love has deepened for You, Jesus, throughout this journey. You are beyond comprehension as the living Word of God who created everything in the universe on the perfect foundation of deep quantum mathematics. How did You do that? You are the Master Quantum Physicist and the Ultimate Mathematician!

ABOUT THE AUTHOR

Phil Mason is married to Maria and has three sons and a daughter. Together, Phil and Maria are the spiritual directors of New Earth Tribe, a spiritual community located in Byron Bay, Australia. New Earth Tribe was pioneered by Phil and Maria in 1998. Phil is director of the "Deep End School of the Supernatural" which is also located in Byron Bay. The school is a nine-month training program that equips and activates disciples of Christ in supernatural ministry. Phil completed a Bachelor of Theology at Flinders University in South Australia in 1991. He has no formal educational qualifications in science but has had a strong personal interest in many aspects of science. In his school he lectures on quantum physics, astrophysics and molecular biology as part of his training program.

One of the features of Phil and Maria's ministry is their passion to impact the New Age community with the love and power of Christ. Phil is a former New Ager and has been working amongst this community for three decades since his conversion to Christ. He has a wealth of experience in reaching New Age people with the revelation and power of Christ. Phil is the director of "Christocentric Light," a ministry that takes teams into New Age festivals throughout Australia releasing demonstrations of the supernatural ministry of Christ. They are now seeing thousands of miracles in the New Age marketplace. Phil is also the director of the Byron Bay Healing Room and Byron Burn 24/7. To find out more about Phil and Maria and their ministry, please visit the following websites:

www.newearthtribe.com
www.deependschool.com
www.philmason.org

Dedication

I would like to dedicate this book to my amazing family. Maria, you have been an amazing pioneer alongside me for the last 28 years. Thanks for all your love, encouragement and prayer for me over the years. I am what I am because of you! Simon, you are an amazing son and I love your passion for truth, justice and knowledge. Pete, you are such a gift from God and I love your passion for rhythm and sound. Phoebe, you are such a beautiful daughter and I love your creativity! Toby, you are also an amazing gift from God and I love your passion for making music! Thanks guys for being such an awesome supportive family and for showing such interest in this writing project.

> Businessmen they drink My wine
> Plowmen dig My earth
> None of them along the line
> Know what any of it is worth.
>
> —Bob Dylan – All Along the Watchtower

CONTENTS

FOREWORD BY BILL JOHNSON

The world only has a voice when the church is silent. My heart's cry has been for God to raise up individuals who have the wisdom and insight to impact the present-day mind molders with truth. Religious answers will not do. Mindless claims will never work. Our discourse must be real, and it has to be practical.

The Bible states that Jesus is the "Desire of the Nations." That basically means that everyone wants a king like Jesus. It is the wise steward of the knowledge of God who can bring the *word of the Lord for the moment* into the lives of others so they can discover that God truly loves them.

This kind of wisdom must come with deep understanding and insight. It has both history and the future in its sights, with an unusual ability to impart perspective with hope. A spokesperson with this gift must also have a unique ability to hear God speak to them in the moment, as they are giving voice to Kingdom concepts, concepts that never fail. That last quality makes them useful significantly beyond their experience.

Solomon functioned with extraordinary wisdom. The news of his gift's impact on Israel soon spread to other nations. The Queen of Sheba was his most notable visitor. She traveled a great distance with a large entourage. Her questions were such that no one else could answer them. But when Solomon spoke, she envied even the servants who had the privilege to live under the influence of his wisdom. The Queen was stunned – into silence. True wisdom has that effect. And it's time for the world to become silent again.

This is a time when God is responding to the need for His people to express the wisdom that silences the godless ideals of the world. He is releasing great wisdom to those who will ask, pursue, and display this gift to His glory – even in the courts of kings. This is where Phil Mason and his wonderful book, **Quantum Glory**, comes into the picture. I believe that God has raised up the author and others like him to be this kind of voice. The need has never been greater. God has given him the ability to articulate the principles of the Kingdom of God to people that many believers cannot relate to. In fact, one could say that Phil and his family of believers run to a battle that many Christians run from – dialogue with both the scientific and New Age communities. They lead this charge in order to present their portion of the harvest to the Lord worthy of His sacrifice at Calvary.

There is no conflict between true science and theology. In fact it's a perfect marriage. But in the absence of sanctified intelligence, some have commandeered the subject for their own godless agenda. One wonders how those with such high IQs can believe in such complex "design" without a "Designer." But this battle over ideals will be won not through argument and heartless debate but by a loving response to unbelievers as people made in God's image, coupled with intelligent discussion of their ideas. When that is displayed with the power of the Kingdom, meeting deep personal need, then we will be able to bring the greatest harvest from that segment of our society.

When some in the scientific community speak of creation without a creator, people under their influence will often in some way make their own god to worship. It's happened all through history. It used to be idols. Often today it is ideals. The reason is that we were designed to worship. While some humanistic scientists end up exalting man, the New Age tries to fill the void by creating a distant impersonal god of energy or force. The author's background gives him an unusual understanding and compassion for this group of people. My wife and I know firsthand the fruit of his life. It is wonderful.

I don't mean to imply that everyone should read **Quantum Glory** only so we can share Christ to the scientific or New Age communities. That might be the overflow. The real glory of this book is that it gives understanding of this wonderful world around us in a way that creates awe for what God has done. It also ignites praise in our hearts to the Creator of all, while at the same time giving us understanding of how things work. God left His message everywhere for anyone interested in truth. His fingerprints are everywhere: from the largest galaxies in existence, to the smallest thing known to man. I appreciate Phil's amazing insights and deep understanding of very difficult subjects addressed in **Quantum Glory**. I am especially thankful for his gift of taking big thoughts and breaking them down so that all of us can understand them. But I am also glad for how He values mystery. Anything that creates awe and wonder, all the while pointing to Jesus, to me is priceless. With that note, I highly recommend **Quantum Glory**. Enjoy. Be awed. Give God praise over and over again.

BILL JOHNSON
Senior Pastor, Bethel Church, Redding, California USA
BJM.org, Author, *When Heaven Invades Earth* and *Face to Face with God*

FOREWORD BY ROLLAND BAKER

Now this is interesting theological/scientific research! I am a missionary preacher with many years of education in biblical studies and systematic theology. But before that I had totally dedicated myself to science, and finally attained a full scholarship to the California Institute of Technology. I was interested in all things technical, precise, logical, and that explained what things were and how they worked. I considered it powerful knowledge that made so much possible. And so it is!

I have followed with great interest the effects of postmodernism not only on science but also on the way we do theology. Old, static, singular models used to explain that nature and God simply do not contain reality, or even approach the essence of relationality that describes both God and the physical world.

So there has been breakthrough both in physics and the study of God. The old divide between science and religion does not exist in this new environment. We are not asked to believe blindly in spiritual matters, nor are we constrained in natural science by ordinary boundaries of common sense.

Phil Mason's work is a tremendous contribution to our understanding of the relationship between the spiritual and the physical, and between God and His creation. But more than expanding our ideas of what is rational, he shows that science is able to allow for and even endorse the concept of a Creator outside creation who affects reality by His own consciousness.

I have long asserted that faith in God does not obviate reason, and that investigation of any field of knowledge, experience or phenomena will point to and not discourage our faith in God's existence and the truth of the Bible. *Quantum Glory* illuminates the sheer richness of the rational, mathematical order of reality as we have come to know it in a new way. Far from arriving at a picture of random, impersonal, unguided universal consciousness, Phil's research clears the way for appreciating the relationship between the world and the God who created it and established its order.

Believers with extraordinarily childlike and undisturbed faith have always been able to grasp and accept the miraculous. In our ministry among the poor and uneducated of rural Africa, we see the dead raised and other miracles of a broad variety. These people have little need of understanding how things work, but they do understand the love of God, something equally miraculous that is circumvented by those who attempt to use rationality to escape the implications of the gospel.

In this world of "supra-rationality," we of the faith understand more than ever that God's love, creative power and sovereignty over our world are not anti-science. Phil is showing in his book that increasing understanding of the "new science," and quantum theory in particular, is not restrictive, but actually frees us from a stubborn, "scientific" rejection of a God who is nothing if not relational and the personification of love. The New Age movement stubbornly pursues supernatural experience without holiness. Its adherents have escaped the boundaries of modernism, and are therefore refreshingly eager for the miraculous, but they still need a hunger and thirst for the unique righteousness of God as a personal being.

Modern theology is concentrating on the nature of personhood, realizing that we are who we are by virtue of our relationship with others and the world around us. Similarly, in physics we now understand that what we know of an instance of reality is determined by our perspective. We cannot limit our approach to single models, and in fact both God and nature are actually not definable in impersonal, non-relational terms. Rationality now includes *relationality*, and only in that way does the science of both nature and religion make sense.

The spiritual mind in Scripture is concerned about the unseen, eternal world and the divine qualities of love and relationship. **Quantum Glory** is a major help to those of us who are excited by a new understanding of how God relates not only to us as persons, but also to every last aspect of our created world. I especially am interested in continuing to explore the idea that the whole universe, and not just our personal lives, is the field of the activity of God's mind and heart. Our world is not cold, but hot with the life and love of God.

Sin to my mind is a rejection of relationality, and some of the most brilliant minds in history have refused the logic of relationality with God. Phil Mason's book will not "force" people to believe. Others have cautioned us toward humility concerning what our finite minds can grasp of reality. But this book is massive encouragement, from God Himself, I believe. More than ever I maintain that all investigation into the seen and unseen will point to the God who loves the world He created.

Dr. Rolland Baker
Director, Iris Ministries, Pemba, Mozambique

PREFACE

I am sitting in the library of the University of Berkeley, California as I write the preface to what has become a four year journey of exploration into the relationship between the science of quantum physics and the glory of God. As the title of this book: **Quantum Glory** might already suggest, it explores a fascinating intersection between science and spirituality through the lens of the biblical worldview. The subtitle of the book is *The Science of Heaven Invading Earth*. Throughout this book I develop the idea that the phenomenon of quantum non-locality represents the bridge between heaven and earth.

The science of quantum physics explores the material world whilst spirituality explores the nature of the spiritual world, so already this book narrows the field of interest to those who accept the existence of spiritual realities. However, interest in spirituality has been on the rise for decades in the Western world and there is compelling evidence that the majority of people in Western society now value some expression of spiritual belief. This book is a serious exploration of the intersection between biblical revelation and some of the most compelling discoveries of quantum physics.

So what am I doing in the library of UCB in Berkeley? Well, Berkeley has a reputation for excellence in the sciences, in particular, physics. The Berkeley Department of Physics has been at the cutting edge of discoveries that have contributed to and supported the emergence of the "new physics" which represents a departure from conventional physics in its acceptance of extra dimensions. And Berkeley ever since the 1960s has represented the radical fringe of Western culture. Walking around Berkeley, the intersection between the rationalism of the modernist era and the spirituality of the postmodern era is everywhere to be seen. It's like two worlds in collision: the age of reason and the age of spirit.

I am an Australian but I travel regularly to the United States. On this trip to California I have had the opportunity to meet with Professor Raymond Chiao, a quantum physicist whose groundbreaking research at Berkeley into quantum non-locality captured world attention. Chiao is a physicist who is also an evangelical Christian. In our conversation I shared with Professor Chiao the central thesis of this book concerning the significance of quantum non-locality as a buffer zone between the spirit world and the material world.

I was greatly encouraged when Professor Chiao told me personally that he knows of Christian physicists who are arriving at a similar conclusion. He said, "As a Christian I believe that this physical universe that we are living in is not all that there is. There is a reality which transcends the visible universe." This other layer of reality is the non-local universe that bridges the spirit world and the material world whilst sharing attributes of both worlds. Meeting with Professor Chiao was a great privilege and a tremendous encouragement on my own journey of exploration. Thank you for joining me on this journey. I hope it will be as fulfilling for you, the reader, as it has been for me, the author!

PHIL MASON
Byron Bay, Australia
November 2010

Part One:

MAPPING THE QUANTUM UNIVERSE

The science of physics focuses upon the study of the physical universe in which we live. It seeks to probe matter at the deepest possible level to discover exactly what our material world is made of. As the study of physics has advanced, it has given rise to *quantum physics* which seeks to probe matter at the sub-atomic level. The strange, counter-intuitive world of quantum mechanics reveals a universe with features and characteristics that are fundamentally at odds with our everyday experience of matter at a macroscopic scale.

Quantum physics has opened an entirely new window to the world we live in. In fact, the quantum world exhibits such strange properties; it is almost as though scientists have discovered another universe. Nevertheless, the quantum world is a fundamental part of our universe and it is the foundation upon which the macro world has been gloriously constructed by our loving Creator. Exploring the fabric of the cosmos at a quantum scale yields profound theological insights into the nature of the universe we live in!

Because we are now certain that our universe is firmly built upon quantum realities, this new counter-intuitive world of quantum mechanics is itself a deeper revelation of the creative genius of God. Every discovery in the quantum world opens our eyes to the glory of God. "The heavens declare the glory of God; the skies proclaim the work of His hands. Day after day they pour forth speech; night after night they display knowledge. There is no speech or language where their voice is not heard. Their voice goes out into all the earth, their words to the ends of the world." (Psalm 19:1-4 NIV)

The heavens and the earth are a revelation of the handiwork of the Creator. David wrote Psalm 19 as a theological reflection as he gazed into the heavens. He viewed the cosmos as a revelation of the glory of God. Now in the twenty-first century as scientists continue to map the quantum universe, we are collectively granted a glimpse into a realm that fundamentally upgrades our understanding of the glory and majesty of God, who, through the emerging science of quantum physics, is now being revealed as the master Quantum Physicist and the Master Mathematician who exquisitely designed the world we live in. Come with me on a journey into the creative mind of God!

Introduction

WHAT'S THE HYPE ABOUT QUANTUM PHYSICS?

If you are anything like me, I imagine that you are attracted to the title of this book because you are aware that there is a lot of hype and interest surrounding the subject of quantum physics these days. New Age books, movies and DVDs are invoking the mysteries of the quantum world in support of their claim that "you are God" and you are endowed with unlimited spiritual power to create your own reality.

Documentaries such as *What the Bleep Do We Know?* and *The Secret* confidently assert that there is a realm of metaphysical knowledge that will open up to you the ability to powerfully create your own reality and change your life circumstances. This is welcome news to disempowered people who are frustrated with their lives and their lack of personal empowerment. It also explains the popularity and success of these highly popularised expressions of New Age beliefs.

I have watched the *What the Bleep* movie a number of times and I even went out and purchased a copy of the book by the same title which was published on the heels of the extraordinary success of the movie. The subtitle of the book is, *Discovering the Endless Possibilities for Altering Your Everyday Reality*. As with the movie, throughout the entire book the science of quantum physics is invoked again and again to assert that we can master the ability to create our own reality.

This book that you are now reading is, in part, a biblical response to the issues raised by those who assert that quantum physics supports New Age teachings and beliefs. It is also designed to introduce readers to some of the key concepts of quantum physics and to examine these concepts in the light of biblical revelation. This is a profoundly fascinating field of study which has extraordinary appeal to both scientifically and metaphysically inclined students of the world we live in.

There was a time in the 1970s when I was committed to New Age teachings. I almost became a New Age teacher myself until I had an extraordinary encounter with the supernatural ministry of Christ. As a dedicated student of the teachings of Christ for over 30 years, I have been actively engaged in evaluating New Age teachings in the light of the New Testament and the biblical worldview.

My life calling has been to build a bridge of dialogue into the New Age community and to equip followers of Christ with the skills to intelligently engage New Age seekers in order to bring them into an encounter with the glory of the risen Christ. I teach on the relationship between quantum physics and biblical theology in a training environment, even though I am not a trained quantum physicist. My personal fascination with the strange world of the sub-atomic building blocks of matter has led me into an in-depth study of the science of quantum physics, so that I am now able to effectively communicate the discoveries of the quantum world in the light of biblical theology.

As we journey together into the world of the quantum, I think you will see that the strangely counter-intuitive world of quantum physics, rather than substantiating the claims of New Age teachings, actually substantiates the revelation that God alone has the power to create reality and to re-structure the quantum field. My own personal journey into the weird world of the quantum has powerfully enhanced my understanding of the reality of the spiritual realm and has strengthened my personal conviction that everything the Bible reveals about the invisible world is powerfully supported by the discoveries of quantum physics in the past century.

Chapter One

THE HIJACKING OF QUANTUM PHYSICS

It is my personal conviction that the science of quantum physics has been hijacked by New Age teachers in their eagerness to assert that nature itself confirms New Age beliefs about the nature of the oneness of all reality and the power of the mind to create and manipulate reality. My own study of quantum physics in the light of biblical revelation has given me an entirely different perspective. I believe with all my being that God is the supreme Quantum Physicist, that the world of the quantum has been beautifully and intentionally crafted by a personal God to respond to His voice, and that God alone has the power to alter reality at a quantum level for His glorious redemptive purposes.

The New Age community has seized the high ground in our culture in their public popularisation of quantum physics. In New Age literature there is now such a significant overlap between the discovery of the strange world of quantum reality and New Age metaphysical speculation that in many respects, at a popular level, many people would now associate New Age teaching with quantum physics and vice versa.

The blending of New Age metaphysical speculation and the science of quantum physics is so extensive in popular literature that a number of scientists are at pains to distinguish themselves from the New Age community whenever they seek to explore the relationship between human consciousness and the peculiarities of the quantum world. By way of illustration, among my collection of books on quantum physics I have a volume titled *The Non-Local Universe: The New Physics and Matters of the Mind*, in which the co-authors make the following observation, perhaps more as a sign of the times than anything else:

> Numerous writers of New Age books, along with a few well known New Age gurus, have played fast and loose with the "implications" of the new physics in an attempt to ground the mental in some vague sense of cosmic Oneness. But if this book is ever erroneously placed in the New Age section of a commercial bookstore and purchased by those interested in New Age literature, they will be disappointed.[1]

The New Age occupation of the high places has only taken place because the followers of the historical Christ of Scripture have been rather slow on the uptake in regard to the powerful discoveries that have taken place in the field of quantum physics. New Age metaphysics has filled the void because followers of Christ have been largely silent in interpreting the discoveries of this new field of science to the wider culture. By and large the New Age community has taken a deeper interest in quantum physics because of their passionate agenda to prove that the revelations of the quantum world support their paradigm about the power of human consciousness to alter reality. The science of quantum physics holds a deep and alluring fascination for anyone who holds a metaphysical worldview.

GOD AND QUANTUM PHYSICS

Those who believe in the inspiration and authority of the Bible believe and accept that there is a personal God who created the heavens and the earth. As such we believe that this God is the Creator of everything that is now being discovered in the frontier science of quantum physics. We also believe that the only correct interpretation of the science of quantum physics will come in the light of the revelation of the Bible. The conflict between the New Age and biblical interpretation of quantum physics is similar to the conflict that surrounds the interpretation of nature in the evolution/intelligent design debate. Both sides of the debate are claiming the upper hand in their ability to rightly interpret the natural world.

It is time for the followers of Christ to re-occupy the high places by shouting from the rooftops that the God and Father of our Lord Jesus

Christ is the architect of the quantum world and that the quantum world constitutes the very foundation or the building blocks that God used in the creation of His physical universe. As we journey through the strange, counter-intuitive world of the quantum, we will focus largely upon God's relationship to the quantum world and His glorious power to create the universe from the invisible substance of quantum waves of energy. As we do this we will dialogue with some of the seminal ideas that are currently being espoused by New Age thinkers and give a response to these ideas in the light of biblical revelation. We will also dialogue with some of the ideas and concepts in the Scriptures concerning the invisible powers of darkness and their ability or inability to interfere with the quantum world.

At the centre of this entire discussion is the issue of the nature and being of God. New Age teachers boldly assert that there is no personal God. In their teachings they deliberately *depersonalise* the concept of God and reduce God to the status of an "impersonal energy." In fact, New Age teachers are fundamentally opposed to the idea of a personal God because if God was a personal being who exists outside of time and space then He would be separate from His creation. To them, the concept of a God who is not a part of the universe is absolutely abhorrent because it perpetuates the notion of *separation,* whereas New Agers are focused upon cultivating a sense of universal oneness. In contrast, followers of Christ who are informed by biblical revelation argue passionately for the existence of God as a personal being with all the attributes of personhood who is clearly differentiated from His creation. This is where I stand. My knowledge of God as a personal being who has made human beings in His own image and likeness has moved well beyond the realm of wishful belief or a blind adherence to theological dogma.

In the past three decades since the time I first encountered the power of the risen Christ I have seen His supernatural power again and again to such an extent that I have moved into the realm of *knowing* God through first-hand experience. I have personally been used by God to release His supernatural healing power so many times that I have lost count. I turned to Christ in 1979 as a result of a life-changing prophetic dream and because I witnessed an incredible healing miracle in the life of a friend with whom I lived.

Over more than 30 years I have seen extraordinary healing miracles with my own eyes that have defied any rational explanation. I have been in the midst of public meetings where hundreds of supernatural healings have taken place simultaneously. I have seen prophets moving in such extraordinary levels of prophetic gifting that I have been completely overwhelmed with a sense of awe and wonder at the majesty and power of the mind of Christ. Nothing could now convince me that there is no God; I have gone way too far into this journey of knowing God. I have literally experienced decades of cumulative evidence for the existence of God.

My personal experience of walking with Christ and participating with Him in His glorious kingdom ministry has brought me to a place of deep conviction in the absolute truth of the Scriptures. I have studied the Bible for almost three decades and have completed almost five years of full time theological training. All of my studies have brought me to the place of an overwhelming confidence in the authority of the Scriptures as an extraordinary revelation of a personal God who has intentionally revealed Himself to humanity in the pages of the Old and New Testaments.

The Bible is a prophetic signpost that points to the person of the resurrected Christ who invites every human being to open their heart to receive Him as Lord and Saviour. Once we open our hearts, Christ begins to unveil Himself and to reveal His glory to our hearts. The revelation of the glory of God in the face of Christ is cumulative and it transforms people's lives from glory to glory. I have personally experienced decades of spiritual transformation and freedom through the supernatural activity of the Holy Spirit and have been drawn into an engagement with the supernatural realm of heavenly glory that is hidden from those who choose not to receive Christ. The cumulative experience of a first-hand personal encounter with the glory of God shifts people out of a second-hand theological knowledge into an intimate personal knowledge so that people can actually know God. Knowing God intimately and personally is entirely different than merely believing in some distant entity called "God."

QUANTUM PHYSICS AND BIBLICAL THEOLOGY

I passionately believe that theology must inform science and that science must inform theology, and that there can be a deep reconciliation between everything that can be learnt through science with everything that can be learnt through sitting at the feet of the prophets. I am convinced that the study of the sciences without the aid of biblical revelation will lead people into faulty conclusions and endless speculations that generate more heat than light. It is my firm conviction that God's creation is intended to be studied in the light of divine revelation. That is the paradigm from which I have embarked upon a study of the science of quantum physics. The revelation of God in the Scriptures is the bedrock foundation that is the anchor of all of my research. It is the filter through which everything that crosses my radar is evaluated and assessed. I believe God desires that all human beings discover the sheer exhilaration of exploring His creation through the lens of biblical revelation.

It is time to move beyond the "science versus religion" debate. That is an old paradigm that is promoted by some within the scientific community who regard biblical revelation as something which is hostile toward science. Those who are living out of this paradigm of the conflict between religion and science have probably been burned by Christian fundamentalists who have attacked the scientific community with their theological dogmatism. Professor Paul Davies, one of the world's most eminent physicists, wrote an interesting book titled *God and the New Physics*, which he published in 1983. The title promises so much yet delivers so little in the way of theological insight because it buys into the old paradigm of "science versus religion." Paul Davies writes in the preface of his book:

> It may seem bizarre, but in my opinion science offers a surer path to God than religion. Right or wrong, the fact that science has actually advanced to the point where what were formerly religious questions can be seriously tackled, itself indicates the far-reaching consequences of the new physics.[2]

Paul Davies' "surer path to God" completely extinguishes any possibility of a contribution of biblical revelation to the discussion because, as he goes on to reveal, he has absolutely no confidence in the reality of divine revelation. His argument exemplifies the "science versus religion" debate.

> The scientist and the theologian approach the deep questions of existence from utterly different starting points. Science is based on careful observation and experiment enabling theories to be constructed which connect different experiences. Regularities in the working of nature are sought which hopefully reveal the fundamental laws which govern the behaviour of matter and forces. Central to this approach is the willingness of the scientist to abandon a theory if evidence is produced against it. Although individual scientists may cling tenaciously to some cherished idea, the scientific

community as a group is always ready to adopt a new approach. In contrast, religion is founded on revelation and received wisdom. Religious dogma that claims to contain an unalterable "Truth" can hardly be modified to fit changing ideas. The true believer must stand by his faith whatever the apparent evidence against it. This "Truth" is said to be communicated directly to the believer, rather than through the filtering and refining process of collective investigation. The trouble about revealed "Truth" is that it is liable to be wrong, and even if it is right other people require a good reason to share the recipients' belief. Many scientists are derisory about revealed truth. Indeed, some maintain that it is a positive evil.[3]

Davies then proceeds to quote with approval the famous big-bang cosmologist, Professor Hermann Bondi, who says:

Generally the state of mind of a believer in a revelation is the awful arrogance of saying "I *know*, and those who do not agree with my belief are wrong." In no other field is such arrogance so widespread, in no other field do people feel so utterly certain of their "knowledge." It is to me quite disgusting that anyone should feel so superior, so selected and chosen against all the many who differ in their beliefs and un-beliefs.[4]

Ironically, the author of *God and the New Physics*, at the very outset of his book, systematically rules out the possibility of the role of biblical revelation as a valid contribution to our understanding of the nature of ultimate reality. Through Davies' rejection of the trustworthiness of biblical revelation he is left alone with his "surer path to God" which is none other than the Enlightenment paradigm of pure human reason unaided by revelation. Davies went on to publish *The Mind of God; Science and the Search for Ultimate Meaning* in 1992. Equipped with a deep knowledge of the fine-tuning and design of the universe, Davies continues to probe the idea that science points toward the existence of design and of God but he refuses to countenance the biblical concept of God.

Sometimes Christians get a bit excited when they read about certain scientists referring to "God." Paul Davies chose the title of his book, *The Mind of God*, from a quote by Stephen Hawking who said, "If we do discover a theory of everything... it would be the ultimate triumph of human reason – for then we would truly know the mind of God." The "God" of the scientists is often not the God of faith who has revealed Himself through Scripture. Instead it is a scientific concept of God arrived at through pure human reason. It is not a God who requires something of us but rather it is a God that can be scientifically and empirically discovered through science. The last thing on these scientists' minds is the unification of science and religious faith.

Richard Dawkins, commenting on the use of "God" language amongst physicists, points out that from their perspective, "God is a synonym for the deepest principles of physics."[5] There is often no reason for believers to get excited over physicists talking about discovering God through science. There is a certain particle that is yet to be identified that the standard model of particle physics predicts must be there even though it remains elusive in the world of sub-atomic particles. This predicted particle, called the "Higgs Boson," is often called the "God particle" by physicists, illustrating again the invocation of "God" language amongst quantum physicists. The hunt for the last missing piece of the standard model of the atom continues, but even if it is one day discovered it will not prove the existence of God. All of this talk about God amongst physicists does not, from their perspective, have anything to do with the convergence of science and spirituality.

However, from the perspective of theologians who are actively pursuing the evidence for the convergence of science and biblical theology there is compelling evidence that such a convergence is possible. I wholeheartedly agree with the conclusions of the Christian quantum physicist, Dr. John Polkinghorne, who confidently argues for a deep reconciliation between biblical revelation and scientific discovery. The argument goes like this: God is the Creator of the heavens and the earth, and every discovery of science ought to be able to be reconciled with the reality of an intelligent Designer since it is God's handiwork in the first place.

Polkinghorne, who is both a Professor of Mathematical Physics and a trained theologian, is the author of over thirty books, including *Quantum Physics and Theology: An Unexpected Kinship*. He has written extensively on the theme of the relationship between science and biblical theology. In one volume, appropriately titled, *One World: The Interaction of Science and Theology*, he writes:

> We live in one world and science and theology explore different aspects of it. The two disciplines have in common the fact that

they both involve attempts to understand experience. They are both concerned with exploring, and submitting to, the way things are. Because of this they are capable of interacting with each other: theology explaining the source of the rational order and structure which science both assumes and confirms in its investigation of the world; science by its study of creation setting conditions of consonance which must be satisfied by any account of the Creator and His activity. Science discerns a world of rational order developing through the unfolding of process. Theology declares that world in its scientific character to be an expression of the Word of God.[6]

Frank Tipler is a Professor of Mathematical Physics who is also a believer in Christ. He is the author of *The Physics of Immortality* and *The Physics of Christianity*. Like Polkinghorne, Tipler also challenges the deliberate segregation of science and religion that is regularly imposed upon Christians by the scientific community and all too readily accepted by Christians who feel intimidated by the "authority" of this community. Tipler points out that the negative perception of Christian theology adopted by the scientific community stems from "the idea that religion and science belong in distinct categories: religion is concerned with moral questions and science with factual questions: religion is concerned with the spiritual world and science with the material world." Tipler points out that those who advocate "segregating science and religion really mean that religion should be kept out of science because religion is factually false. These people truly believe that God does not exist and hence does not have any effect on reality."[7]

QUANTUM PHYSICS AND NEW AGE SPIRITUALITY

Currently most popular literature written by quantum physicists for the popular audience reject the Bible and the concept of a personal God. They do not see any value in exploring the relationship between the concept of an intelligent Designer and the quantum physical world. Instead, almost all quantum physicists who have any interest in spirituality gravitate toward Eastern philosophy and New Age metaphysics. Subsequently the dominant spiritual interpretation remains New Age or Eastern in its orientation.

In distinct contrast, this book is written from the perspective of a confident assurance in the existence of God as a personal being and of the reality of the supernatural realm. The relationship between a personal God and quantum physics is a topic worthy of deep exploration. My primary goal in writing the first part of this book is to glorify God through bringing to light recent discoveries in the quantum world that give us a much deeper insight into the intricacies of God's creation at a sub-atomic level. Through the lens of quantum mechanics I believe that God is revealed as the supreme Quantum Physicist who created the material world on the foundation of invisible quantum realities.

I really like New Age people. I once was one myself! I enjoy nothing more than meaningful dialogue with New Age travellers. I love the fact that most New Age people have such a high respect for the spirituality of Christ and a love and respect for nature. I love the way that they are so hungry for spiritual reality. Whilst I no longer personally agree with the New Age worldview, I seek to dignify New Agers in their spiritual journey and I would hope that there is not even a trace of condescension in the way I engage in dialogue with New Age beliefs.

I have spent more than 30 years of meaningful dialogue with New Agers as a sincere follower of Christ, and I have a number of friends who are still actively engaged in the New Age community. I am personally convinced that the New Age interpretation of the world of quantum physics is misguided and that it ultimately leads New Age practitioners into a life of frustration in their attempt to create their own reality apart from the grace of God that is freely given in Christ. But I love the way that New Agers are fascinated by quantum physics. I share their joy and exhilaration at the uncovering of some of the strange features of the quantum world.

Recent developments in the field of quantum exploration have unearthed some extraordinary attributes of the world of the extremely small. Perhaps one of the most startling discoveries is the concept of non-locality. Many physicists who have been inducted into an understanding of the quantum world now recognise and appreciate that there is a non-local dimension to atoms and their sub-atomic components. "Non-locality" means that a quantum system cannot be localized in space and time, whereas "locality" means that something can be precisely "located." The fact is that an electron or a photon cannot be technically "located."

Locality is not an attribute of the electron or the proton or the neutron for that matter. These "particles" are now widely understood to be non-local which essentially means that they exist in another dimension other than our space/time dimension. Quantum physicists have now confirmed the existence of other dimensions where quantum "particles" exhibit strange non-local characteristics such as quantum entanglement and quantum tunnelling. Don't worry; we will explain all of these concepts as we journey through the unfolding revelation of the quantum world.

The Bible reveals a "God" who is non-local and who exists in an invisible spiritual dimension. In fact, it is not just God who exists in this non-local universe. The entire dimension that the Bible calls "heaven," inhabited by God and His invisible angelic servants, is non-local. The Bible also reveals the existence of fallen angelic beings; Satan and his demonic cohorts who exist in this invisible non-local dimension. In fact, there is a whole other spiritual world that exists right alongside our physical space/ time dimension. Quantum physicists have now been universally compelled to accept the existence of non-local realities that confirm the existence of other dimensions. In fact, they are now proposing that this visible world of matter has come into being through the materialisation of non-local realities that essentially exist in another dimension outside of space and time!

Those who embrace the testimony of Scripture as the deliberate unveiling of the invisible world by God have already adapted themselves to these ideas. But now these notions of non-locality are being confirmed by mainstream science. It is no wonder that New Age thinkers are latching onto these concepts in the belief that they confirm New Age teachings. New Agers have a "magical" view of the universe and they also universally accept the concept of non-locality. They are right at home with this idea! They believe in the world of angels and spirit guides who are communicating with humanity. They accept the concept of the miraculous and the reality of other planes of existence beyond our time/space universe.

This is why the New Age community has adopted the discoveries of quantum physics as something of a scientific mascot in the same way they initially co-opted the rainbow and the crystal in earlier decades. Only now, the co-opting of quantum physics has given rise to a new level of sophistication to New Age teachings. Biblical revelation and New Age spirituality are the two major contenders in the Western world in the arena of interpreting the discoveries of quantum physics to the world. One of our goals in this book is to discover which interpretation more accurately reflects reality. So let's explore how the New Age community has "hijacked" quantum physics.

QUANTUM PHYSICS AND NEW AGE METAPHYSICS

We need to understand the shift that has taken place in our culture in the light of the transition from the modernist to the postmodernist era. Modernism was the philosophy that emerged during the period known as the Enlightenment in the mid 17th century. Modernist thinkers embraced the principles of Newtonian physics with its clockwork view of the universe. Many of the principles of classical physics that still hold true in the macroscopic world of physics were developed under Newton and other Enlightenment physicists.

In contrast, the physics of the postmodern era has been called the "New Physics." The "New Physics" developed its understanding of the material world upon the emerging discoveries of quantum mechanics and the apparent random, even chaotic, nature of the universe especially at the sub-atomic level. A giant chasm emerged between the physics of the quantum world and classical physics. Because the strange new world of quantum physics challenged many of the cherished views about the orderly, mechanistic view of the universe that was promoted by classical physics, the "New Physics" was co-opted as a powerful ally in the promotion of New Age ideas.

New Age spirituality is the spirituality of choice for the postmodernist who has rejected the concept of absolute truth which characterised the modernist era. New Age spirituality is a uniquely postmodern phenomenon that reflects the shift from a rationalist approach to understanding and perceiving reality to a more subjective, intuitive approach. In terms of direction and movement, the Western world is undergoing a movement away from the concrete to the abstract, from the rational to the intuitive, from the objective to the subjective, from a rejection of the supernatural to an acceptance of invisible spiritual realities. The discoveries of quantum physics somehow reflect and support this movement away from a traditional Western, rationalistic view of the universe to a more intuitive acceptance of the interconnectedness of all things and the role of consciousness in the shaping of reality.

The New Age adoption of quantum physics is not a particularly new phenomenon. The earliest work in this area dates back to the writings of some of the mainstream 20th century quantum physicists in Europe who began to engage in metaphysical speculations as the emerging discoveries of the quantum world were coming to light. Most notably, the two concepts of quantum entanglement and the interplay between consciousness and the quantum field have captured the imagination of many physicists, alluring them into the realm of metaphysics in order to find analogies with which to describe the emerging revelation of the non-local world of quantum mechanics.

"Metaphysics" addresses the philosophical issue of the *essence* of physical existence and it seeks to answer the question, "What is the nature of ultimate reality?" Metaphysics is concerned with explaining the ultimate nature of being. Metaphysical philosophers seek to answer such questions as "What is the nature of reality?" and "Does the world exist outside of the perception of the mind?" The counter-intuitive realities of the quantum world discovered by 20th century physicists forced them to ask questions that overlapped with the concerns of metaphysical thinkers. It was inevitable that New Agers would be drawn and even magnetically attracted to the metaphysical conclusions of some of these physicists.

Some of the greatest names of 20th century physics have drawn strong analogies between the newly emerging discoveries of quantum physics and the Eastern worldview of universal oneness. Because of the dominance of Enlightenment rationalism in the West and the rejection of biblical authority, there has been an attraction over the past few centuries amongst certain Western intellectuals to the wisdom of the East. This attraction reflected an underlying dissatisfaction with the anti-spirituality that characterised modernism and it reached new heights with the birth of the postmodern era in the latter decades of the 20th century.

The spirituality of the Postmodern era is decidedly Eastern in its orientation, with New Age ideas dominating discussions of spiritual matters at a popular level. Those quantum physicists who exhibited an attraction to Eastern philosophy were the precursors of a wider movement amongst disaffected Westerners who were becoming increasingly well educated and simultaneously disenchanted with the wholesale rejection of spirituality that had come to characterise Western rationalistic materialism.

The Emergence of the Mystical Physicists

We will give a brief overview of the metaphysical or mystical leanings of some of the greatest scientific minds of the 20th century but, before we do, it is perhaps helpful to examine the motives of some of these thinkers in their exploration of the parallels between quantum physics and Eastern mysticism. Humanity has always been inclined toward religion in its yearning for ultimate answers to the purpose of existence. Ken Wilbur, in his authoritative book, *Quantum Questions*, alludes to this perennial mystical quest.

> The common tendency, when faced with the truly ultimate issues of existence, is to assume – or at least hope – that physics or mysticism would somehow converge on a similar set of answers; that physics would somehow support or even prove a mystical worldview.[8]

It was Einstein [1879-1955] himself who said, "I maintain that the cosmic religious feeling is the strongest and noblest motive for scientific research."[9] Einstein is regarded as perhaps the greatest physicist who has ever lived. He personally experienced this "cosmic religious feeling" and he identified it in a number of spiritual traditions.

> It is very difficult to elucidate this feeling to anyone who is entirely without it. The beginnings of cosmic religious feeling already appear at an early stage of development, e.g., in many of the Psalms of David and in some of the prophets. Buddhism...contains a much stronger element of this. The religious geniuses of all ages have been distinguished by this kind of religious feeling.[10]

Niels Bohr [1885-1962], a leading Danish quantum physicist, was typical of many of his peers who reflected this attraction to the wisdom of the East. In 1937 Bohr had travelled to China and had been influenced by Eastern thinking. He later adopted the yin and yang symbol as his family coat of arms with the motto: *Contraria sunt complementa* [Opposites are Complimentary]. Bohr pioneered research into the sub-atomic world and embraced the principle of "complementarity," the unity of seeming opposites, in his attempts to describe the unity of the atom. In 1958 he wrote, "For a parallel to the lesson of atomic theory [we must turn] to those kinds of epistemological problems with which already thinkers like Buddha and Lao-Tzu have been confronted, when trying to harmonise our position as spectators and actors in the great drama of existence."[11]

In the same year, Werner Heisenberg [1901-1976], another leading European physicist wrote, "The great scientific contribution in theoretical physics that has come from Japan since the last war may be an indication of a certain relationship between philosophical ideas in the tradition of the Far East and the philosophical substance of quantum theory."[12] Heisenberg travelled to India in the 1930s and engaged in discussions with Eastern mystics and philosophers. Reflecting upon the influence of the Eastern world-view upon his capacity to comprehend the mystery of quantum physics, he wrote in 1959, "It may be easier to adapt oneself to the quantum theoretical concept of reality when one has not gone through the naive materialistic way of thinking that still prevailed in Europe in the first decades of this century."[13] Ken Wilbur described Heisenberg as "an excellent philosopher and a metaphysician or mystic."[14]

Erwin Schrödinger [1887-1961], the famous Austrian theoretical physicist, expressed the desire to see: "Some blood transfusion from the East to the West to save Western science from spiritual anaemia."[15] In the period immediately following the end of World War I Schrödinger immersed himself in the Indian Vedanta philosophy of the Vedas and the Upanishads. In his book, *My View of the World* [1925], Schrödinger wrote, "In all the world there is no kind of framework within which we can find consciousness in the plural; this is simply something we construct because of the temporal plurality of individuals, but it is a false construction....The only solution to this conflict insofar as any is available to us at all lies in the ancient wisdom of the Upanishad."[16] Schrödinger was a full blown pantheist who was deeply immersed in Eastern mysticism. He wrote extensively on issues of mysticism and Ken Wilbur judges his writings to contain "some of the finest and most poetic mystical statements ever penned!"[17]

There is a debate as to the extent of Eastern influence in the shaping of Schrödinger's quantum research. J.J. Clarke writes, "The precise influence of this reading on his scientific investigations is difficult to assess, but it is certain from that time onwards Indian philosophy became a central part of his thinking about life in general and it is difficult to imagine that this did not influence his work in physics to some degree."[18] According to Schrödinger's biographer, the Vedanta philosophy became the foundation for his life and work, "for it offered a unified picture of the world which was entirely consistent with the emerging view of physics."[19]

One quantum physicist who deliberately sought to merge quantum physics and Eastern mysticism was David Bohm [1917-1992], an American physicist who was equally as interested in Eastern philosophy as he was in probing the mysteries of the quantum world. In 1980 Bohm, a protégé and friend of Einstein, wrote a book titled *Wholeness and the Implicate Order*. Throughout this book it is not difficult to recognise the extent of Eastern influence upon Bohm's understanding of quantum reality.

I would say that in my scientific and philosophical work, my main concern has been with understanding the nature of reality in general and consciousness in particular as a coherent whole, which is never static or complete, but which is in an unending process of movement and unfoldment.[20] If man thinks of the totality as constituted of independent fragments, then that is how his mind will tend to operate, but if he can include everything coherently and harmoniously in an overall whole that is undivided, unbroken, and without a border then his mind will tend to move in a similar way, and from this will flow an orderly action within the whole.[21]

Bohm had a close association with J. Krishnamurti, a New Age teacher who was trained within the Theosophical Society and who exercised considerable influence upon Bohm's spiritual beliefs. Bohm adopted the Eastern concept of what he called "the undivided wholeness of the universe." Rejecting the classical idea that the world is divided into independently existing parts, Bohm saw no distinction between human consciousness and the physical world of matter and fully embraced the New Age concept that "all is one."

After Bohm's introduction to J. Krishnamurti in 1959 he was drawn deeper into a fascination with the wisdom of the East where "such views still survive in the sense that philosophy and religion emphasise wholeness and imply the futility of analysis of the worlds into parts."[22] Bohm rhetorically asks: "Why then, do we not drop our fragmentary Western approach and adopt these Eastern notions which include not only a self-world view that denies division and fragmentation but also techniques of meditation?"[23]

Robert Oppenheimer [1904-1967] was an American theoretical physicist who is remembered for his famous role as the Director of the Manhattan Project, a World War II research program designed to produce the first atomic bomb. In 1954 he wrote,

The general notions about human understanding...which are illustrated by discoveries in atomic physics are not in the nature of things wholly unfamiliar, wholly unheard of, or new. Even in our own culture they have a history, and in Buddhist and Hindu thought a more considerable and central place. What we shall find is an exemplification, and encouragement, and a refinement of old wisdom.[24]

Oppenheimer continues:

If we ask, for instance, whether the position of the electron remains the same, we must say "no;" if we ask whether the electron's position changes with time, we must say "no;" if we ask whether the electron is at rest, we must say "no;" if we ask whether it is in motion, we must say "no." The Buddha has given such answers when interrogated as to the conditions of man's self after his death; but they are not familiar answers for the tradition of seventeenth- and eighteenth-century science.[25]

The metaphysical speculations of some 20th century physicists set the stage for further advancements in this field of exploration. In 1975, Fritjof Capra, a New Age author with a Ph.D. in Theoretical Physics, wrote a ground-breaking book on the alleged parallels between quantum physics and Eastern spirituality. In his book titled, *The Tao of Physics: An Explanation of the Parallels Between Modern Physics and Eastern Mysticism*, Capra wrote,

> The purpose of this book is to explore the relationship between the concepts of modern physics and the basic ideas in the philosophical and religious traditions of the Far East. We shall see how the two foundations of twentieth-century physics – quantum theory and relativity – both force us to see the world very much in the way a Hindu, Buddhist or Taoist sees it. The most important characteristic of the Eastern world view – one could almost say the essence of it – is the awareness of the unity and mutual interrelation of all things and events, the experience of all phenomena in the world as manifestations of a basic oneness. All things are seen as interdependent and inseparable parts of this cosmic whole; as different manifestations of the same ultimate reality.[26]

Fritjof Capra's book was the first explicitly New Age interpretation of quantum physics for the popular audience and it quickly became a bestseller. Since its initial publication it has now been published in 43 different editions in 23 different languages. In the epilogue of the book Capra says, "Physicists do not need mysticism, and mystics do not need physics, but humanity needs both."[27]

Following on the heels of the success of *The Tao of Physics* another extremely popular New Age author, Gary Zukav, published a book four years later titled, *The Dancing Wu Li Masters: An Overview of the New Physics.*

According to Zukav, *Wu Li* means "patterns of organic energy" or "patterns of universal order" in Chinese. It is the Chinese description of physics. According to Gary Zukav, who is not himself a quantum physicist, "the *Wu Li* was 'a vehicle through which we could present the seminal elements of advanced physics.'"[28] Using the metaphor of "Master," he asserted that the Master is one who teaches the essence of something. Hence, the "Wu Li Master" teaches us the essence of physics.

> The Wu Li Master dances with his student. The Wu Li Master does not teach, but the student learns. The Wu Li Master always begins at the centre, the heart of the matter.... This book deals not with knowledge, which is always past tense anyway, but with imagination, which is physics come alive, which is Wu Li... Most people believe that physicists are explaining the world. Some physicists even believe that, but the Wu Li Masters know that they are only dancing with it. *The Dancing Wu Li Masters* is a book of essence: the essence of quantum mechanics and some ideas that indicate the direction that physics seems to be moving.[29]

CONSCIOUSNESS AND MATTER

This "direction" that Zukav refers to is the exploration of the relationship between human consciousness and the essence of physical reality. Zukav asks the question: is so-called "matter" really just a manifestation of consciousness?

> The world we "see" may seem solid and predictable, but at bottom, we are entitled to wonder whether "matter" even exists at all in any permanent way, or is just a momentary meeting of forces that we call "matter" as a convenience. Interestingly enough, this echoes some things said centuries ago by the Buddha and other eastern philosophers about the fundamental nature of reality.[30]

Zukav's bestselling book went on to win the prestigious American Book Award.[31] He was helped with the quantum physics aspect of his book by Jack Sarfatti, a colleague of David Bohm and a researcher into the relationship between consciousness and matter. Sarfatti, an American theoretical physicist, is heavily involved in what has come to be called "Quantum Mysticism." He has authored many books that explore the theme of quantum physics and consciousness. The basic premise of all research into the relationship between quantum reality and consciousness is that "God" and the physical universe are one, not two distinct realities. Because humans are the only self-conscious beings who are capable of contemplating their own inner divinity, they can cultivate the power of consciousness to create their own reality. This has now been allegedly proven by quantum physics because it has been established that the consciousness of the observer has the capacity to affect and shape the quantum field.

Zukav argues that the study of quantum physics itself is a mind expanding experience that has the potential to bring a shift in consciousness. "The development of physics in the twentieth century already has transformed the consciousness of those involved with it."[32] One only has to look back to the mystical musings of some of the pioneers of the science of quantum research to appreciate the shift that has taken place in our understanding of the role of consciousness in shaping our reality.

It seems that the science of quantum physics has the same effect upon many people who are drawn into studying this subject. Shirley MacLaine, popular actress and New Age author of *Dancing in the Light*, commented, "I thought of all the books I have read – and tried to understand – on quantum physics, (the new physics they called it), it sounded so much like ancient Eastern mysticism."[33] Perhaps it sounds so much like Eastern mysticism because there is a definite agenda amongst many authors in this field to promote the idea that cutting edge science establishes long cherished New Age teachings.

Another well known quantum physicist who has drifted increasingly toward a New Age interpretation of physics is Nick Herbert Ph.D. Herbert became a popular author through his 1985 publication, *Quantum Reality: Beyond the New Physics* which explored the different models of reality that have been proposed by physicists in their attempt to unravel the mysteries of the quantum world. His first book did not contain any New Age metaphysics; however he then went on to write, *Elemental Mind: Consciousness and the New Physics* in 1994, which explored the relationship between consciousness and matter. In this book Herbert argued that paranormal phenomena prove the reality of disincarnate spirits and he proposed the idea that consciousness, (whether of living or disincarnate beings) can manipulate the quantum world.

Herbert proposed that the mind or consciousness is an elemental force that interacts with the world much like the force of electromagnetism or gravity. His second book indicated a decisive shift toward New Age metaphysics. Herbert's latest book is titled, *Quantum Tantra: Quantum Physics as Deep Union with Nature.* Herbert takes the "consciousness and matter" relationship to a whole new level by using the metaphor of playful tantric sex as a paradigm for exploring the relationship between the observer and nature. According to Herbert:

> *Quantum Tantra* attempts to blaze a new pathway for science by incorporating previously discarded and marginal ways of thinking into a new synthesis. Tantra teaches that the universe is not mere motion of dead matter but the sexual play of two divine beings and seeks techniques to directly participate in that holy play. The goal of *Quantum Tantra* is to initiate an entirely new direction of research by approaching quantum theory and its paradoxes as if they were incomplete fragments of a "successor science" based on tantric and alchemical principles.[34]

In recent decades New Age speculations about the nature of reality in the light of quantum physics have become extremely sophisticated. The appearance of the *What the Bleep Do We Know?* movie, which was released in 2004, has been tremendously successful and has also been the most triumphant endeavour to date to promote the New Age viewpoint and to claim the high ground in the interpretation of quantum physics in Western culture. The movie grossed over US$10 million and appeared in theatres around the world for up to a year. The movie has spawned an online subculture with forums, discussions, lecture circuits, seminars and plenty of recruits for the *Ramtha School of Enlightenment*[35] which funded the production of the high budget movie. Similarly, *The Secret* DVD released in 2006 is another popularisation of the same idea that consciousness creates reality. It was followed by a 2009 DVD sequel titled *Beyond the Secret* which explained why adherents need to be patient with the "law of attraction" if they want to use it to create reality.

Fred Alan Wolf is one of the leading apologists for the New Age interpretation of quantum physics. He earned a Ph.D. in theoretical physics and he appears in both *What the Bleep* and *The Secret* to promote his views on the relationship between consciousness and matter. He is the author of *Taking the Quantum Leap: The New Physics for Non-Scientists* which was published in 1982 and which won the National Book Award. He also wrote *Mind into Matter: A New Alchemy of Science and Spirit* [2000].

Wolf appears on radio shows all over the U.S. and on the Discovery Channel using quantum physics to argue that humans have the power to harness their consciousness to create reality at a quantum level. An entirely new media industry has emerged around the popularisation of this single New Age concept. There is a big market for these ideas and they are currently being exported through books, DVDs, CDs, training programs, movie theatres, radio and television, and they all carry the same basic message: "All is one and your consciousness is an expression of the universal mind of God! You have the power to alter your reality through applying the technique of mind over matter!"

The shift that is occurring in popular thought is a reflection of the widespread adoption of a concept that has become a "self-evident truth" in Western culture. Remember the shift that came when evolutionary teaching was elevated from the status of a *theory* into an unassailable truth? The same shift is now occurring in Western culture which is resulting in a key New Age concept capturing the popular imagination and being transformed into a new self-evident truth right before our eyes. This new "truth" boldly asserts that quantum physics confirms the fact that science has now proven, that consciousness creates reality. Marilyn Ferguson, the author of *The Aquarian Conspiracy*, writes, "Science is only confirming paradoxes and intuitions humankind has come across many times but stubbornly disregarded."[36]

These intuitions are the ideas expressed through contemporary New Age teachings: the seductive idea that you are God and that everything is one! Pantheism[37] is a powerfully compelling idea that has the innate power to capture the popular imagination. Fred Alan Wolf, in *The Spiritual Universe* [1996] speaks fondly of "our present modern vision of an abstract God and mysterious eternal soul"[38] that is present throughout all matter in the universe. Wolf delights in the fact that this pantheistic vision of nature is "returning to our time"[39] and that the biblical conception of a personal God is being replaced with a far more palatable and non-threatening vision of divinity.

Amit Goswami, yet another quantum physicist with a Ph.D. in theoretical physics, also appears in the *What the Bleep* movie. Goswami, in his book, *The Self-Aware Universe: How Consciousness Creates the Material World*, asserts that "science proves the potency of monistic philosophy over dualism – over spirit separated from matter."[40] "Monism" is the Eastern concept that all is one whereas "dualism" teaches two distinct and separate realities, that of the realm of "spirit" and of "matter." Western thought has traditionally been dualistic in that it has embraced the biblical idea of a spiritual realm and a material realm.

Eastern philosophy has never embraced this dualistic interpretation of reality, and Amit Goswami is convinced that quantum physics has shifted the centre of gravity away from Western dualism back to a monistic view of reality – that all is one.

Goswami envisions a universe that is animated by spirit so that the entire universe is a manifestation of "God." The collective impact of a number of high profile professors who are qualified in the field of quantum physics, all advocating an Eastern, New Age interpretation of reality is shifting popular sentiment further toward the new "self-evident truth" of quantum mysticism. All committed New Agers are now firmly convinced through the vast body of literature that has been published in the last three decades that science indeed proves that matter is shaped by consciousness.

And to drive the point home, radical quantum theorists are now boldly asserting the primacy of consciousness in stark contrast to the dominant scientific paradigm of the primacy of matter. Goswami calls his new paradigm, "monistic idealism," the idea that consciousness is the foundation of everything that exists. He teaches that in order for the universe to exist it must have a conscious observer. Without an observer it remains only a possibility. Therefore it is only "observation" and the intentional exercise of consciousness that forces the universe into a state of material reality. This reflects the notion of the superiority of consciousness over matter. This is where the new paradigm converges with Eastern mysticism. Goswami says:

> Mystics, contrary to religionists, are always saying that reality is not two things (God and the world) but one thing; consciousness. The problem with science has always been that most scientists believe that science must be done within a different monistic framework; one based on the primacy of matter. Quantum physics showed us that we must change that myopic prejudice of scientists, otherwise we cannot comprehend quantum physics. So now we have science within consciousness, a new paradigm of science based on the primacy of consciousness that is gradually replacing the old materialist science.[41]

QUANTUM MYSTICISM

These and similar writings point toward the development of an emerging trend. It is interesting to trace the development amongst many quantum physicists from a purely rationalistic scientific paradigm to New Age metaphysical speculation and finally to advocacy for the New Age cause in their writings over the past three decades. Nowhere is this trend more evident than in the lives of Fred Alan Wolf and Amit Goswami who most recently appeared on the latest New Age documentary titled the *Dalai Lama Renaissance*.[42] With almost 20 published books between them and guest appearances in almost every form of popular media, these two men who began as secular quantum physicists have transitioned over the decades to become full blown advocates of the New Age worldview. The orientation of their lives toward this arena of metaphysics highlights the seductive nature of the marriage between quantum science and New Age spirituality. Essentially this represents a marriage of convenience between spiritual philosophy and quantum physics.

But not everyone has been swept up in the explosion of quantum mysticism. Richard Dawkins, the supreme rationalist evolutionist (with an axe to grind against all forms of spirituality) cynically writes, "Quantum mechanics, that brilliantly successful flagship theory of modern science, is deeply mysterious and hard to understand. Eastern mystics have always been deeply mysterious and hard to understand. Therefore, Eastern mystics must have been talking about quantum theory all along."[43] Of course, not all quantum physicists are inclined toward quantum mysticism. There are still many purely secular scientists who reject the New Age interpretation. One opponent of what he calls "Quantum Quackery" is Victor Stenger, a Professor of Physics at the University of Hawaii. He is a fierce opponent of the marriage between quantum physics and New Age mysticism. He writes,

> "Quantum" is the magic incantation that appears in virtually everything written on alternative medicine. It seems to be uttered in order to make all the inconsistencies, incoherencies, and incompatibilities of the proposed scheme disappear in a puff of smoke. Since quantum mechanics is weird, anything weird must be quantum mechanics.[44]

Victor Stenger is the author of *The Unconscious Quantum* and *Quantum Gods*. According to Stenger,

> Certain interpretations of quantum mechanics... are being misconstrued so as to imply that only thoughts are real and that the physical universe is the product of a cosmic mind to which the human mind is linked throughout space and time. This interpretation has provided an ostensibly scientific basis for various mind-over-matter

claims, from ESP to alternative medicine. "Quantum mysticism" also forms part of the intellectual backdrop for the postmodern assertion that science has no claim on objective reality. Quantum mechanics is misinterpreted as implying that the human mind controls reality and that the universe is one connected whole that cannot be understood by the usual reduction to parts. No compelling argument or evidence requires that quantum mechanics plays a central role in human consciousness or provides instantaneous, holistic connections across the universe. Modern physics, including quantum mechanics, remains completely materialistic and reductionistic while being consistent with all scientific observations.[45]

The presence of trained quantum physicists who have not embraced any elements of quantum mysticism is itself a clear indicator that the real issue is someone's predetermined worldview. If someone has embraced a spiritual worldview there will be a greater temptation to argue that quantum physics supports that particular spiritual worldview. In the same way, if someone is a devout secularist they will not see any evidence to support a spiritual worldview even if there are elements of compelling evidence. The quantum physics community is clearly divided in their interpretation of the mysteries of the quantum world. Of course there will always be secular antagonists who oppose anything that smacks of "quantum mysticism" but there is an increasing number of physicists who are resorting to mystical interpretations to explain the counter-intuitive nature of the quantum world.

Those within the New Age community no longer question the widely accepted conclusions of New Age quantum physicists: the plethora of books written by expert scientists who have converted to the New Age worldview now effectively substantiate and prove the new paradigm. Ken Wilbur, who highlighted the mystical orientation of a number of 20th century quantum physicists in his book, *Quantum Questions*, notes that the New Age community is now,

> ...firmly convinced that modern physics automatically supports or proves mysticism. This view is now so widespread, so deeply entrenched, so taken for granted by New Agers, that I don't see that any one book could possibly reverse this tide. It was, I believe, with every good intention that this "physics-supports-mysticism" idea was proposed, and it was with every good intention that it was so rapidly and widely accepted. But I believe these good intentions

were misplaced and the results have been not just wrong but detrimental. Modern physics offers no support (let alone proof) for a mystical worldview.[46]

In this chapter we have traced the development of what I have called the "hijacking" of quantum physics. We have seen how the New Age community has co-opted the discoveries of the "new physics" to assert that the quantum world actually teaches an eastern mystical worldview. Ernest Lucas, in his book, *Science and the New Age Challenge,* writes, "When claiming scientific support for their view of reality, New Agers often appeal to the "new physics." This is not a term which they invented, but it does have the advantage of paralleling the term "New Age."[47] Fritjof Capra argues that the new physics presents an entirely new vision of the universe that reveals "philosophical conceptions which are in striking agreement with those in Eastern mysticism."[48] The emerging New Age vision coalesces around a number of key concepts that have now become self evident truths to all who have adopted the New Age interpretation of quantum physics.

Ernest Lucas traces these key concepts in his book, *Science and the New Age Challenge.* The first major concept is the notion that the material world is an illusion. Capra says, "Like modern physicists, Buddhists see all objects as processes in a universal flux and deny the existence of any material substance."[49] Zukav says, "The world of matter is an illusory one: illusory not in the sense that it does not exist, but illusory in the sense that we do not see it as it really is."[50] New Ager mysticism teaches that the material world is really an interplay of fields of quantum energy.

The second major concept teaches that "the universe must be seen as a unified, inter-connected whole."[51] Zukav explains that quantum non-locality teaches us that "what happens here is intimately and immediately connected to what happens elsewhere in the universe, and so on, simply because the 'separate parts' of the universe are not separate parts."[52] This translates in New Age thinking to the idea that all is God and all is one. New Age pantheism teaches that you are God and that your consciousness is, in fact, divine consciousness.

The third major concept to emerge from the New Age interpretation of quantum physics is the idea that "human consciousness plays a part in creating reality."[53] This is the key concept that leads the New Age practitioner to expend considerable energy in seeking to apply their consciousness to the creation of new realities such as health and wealth. Michael Talbot, author of *Mysticism and the New Physics* explains the interplay between consciousness and matter.

> For centuries the mystic has asserted that matter and consciousness are different aspects of the same something. For all those who have spent their lives trying to penetrate the secrets of matter, the new physics has a message, not a new one, but one that may well turn out to be the most important rediscovery humankind has ever made....the message of the new physics is that we are participators in a universe of increasing wonder.[54]

These key concepts, (1) that the material world is really a field of cosmic energy that can be manipulated by consciousness, (2) that we are all a part of a cosmically interconnected whole and (3) that our consciousness is an untapped resource that can shape reality, have emerged into a cluster of powerful ideas that have gripped the popular imagination in the Western world. These ideas are popularised by people like Shirley MacLaine and Oprah Winfrey who exercise extraordinary spheres of influence in our culture. These ideas are potent in that they appeal directly to people who feel disempowered and who are searching for a sense of personal empowerment to change their often unhappy life circumstances. Quantum physics is now cited as a scientific proof that these concepts are true, setting the compass for a socio-spiritual revolution.

To understand the New Age obsession with quantum physics we must have a basic understanding of the nature of the quantum world. When we understand some of the weird properties of the quantum world it becomes more apparent why New Agers have adopted quantum physics to try to substantiate their spiritual worldview. It also explains why so many physicists with Ph.D.'s have been drawn into the maelstrom of New Age ideas and teachings. We are touching upon a powerfully seductive idea for which there is a growing market. So, in order to grasp the essence of this highly appealing concept we must go on a journey together into the heart of the quantum world with a view to coming out the other side with a clearer understanding of the rationale behind the New Age hijacking of quantum physics.

Chapter Two

ENTERING THE WORLD OF THE QUANTUM

What can the average person on the street hope to understand about the quantum world? Is the science of quantum physics largely impenetrable to the uninitiated? Does someone have to have a university degree in mathematical physics to penetrate the veil of this frontier science? Some scientists would argue in the affirmative, suggesting that too many fanciful speculations about quantum physics have emerged precisely because the uninitiated have not fully grasped the mathematics of quantum realities and are therefore disqualified to speculate on the metaphysical implications of this field of science.

However, there have been countless volumes written by the initiated for the uninitiated to ponder this strange new sub-atomic world. If qualified quantum physicists believe that popular books, stripped of all of the mathematical equations, can indeed benefit the general public, then we can assume that there are discoveries from the frontiers of physics that can be understood by the public even when the uninitiated cannot understand the mathematical equations behind the discoveries.

In my quest to grasp the basic concepts behind quantum physics I have spent the last few years reading widely in this field, building a library of resources and pondering the descriptions of the quantum world by many popular authors who use various analogies to try to communicate to the public audience those findings which have created such a groundswell of interest in this subject. On numerous occasions I have found myself standing in the physics or science sections of large bookshops pondering various new acquisitions in my quest to penetrate the mysteries of quantum physics.

I have greatly enjoyed reading such popular authors as Paul Davies, Brian Greene, John Gribbin, Isaac Asimov, Sir Roger Penrose and Richard Feynman, but I was disappointed to learn that there is not one conclusive interpretation of the quantum world. Instead there are quite a few competing interpretations that have given rise to conflicting theories within the field of quantum physics. This heightened the challenge to arrive at a fixed point of reference because it meant attempting to penetrate and comprehend the competing interpretations.

Every scientist has an interpretation. I found the biggest hurdle to be the realisation that well intentioned scientists impose their own interpretations upon the facts and interweave the description of the greatest discoveries of the quantum world with their own unique interpretations. But this is the nature of the scientific method. A theory is set forth and then tested and cross examined to see if it accurately reflects reality.

Many of the conflicting theories are driven by metaphysical speculations where those who are doing the speculating are seeking to interpret quantum realities through their own unique paradigm. I was encouraged to find that there were some clear concepts that have emerged from the study of the quantum world that are almost universally accepted by most quantum physicists. The divergences come from the various schools of interpretation that have arisen as different theorists from different traditions have sought to place an interpretation upon the emerging discoveries of the sub-atomic world.

There are spiritual theorists, secular theorists, metaphysical theorists, anti-metaphysical theorists, New Age theorists, biblical theorists and so on, all seeking to grasp the meaning of quantum mechanics. But leaving aside all of these theories of the meaning of the quantum world, we are left with some very startling discoveries in the sub-atomic world of nature that are supported both scientifically and mathematically. It is these almost universally accepted quantum realities that we wish to explore in this chapter. We will leave the theoretical speculations to subsequent chapters.

ENTERING THE SUB-ATOMIC WORLD

To grasp the nature of the quantum world we must reduce our scale of thinking down to the infinitesimally small. The world of the quantum is so unimaginably small that it is difficult to understand how something so incredibly small could still have structure and measurable attributes. Quantum physicists keep on pressing the envelope in probing the depths of the world of matter. Physics is that field of science which explores the nature of the physical world that we live in. Physicists are fascinated by the nature of matter. They want to know what the universe is made of and what holds it together.

What is the nature of matter and what is the smallest constituent part of matter? Is it a point particle as the standard model of the atom asserts or is it made up of tiny strings of vibrating energy as the string theorists speculate? Physics concerns itself with matter, energy, force, motion, space, time, gravity, mass and electrical charge. These are all the domain of the physicist who explores the relationship between all of these realities and who seeks to arrive at an exact mathematical measurement of the characteristics and the forces of nature.

Quantum physics concerns itself with the study of the constituent elements of nature which are divided into discrete units or packets of energy called "quanta." This is where the word "quantum" comes from. The world of the quantum is the world of sub-atomic particles and photons that interact with one another in the smallest scale of the universe. Everything is made up of these microscopic quantities of energy. But to use the word "microscopic" can be somewhat misleading because the world of quantum realities are unimaginably smaller than microscopic ingredients.

All of matter is made up of molecules and molecules are made up of atoms. So how small is an atom? Richard Feynman, one of the greatest physicists of the 20th century says, "If an apple is magnified to the size of the earth, then the atoms in the apple are approximately the size of the original apple!"[1] That's small! So small that no one will ever see an atom even with the most powerful microscopes ever developed. How many atoms are there is a single droplet of water? "There are 2,000,000,000,000,000,000,000 (that's 2 sextillion) atoms of oxygen in one drop of water – and twice as many atoms of hydrogen."[2] A speck of dust can contain up to three trillion atoms.[3] Imagine just how many atoms there are in the entire universe! God only knows!

A simple water molecule [H_2O] consists of two hydrogen atoms and one oxygen atom bonded together to form a molecule. A hydrogen atom consists of a single electron and a single proton. It is the simplest atom that has ever been discovered. Therefore its "atomic number" is 1. A helium atom has two protons, therefore its atomic number is 2. We all know helium as an extremely light gas which carries helium balloons high into the stratosphere. A carbon atom has 6 protons. (atomic number = 6) A nitrogen atom has 7 protons. (atomic number = 7) An oxygen atom has 8 protons. (atomic number = 8)

Every different kind of atom that has been discovered appears on the "Periodic Table of Elements" and each atom has its own unique properties. A lead atom, for example, has 82 electrons, 82 protons and 125 neutrons. Lead is a heavy element. Unlike helium, we all know that lead goes down instead of up. The human body is made up of 63% hydrogen, 25.5% oxygen, 9.5% carbon and 1.4% nitrogen which constitutes 99.5% of the entire human body. We are made of atoms just like everything else in the universe. There are 117 known elements that occur naturally in the earth.

Now we might wonder, what exactly is inside an atom? The atom consists of an extremely small nucleus and a cloud of electrons jiggling around the nucleus at almost the speed of light! The traditional notion of negatively charged electrons neatly orbiting the positively charged nucleus in much the same way that the planets orbit around the sun is now considered to be incorrect. Rather, the electrons are in a state of frenzied activity and the world of the atom is in a state of violent quantum fluctuations.

The ratio of the size of the nucleus to the rest of the atom is astonishingly small. The nucleus of the atom consists of only one part in 100 trillion. The area occupied by the electrons constitutes most of the volume of the atom. To use an analogy, the nucleus would be the equivalent of a grain of sand in the centre of a large sports stadium. The outermost fringe of the stadium's seating would be the edge of the atom's entire volume and the electrons that violently oscillate in a cloud around the nucleus can occasionally extend right to the outer fringe of the atom's volume. But what we now call the atom consists mostly of empty space! Richard Feynman gives us an extraordinary description of the nature of an atom:

An atom has a diameter of about 10_{-8} cm. The nucleus has a diameter of about 10_{-23} cm. If we had an atom and wished to see the nucleus, we would have to magnify it until the whole atom was the size of a large room, and then the nucleus would be a bare speck which you could just about make out with the eye, but very nearly all the weight of the atom is in that infinitesimal nucleus.[4]

Gerald Schroeder, the Israeli physicist, uses another analogy to explain the extent of apparent empty space within the atom:

> Solid matter, the floor upon which we stand and the foundation which bears the weight of a skyscraper, is actually empty space. If we could scale the centre of an atom, the nucleus, up to four inches, the surrounding electron cloud would extend to four miles away and essentially all the breach between would be marvellously empty. The solidity of iron is actually 99.9999999999999 percent startlingly vacuous space made to feel solid by ethereal fields of force having no material reality at all. But don't knock your head against that space. Force fields can feel very solid.[5]

The nucleus of the atom consists of a bundle of positively charged protons and neutrons (that have a neutral charge) tightly bound together to form the tiny core at the heart of the atom. The electron is much smaller in size than the proton and the neutron and has considerably less mass. The comparison between the mass of an electron to a proton or a neutron is staggering; protons and neutrons are almost 2,000 times heavier than electrons! If we were to journey deeper still into the heart of protons, electrons and neutrons we would find that they consist of even smaller components. The electron is made up of "leptons" and the protons and neutrons are made up of "quarks." Quarks are believed to be less than one thousandth the size of protons and neutrons, and there are believed to be approximately a thousand quarks in the nucleus of the average atom. Quarks were once believed to be the smallest fundamental ingredient of the atom. But according to string theorists, the fundamental elements that constitute the quarks get even smaller still.

The standard model of the atom claims that the smallest possible components are zero-dimensional "point particles" which are for all intents and purposes nothing more than miniscule "dots." String theorists challenge the standard model and argue that the smallest constituent elements are tiny loops of oscillating, vibrating energy called "strings." According to string theory the leptons and the quarks are themselves made up of loops of vibrating strings that are folded up within extra dimensions that are so small they cannot be detected.

According to Brian Greene, author of *The Elegant Universe* and one of the most passionate advocates of string theory, "The length of a typical string loop is about a hundred billion, billion times smaller than an atomic nucleus."[6] In terms of size, a string is so small that it can only be illustrated by analogies such as our earlier comparison between the apple and the earth. If a single atom was enlarged to the size of our entire solar system, then a string would be no larger than that of a tree on earth.[7] Now that's super small! Physicists describes the length of a string as a "Planck length" or 10_{-33} cm.[8]

So what is a quantum particle in relation to the tiny world of the atom? Well, a quantum particle is an indivisible unit or packet of energy. The word "quanta" describes a mathematically determined "quantity" of energy such as a photon or an electron. Max Planck was awarded the Nobel Prize in 1918 for his contribution to science for discovering that all of nature is made up of these invisible quanta of energy. These are the smallest units into which something can be partitioned. There are many different kinds of quanta. We have mentioned the photon but we could also mention electromagnetic radiation and electrons that carry a certain amount of quantum energy. So, we understand that the atom is made up of quantum ingredients; therefore, the entire universe is made up of quanta (or quantities) of energy. Quantum physics is therefore the study of the physical world at the scale of these quanta.

One of the strangest features of the sub-atomic world is the fact that these electrons which violently jiggle around the nucleus cannot be precisely measured in terms of their position and their momentum. Because they are in a state of continuous motion with wildly oscillating velocities and trajectories, they cannot be measured. Brian Greene describes the electron cloud as a "roiling frenzy, awash in a violent sea of quantum fluctuations." This peculiar property of the quantum world gave rise to what Werner Heisenberg called the Uncertainty Principle. This is a principle of quantum mechanics that was discovered and identified by Heisenberg.

According to Brian Greene, the Uncertainty Principle emphatically teaches that "the features of the universe, like the position and velocity of a particle...cannot be known with complete precision" because "particles and fields undulate and jump between all possible values consistent with the quantum uncertainty."[9] This has been a source of frustration to quantum physicists.

Another feature of the quantum world is its ability to exist at an extraordinary range of temperatures. If we consider the vast range of temperatures in the entire universe and then realize that the entire universe is made of atoms, it becomes apparent that atoms are extremely durable little things! Absolute zero is a theoretic state that has never been achieved by scientists. It is 0 degrees Kelvin or -273.15 degrees Celsius. The temperature in deep space is said to be 2 degrees above absolute zero. At absolute zero, quantum mechanical systems are said to reach "zero-point energy." In quantum field theory the zero point field is the lowest possible energy that a quantum system may possess.

At these extremes of cold, some quantum systems exhibit a property called "superconductivity" where there is zero electrical resistance. But Richard Feynman speculates that even if absolute zero was attainable, "the atoms do not stop moving; they still jiggle. Why? If they stopped moving, we would know where they were and that they had zero motion, and that is against the Uncertainty Principle. We cannot know where they are and how fast they are moving, so they must be continually wiggling in there."[10] According to Feynman, the Uncertainty Principle rules over all possible states of a quantum field.

Let's go to the other end of the scale and consider the hottest attainable temperature in the universe. We might think of the temperature of the largest sun in the universe, but apparently that doesn't even come close to the hottest possible temperature. The theoretical highest achievable temperature is called the Planck temperature and it is estimated to be 10^{32} Kelvin. That is 100 million, million, million, million, million degrees Kelvin, which Big Bang cosmologists suggest was the temperature of the Big Bang at the creation of the universe.[11]

The universe has cooled considerably since then with the highest known temperatures hovering around 10 million degrees C experienced on the surface of the sun and in a nuclear explosion. But even at these unimaginably high temperatures, an atom is a stable system with electrons still jiggling (perhaps a bit faster) around the nucleus of the atom. The sun consists of 70% hydrogen atoms and 28% helium atoms, and even at these unfathomable temperatures the atoms still do what atoms do!

Divine Omniscience and the Atom

If the universe is made up of atoms, and atoms are made up of quantum particles, then it is not at all improbable to consider that God can view the world of atoms and even the world of quanta just as He would view the macroscopic world that we are accustomed to observing. The biblical revelation of the "omniscience" of God would incline us to believe that nothing is hidden from the observation of God, whether macroscopic or microscopic or even sub-atomic. The Bible teaches that *Nothing* in all creation is hidden from God's sight. Everything is uncovered and laid bare before the eyes of Him to whom we must give account." (Hebrews 4:13 NIV) "Nothing" in the Greek language means "nothing!"

If God is indeed omniscient, then we could also safely assume that God knows the entire number of atoms in the entire universe. That is a staggering thought to meditate upon, but this seems to be the logical implication of the words of Jesus who said that, "The very hairs of your head are all numbered." (Matthew 10:30) The psalmist declared that God "counts the number of the stars; He calls them all by name. Great is our Lord, and mighty in power; His understanding is infinite." (Psalm 147:4-5) His understanding would indeed need to be infinite when we consider that there are between 150 and 200 billion stars in the Milky Way galaxy, of which our sun is but one! And there are estimated to be over 150 billion galaxies in the universe, some of which have more than five trillion stars all by themselves![12]

The Bible has an exceptionally high, indeed, *unlimited* view of the omniscience of God. Isaiah asks the question: "Who has measured the waters in the hollow of his hand, or with the breadth of his hand marked off the heavens? Who has held the dust of the earth in a measure, or weighed the mountains on the scales and the hills in a balance? Who has understood the mind of the Lord?" (Isaiah 40:12-13 NIV)

If God can count the stars and if He knows them each by name, if He can span the entire universe with His hand, then it follows that He can also plumb the depths of the quantum world and perceive even the number of leptons and quarks in the entire universe, or beyond that, even the number of tiny vibrating strings in the universe, if string theory is correct! Isaiah said that God can hold particles of dust in a measure. Surely the juxtaposition between the vastness of the universe and a minute particle of dust would suggest that God's omniscience extends from the macroscopic world to the microscopic world.

There is a debate about whether the omniscience of God extends to the violent fluctuations of the electron. In the light of quantum indeterminacy or the Uncertainty Principle, the question has been raised about God's ability to penetrate the mysterious quantum world. Arthur Peacocke, who is both a scientist and a theologian, writes, "God has so made the natural order that it is, in principle, impossible even for God, as it is for us, to predict the precise future values of certain variables."[13] Peacocke suggests that even God "does not know which of a million radium atoms will be the next to disintegrate in, say, the next 10 seconds but only...what the average number will be that will break up in that period of time."[14]

Is the Uncertainty Principle even binding on God? Peacocke finds it inconceivable that God's omniscience could extend to the world of quantum indeterminacy. Admittedly, it is challenging to grasp the idea that God could look into the sub-atomic world and know with absolute certainty the outcome of all quantum possibilities at all times. The idea of partial foreknowledge and limited omniscience has been proposed by others in the history of the church, but the answer to this theological dilemma lies in the transcendence of God.

John Jefferson Davis, in an essay titled "Quantum Indeterminacy and the Omniscience of God" argues that "the realities of quantum physics do not require the abandonment of the concept of maximal divine omniscience."[15] He proposes that the solution can be found in the complementary nature of God's transcendence and His immanence. "God is understood to be both immanent within the space-time order and transcendent of it." Because God is transcendent over the created order He stands outside of the space-time manifold, yet He is "free to be present within the space-time manifold"[16] as He interacts with His creation within the context of time and space to which we are bound. Because God transcends time He can see the end from the beginning. That is why He is called "The Alpha and the Omega, the Beginning and the End." (Revelation 1:8) His omniscience extends to all quantum possibilities because He is transcendent beyond space and time.

THE CENTRAL MYSTERY OF QUANTUM PHYSICS

When you get down to the tiny scale of photons and electrons, the rules that govern the world we live in, the "classical" world of physics, give way to the rules of "quantum mechanics." At some point along the line, as things get smaller and smaller, the rules of the classical world change over to the rules of the quantum world. All those who are initiated into the complex world of quantum mechanics seem to have the same kind of reaction; they use words such as "shock," "mystery" and "weird."

In a now famous quote, Niels Bohr said concerning the quantum world, "Those who are not shocked when they first come across quantum theory cannot possibly have understood it."[17] Physicists are absolutely certain of the properties of the quantum world because the mechanics of quantum physics are tested and validated mathematically. The mathematical laws of the quantum world are extraordinarily accurate! But no-one can rationally explain the mystery of what they have discovered in the world of quantum mechanics. John Archibald Wheeler says, "The quantum is the greatest mystery we've got."

Quantum theory has consistently proven to be a very successful mathematical description of the structure of the atomic world. Marvin Chester wrote in his *Primer on Quantum Mechanics*: "The mathematical predictions of quantum mechanics yield results that are in agreement with experimental findings. That is the reason we use quantum theory. That quantum theory fits experiment is what validates the theory, *but why experiment should give such peculiar results is a mystery*. This is the "shock" to which Niels Bohr referred."[18] However strange it may seem, quantum theory has survived all the experimental tests it has been subjected to. Richard Feynman said,

> I think it is safe to say that no one understands quantum mechanics. In fact, it is often stated that of all the theories proposed in this century, the silliest is quantum theory. Some say that the only thing that quantum theory has going for it, in fact, is that it is unquestionably correct. Do not keep saying to yourself, if you can possibly avoid it, "But how can it possibly be like that?" because you will go down the drain into a blind alley from which nobody has yet escaped.[19] We have always had a great deal of difficulty understanding the world view that quantum mechanics represents. At least I do, because I'm an old enough man that I haven't got to the point that this stuff is obvious to me. Okay, I still get nervous with it... You know how it always is, every new idea, it takes a generation or two until it becomes obvious that there's no real problem. I cannot define the real problem, therefore I suspect that there is no real problem, but I'm not sure there's no real problem.[20]

Thanks for the clarification Mr. Feynman! So what is so weird about the quantum world that makes so many people become strangely fascinated by it? Why does it magnetically attract all sorts of mystical metaphysical speculation? A brief journey through some of the most significant historical developments in the evolution of quantum physics will shed more light on the weird properties of this strange frontier science.

We begin this brief journey with Max Planck who was the father of quantum theory. In the early part of the 20th century, Planck made the assumption that energy was made of individual units, or "quanta." The existence of these discrete units became the first assumption of quantum theory. The discovery that energy came in discrete packets or quantities revolutionised scientist's understanding of the nature of matter and energy. As physicists continued to probe the new frontiers of the sub-atomic world, they began to discover attributes of this world that were entirely counter-intuitive. These discoveries went against all instinctive understanding that we humans have developed through our regular interaction with the classical world of physics.

One of the most striking features of the quantum world is what has been called the "wave-particle duality." In 1924, Louis de Broglie proposed that there was no fundamental difference in the makeup and behaviour of energy and matter; on the atomic and subatomic level, both behave as if they are made of either particles or waves. This theory became known as the *principle of wave-particle duality*: elementary particles of both energy and matter behave, depending on the experiment, like either particles or waves. In 1906, Joseph John Thomson received the Nobel Prize for proving that electrons are particles. Ironically, in 1937 he saw his son, George Paget Thomson, awarded the same Nobel Prize in Physics for proving that electrons were waves! Both father and son were correct. From then on, the scientific evidence for the wave-particle duality has become overwhelming.

To understand this scientific journey toward the discovery of the wave-particle duality we must go back even further. Quantum physics had its origins in the seventeenth century debate over the nature of light. Isaac Newton believed that light consisted of a stream of extremely small particles, moving according to definite laws rather as macroscopic objects do. But over time other physicists began to prove that light consisted of waves. In 1801, an English physicist named Thomas Young performed an experiment that strongly inferred the wave-like properties of light. Because he believed that light was composed of waves, Young reasoned that some type of interaction would occur when two light waves met. Young developed the now famous "double-slit experiment" in which he caused light photons to pass through a single slit screen and then through a double-slit screen to observe the wave-like interference patterns of light waves. Young's experiment was based on the hypothesis that if light were wave-like in nature, then it should behave in a manner similar to ripples or waves on a pond of water.

Thomas Young's famous double-slit experiment confirmed the interference pattern and thus he scientifically proved the wave property of photons. This dual nature of light eventually came to be known as the ***wave-particle duality***. But any attempt to pin down light as being definitely one or the other failed. The best that could be said was that light *acts like* a wave when one type of experiment is being performed, but it *acts like* a stream of particles when a different type of experiment is being performed. Light travels as a wave, but departs and arrives like a particle. Of course, this raises the immediate response: how can something be simultaneously a wave or a particle? We can accept that something in the macroscopic world is either one or the other but not both at the same time! This is the shock of quantum physics: a shock that has reverberated throughout the scientific community ever since the dawn of quantum physics.

But it was not just photons that were discovered to have this wave-particle duality. To complicate matters, streams of electrons that were already long accepted as being particles were also shown to exhibit wave-like phenomena in experiments involving diffraction. The same double-slit experiment was used in the 20th century. Electrons were fired through double-slit screens to observe how they "interfere" with each other to produce regions of high and low intensity.

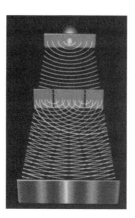

It was discovered that one electron fired through a double-slit screen travels through both slits at the same time and creates interference waves! As soon as the electron is fired it spreads out in a broad wave pattern, and when it hits the double-slit screen it passes through both slits! Because of this strange behaviour, a single electron is said to exist in a *superposition* of two "states." The double-slit experiment essentially confirmed that "matter"

also exhibits this same wave-particle duality. Through the double-slit experiment it has been established that the electron displays all the attributes of waves. How bizarre! It appears that an electron actually has the capacity to materialise and to dematerialise!

Richard Feynman, one of the 20th century's most prominent physicists, points out that the entire mystery of quantum mechanics is unveiled in the double-slit experiment. The wave-particle duality is the central mystery of quantum mechanics! Is an electron a particle of matter or a wave of energy? It was discovered and confirmed experimentally that it is both! From this reality all the other principles of quantum mechanics follow. "Superposition" therefore is a characteristic of the quantum world that describes a challenging concept about the nature and behaviour of matter and forces at the subatomic level.

The discoveries of 20th century quantum physics also tell us a great deal about the true nature of the material universe. Is the visible world of matter really material or is it essentially a manifestation of quantum energy? In their book *The Matter Myth* popular science authors, Paul Davies and John Gribbin write, "It is fitting that physics – the science that gave rise to materialism – should also signal the demise of materialism. During this century the new physics has blown apart the central tenet of materialist doctrine in a series of stunning developments."[21] Davies and Gribbin point specifically to the emergence of quantum theory,

> ...which totally transformed our image of matter. The old assumption that the microscopic world of atoms was simply a scaled down version of the everyday world had to be abandoned. An extension of the quantum theory, known as quantum field theory, goes beyond even this. It paints a picture in which solid matter dissolves away, to be replaced by weird excitations and vibrations of invisible field energy. In this theory, little distinction remains between material substance and apparent empty space, which itself seethes with ephemeral quantum activity. Quantum physics undermines materialism because it reveals that matter has far less "substance" than we might believe.[22]

THE OBSERVER EFFECT

Another strange property of quantum physics is what has been called the *observer effect,* otherwise known as the *measurement problem.* The principle of quantum superposition claims that while we do not know what the state of any object is, it is actually in all possible states simultaneously, as long as we don't look to check. It is nothing more than a cloud of ambiguous possibilities. When someone "looks" to take a measurement, it is the act of measurement itself that causes the electron to be limited to a single possibility. Whenever physicists seek to measure something at the quantum level, they "collapse" the superposition simply by the act of measuring it. Measuring actually destroys the superposition, forcing the electron into a single state. That is why physicists expect to see light as either a particle or a wave, depending on the kind of experiment they subject the photon to, because they are collapsing the superposition of the light from being particle and wave at the same time to being either one or the other. I will try to explain this bizarre feature of the quantum world but you may have to read and re-read the following paragraphs a couple of times to really absorb the impact of this strange mystery.

Remember the double-slit experiment? This experiment has been conducted using a gold foil screen with two extremely narrow slits a thousandth of a millimetre wide. Now, picture a single electron being fired at the double-slit screen so that once it has passed through the double-slit screen it hits another screen at the rear and records where the electron hits. Hidden behind the double-slit screen, (between the double-slit screen and the detector screen at the rear) is a particle detector: a measuring device that measures when an electron passes through the double-slit screen.

When a single electron is fired through the double-slit screen whilst the detector is switched on the act of measurement mysteriously collapses the dual nature of the electron into a particle state so that it only passes through a single slit, much like a bullet passes through a doorway in a wall. The detector can determine which slit the electron passed through so that it picks up that it is acting like a single particle passing through only one slit. But, do the experiment again and this time remove or switch off the detector and the electron will pass through both slits at the same time!

The reason scientists know that the electron has passed through both slits of the double-slit screen is because the electron has created an interference pattern which shows up on the rear screen. The obvious interference pattern reveals that a single electron, spread out into a wave, passes through both slits simultaneously and creates an interference pattern where the electron in its wave form actually interferes with itself, resulting in a fringe pattern appearing on the rear screen that reveals obvious interference. As the two waves collide with one another they interfere with the trajectory, altering the direction of the electron that hits the rear screen. The interference pattern of electrons can be compared to a body of water surging against a wall with two openings in the wall. As the water surges through these two openings it will create a natural interference pattern on the other side of the wall as the surging water creates ripples that begin to interfere and overlap with one another.

It is a unique property of the quantum world that sub atomic particles have the capacity to be in two places at the same time. In our macroscopic world of classical physics the last thing we would expect is to see someone bilocate right before our eyes so that suddenly they can be in two places at the same time. Yet, in the counter-intuitive world of the quantum universe this is exactly what is going on all the time. Electrons have the ability to be in two places at once! Based on this attribute of the quantum world the Uncertainty Principle teaches us that we cannot know where an electron is at any given moment because the truth is that it can be in more than one geographical place at the same time and that most probably, it is!

This experiment with electrons has been repeated over and over again with 100% consistency. When the detector is activated the electron passes through one slit as a particle and no interference pattern is recorded on the rear screen. When the detector is deactivated the electron passes through the two slits simultaneously and produces an interference pattern! This has baffled the greatest minds in contemporary science and has sent some mystically minded people into all sorts of strange metaphysical speculations. The problem simply cannot be explained rationally. When an electron is being observed the superposition of two states are collapsed into a definite particle state. When it is not being observed it remains in a superposition of two states.

The question is: how does the electron intuitively know that it is being observed? Does it have its own internal intelligence? How does it know when a detector is hidden behind the double-slit screen? How does it know when the detector is not switched on so that it can pass through both slits without being observed? Scientists have devised all sorts of interesting experiments to try to figure out what is going on, but it seems that the mystery of the quantum world is still largely impenetrable to rational explanation.

Are you shocked? Does the word "mystery" or "weird" spring to mind? If it does, you are beginning to come to terms with the counter-intuitive world of quantum physics. Welcome to the mystery that has rocked the scientific community and fascinated millions with its "science-fiction" like reality! John Archibald Wheeler, the eminent American theoretical physicist and friend of Einstein wrote:

> Nothing is more important about the quantum principle than this, that it destroys the concept of the world as "sitting out there" with the observer safely separated from it by a 20 centimetre slab of plate glass. Even to observe so minuscule an object as an electron, he must shatter the glass. He must reach in. He must install his chosen measurement instrument. Moreover the measurement changes the state of the electron. The universe will never afterwards be the same. To describe what has happened one has to cross out the old word "observer" and put in its place the new word "participator." In some strange sense the universe is a participatory universe.[23]

I first came to grips with the full realisation of the mystery of the quantum world whilst reading Jim Al Khalili's excellent book, *Quantum: A Guide for the Perplexed*. I was standing in a bookshop reading this appropriately named book, and the fullness of the mystery began to hit me for the first time. I bought a copy of the book and studied it until the mystery began to really sink in. Khalili pointed out that the behaviour of the electron in the double-slit experiment is so bizarre that it literally "sounds like magic!"[24] He calls it "nature's own conjuring trick." Khalili writes,

> It is one thing for atoms to magically transform themselves from tiny particles into spread out waves whenever they encounter two possible routes through the first screen. But it is another matter entirely to suggest that the atom can somehow be aware of the detector hiding behind one of the slits ready to catch it in the act of its spread-out state. It is as though it knows beforehand that we are lying in wait ready to ambush it and cunningly maintains its particle persona. Presumably the detector has the ability to convert a spread-out wave atom back to a localised particle. What is going on? This seems like magic and I suspect you probably do not believe me. Well, physicists have spent many years trying to come up with a logical explanation for what is seen. Physicists have been forced to

admit that, in the case of the double-slit trick; there is no rational way out.[25]

What are we to make of atoms that appear to have an inbuilt capacity to know when they are being observed? Surely one of the most curious attributes of quantum weirdness is this appearance of conscious awareness in atoms themselves which causes them to materialise in the presence of a conscious observer. Electrons cannot be tricked! No matter what experiment they are subjected to, they consistently appear to be highly attuned to their environment. The electron appears to sense exactly what is going on around it!

Freeman Dyson is an American mathematician and physicist who also believes in God. In the year 2000 he was awarded the "Templeton Prize for Progress in Religion." The prize is awarded annually "to a living individual for outstanding originality in advancing the world's understanding of God or spirituality." In his acceptance speech in May 2000 he attempted to articulate his personal theology in which he touched upon this apparent "consciousness" embedded in sub-atomic particles:

> Here is a brief summary of my thinking. The universe shows evidence of the operations of mind on three levels. The first level is elementary physical processes, as we see them when we study atoms in the laboratory. The second level is our direct human experience of our own consciousness. The third level is the universe as a whole. Atoms in the laboratory are weird stuff, behaving like active agents rather than inert substances. They make unpredictable choices between alternative possibilities according to the laws of quantum mechanics. It appears that mind, as manifested by the capacity to make choices, is to some extent inherent in every atom. So I am thinking that atoms and humans and God may have minds that differ in degree but not in kind.[26]

Wave-particle duality, superposition and the Uncertainty Principle are baffling realities. In 1935, Erwin Schrödinger [1887–1961] created a "thought experiment" in an attempt to illustrate how quantum superposition might operate in the every-day world of macroscopic objects. His experiment came to be known as "Schrödinger's Cat." In the experiment he suggested putting a live cat into a lead-lined box. Schrödinger then suggested throwing in a vial of cyanide and sealing the lead box. Of course, at this stage there would be no question that the cat was well and truly alive (and probably meowing in great distress!). According to the Uncertainty Principle, once the box has been sealed it is impossible to know whether the cat is alive or if it has broken the cyanide capsule and has tragically died.

Because we cannot have absolute certainty, according to the laws of the quantum world the cat is both dead and alive; it is in a superposition of two states. In order to discover the outcome of the experiment we would need to open the sealed lead box at which time the superposition would be lost, and the cat would be found to be either dead or alive but certainly not both. The tale of Schrödinger's Cat has become as famous as many of the great luminaries of the 20th century quantum physics community. Schrödinger's thought experiment illustrates the principle of quantum indeterminacy. Apparently, it was rumoured that Schrodinger said in later life that he wished "he had never met that cat!" He is definitely not the only person who has spent far too much time pondering the quantum paradox.

Chapter Three

TIME AND THE QUANTUM

"The distinction between past, present, and future is only a stubbornly persistent illusion." – Einstein

A number of scientists who are kept awake at night perplexed by the counter-intuitive world of quantum mechanics have devised additional experiments in order to probe more deeply the bizarre attributes of the sub-atomic world. We will examine some of these experiments shortly but, before we do, we need to note that these additional discoveries will totally mess with our heads concerning the nature of time itself.

We are so hard wired in our conscious experience of the linear progression of time that anything which appears to contradict our collective perception of time is spontaneously rejected as false. Nevertheless it now appears that a significant key to understanding the quantum enigma hinges upon the issue of time as it relates to quantum space.

As you are about to discover, the quantum world radically violates our classical understanding of time and space. Somehow, an electron or a photon appears to know *ahead of time* that an observer lies in wait on the other side of the double-slit screen. Precisely how these sub-atomic particles exercise such accurate prophetic prescience is a mystery that has preoccupied some of the greatest minds in modern science. The central mystery of quantum physics is revealed in the double-slit experiment and it has everything to do with time.

Louie De Broglie in 1927 proposed a theory called the "Pilot Wave Theory" in which he argued that each quantum particle has an associated wavefunction that travels ahead of the particle and detects whether it will be observed or not. The Pilot Wave Theory was later adopted and developed by a physicist called David Bohm in the 1950s. Bohm advanced the theory that the pilot wave was actually *non-local* and therefore not bound by the constraints of time and space.

The pilot wave somehow travelled *ahead* of the particle and determined whether the electron would be observed in the imminent future. The wavefunction therefore pushes the particle around and guides it through either one slit or the other depending upon whether an observer is present. Because the wavefunction is non-local it travels ahead of the arrow of time itself to seemingly know what is coming in advance.

In his brilliant book, *The Fabric of the Cosmos*, Brian Greene devotes an entire chapter to the subject of "Time and the Quantum." In this chapter Greene seeks to explain this other-worldly reality that challenges our conventional notion of time and space.

Bohm imagined that the wavefunction of a particle is another *separate element of reality*, one that exists *in addition to the particle itself.* It's not particles or waves; according to Bohm, it's particles and waves. Moreover, Bohm posited that a particle's wavefunction interacts with the particle itself – it "guides" or "pushes" the particle around – in a way that determines its subsequent motion. While this approach agrees fully with the successful predictions of standard quantum mechanics, Bohm found that changes to the wavefunction in one location are able to immediately push a particle at a distant location, a finding that explicitly reveals the non-locality of his approach. In the double-slit experiment, for example, each particle goes through one slit or the other, while it's wavefunction goes through both and suffers interference.[1]

We will discuss the concept of non-locality in greater depth in the next chapter, but for now it is important to appreciate that the reason Bohm advanced the pilot wave theory in relation to the quantum measurement problem was to highlight the fact that only the reality of quantum "non-locality" can sufficiently explain what is going on in the double-slit experiment.

Bohm proposed the theory that the quantum measurement problem revealed an entirely different order of existence that defied all conventional paradigms of reality. He called this the "explicate order" which revealed a deeper "implicate order" that is hidden from view but which is powerfully revealed in quantum mechanics. In his book, *Wholeness and the Implicate Order*, David Bohm gives the following explanation:

> In the enfolded [or implicate] order, space and time are no longer the dominant factors determining the relationships of dependence or independence of different elements. Rather, an entirely different sort of basic connection of elements is possible, from which our ordinary notions of space and time, along with those of separately existent material particles, are abstracted as forms derived from the deeper order. These ordinary notions in fact appear in what is called the "explicate" or "unfolded" order, which is a special and distinguished form contained within the general totality of all the implicate orders.[2]

According to Bohm there is another order of reality revealed in the world of quantum space that is not subject in any way to our conventional understanding of space and time. We regard locality to mean that which relates to our classical understanding of time and space whereas non-locality refers to the existence of another dimension of reality that transcends time and space as we understand it. The additional experiments that we mentioned earlier consistently point to this other level of non-local reality that fundamentally challenges our classical experience of time. Let's briefly consider these experiments.

THE DELAYED CHOICE EXPERIMENT

John Archibald Wheeler developed a thought experiment in 1978 called the "delayed choice experiment." Since light travels at 299,792,458 metres per second (or approximately 300,000 kilometres per second or 186,000 miles per second), Wheeler realised that an experiment could potentially be set up whereby a measurement could be made long after a photon had passed through the double-slit screen unobserved by an observer.

His experiment was a variation of the standard double-slit experiment with two telescopes pointed toward each of the two slits. Photons were fired toward the double-slit screen and were only observed through the telescopes as a "delayed choice" by the observer "long" after they had passed unobserved through the two slits. The detection (or measurement of) the photon was sufficiently delayed in time so as to not force the photon to make a choice between which path it will travel through the slits.

Quantum theory predicted that even if the measurement was taken "significantly" after the photons had traversed the double-slit screen the act of subsequent measurement or observation would still cause the wave-function to collapse. In Wheeler's experiment, once the photon has passed through the two slits, within the space of a few billionths of a second the rear detector screen is removed and the two telescopic devices, aimed at each slit, detect which slit the photon passed through by recording a brief flash of light.

If the photon passed through both slits as a spread out wave, it would be anticipated that a flash of light would appear at both slits at once. But if the measurement caused the wave function to collapse *after* the photon had passed through, it would confirm the predictions of quantum theory. So what was the outcome? According to Wheeler:

> The double-slit experiment...imposes a choice between complementary modes of observation. In each experiment we have found a way to delay that choice. That delay makes no difference in the experimental predictions. On this score everything we find was foreshadowed in that solitary and pregnant sentence of Bohr, "It... can make no difference, as regards observable effects obtainable by a definite experimental arrangement, whether our plans for constructing or handling the instruments are fixed beforehand or whether we prefer to postpone the completion of our planning until a later moment when the particle is already on its way from one instrument to another."[3]

In the delayed choice experiment, Wheeler said, "We decide, after the photon has passed through the screen, whether it shall have passed through the screen."[4] The delayed choice experiment was designed to catch the photon in the act of traversing both slits as a spread out wave. Logic would dictate that this experiment would be a possible means of observing something in the past, and the assumption was that because the observation was sufficiently delayed the observer would indeed see the single photon pass through both slits at the same time. But the quantum world does not obey our classical rules of logic. Ross Rhodes, a science writer and lecturer in quantum physics, explains the bizarre implications of this experiment:

It seems paradoxically that our later choice of whether to obtain this information *determines whether the particle passed through one slit or the other slit or both slits*, so to speak. If you want to think of it this way (I don't recommend it), the particle exhibited after-the-fact wave-like behaviour at the slits if you chose the screen; and it exhibited after-the-fact particle-like behaviour at the slits if you chose the telescopes. Therefore, our delayed choice of how to measure the particle determines how the particle actually behaved at an earlier time.[5]

Brian Greene also attempts to explains this bizarre outcome:

Somehow, the photons always get it right. Whenever the detector is on – again, even if the choice to turn it on is delayed until long after a given photon has passed through [the double split screen] – the photon acts fully like a particle. It is found to be on one and only one route to the screen (if we were to put photon detectors way downstream along both routes, each photon emitted by the laser would be detected by one or the other detector, never both); the resulting data show no interference pattern.

Whenever the new detector is off – again, even if this decision is made after each photon has passed [the screen] the photons act fully like a wave, yielding the famous interference pattern, showing that they have travelled both paths. It's as if the photons adjust their behaviour in the past according to the future choice of whether the new detector is switched on; it's as though the photons have a "premonition" of the experimental situation they will encounter farther downstream, and act accordingly. It's as if a consistent and definite history becomes manifest only after the future to which it leads has been fully settled.[6]

Robert Nadeau and Menas Kafatos also explain the results of the delayed choice experiment in their book *The Non-Local Universe*. They suggest that the results of these experiments have startling implications for our understanding of the quantum aspect of nature because, as they observe, "What is disclosed in these experiments are general properties of all quanta, and therefore, fundamental aspects of everything in physical reality."[7] Nadeau and Kafatos explain the implications of the delayed choice experiment for the relationship between non-locality and time.

Although the delayed choice experiment was originally merely a thought experiment, we have been able to conduct actual delayed choice experiments with single photons. Amazingly enough, these single photons follow two paths, or one path, according to a choice made "after" the photon has followed one or two paths. These results indicate that the wave-like or particle-like status of a photon at one point in time can be changed later in time by choosing to measure or observe one of these aspects in spite of the fact that the photon is travelling at light speed. The results of these and other experiments not only show that the observer and the observed system cannot be separate and distinct in space. They also reveal that this distinction does not exist in time. It is as if we have caused something to "happen" after it has already occurred. These experiments...unambiguously disclose yet another of the strange aspects of the quantum world – the past is inexorably mixed with the present and even the phenomenon of time is tied to specific experimental choices.[8]

All of this suggests that quantum time is clearly not the same as our collective perception of time. John Wheeler asks the following question in response to his delayed choice experiment. "Should we be prepared to see some day a new structure for the foundations of physics that does away with time? Yes, because 'time' is in trouble!"[9] The discovery of the curious relationship between time and the quantum world parallels the discoveries of Einstein in the early 20th century when he wrestled with the issue of time's relationship to space.

Einstein's theories of general and special relativity explained the fact that if someone was travelling at the speed of light they would experience time to stand still. Einstein relativised time in relation to space, hence the term "relativity." Could it be that quantum mechanics also relativises time? The double-slit experiment and the delayed choice experiment suggest that in quantum mechanics time is also fundamentally relativised.

Paul Davies, in his book, *About Time: Einstein's Unfinished Revolution*, says, "The core difficulty with quantum time harks back to the very notion of Einstein's time; there is no absolute and universal time. The absence of any absolute, underlying time implies that physical processes cannot ever depend explicitly on time as such. The point is, rather, that the only meaningful way to measure physical change in Einstein's universe is to forget time "as such."[10]

Einstein himself concluded that "The distinction between past, present and future is only a stubbornly persistent illusion."[11] Daniel M. Greenberger came to this conclusion; "Einstein said that if quantum mechanics were correct then the world would be crazy. Einstein was right - the world is crazy!"[12]

Wheeler decided to expand his thought experiment to the universal scale by considering a photon that was emitted billions of years ago from a distant star that is now travelling toward earth. At some point on its journey toward earth it must pass by a distant galaxy which will affect the trajectory of the photon. According to Ross Rhodes,

> "Gravitational lensing" predicted by general relativity (and well verified) will make the light bend around the galaxy or black hole. The same photon can, therefore, take either of two paths around the galaxy and still reach earth – it can take the left path and bend back toward earth, or it can take the right path and bend back toward earth. Bending around the left side is the experimental equivalent of going through the left slit of a barrier; bending around the right side is the equivalent of going through the right slit.[13]

If an astronomer on earth chooses to apply the delayed choice experiment to the travelling photon as it arrives on earth, his choice will determine which path the photon travelled, either to the left or to the right of a distant galaxy billions of years ago! Does that sound absolutely bizarre? Welcome to the strange world of quantum mechanics!

Ross Rhodes concludes by saying, "So it seems that time has nothing to do with effects of quantum mechanics. And, indeed, the original thought experiment was not based on any analysis of how particles evolve and behave over time – it was based on the mathematics. This is what the mathematics predicted for a result, and this is exactly the result obtained in the laboratory."[14] The delayed choice experiment confirmed mathematical quantum predictions that if an observer is making a measurement it will affect the outcome even if the observer makes a measurement after the fact!

The popular science author, John Gribbin, also gives a detailed account of the delayed choice experiment as it was applied to the cosmic scale. He says, "However you try to describe it, clearly something *very* strange is going on in the cosmic version of the delayed choice experiment. The whole universe seems to "know," in advance, what experiment an individual human being is going to carry out."[15] These discoveries highlight the emerging realisation that quantum realities are truly "non-local" in the full sense of the term.

Something qualifies to be defined as non-local if it is outside of the time-space manifold. Space is three dimensional and ever since Einstein time is understood to constitute the fourth dimension. But the non-local realities of the quantum world point to the existence of yet another dimension of reality that is not bound by either locality or by time. Scientists appear to have stumbled upon empirical evidence for the existence of additional dimensions! This ought to be headline news around the world!

Now, let me ask: Does all of this mess with your head? Because if it does you are beginning to appreciate the shock of quantum physics! The English physicist, Paul Davies, has wrestled extensively with the issue of what is commonly identified in the physics community as the "arrow of time." He has authored *The Physics of Time Asymmetry* (1974), *About Time* (1995) and *How to Build a Time Machine* (2002). Davies is perhaps one of the world's leading authorities on time and its relationship to space, and he has concluded that time is a product of the observer rather than an objective attribute of space, as Einstein's theory of general relativity also suggests. In an essay titled *The Mysterious Flow of Time* he writes:

> Some researchers...have suggested that the subtle physics of irreversible processes make the flow of time an objective aspect of the world. But I and others argue that it is some sort of illusion. After all, we do not really observe the passage of time. What we actually observe is that later states of the world differ from earlier states that we still remember. The fact that we remember the past, rather than the future, is an observation not of the passage of time but of the asymmetry of time. Nothing other than a conscious observer registers the flow of time. A clock measures durations between events much as a measuring tape measures distances between places; it does not measure the "speed" with which one moment succeeds another. Therefore, it appears that the flow [of time] is subjective, not objective.[16]

Paul Davies highlights the subjective, almost illusory nature of time. In his groundbreaking book, *About Time: Einstein's Unfinished Revolution* he writes, "Running like a common thread through the history of human thought...is a belief that the entire paradigm of human temporality is rooted in some sort of monstrous illusion; it is but an elaborate product of the human mind."[17] As we gaze into the quantum world we peer into a world that is not subject to the constraints of time as we consciously observe it. We are as unaccustomed to a world unfettered by time as we are to the concept of eternity. The German Christian mystic poet, Angelus Silesius, wrote in the 17th century:

> Time is of your own making, Its clock ticks in your head,
> The moment you stop thought, Time too stops dead.[18]

Because the quantum world is fundamentally non-local it does not obey our rules when it comes to measuring time. The quantum world is as difficult to conceptualise as the notion of eternity. According to the prophet Isaiah, God is "the High and Lofty One who inhabits eternity." (Isaiah 57:15) God is outside of time and space and as such He transcends the temporal realm of time. Somehow, the quantum world appears to straddle the two worlds of time and eternity. Angelus Silesius continues:

> Do not compute eternity, As light year after year,
> One step across that line called Time, Eternity is here.[19]

As human beings we are deeply conscious of time. Time imposes itself on almost every aspect of day to day life. However, when we seek to consciously impose our perception of time upon the quantum world we discover that it refuses to play ball. Paul Davies explains the distinction between our conscious participation with the world around us and the stubborn refusal of the quantum world to live in subjection to our experience of the arrow of time:

> Our perception of the flow of time is linked in some way to quantum mechanics. It was appreciated from the earliest days of the formulation of quantum mechanics that time enters into the theory in a unique manner, quite unlike space. When a human observer makes a measurement, one and only one result is obtained. Within the observer's mind, the possible makes a transition to the actual, the open future to the fixed past – which is precisely what we mean by the flux of time. There is no agreement among physicists on how this transition from many potential realities into a single actuality takes place. Many physicists have argued that it has something to do with the consciousness of the observer, on the basis that it is the act of observation that prompts nature to make up its mind.[20]

The crazy world of quantum mechanics would be virtually impossible to believe were it not for scientific experiments that prove these mystifying realities. Here we encounter the overlap between mystical experience and quantum physics. Paul Davies refers to the experience of Christian mystics who experience God and eternity in ways that bring them in touch with a sense of timelessness.[21] Quantum experiments are the closest thing to mystical encounters because the physicist experiences the privilege of gazing into realities that completely boggle the mind.

Perhaps this explains why a number of leading quantum physicists are so inclined toward mysticism. As Davies shocks his readers with the realities of the new physics he asks the rhetorical question: "What has happened to time? You make it sound as though it never really existed!" He then answers his own question: "It has evaporated in a puff of quantum fuzziness, in the same way that other precise notions, like position and trajectory for particles, disappear in conventional quantum mechanics. Quantum cosmology has abolished time as surely as the mystic's altered state of consciousness. For a typical quantum state in this theory, *time is simply meaningless!*"[22]

ERASING THE PAST

The unfolding mystery of the quantum deepened even further in the early 1980s as scientists engaged in additional experiments that probed the quantum world. A number of physicists developed the Quantum Eraser Experiment on the basis of quantum theory. According to the theoretical predictions of quantum mechanics it was believed that it would be possible to actually erase the past in the quantum realm. The quantum eraser experiment actually confirmed the theoretical prediction. Brian Greene, who describes the experiment says, "As is usual with quantum mechanics, the puzzle doesn't pit theory against experiment. It pits theory, confirmed by experiment, against our intuitive sense of time and reality."[23]

In this experiment photons were "tagged" just before they passed through the two slits by manually manipulating the direction of their "spin." (All photons have either a left or right hand spin which is how polarised lenses work by blocking a percentage of all photons that have a certain spin.) Of course this tagging process guarantees that the photon would only pass through one slit or the other and would not create an interference pattern on the rear detector screen. However, after the photons passed through the two slits the "tagging" was removed and the previous manipulation of the photon was reversed or "erased" just before the photon hit the detector screen. Brian Greene describes the outcome of this experiment:

> Remarkably, the photons detected by the screen after this erasure *do* produce an interference pattern! When the eraser is inserted just in front of the detector screen, it undoes – it erases – the effect of tagging the photons way back when they approached the slits. As in the delayed choice experiment, in principle this kind of erasure could occur billions of years after...in effect undoing the past, even undoing the ancient past![24]

Needless to say, this kind of phenomena is comprehensively counter-intuitive. We could also discuss additional experiments such as the Delayed Choice Quantum Eraser Experiment[25] that take us into even deeper realms of quantum mystery that completely violate our logical understanding of space and time. This experiment has been carried out in a laboratory setting but if it were carried out over greater distances across space the results would be utterly astonishing. In the quantum universe our conscious intrusion into this previously unknown world seems to result in the contradiction of all of our familiar concepts of past and future. If a quantum particle can "know" the future before it occurs and, similarly, if an act in the present can erase the past, it is evident that we are not dealing with a linear arrow of time in our developing understanding of the non-local dimension of quantum space. Brian Greene writes,

> These experiments are a magnificent affront to our conventional notion of space and time. Classical reckoning is the wrong kind of reckoning to use in the quantum universe. For a few days after I first learned about these experiments I remember feeling elated. I felt I'd been given a glimpse into a veiled side of reality. Common experience – mundane, ordinary, day to day activities – suddenly seemed part of a classical charade, hiding the true nature of our quantum world. The world of the everyday suddenly seemed nothing but an inverted magic act, lulling its audience into believing in the usual, familiar concepts of space and time, while the astonishing truth of quantum reality lay carefully guarded by nature's sleights of hand.[26]

Quantum Entanglement

But guess what! The weird world of the quantum gets even weirder! Another manifestation of quantum weirdness is the phenomena called "quantum entanglement." This is a property of the quantum world that is extremely strange and mysterious and which also eliminates conventional concepts of time. To illustrate this discovery we will describe two photons that are the product of an original single photon. When a photon passes through matter it is absorbed by an electron.

This interaction can cause a photon to decay into two photons as it is emitted from the electron. The total energy of the two new photons then equals the energy of the original photon. These two new, smaller photons are said to be "entangled" with one another and they mysteriously remain "partners" for life. Schrödinger first described this property of quantum mechanics as "quantum entanglement." Schrödinger himself said that, "Entanglement is not *one* but rather *the* characteristic trait of quantum mechanics."[27]

Because photons are continuously interacting with electrons throughout the entire universe the phenomenon of quantum entanglement is ubiquitous to our universe. Entangled pairs of photons are made by taking one photon and converting it into a pair that are then sent off in opposite directions. If two particles are entangled, they act in some respects as if they were a single object.

This requires further explanation. As we have just stated, all particles have a property known as "spin." They rotate on an axis. They spin either forwards or backwards, and in the case of photons the spin is called either "left handed" or "right handed" spin. In the case of two entangled photons the spin property of one will always be the exact opposite of the other entangled partner. Amazingly, entangled photons which have interacted in the past and then moved far away from each other, remain, in a certain sense, still connected, and can instantaneously "communicate" with each other.

Two entangled particles must have opposite values; for example, if one is spinning in the "up" direction, the other must be spinning in the "down" direction. Suppose you measure one of the entangled particles and, by doing so, you nudge it into the "up" direction. This instantaneously causes its entangled partner to spin "down." The measurement "here" affects the other particle "over there" *instantaneously*, even if the other particle was theoretically a million miles away! Measuring the properties of one entangled photon will immediately tell you the properties of the other with absolute consistency.

Whatever happens to one particle would thus immediately affect the other particle, wherever it may be in the universe. Einstein called this "spooky action at a distance." Albert Einstein disliked the newly emerging implications of quantum mechanics. To Einstein, quantum entanglement seemed to run counter to a central tenet of his theory of relativity: nothing, not even information, can travel faster than the speed of light.

In quantum mechanics, all the forces of nature are mediated by the exchange of particles such as photons, and these particles must obey this cosmic speed limit. So theoretically an action "here" cannot cause an effect "over there" any sooner than it would take light to travel there in a vacuum. However, two entangled particles can influence one another instantaneously, whether they're in the same room or at opposite ends of the universe! Amazingly, this was scientifically proven in experiments conducted by Alain Aspect in 1982. Science writer, Jeane Staune, in a fascinating essay titled, "On the Edge of Physics," writes,

> Aspect's experiments demonstrated instantaneous interaction between particles 12 meters apart: a communication time of less than a billionth of a second, or 20 times faster than the supposedly unbreakable speed of light. This was followed in 1997 by the work of Nicolas Gisin, who worked with distances of 10 kilometres and showed a speed of the observed phenomenon 10,000 times faster than the speed of light. These first experimental evidences of "ghost links" over such distances have been used by others, such as Gilles Brassard and his team, to demonstrate the principle of "quantum teleportation." When the first twin of the two linked particles meets a third particle, the second twin will receive – via "teleportation," through the "ghost link" – the properties of the new particle, although it has not come in contact with it.[28]

These and other recent experiments have confirmed the laws of quantum mechanics, which totally contradict the laws of classical physics. The growing knowledge of quantum phenomena demonstrates the existence of a level of reality that transcends time, space, energy, and matter, and yet still has a causal effect on our material level of reality. Quantum entanglement proves the existence of *another level of reality* – "one, which lies outside space and time since non-locality is its principal characteristic."[29]

The discovery of the fact of quantum entanglement confirms the discoveries of the double-slit experiment. In fact all discoveries in 20th and 21st century quantum physics support the notion of non-locality. Amir Aczel, author of *Entanglement: The Greatest Mystery in Physics,* writes,

> What does entanglement mean? What does it tell us about the world and about the nature of space and time? These are probably the hardest questions to answer in all of physics. Entanglement breaks down all our conceptions about the world developed through our usual sensory experience. To understand, or even simply accept, the validity of entanglement and other associated quantum phenomena, we must first admit that our conceptions of reality in the universe are inadequate. Entanglement teaches us that our everyday experience does not equip us with the ability to understand what goes on at the micro-scale, which we do not experience directly. An electron, a neutron, or even an atom, when faced with a barrier with two slits in it, will go through both of them at once.
>
> Notions of causality and of the impossibility of being at several locations at the same time are shattered by the quantum theory. The idea of superposition – of "being at two places at once" – is related to the phenomenon of entanglement. But entanglement is even more dramatic, for it breaks down our notion that there is a meaning to spatial separation. Entanglement can be described as a superposition principle involving two or more particles. Entanglement is a superposition of the states of two or more particles, taken as one system. Spatial separation as we know it seems to evaporate with respect to such a system. Two particles that can be miles, or light years, apart may behave in a concerted way: what happens to one of them happens to the other one instantaneously regardless of the distance between them.[30]

Quantum entanglement so challenges our thinking about the nature of reality that one secular author has called it the *God Effect*. Brian Clegg, author of *The God Effect: Quantum Entanglement, Science's Strangest Phenomenon,* writes,

> Entanglement. It's a word that is ripe with implications. In physics it refers to a very specific and strange concept, an idea so bizarre, so fundamental and so far reaching that I have called it the God Effect. Once two particles become entangled, it doesn't matter where those

two particles are, they retain an immediate and powerful connection. Even if these entangled particles are then separated to opposite sides of the universe they retain this same connection. The God Effect has an unsettling omnipresence![31]

Entangled quantum particles have "superluminal" qualities in that they communicate with one another at speeds infinitely beyond the speed of light. In fact, the speed of light doesn't even come into the equation. The communication is absolutely instantaneous! Once again, this messes with our conventional concept of time. There simply is no such thing as a "time lapse" between an entangled pair of particles. We are faced with an alternative geometry of spacetime that contradicts our classical 3 + 1 Euclidean geometry. Paul Davies says,

> In a quantum description, there is no single spacetime with a well defined geometry that is "there;" instead, you must imagine all possible geometries – all possible spacetimes, space-warps and time-warps mixed together in a sort of cocktail or "foam." The quantity called "time" that is so crucial to our lives and our description of the physical world, may turn out to be an entirely secondary concept, unrelated to the basic laws of the universe.[32]

QUANTUM TUNNELLING

There is yet another attribute of the quantum world that reveals the non-local nature of quantum mechanics. The phenomenon of "quantum tunnelling" confirms that so-called "matter" has the capacity to de-materialise and to re-materialise in the sub-atomic world. Much has been written on this strange quantum property and many illustrations have been proposed to illustrate the mysterious capabilities of the quantum world. One writer says,

> Quantum physics predicts there is a chance that a particle trapped behind a barrier without the energy to overcome the barrier may at times appear on the other side of the barrier without overcoming it or breaking it down. For example, assume you're in jail. It does not violate the laws of classical physics for you to exist inside your cell or outside your cell, but you do not have enough energy to penetrate or break down the walls. According to quantum physics, there is a certain probability you could disappear from the inside and reappear on the outside leaving the wall unbroken.[33]

Even though a sub-atomic particle doesn't have enough energy to get over an impenetrable barrier, there is still a small probability that it can "tunnel" through it! Jean Staune documents recent scientific developments that push our understanding of the mysteries of the quantum world to new extremes.

Raymond Chiao, whose experiments have confirmed the "tunnel effect," offers one of the best proofs of this. When a particle meets a wall, Heisenberg's Uncertainty Principle says there is a slight chance it will find itself on the other side of the wall, because there is an inherent uncertainty in its position. The particle really does pass through the wall in some cases, for we can "pick it up" on the other side. How is this possible? Chiao used two beams of photons that move at the speed of light, both covering identical distances from Point A to Point B. The particles that leave together from A thus arrive at the same time as B. If we put a wall in the pathway of one of these beams, most of those photons are stopped, but a small number, through the tunnel effect, do make it through to Point B.

Chiao has shown that these photons actually arrive *before* those which left at the same time in the beam without a wall – even though both beams travel at the speed of light and both their trajectories are identical in length. How can light go faster than...*light*? The only possible conclusion is that the particle does not actually go through the wall and its molecules, but materializes itself directly on the other side. This dematerialization could explain why the "blocked" photons seem to arrive earlier, having effectively "skipped" the space of the wall. The experiment shows, in fact, that the thicker the wall, the earlier the particles arrive. Since this experiment can be done with any fundamental components of matter (protons, electrons, etc.), it proves that we must renounce the idea that these components are somehow little pieces of ultimately indivisible matter, like infinitely small grains of sand.[34]

Once again, the issue of time, or at least our perception of time comes into focus in the quantum tunnelling phenomenon. Paul Davies addresses this issue of the "time" it takes for a quantum particle to dematerialise and rematerialise on the other side of the barrier:

When the tunnel effect was first discovered several decades ago, an obvious question was, how *long* do the particles take to tunnel through the barrier. You might imagine that the presence of a barrier would slow the particles up. But when the quantum particles penetrate the barrier by the tunnelling mechanism, simple reasoning fails. In fact, there is good reason to believe that the barrier has the effect of making the tunnelling particles travel *faster*.[35]

As with quantum entanglement, perhaps time doesn't even come into the equation, especially when a photon or an electron transcends the cosmic speed limit of the known speed of light. It is more probable that quantum non-locality is the explanation once again and that the quantum particle simply disappears and reappears on the other side of the barrier. Paul Davies describes quantum tunnelling as a miracle!

> Imagine throwing a stone softly at a window. You expect the stone to bounce back again. Suppose that, instead of the stone rebounding from the window, it passed right through and appeared on the far side, leaving the window intact! Anyone seeing a stone penetrating a window without breaking it would conclude a miracle had happened, but this particular miracle occurs all the time in the subatomic domain, where quantum rules defy common sense.[36]

QUANTUM TELEPORTATION

The phenomena of quantum entanglement and quantum tunnelling have paved the way for advances in the field of quantum teleportation. In 2004 scientists actually teleported photons for the first time. In a National Geographic news report we read:

> Austrian researchers have teleported photons (particles of light) across the Danube River in Vienna using technology that calls to mind Scotty beaming up Captain Kirk in the science fiction series. "We were able to perform a quantum teleportation experiment for the first time ever outside a university laboratory," said Rupert Ursin, a researcher at the Institute for Experimental Physics at the University of Vienna in Austria. Teleportation involves de-materializing an object at one point and transferring the precise details of its configuration to another location, where the object is then reconstructed.[37]

As time marches on new experiments push the frontiers of effective quantum teleportation. "The longest distance yet claimed to be achieved for quantum teleportation is 16 kilometres (10 miles) in May 2010 by Chinese scientists over free-space with an average of 89% accuracy."[38] It needs to be pointed out that the days of full scale teleportation of physical objects are still the stuff of science fiction. Up until now quantum teleportation has involved the actual transference of quantum information, but this has certainly paved the way for greater experiments in the future. The success of one experiment lays the foundation for even greater successes.

Recent trends in the exploration of the quantum world are bringing to light some strange new realities. Wave-particle duality, quantum entanglement, quantum tunnelling and quantum teleportation all reveal that matter is effectively non-local! That is to say, quantum interactions occur instantaneously over arbitrarily long distances. Quantum entanglement proves that in the quantum world there is no such thing as "over here" and "over there." There is no mechanism in quantum mechanics which explains how particles "communicate" with each other superluminally [faster than light].

The fact is, there is no superluminal communication; rather there is an extra-dimensional property called "non-locality" which implies that two sub-atomic particles separated by vast distances in space are actually "non-locally" joined together in another dimension! New experiments consistently prove that matter itself, at a quantum level, does not have a strictly "material" reality.

The further scientists probe the essence of matter the more it is found in some mysterious way to have extra-dimensional properties. Einstein didn't like the implication of the early findings of quantum physics because they so radically challenged rational explanation. If he were alive today he would be compelled by the sheer weight of scientific evidence to renounce his rationalistic presuppositions.

An Entirely New Reality

Richard Feynman said that quantum weirdness "is impossible, absolutely impossible to explain in any classical way."[39] It simply cannot be explained rationally unless we allow for a non-local interpretation of reality; something which devout rationalists such as Einstein could not accept. Feynman continues, "The paradox is only a conflict between reality and your feeling of what reality ought to be!"[40]

The development of the science of quantum physics has been like the discovery of a whole new world that is entirely at odds with our world. It has opened up to us an entirely new paradigm of reality that is in conflict with everything that we have understood to constitute reality in the macroscopic world. But as surely as our macroscopic world is real so the quantum world is real, just incredibly different! Thus the frontiers of modern science have stumbled upon a different kind of reality that is just as much a part of the fabric of nature as anything we are familiar with in the macroscopic world.

The discovery of the wave-particle duality and the discovery of the bizarre effect that the observer exercises upon the quantum world reveal a strange world that is completely foreign to everything we consider familiar. Analogies fail because there are suddenly no analogies. The quantum enigma has become the fountainhead of a torrent of speculations concerning the apparent relationship between consciousness and matter. These mysterious scientific discoveries begged for new theories to be conceived to attempt to explain the impact of consciousness upon the material world.

The popular New Age metaphysical speculation that consciousness creates reality springs from the realisation that the placement of a particle detector behind the double-slit screen represented a *conscious act* that interfered with the normal function of an electron which would ordinarily pass through both slits as a spread out wave. The presence of a particle detector symbolises a *conscious interaction* with the quantum world which results in a significant impact upon that world. In effect it changes the world of the quantum. Needless to say, this is an idea that has the power to ignite the popular imagination.

Consciousness has come to be regarded as the unique factor which has the latent capacity to alter the very nature of quantum reality. It is the new key player in the arena of quantum mysticism. From this realisation a perception emerged that human consciousness is more intimately intertwined with the world of matter than had previously been thought. Enlightenment philosophers always emphasised the fundamental division between mind and matter.

Suddenly the revelation of the quantum world threatened to overturn this long cherished paradigm. This emerging perception of reality has been extremely powerful. Many within the New Age community now believe that quantum physics is actually telling us that we have the power to create our own reality. Our problem, we are told, is that we have not sufficiently developed this latent power to consciously shape our world around us through the power of consciousness. This is just one of the ideas that have captured the popular imagination as a result of the new physics.

Chapter Four

Quantum Non-Locality and the Spiritual Realm

In the previous chapter we briefly began to explore the concept of quantum non-locality. In this chapter we will endeavour to delve a little deeper into this subject and explore the relationship between the phenomena of quantum non-locality and the spiritual realm. As we walk through this journey I think you will agree that this is a relationship that demands our attention.

Physicists have stumbled upon an attribute of the sub-atomic world that compels us to re-think the very nature of the world that we live in. Some eminent thinkers have even speculated that the discovery of the existence of non-local realities would suggest that scientists have accidentally bumped into the reality of the spiritual realm. Other more metaphysically inclined writers would go as far as saying that scientists have discovered "God."

In their book, *The Non Local Universe: The New Physics and Matters of the Mind*, authors Robert Nadeau & Menas Kafatos write:

> In the strange new world of quantum physics we have consistently uncovered aspects of physical reality at odds with our everyday sense of this reality. But no previous discovery has posed more challenges to our usual understanding of the "way things are" than the amazing new fact of nature known as non-locality.[1]

Research into the extent of quantum entanglement throughout the universe has indicated that non-local reality is now an established feature of the entire universe at the quantum level. In a 1998 article in the *New Scientist* magazine titled, "Why God Plays Dice," we read the following comments:

> Quantum theory isn't just a tiny bit nonlocal. It's overwhelmingly nonlocal. Non-locality is the rule for our Universe. That is an unsettling conclusion. Non-locality cuts into the idea of the separateness of things, and threatens to ruin the very notion of isolation. To isolate an object we ordinarily move it a long way away from everything else, or build impenetrable walls around it. But the link of entanglement knows no boundaries. It isn't a cord running through space, but lives somehow outside space. It goes through walls, and pays no attention to distance![2]

As we have seen, all the discoveries of quantum physics in the past century point toward the existence of another layer of reality that undergirds the physical level of reality that we are all so familiar with. These discoveries lend support to everything that the Bible reveals about the reality of the existence of God, the supernatural and the invisible world of spirit. A thinking Christian, faced with the strange revelations of the world of the quantum, immediately begins to reflect upon these new scientific discoveries in the light of biblical revelation.

For the follower of Christ who engages with the science of quantum physics there are a number of fixed realities. First of all, there is the newly discovered reality of the nonlocal properties of the sub-atomic world and then there is the reality of the existence of God who created this mysterious world and who still miraculously engages with this world at a macroscopic level via the sub-atomic level. All miraculous intervention into this space-time manifold is an intervention at a sub-atomic level that ultimately manifests in the macroscopic world.

THE "VEIL" BETWEEN TWO WORLDS

Faced with the triple realities of quantum non-locality, the existence of God and the supernatural intervention of God, we can move forward to theorise the relationship between these three fundamental realities of our supernaturally crafted universe. As we explore this dimension of non-local quantum reality in greater depth I will propose that this invisible layer of quantum reality acts as some kind of *interface* between the presence and power of God (who exists in the spiritual realm) and the world of matter.

The non-local quantum world appears to be a kind of invisible, intermediate "buffer zone" between spirit and matter. It appears that the non-local quantum realm has been strategically crafted by God to be directly responsive to the influence and activity of the Spirit of God so these non-local quantum realities are capable of "materialising" into a localised spatial formation. Quantum realities are the building blocks of matter. This is an established scientific fact!

In this chapter and the next we will begin to explore the nature of the creation of the heavens and the earth through the lens of quantum non-locality and the wave-particle duality. But before we can get to that subject we need to delve deeper into this phenomena of quantum non-locality. I am proposing the simple theory that this twilight zone of quantum non-locality is the interface between two worlds. This is by no means an outrageous speculation in the light of trends in the scientific community.

Even purely secular physicists such as Richard Feynman, Stephen Hawking and many others have embraced an idea called the "Many Worlds Interpretation" as a way of resolving the quantum paradox. Richard Feynman said, "I think we are forced to accept the Many Worlds Interpretation if quantum mechanics is true."[3] Stephen Hawking is a big fan of this interpretation. In fact, in a poll of 72 leading cosmologists and quantum theorists 58% claimed to believe in the Many Worlds Interpretation.[4] That is almost 6 out of 10!

This theory was developed by an American physicist called Hugh Everett. Everett argued that there is no such thing as the wave function collapse when it is measured by an observer. Instead the act of quantum measurement causes a splitting into two parallel universes: one in which the sub-atomic particle exists as a particle and the other in which it still exists as a non-collapsed wave. This theory has given rise to the science fiction popularisation of the concept "parallel universes." Scientists who have embraced the Many Worlds Interpretation have sought to explain the phenomena of the double-slit experiment as evidence that we live in a "Multiverse" rather than a universe.

The Multiverse is a hypothetical set of possible universes that exist alongside one another in different dimensions, of which our physical universe is but one of a series of parallel worlds. I am not an advocate of the Many Worlds Interpretation because I believe in just two worlds: the world of spirit and the world of matter. But I wanted to make the point that the idea of parallel universes or merely the idea of another universe alongside our own is not an idea that is on the fringe of contemporary scientific thought. Many well known scientists who have become popular authors subscribe to this view and actively promote it as a solution to the quantum paradox.

Jesus said, "My Kingdom is not of this world!" (John 18:36) The writer to the Hebrews indicates that Christ is the one through whom God "made *the worlds.*" (Hebrews 1:2) Note that the term "worlds" is plural, not singular. We see this same term in a later chapter of Hebrews. "By faith we understand that *the worlds* were framed by the word of God, so that the things which are seen were not made of things which are visible." (Hebrews 11:3)

There are two worlds revealed in the Bible. Jesus frequently talked about this world and the world above. He said to those who opposed Him, "You are from beneath; I am from above. You are of this world; I am not of this world." (John 8:23) On another occasion He said, "I came forth from the Father and have come into the world. Again, I leave the world and go to the Father." (John 16:28) Clearly Jesus revealed that there are two worlds. There is this material world and there is another world that is above and beyond this physical universe because it exists in another spiritual dimension.

These two worlds are separated by a gossamer thin veil. They are continuously intersecting yet they are two entirely separate worlds. One is the world constituted by matter and the other is constituted by spirit. When Jesus walked upon the earth he displayed the supernatural powers of the world above, which He identified as "heaven." Even when He was upon the earth He was still living in this other dimension called heaven. He said, "No one has ascended to heaven but He who came down from heaven, that is, the Son of Man who is in heaven." (John 3:13) The Heavenly Man, Jesus Christ, displayed heaven on earth and revealed the Kingdom of Heaven everywhere He walked on earth. The gospels continually reveal His world breaking into our world.

The Bible talks about a "veil" that separates heaven and earth. The book of Hebrews talks about entering "the Presence behind the veil." (Hebrews 6:19) Matthew, Mark and Luke all record that at the exact moment that Jesus died on the cross the veil in the temple was torn from top to bottom, prophetically symbolising that through the atonement of Christ the way had been made for humanity to pass "through the veil" (Hebrews 10:20) into this supernatural world called heaven. Elsewhere in the New Testament we encounter another interesting concept that appears to communicate a similar idea to the veil. Paul talked about a "mirror" or a "looking glass." He said, "For now we see through a glass, darkly, but then face to face." (1 Corinthians 13:12 KJV)

Paul picked up this idea again in his second Epistle to the Corinthians where he deliberately dovetailed the twin concepts of the "looking glass" and the "veil." He taught that whenever someone turns to Christ the veil is taken away. (2 Corinthians 3:16) He then proceeded to teach that those who have turned to Christ are now able to peer through the looking glass into heaven in order to behold the glory of God. "But we all, with **unveiled** face, beholding **as in a glass** the glory of the Lord, are being transformed into the same image from glory to glory, just as by the Spirit of the Lord." (2 Corinthians 3:18) The obvious suggestion is that God is on the other side of the veil. He is on the other side of the looking glass, peering into this world. We are in this material world but through Christ we can now peer through the looking glass into heaven.

ALICE'S LOOKING GLASS

We would all remember the tale of Alice in Wonderland who fell into another world as she peered through the looking glass. This is a powerfully compelling image in Western culture. Curiously, it has also become a metaphor for writers who search for parallels for peering into the quantum world. The *What the Bleep* book is advertised as "Taking you through the looking glass of quantum physics into a universe that is more bizarre and alive than ever imagined."[5] Other books have been written that have adopted such titles as, *Science Through the Looking Glass* and *Einstein and Jabberwocky: Through the Quantum Looking Glass*. Jabberwocky, of course, was Lewis Carroll's famous nonsensical poem that appeared in his novel, *Through the Looking Glass*.

> Like Alice stepping through the looking glass, the journey into the quantum realm of subatomic particles is fraught with strange phenomena. Now, new research indicates that the looking glass is more than a helpful analogy - there is indeed a perceptible barrier between the large-scale world we know and understand, and the wacky quantum world of half-dead, half-alive cats and particles that can be in two places at once. Rather than a gradual transition between the two realms as was previously thought, a computer

scientist working at the University of California, Berkeley, has proven the existence of an actual turning point where classical behaviour stops and quantum behaviour starts.[6]

Paul's concept of the looking glass is a powerful image that helps us to understand the possibility of gazing upon the glory of Christ in the invisible world. Using another metaphor, Jesus Himself revealed that He is the doorway into heaven and through Him we can enter this other world. These are deep spiritual mysteries that beckon us to explore this other world of spirit. Jesus said to Nathaniel, "Most assuredly, I say to you, hereafter you shall *see heaven open*, and the angels of God ascending and descending upon the Son of Man." (John 1:51)

When Stephen, the first martyr, was being murdered, we are told that he "being full of the Holy Spirit, gazed into heaven and saw the glory of God, and Jesus standing at the right hand of God." (Acts 7:55) The veil and the looking glass describe this strange intersection between the physical world and the spiritual world and now through the lens of advanced quantum physics we can comprehend the intersection of these two worlds! If there are indeed two distinct and separate worlds there must be a point of intersection between these worlds, and the best candidate for this twilight zone is the mysterious realm of quantum non-locality.

The discovery of the non-local nature of our universe has naturally given rise to an explosion of divergent metaphysical interpretations amongst both secular and spiritually oriented thinkers. These speculations are interesting but ultimately they generate more heat than light when they are not guided by biblical revelation. We ought not to be surprised by this explosion of interesting and sometimes bizarre interpretations.

Nick Herbert in his fascinating book, *Quantum Reality*, documents all of the different schools of quantum interpretation. We need to appreciate the fact that the unique qualities of the quantum world actually lend themselves to a range of metaphysical speculations concerning the precise nature of quantum reality. The emergence of the "new physics" has violently overthrown the purely materialistic worldview of the universe that was espoused by classical Newtonian physics and it has opened people's minds to the realm of metaphysics as quantum theorists wrestle with the implications of the quantum revolution.

We are living in a postmodern era where prominent researchers and professors in many different academic disciplines are drifting away en masse from the modernist Enlightenment paradigm. Einstein had an inbuilt aversion to the direction that the new physics was taking. He opposed any notion that the universe was fundamentally non-local and he clung tenaciously to the idea that the newest discoveries of quantum physics could be reconciled to his concept of relativity.

Einstein, in an archetypal sense, represented modernism's last stand and he was inevitably proven wrong by John Stewart Bell who developed the mathematical theorem that proved that the universe was actually non-local. Einstein, who died in 1955, did not live to see the final nail in the coffin of his tenacious adherence to a classical modernist interpretation of physics. Bell's theorem was the scientific and mathematical proof that triggered the explosion of New Age metaphysical speculations and, as they say, the rest is history.

New Age spirituality is the spirituality of choice in the postmodern era. As we have already seen, New Agers have taken to the new physics like ducks to water. The discoveries of quantum physics do in fact lend themselves to metaphysical speculation as witnessed by the present drift of quantum physicists into the arena of New Age metaphysical speculation. Fritjof Capra, Nick Herbert, David Bohm, Fred Alan Wolf, David Albert, John Hagelin and Amit Goswami are just a handful of prominent quantum physicists with Ph.D.'s who have turned to metaphysical speculation in their attempts to interpret the nature of quantum reality.

All of these prominent figures are committed pantheists who have placed a New Age interpretation upon the bizarre discoveries of the quantum world. Why has quantum physics fallen so vulnerably into the hands of New Age metaphysicians and not, for argument's sake, Buddhists or Muslims? The ubiquity of non-local connections throughout the universe has inclined these scientists toward the belief in the ultimate inter-connectedness of all things which has in turn led to the adoption of pantheistic beliefs. Pantheism appears to be the number one contender in Western culture for the right to interpret quantum physics.

The Edge of the Spiritual World

As I have already mentioned, I would like to submit the idea that the weird world of quantum mechanics represents the intersection between two worlds. It is the intersection between the world of spirit and matter. It is like the buffer zone between spiritual realities and material realities. The quantum world appears to exhibit the dual attributes of both spirit and matter! The realm of spirit is by its very nature non-local. It transcends space and time, those four familiar dimensions that we are all accustomed to navigating in everyday life.

All quantum systems exhibit attributes of both waves and particles. They are in a superposition that cannot be accurately discovered because they can be in more than one state and one specific location at any given moment. In fact, according to quantum theory they are in every state simultaneously until they are observed by an observer. Photons and electrons exhibit this weird property called non-locality! Timothy Ferris, a Professor at the University of California at Berkeley writes,

> The essence of quantum weirdness can be summed up in the statement that quantum systems – typically, photons and electrons, things smaller than an atom – exhibit "non-local" behaviour. In all previous scientific investigations, nature acts locally. For a cause here to produce an effect over there, an intervening mechanism must link the two. Such a mechanism is "local" in that you can identify it here and now; the waves that make a skiff bob in its moorings can be traced to a passing ship. If no waves or other mechanisms could be found connecting the ship to the skiff, we would have non-local behaviour, which seems as inexplicable as if a car were to continue accelerating down the road after losing its drive shaft.[7]

Quantum physics has brought scientists to the very edge of the world of spirit. From a biblical perspective we understand "spirit" as a dimension beyond space and time. In the world of spirit all the attributes familiar to human existence suddenly change. Similarly, within the quantum world the rules of the game are not at all the same as the rules of the classical physical world that we live in. Quantum weirdness is exemplified by realities that are entirely counterintuitive to the macroscopic world in which we live. In the quantum world electrons can materialise as particles and dematerialise into a spread out wave formation.

In this wave form they can behave in ways that resemble the dimension of spirit rather than what we traditionally understand as "matter." They can materialise in one location and rematerialise in another location instantaneously. In a dematerialised state scientists have discovered that they can pass through solid objects like walls. In the previous chapter we introduced the strange property called quantum tunnelling.

We also saw that two "entangled" quantum particles can instantly communicate with each other over vast distances, even theoretically if these two entangled partners are at the opposite end of the universe. This property is called quantum entanglement. They can also disappear and reappear in another location. This is called quantum teleportation. In fact, quantum waves have recently been discovered to travel much faster than the speed of light.

The New Age community is powerfully attracted to the world of quantum physics precisely because of the realisation that the quantum world appears to exhibit the extra dimensional attributes of *spirit*. Eastern mysticism does not divide spirit from matter as we do in the West. New Agers see a direct correlation between the phenomenon of quantum non-locality and the invisible realm of spirit. In this sense they are close to the biblical worldview that has always insisted upon the existence of the spiritual world.

Western science, however, is still operating in a *modernist* paradigm that categorically rejects the realm of spirit and relegates it to religious superstition. Western science is dogmatically materialistic and naturalistic. It denies the realm of spirit and binds itself to a natural explanation for everything. But with the emergence of quantum physics the materialistic philosophy of modernism has become scientifically unsustainable. The emerging science of quantum physics actually contradicts a purely materialistic explanation of the universe. Non-local equals non-material!

Jean Staune is a French professor of philosophy who also firmly believes in a personal God. He writes on the subject of the intersection of science and religion. In his essay: "On the Edge of Physics," he wrote,

> The central idea of all monotheistic religions is that the world in which we live – the world of time, space, energy, and matter – cannot be its own cause because it has been created by a transcendent principle: God. The science of the 19th century seemed very close to demonstrating that the world caused itself. Science not only failed in this demonstration, however, it has *actually demonstrated the opposite*. Science has suggested through quantum physics that it alone cannot provide a complete picture of reality. It has provided the basis for a credible way to understand the existence of God, because the world no longer limits itself to our level of reality. Quantum physics does not prove the existence of God. It nonetheless takes us through a giant step from a scientific materialism that ruled out

the existence of God, to a position where, on a scientific basis, we can start to understand the concept of God's existence. A belief in materialism is still possible under quantum physics, of course – but only if it is transformed into a kind of "science fiction" materialism, somehow able to integrate the "de-materialization of matter." New experiments show that matter itself does not have a strictly material reality.[8]

EXPLORING THE TWILIGHT ZONE

Jean Staune believes that the discovery of non-locality brings us to a necessary acknowledgement that the realm of spirit is just as empirically real as the material world. He continues:

In 1964, an Irishman named John Stewart Bell developed a mathematical proof that supported a non-physical part of the universe. This theoretical physicist stated that any model explaining the universe entirely as local or as physical reality is incomplete for it does not include the non-local part. This proof was called the Bell Theorem and it was verified by many scientific experiments. Simply put, the Bell Theorem proves that there is another reality (non-local), which can be referred to as "spirit," beyond our current, physical (local) reality. Non-local reality interacts with our reality and is the source and cause of the physical existence of reality. The non-physical part of the universe is the definitive proof that all science was seeking. Bell's Theorem proves another realm exists that theology has talked about, but was unable to prove in a theoretical or empirical sense.[9]

Bell's Theorem has been described by some scientists as "the most profound discovery of science." Nick Herbert, in his book *Quantum Reality: Beyond the New Physics* writes, "Bell's discovery of the necessary non-locality of deep reality is the most important achievement in reality research since the invention of quantum theory!"[10] Bell was thoroughly preoccupied with the fact that quantum physics pointed to another level of reality that was non-local.

John Bell focused his research on the mystery of quantum entanglement and the discovery of the fact that entangled particles communicated with each other over vast distances at speeds that vastly exceed the speed of light. Einstein had said that nothing can exceed this universal speed limit, but experiments in the field of quantum entanglement were revealing that the quantum world had attributes that lead to only one possible conclusion, that reality is non-local. "Non-local" actually means non-material. Non-locality is not a property of the physical realm of matter. It reveals another invisible dimension beyond space and time.

John Stewart Bell himself said, "That the guiding wave, in the general case, propagates not in ordinary three-dimensional space but in a "multi-dimensional configuration space" is the origin of the notorious "non-locality" of quantum mechanics." Bell asserted that the wave function exists in a dimension beyond that of our four dimensional world of space and time. Those who are informed by biblical revelation would understand this other dimension as the "spiritual realm." The existence of the spiritual realm is the central thesis of this book and it is my intention to explore the relationship between the discoveries of quantum physics and the spiritual realm.

I believe that exploring this relationship actually sheds new light upon the relationship between God and the world of quantum physics. The central proposition of this book is that the realm of spirit undergirds the realm of matter and that the material world is actually structured upon the building blocks of spirit.

New Age spirituality also believes in the spiritual realm and embraces a magical view of the universe. Because they embrace the reality of the spiritual realm they have gained the high ground in the spiritual marketplace through hijacking and co-opting quantum physics. They assert themselves as the only reliable guide to the strange world of quantum physics. But the New Age interpretation of quantum discoveries is only one interpretation. There are a growing number of Christian physicists who are arguing that discoveries in the quantum world are actually confirming biblical revelation. One such interpreter is Raymond Chiao. He is a quantum physicist and former researcher at the University of California in Berkeley where he was based for almost 40 years. He is now a researcher at the University of California, Merced. He writes:

> As a Christian, I believe that we can learn spiritual truths from science, in particular from quantum physics – that is, from a deep study of the physical universe, which I believe bears testimony to the divine characteristics of its Creator. When we consider the lessons taught by the scientific achievements of the 20th century, perhaps the most important is the fact that after many centuries of

separation, a genuine convergence between science and religion is beginning to occur.

Chiao's field of expertise is in the study of quantum tunnelling and non-locality. He is deeply aware that there is another level of reality that cannot be located in time and space. The convergence between science and faith has actually been intensified by the discovery of the non-local dimension of quantum physics. I believe that the "Intelligent Design" interpretation is a superior explanation of this deeper level of quantum reality. Science (driven by modernist presuppositions) believed it could disprove the existence of God but most cutting edge scientific discoveries in the past century have pointed in the direction of Intelligent Design.

Astrophysicists, for example, are overwhelmingly aware of the evidence for the fine tuning of the universe. Recent discoveries at the quantum level point to the evidence for the existence of an Intelligent Designer who determined all the laws of classical and quantum physics before He created the universe! The Bible asserts that God created the quantum world and that it has been uniquely designed and crafted to respond to the creative voice of God. Raymond Chiao writes:

> The quantum world view of a nonlocal universe has been borne out time and again. Specifically, the Uncertainty Principle has taught us that the classical world view is untenable. Work by Einstein, Bell and many others, including our experiments on quantum tunnelling at Berkeley, have told us that it is impossible to believe in a local, "realistic" universe. This has opened up new possibilities for religious understanding. At the heart of quantum physics is the wave-particle duality. In particular, in the Born interpretation of the wave function, a detection of a particle can be thought of as the materialization of the particle at a particular place at a definite time, *out of a wave which is not localized in space nor in time*. Although the wave function is itself not directly observable, its properties can be inferred from the manifestations of the particle, which *are* directly observable.[11]

A wave that is not localized in space or time is something which could be defined as "extra dimensional." Quantum physicists are now frequently interacting with realities that are non-local! But what exactly is non-locality? Heisenberg taught the Uncertainty Principle: that quantum realities are non-locatable or non-localized. Uncertainty rules, because it is impossible to precisely locate a particle without collapsing the wave function. Jean Staune writes,

> Quantum phenomena prove the existence of another level of reality; one, which lies outside space and time since non-locality is its principal characteristic. We have a very extensive knowledge of some characteristics of quantum phenomena, and it is this scientific knowledge that demonstrates the existence of a level of reality that escapes time, space, energy, and matter, and yet still has a causal effect on our material level of reality.[12]

NON-LOCALITY AND PANTHEISM

Discoveries such as quantum non-locality, quantum entanglement, quantum teleportation and quantum tunnelling point toward the existence of other dimensions outside space and time. The weird behaviour of the quantum world can only be explained if we allow the existence of other dimensions. Peering into the quantum world is like peering into an extra-dimensional reality. Quantum non-locality clearly points towards these other dimensions. Serious physicists are now exploring a range of philosophical ideas to explain the appearance of extra dimensions. But this is nothing new. We saw that even back in the 1950s European quantum physicists were exploring concepts of Eastern mysticism to try to explain quantum mysteries. And most recently, as a maturation of this trend we see these Eastern metaphysical speculations being popularised in movies such as *What the Bleep Do We Know?*

This movie is decidedly pantheistic and deliberately anti-Christian but it represents a prime example of the New Age agenda to claim the high ground of quantum physical interpretation. Pantheism is "flavour of the month" in the Western world right now. Approximately 200 million people throughout the West have embraced one degree or another of New Age beliefs and ideas, all of which are built upon the foundation of pantheism.

One author, Lee Warren, wrote an article titled, "Has Science Found God in Non-Local Reality?" His agenda is to proclaim that quantum physics has discovered God. But Warren is a committed pantheist who intentionally blurs the line between biblical theology and New Age pantheism. His speculation concerning the relationship between quantum non-locality and the realm of spirit is typical of this burgeoning field of New Age speculation. He writes:

Some may argue that science has not proven the actual existence of God. However, quantum mechanics has discovered another realm that is not physical or in the realm of space and time. This article will compare the invisible, non-local order of our reality identified by quantum mechanics (specifically proven by the Bell Theorem) and Spirit that is invisible, omnipresent, and all in all. Whether science wants to admit that the non-local phenomenon is in reality Spirit operating does not matter. For those that have eyes to see, it is further evidence to show the existence of Spirit. We must become aware that we are interconnected with the Holy Spirit. In short, Elohim is always omnipresent or ever present in creatures. He is never absent or separate from His creation.[13]

Warren seeks to forge a synthesis between New Age pantheism and biblical theism and is essentially claiming that the entire universe is God. Warren's conclusions are typical of the pantheistic worldview of many who have adopted quantum physics as the new spiritual mascot for New Age beliefs. Patricia Williams is a philosopher of science. She also argues that quantum physics has discovered the realm of spirit.

Science discounted spirit, assigning it no role in the material universe. What science (as well as theology) does not adequately appreciate is that today's matter is "spirit" – active, indescribable, non-local, and immaterial. It may be that the mysterious "wavicles" are merely the deepest physical manifestation of spirit we encounter, and something even more mysterious underlies them. Instead of chasing spirit out of the universe, physics has encountered it However, determined to render occult causes obsolete, physics cloaked its discovery in other names, like "electron," "proton," and "photon" – the quantum particles that make reality so mysterious. Then it redefined the term "matter" to include anything that has mass, whether meeting the former definition of "spirit" or not.[14]

NON-LOCALITY AND BIBLICAL THEISM

The notion that quantum non-locality should be automatically equated with "spirit" simply because both are non-material is highly speculative. The diversity of speculations engendered by quantum non-locality highlights the fact that metaphysical speculation becomes meaningless and abstract unless it is guided by biblical revelation. In contrast to popularised New Age interpretations of the quantum world the concept of non-locality actually supports a much older tradition of spirituality that dates back to the in-breaking of the revelation of a personal God who has revealed Himself in space and time as the very Author of space and time but who exists outside of space and time! God revealed Himself to Abraham and so began a journey of unfolding revelation as God began to reveal Himself and His purposes for the creation which He himself has made for His own glory.

This unfolding revelation is exclusively documented in the Bible and the teachings of the Old and New Testaments actually contain some powerful revelatory insights into the process of creation and the way in which God built the physical universe from non-local and invisible "building blocks." The thesis of this book is extremely simple yet extremely profound: God created this physical world as a physical materialisation of non-local components and He sustains this materialisation of the wave function with His powerful voice. As we journey together we will seek to explore the relationship between this glorious personal God and His amazing creation that is built on the foundation of invisible quantum realities that have their origin in another dimension beyond space and time.

The biblical paradigm powerfully critiques pantheism. From a biblical perspective there is nothing intrinsically "divine" or "spiritual" about quantum reality in spite of the predominance of New Age speculations to the contrary. The Bible makes a clear differentiation between the Creator and the creation. The creation never becomes the Creator and the Creator never becomes the creation.

God is an uncreated being who has an eternal existence independent of the realm of creation. According to the biblical worldview, God is transcendent and exists outside of creation. Yet another distinction that the Bible makes between God and creation is the fact that the Creator is eternal whereas the creation is temporal. Creation has a clearly defined beginning and an end according to the biblical worldview.

In light of this powerful revelation of the distinction between the Creator and the creation we must re-think the exact nature of quantum reality. Is the quantum world of non-local connections intrinsically divine or is there another more accurate interpretation that is consonant with biblical revelation? In Nick Herbert's survey of interpretative models of quantum reality he does not even countenance a biblical interpretation of the quantum facts. Perhaps Christians have been asleep at the wheel and have lacked the initiative to contend for the high place of biblical interpretation.

My own survey of Christian literature that interacts with the newest discoveries of quantum physics has been rather a disappointing adventure. There has been so little written on this subject by Christian thinkers that it would appear that the Christian community has all but surrendered to the New Age community in claiming the high ground of quantum interpretation. There is a pressing need for theologians to reflect upon the discoveries of quantum physics in the light of the revelation of Scripture.

Quantum reality is part of God's glorious creation, albeit an invisible part of creation. It is not divine in any way, nor is it some kind of living entity. It is merely another aspect of creation. In the light of biblical revelation we can safely say that the quantum world is, by divine design, created in such a way that it is highly responsive to the presence and power of the Holy Spirit which, according to the Bible, is omnipresent. "Where can I go from Your Spirit? Or where can I flee from Your presence?" asked David as He pondered the omnipresence of God. (Psalm 139:7) Behind the entire material universe there is another layer of invisible reality called the world of the quantum, and behind this layer of quantum reality is the reality of God who upholds all things by the word of His power. We must avoid the temptation to leap blindly into some form of pantheism by suggesting that this other dimension of reality is itself God.

The majority viewpoint doesn't necessarily make it the correct interpretation of ultimate reality. Pantheism is a long established spiritual worldview and its faithful adherents seek to assume ownership of the recent discoveries of quantum reality, arguing that these discoveries substantiate pantheism. The fact that this ancient theological concept of pantheism has been around for thousands of years adds a certain weight of authority to the task of interpreting reality. The argument is that recent discoveries in the field of quantum physicists now confirm what has been taught in the Vedic Scriptures for thousands of years and that the wise men of the East had it right all along. Could it be that scientists have inadvertently stumbled upon something which substantiates the ancient wisdom of the East or is there another interpretation that is more consistent with biblical revelation?

NON-LOCALITY AND "SPIRIT"

In order to be faithful to what God has revealed in Scripture it is necessary to affirm that the quantum world of non-local reality is *not* in any way divine. But could the non-local quantum world be appropriately described as "spirit" without asserting that it is divine? This is an important question that needs to be resolved if we are to deepen our understanding of the true nature of the quantum world. The traditional New Age interpretation of "spirit" mirrors the ancient Eastern traditions which have always been right at home with the dualism of spirit and matter.

Whatever is not material, according to this model of interpretation, is by definition "spirit." According to this paradigm there are only two options, spirit or matter, and both are said to be a manifestation of "God." There isn't even a debate amongst pantheists about whether the realm of "spirit" is God or not. According to pantheism, everything is God; therefore the non-material world is by necessity "God." But according to biblical revelation everything is not God. God chooses to clearly differentiate Himself from *all* that He has made!

According to the biblical worldview there is a realm that is identified as "spirit" that is definitely not a part of God. For example, there are created spiritual beings such as angels and archangels that constitute an invisible order of created beings, and some of these spirit beings are revealed to be the enemies of God. Satan and the entire demonic realm appear to be the dark counterparts of God's holy angels and archangels. Both God's angels and the entire host of invisible demonic beings are identified as "spirit beings." Angels and demons are living spiritual beings that deserve the designation of "spirit." But in stark contrast to pantheistic teachings, neither the angels or the demons are revealed to be a part of God. They are created beings.

Then there is what we call the "spiritual realm." This is another plane of reality that exists in a hidden and invisible dimension. Within the sum total of what we call the spiritual realm there are two realms: one of darkness and the other of light. We will discuss the realm of spiritual darkness first. The Bible describes a region called the "heavenly places" in Ephesians 6:12 where dark principalities and powers dwell. This is commonly identified as the "second heavens" in contrast to the "third heavens" which is God's holy habitation called "heaven."

We will address in greater detail the differentiation between the "third heavens" and the "second heavens" in a later chapter, but it would be appropriate to make a few comments at this point. Paul said that he had been "caught up to the third heaven." (2 Corinthians 12:2) The term automatically implies that there are two other realms called "heaven." Most biblical commentators identify the *first heaven* as the universe, the so-called "heavens and earth."

The term *second heaven* does not appear in the Bible, but it is a common designation for the "heavenly places" of Ephesians 6 which is occupied by dark principalities and powers. This is probably to be identified with the immediate atmosphere surrounding the earth. Paul spoke of the "prince of the power of the air" (Ephesians 2:2) which would strengthen the idea that Paul was thinking of the immediate atmosphere surrounding the earth which is clearly the theatre of operation for Satan and his demonic hordes.

The *third heaven* that Paul described in 2 Corinthians 12 is clearly identified as the spiritual abode of God and His holy angels. "Look down from heaven and see from Your holy and glorious habitation." (Isaiah 63:15 NASB) The most important thing to recognise about the realm of heaven is that it is holy. Paul described it as a realm of "unapproachable light." (1 Timothy 6:16) The Greek word for "unapproachable" is *aprositos* which means "inaccessible."

Heaven is a realm of such extraordinarily intense light that none can enter apart from the gift of grace. It is so holy that only those who have been thoroughly cleansed from sin by the blood of Christ can enter. Heaven exists in another dimension in the spiritual realm. It is often described as being "above." John the Baptist said of Jesus: "The One who comes from above is above all; the one who is from the earth belongs to the earth, and speaks as one from the earth. The One who comes from heaven is above all." (John 3:31 NIV) Heaven is not above the earth geographically or spatially. Rather it is "above" in terms of its absolute transcendence. Heaven is superior in many respects. It is eternal whereas the physical "heavens and the earth" will pass away.

There is also another region called "hell" which is the abode of disembodied spirits who are separated from God. It seems that hell is in some way distinguished from the "second heavens" but it is also the dwelling place of dark supernatural beings and will become the future prison of the devil and his angels after Christ returns. The realm of spiritual darkness is in some way partitioned from the realm of spiritual light which is identified as the third heaven. Whilst it is purely speculative, we could easily imagine that the realm of darkness exists in a separate "dimension" to the kingdom of light.

The realm of spiritual darkness can never penetrate the realm of heaven. When Lucifer fell into darkness he was immediately expelled from heaven with no possibility of returning. At this critical moment the kingdom of darkness came into being and it is conceivable that God created an extra-dimensional veil between the realm of darkness and the realm of light. Of course such a suggestion is purely speculative and there is no empirical evidence to support the idea that the kingdom of darkness exists in a different dimension to the kingdom of light. But light conquers the darkness. Light is infinitely superior to the darkness. Darkness cannot penetrate the unapproachable glory of God's holy presence whereas light always penetrates the realm of darkness.

A counter argument to the suggestion that the kingdom of light exists in a different dimension to the kingdom of darkness would be the reality that both heaven and hell exists in what is called the "spiritual realm." Heaven and hell both exist in a non-local invisible dimension outside of our space-time manifold. According to biblical revelation, all we are told is that there are spirit beings that inhabit a spiritual realm. Some of these beings are of the light and others are of the darkness. The concept of "spirit" therefore includes both invisible spiritual beings and it extends to the realm that they inhabit. The spiritual world somehow encases the physical world and has the capacity to intersect with the physical world in many ways.

Our question is whether the non-local world of quantum reality is a legitimate part of the spiritual realm alongside the obvious non-local realities of heaven and hell. Is there perhaps a third category beyond the dualistic concepts of matter and spirit? Should we just automatically agree with those metaphysicians who assert that whatever is not part of the material order is automatically part of the spiritual realm?

The concept of extra-dimensionality is helpful in seeking to come to an understanding of the exact nature of quantum reality. By "non-local" physicists mean something which transcends our familiar space-time plane of existence. Non-local means something that is not a part of this four dimensional world of space and time. We live in a local, physical universe that is bound by four dimensions, but quantum physicists are now conscious of the existence of another dimension beyond our four dimensions and this additional dimension is said to be "non-local." In this other dimension quantum realities do not appear to be bound by the constraints of space and time.

Extra-Dimensionality

Let's return to our original investigation in which we were asking the question whether the discovery of the reality of quantum non-locality constitutes the scientific discovery of the spirit world as some metaphysicians have suggested. It is evident from biblical revelation that the spirit world exists outside of time and space and is in no way constrained by the limitations imposed by spatial travel or time travel. God Himself is outside of time and the order of created spirit beings appear to be endowed with the capacity to "move" from point A to point B without the constraints of time.

This doesn't mean they are omnipresent but it does confer an advantage to exercise greater mobility of movement than those beings that live within the space-time manifold. Similarly, the non-local world of quantum mechanics does not appear to be bound by these constraints either. At least on this account there are some compelling parallels between the attributes of spirit and the attributes of quantum non-locality. So let's continue our investigation.

The concept of "extra-dimensionality" is an excellent paradigm for describing the non-local world of quantum mechanics. As we have seen, many New Age interpreters and even some Christian interpreters have argued that science has now stumbled upon the realm of spirit. But from a scientific perspective, the discovery of this non-local dimension of existence does not necessarily constitute the scientific discovery of the spirit world.

This is evidenced by the fact that the arguments set forth are not so compelling that they would persuade all physicists to take the quantum leap in embracing this conclusion. Admittedly, there is an anti-supernatural bias that strongly influences some physicists so that they have an inbuilt gravitation toward non-spiritual conclusions. I am not a scientist, but even as a biblical thinker I am cautious about identifying myself with those metaphysicians who are quick to adopt the view that quantum non-locality constitutes the discovery of the spiritual world.

The traditional biblical idea of "spirit" is something which is both *supernatural* and outside of space and time. Communication in the spirit world is not constrained by space and time, nor is communication between non-local quantum realities such as electrons and photons. They can be entangled in such a way that they can communicate superluminally (or beyond the constraints of space or time).

Something is considered "superluminal" if it transcends the cosmic speed limit of the known speed of light, and it is now universally accepted by quantum physicists that quantum realties can communicate much faster than the speed of light! Similarly, the spirit world exists in another dimension and so does the non-local world of the quantum. Quantum entanglement reveals that there are countless cosmic connections from one side of the universe to the other that can communicate superluminally in an instant with no reference to time. This is a classical example of extra-dimensionality.

The parallels are sufficient to satisfy some people that the non-local world is indeed the spiritual realm. New Agers are comfortable with this idea because they are devoted pantheists. It is therefore conceivable that some Christians might also be comfortable in describing the non-local quantum world as a manifestation of the invisible spiritual world, and on the surface of things there seems to be nothing that would prevent someone from seeing such a relationship between quantum realities and the spiritual realm. But we ought not to settle for superficial similarities in our quest to probe the true nature of quantum reality.

Perhaps a further question we could ask is whether the world of quantum non-locality is by definition "supernatural." Supernaturalism is a term that describes a reality that is beyond the "natural" world which cannot be explained in purely natural terms. Modern science, living in the shadow of Enlightenment rationalism, consistently pursues an exclusively natural explanation for everything that can be discovered and explored in the world of nature. Rationalist scientists have an inbuilt aversion to the idea of supernatural explanations and supernatural intervention. They refuse to countenance the idea of supernatural causality, insisting that there must be a natural explanation for everything in nature, including non-local realities.

Modern scientists have no room for the notion of miracles. It is therefore quite an interesting development in quantum physics to witness scientists using such words as "magic" and "ghost-like" to describe the properties of the quantum world. But it is worth noting that many scientists who are most in tune with the startling new revelation of quantum non-locality are not necessarily compelled toward a supernatural explanation.

Remember the comments by the authors of *The Non-Local Universe:* "If this book is ever erroneously placed in the New Age section of a commercial bookstore and purchased by those interested in New Age literature, they will be disappointed."[15] The term "supernatural" is synonymous with the concept of miracles. Quantum non-locality is indeed deeply mysterious but not necessarily miraculous. While it is a newly discovered property of nature, it is nonetheless part of the natural world. The big shock is that up until the quantum revolution we didn't think nature behaved like this!

We might also explore our question through the lens of the world of the invisible. Is something necessarily "spiritual" just because it is invisible? The non-local quantum realm is clearly invisible. Even if scientists had equipment capable of studying electrons under extreme magnification, they would not see them because they are non-local waves. But just because something is invisible does not necessarily make something "spiritual."

There are many things in the natural world that are completely invisible. We could suggest the existence of radio waves, electromagnetic waves, gravitational waves, gamma waves and other kinds of invisible forces, yet none of these things would qualify to be identified as part of the spirit world. Suggesting that the non-local dimension of the quantum world is part of the spirit world is tantamount to suggesting that radio waves are part of the spirit world, but nobody seems to be in a hurry to suggest that these phenomena are synonymous with the spirit world.

The world of quantum physics is certainly a departure from anything in the world of classical physics. It could even be said that non-local realities are *almost* supernatural in nature, but at the end of the day even the quantum world is a part of the world of nature and from a biblical perspective it is a natural part of God's creation. In light of the fact that there is nothing intrinsically supernatural about the rest of God's creation it would be true to say that even the world of quantum reality is not intrinsically supernatural in and of itself. It is bizarre. It is weird. It is even "spooky," to quote Einstein, but it is not necessarily supernatural and some would argue that something must fall into the category of "supernatural" to warrant the definition of belonging to the spiritual realm. I would agree with this because the spiritual realm is something which is entirely supernatural.

We have probed the world of quantum non-locality through the lens of supernaturalism, invisibility, extra dimensionality and that which exists outside of time and space, yet even when it is explored through these various lenses I would suggest that none of these attributes compel us to conclude that quantum non locality is the same as the spirit world. Forced with a choice between considering the non-local universe as being synonymous with the spirit world or considering it as a buffer-zone between the spirit world and the material world, I have chosen to opt for the latter.

I am personally uncomfortable with the idea that the non-local quantum dimension is the same realm as the spiritual realm. But even if we prefer to use the language of extra dimensions to the language of the "spiritual world" we must still concede that the non-local world of quantum reality has certain attributes and qualities that mimic that of the realm of spirit. In light of all this perhaps it would be best to say that the non-local dimension of quantum reality is a buffer zone between the supernatural realm and the natural realm and that it acts as something of a twilight zone, a realm that is neither spiritual or material.

It would appear that the invisible sub-structure of the universe has been intentionally designed by God to be non-local in nature in order to allow for the possibility of non-local, supernatural intervention from the spiritual world. God exists on the other side of the looking glass. In the light of that which God has revealed in His written Word coupled with the scientific revelation of quantum non-locality, I would submit that the non-locality of the quantum field mediates the direct supernatural intervention of God. The entire revelation of God in the Bible presupposes the ongoing supernatural divine intervention of God into the world of matter. His world is continually breaking into our world!

It is only in recent decades that scientists have almost accidentally uncovered the non-local dimension of the universe, and this discovery confirms something that has been maintained in the pages of Scripture for thousands of years. God invades the material world at will in order to interrupt the natural progression of human existence with supernatural intervention and miracles. The miraculous ministry of Christ which included literally thousands of supernatural signs and wonders would suggest that the world of nature has been deliberately designed by God to be interrupted by miracles from the realm of heaven. These waves of heavens power and glory ripple across the world of non-local quantum realities in order to restructure the physical world according to the will of God.

A POSSIBLE ANALOGY

Illustrations are especially helpful in trying to visualise these concepts of the quantum world. But there are not many illustrations from the world of nature that can illustrate the relationship between the Spirit of God, the non-local quantum world and the material world. These are the three fundamental realities that we are faced with, and it is important to tease out the relationship between these three fixed realities. Illustrations are hard to find but I believe there is a powerful illustration to be found in the relationship between the Spirit of Christ and the body and soul of the believer in Christ.

I can see a direct parallel between the interaction of God with the material world (via the non-local quantum world) and the interaction of Christ indwelling the hearts and bodies of those who have received Him as their Lord and Saviour. Let me explain. Through the new birth Christ is supernaturally joined to the human spirit. "He who is joined to the Lord is one spirit with Him." (1 Corinthians 6:17) Through this miraculous intervention called the new birth the Spirit of Christ becomes supernaturally joined to the natural spirit of a man or a woman.

There is nothing intrinsically supernatural about the human spirit or the soul; they are a natural part of human beings even though they are invisible components. We would not describe the spirit or the soul as "supernatural" in and of themselves. They are the product of supernatural ingenuity and creative power, but we accept these attributes as ordinary, almost "natural," components of every human being. It could be strongly argued that the spirit and the soul of a person are actually "non-local" attributes. For example, we could pose the question: Where does the spirit and the soul physically dwell inside a human being? Are they in the physical heart that pumps the blood? Are they in the brain? Is the "spirit" of a man or a woman locatable in spatial terms? Is the mind spatially located in the physical brain? What I am suggesting is that the spirit and the soul of a human being is a non-local buffer between the supernatural Spirit of God and the physical body.

Once a person is born again, Christ begins to express Himself through the human spirit and through the person's soul which is traditionally understood as the mind, the will and the emotions. The supernatural influences of Christ are expressed through the non-local, invisible dimensions of a human being. And these supernatural influences extend to the human body. Christ comes to live inside these human bodies with the goal of ultimately controlling the very body of the believer. If someone's heart is fully yielded to Christ, even their body becomes a living sacrifice and Christ powerfully expresses Himself through that person's physical or material body. They physically travel to geographical locations that Christ guides them to. They can even heal the sick through the laying on of their hands. They become the medium through which the supernatural virtues of Christ flow through them to bless the world.

This illustration parallels the divine intervention of God in the world of matter. God breaks into the physical world of matter through the veil of non-local quantum realities in order to actually affect and transform physical reality. For example, when God heals someone who is physically sick He does so via the invisible quantum world which instantaneously manifests in the world of matter. No miracle has ever occurred through the supernatural ministry of Christ that has not been mediated through the non-local quantum world. This non-local dimension of quantum reality really is the buffer zone between the supernatural realm of the Holy Spirit and the realm of matter. It represents the invisible building blocks of the entire material structure of the universe, but even though it is invisible it is not necessarily something which deserves the designation of "spiritual."

The Scriptures declare that God made the world from invisible things. "By faith we understand that the worlds were framed by the word of God, so that the things which are seen were not made of things which are visible." (Hebrews 11:3) The writer to the Hebrews is essentially proclaiming that the material universe is created from invisible building blocks. In the next two chapters we will begin to explore the creation of the heavens and the earth through the lens of the invisible attributes of quantum mechanics. This is a worthy subject that needs much greater investigation in the light of the discovery of quantum non-locality which American physicist Henry Stapp has proclaimed as "the greatest discovery of all science."[16]

Chapter Five

GOD: THE ULTIMATE OBSERVER

Quantum physics studies nature at a quantum level. The most distinguishing attribute of the quantum world is the "wave/particle duality" which reveals that all of what we call "matter" has a dual existence. Quantum realities simultaneously exist as both a wave (a non-materialised state) and a particle (a materialised state). Is the quantum a particle or a wave? The answer is "yes!" It is both a wave and a particle depending on the experiment that it is subjected to.

Quantum physics reveals that in order for the material universe as we know it to be collapsed into a materialised state, it must be observed by an observer. When it is not being observed it exists in a dematerialised wave-like state but as soon as it is observed the wave pattern mysteriously collapses into a particle (or material) state. This is the strangest of all mysteries in the science of quantum physics. This means that the only time a quantum system exists as a materialised particle is when we are looking. The rest of the time it behaves as a dematerialised cloud of invisible energy. It is this "ghost-like" property that has attracted so much interest and has generated so much speculation concerning the metaphysical and ontological implications of quantum physics.

Discoveries in this field of science reveal that the entire universe is a single gigantic field of energy in which matter is nothing more than a "collapsed" form of quantum energy. The physical universe as we know it and experience it day to day exists in a "collapsed" material state! We now know that the invisible building blocks of matter are individual packets of energy that exist inside the quantum field. But according to the science of quantum physics "matter" can only exist in a materialised state whilst it is being observed.

This raises an obvious question: How then can the physical world of matter continue to exist as a complex tapestry of material particles without the presence of an observer? To expand the problem even further, how can the entire physical universe exist in a collapsed material state without the entire universe being simultaneously observed? The materialised universe is both visible and material whereas a quantum wave is invisible.

According to the Uncertainty Principle, the world of the quantum exists in a superposition; that is, it exists simultaneously as a wave and as a particle; this is what quantum physicists call the wave/particle duality. Where does the energy wave go when it is collapsed into a particle? Well, theoretically, it is still both a wave and a particle at the same time. When it is not being observed it is a wave but when it is being observed it is a particle. But according to the Uncertainty Principle this means that even in its collapsed or materialised state it is still an energy wave or a quanta of invisible energy. It is only when this wave packet of energy is being observed that it is collapsed into a material state.

THE OBSERVER EFFECT REVISITED

This raises a significant philosophical dilemma: How can the world of matter come into existence without an observer? According to all the findings of quantum physicists, without the interference of an observer, the quantum field would remain an invisible, non-local cloud of energy. When we expand our understanding of the quantum world to a macroscopic scale, to the size of the entire universe, it is evident that the entire universe is a super massive field of quantum energy that has collapsed into matter and is somehow mysteriously maintained in a material state.

According to quantum mechanics it is the interference of the observer that collapses energy waves into a materialised state. Who or what then is the observer? It is at this point that theorists begin to spiral off in a variety of directions with all sorts of metaphysical speculations concerning the so-called "observer effect" and the identity of the "observer."

John Archibald Wheeler is one of the 20th century's most renowned theoretical physicists. Among his students were Richard Feynman and Hugh Everett who developed the many worlds interpretation of quantum mechanics. Wheeler was the scientist who invented the term "black hole" in 1967. He gave a lot of time to exploring the question of the relationship between the observer and the universe and came to the conclusion that an observer was essential to the existence of the universe because it is the observer who confers reality upon the phenomena he observes. John Gribbins said,

> Wheeler has actually gone so far as to suggest that the entire Universe only exists because someone is watching it – that everything, right back to the Big Bang some 15 billion years ago, remained undefined until noticed. This raises huge questions about what kind of creature qualifies as being alert enough to notice that it exists, and collapses the cosmic wave function.[1]

And this is where the fun begins philosophically. The fact that the observer is necessary to collapse the wave function has led to endless speculation about such things as whether the moon actually exists if we are not looking at it. The scientific branch of the New Age community has found immense delight in speculating about the relationship between consciousness and the material universe. Their usual line of reasoning is that the universe cannot exist without an observer.

The observer is usually identified as human consciousness that collapses the wave function into a material reality. But New Age metaphysics fails to adequately explain the existence of the material universe in the absence of human consciousness which clearly does not pre-date the creation of the universe, nor is it ubiquitous throughout the known universe. At this point the concept of the "universal mind" is introduced. The universal mind is a kind of eternal divine consciousness that transcends time and space but which is localised in human consciousness, yet in some mysterious way, transcends human consciousness.

CONSCIOUSNESS AND CREATION

Amit Goswami is the author of *The Self Aware Universe: How Consciousness Creates the Material World*. Goswami holds a Ph.D. in Quantum Physics and he has also become a prominent New Age teacher. He asserts that consciousness is transcendent over everything in creation because all consciousness is God. He also teaches that God created the universe but not in the way that has customarily been taught in church. He believes that the universe only comes into manifestation when conscious observers first appeared on the scene.

Goswami appeals to Wheeler's "delayed choice experiment" to suggest that the entire 15 billion years of the universe's history, dating right back to the Big Bang, only came into existence when conscious human beings first looked at the universe. Now that is a major mind bending concept and a brilliant piece of New Age mental gymnastics. Craig Hamilton wrote an article titled *Scientific Proof for the Existence of God* in which he eloquently articulated the New Age beliefs of Goswami on how creation came into existence.

> Life somehow evolved to the point that a conscious, sentient being came into existence. At that moment, solely because of the conscious observation of that individual, the entire universe, including all of the history leading up to that point, suddenly came into being. Until that moment, nothing had actually ever happened. In that moment, fifteen billion years happened. According to physicist Amit Goswami, the above description is a scientifically viable explanation of how the universe came into being. Goswami is convinced, along with a number of others who subscribe to the same view, that the universe, in order to exist, requires a conscious sentient being to be aware of it. Without an observer, he claims, it only exists as a possibility.[2]

This is an extraordinarily far-fetched paradigm for creation but in view of the fact that Goswami rejects the idea of a personal transcendent Creator he is forced to shift the focus onto humans who are, in his mind, the only conscious beings who have the capacity to observe and who are thus able to collapse the infinite possibilities of the wave function into one actualised state of existence. In Craig Hamilton's interview Goswami says:

> The concept of delayed choice is very old. It is due to a very famous physicist named John Wheeler, but Wheeler did not see the entire thing correctly, in my opinion. He left out self-reference. The question always arises, "The universe is supposed to have existed for fifteen billion years, so if it takes consciousness to convert possibility into actuality, then how could the universe be around for so long?" Because there was no consciousness, no sentient being...in

that primordial fireball which is supposed to have created the universe: the Big Bang. But this *other* way of looking at things says that the universe remained in possibility until there was self-referential quantum measurement – so that is the new concept. An observer's *looking* is essential in order to manifest possibility into actuality, and so only when the observer looks, only then does the entire thing become manifest – including time. So all of past time, in that respect, becomes manifest right at that moment when the first sentient being *looks*.[3]

Because New Age teachers categorically reject the concept of God as a personal being, they end up reducing "God" to the status of an impersonal energy. This impersonal divine energy is mysteriously expressed through what is often called the "universal mind" or the "universal consciousness." In order to present a convincing creation story, this depersonalised "God" of the New Age must somehow become the eternal divine Observer. But there is a glaringly obvious problem with the concept of a "depersonalised observer." An "impersonal" observer is a contradiction in terms.

An observer, by nature, must be a person and not an impersonal energy. So in order to solve this problem Goswami requires what he calls a "conscious sentient being" to engage in the act of personal observation that is the necessary missing ingredient to collapse the possibility waves into an actual state which we can observe as the universe in which we live. This is a very convoluted and torturous way of dispensing with the concept of a personal God who perfectly fits the qualifications as the ultimate Observer who exists outside of space and time and who can collapse non-local quantum waves into an actualised material state.

Meet the Ultimate Observer

The biblical revelation of the existence of an omnipotent, personal Creator powerfully solves this problem and in so doing it exposes the irrationality of New Age metaphysics. New Agers acknowledge the fundamental role of the observer in determining the properties of the quantum world yet because they deny the existence of the ultimate Observer they are led astray into some highly mind bending speculations!

The biblical concept of God as an eternal, limitless divine being perfectly fits the role of the one true Observer who observes the entire universe simultaneously. The God of the Bible is an omniscient being; this means

He has all knowledge simultaneously. There is nothing that the Creator of the heavens and the earth does not know. His knowledge is absolute and unlimited. That is because He is an omnipresent being who sees everything and who subsequently knows everything.

The Bible reveals a God who is the ever present interactive Observer of His own creation. It is the very nature of God to observe. "He who planted the ear, shall He not hear? He who formed the eye, shall He not see?" (Psalm 94:9) God is revealed as the omnipotent Creator who has uniquely designed and crafted the material universe. It is absolutely fascinating in the light of quantum physics to realise that God has revealed Himself as the One who has created both the *visible* and the *invisible* world.

"For by Him all things were created that are in heaven and that are on earth, **visible and invisible**, whether thrones or dominions or principalities or powers. All things were created through Him and for Him." (Colossians 1:16) The Bible actually reveals that the visible or material realm has been created from invisible immaterial realities. "By faith we understand that the **worlds** were framed by the word of God, so that the things which are seen [visible] were not made of things which are visible." (Hebrews 11:3) Why did the author of the book of Hebrews choose to use a plural form in describing the **worlds**? The answer lies in the fact that there are in fact two worlds: the visible world and the invisible world.

As we have already seen, quantum physics teaches that the non-material world of non-local waves that exist outside of time and space have the capacity to materialise into physical substance or "matter." The building blocks of the material world are non-material invisible realities. Thus, from a biblical perspective there are two distinct aspects of creation: the visible creation and the invisible! And the visible world is actually founded upon the invisible!

This revelation is powerfully substantiated by the discoveries of the quantum world. The Bible actually reveals that the things that are visible are made of things which are invisible. This implies that the invisible preceded the visible and that the visible is in some way an expression of the invisible. This is exactly what quantum physics explains. Matter is the product of invisible packets or quanta of energy that have been collapsed through interaction with conscious observation!

God is the Creator but He is also the ultimate Observer! As long as God is observing the universe it remains collapsed into a material state. This means that the universe is maintained both by the voice of God and by the observation of God. God observes all that He has made. "The Lord looks down from heaven and sees the whole human race. From His throne *He observes* all who live on the earth." (Psalm 33:13-14 NLT)

The infinitesimally small is just as visible and as tangible to God as the macroscopic world of classical physics. God can look into the sub-atomic world on a scale equivalent to our observation of the world around us. Similarly God can look at the entire universe as though it was contained within the space of a large room. "Nothing in all creation is hidden from God's sight. Everything is uncovered and laid bare before the eyes of Him to whom we must give account." (Hebrews 4:13 NIV)

But all of this raises an important question. If God is the ultimate Observer, how is it that scientists can still collapse the wave function into a materialised particle state if God is presently observing the universe? Surely if God is currently observing the entire universe and thus holding it in a materialised state, scientists should not be able to collapse the quantum wave function if it has already been collapsed! Let's carefully think this through together.

Assuming that God exists, we can say that we live in an "observed" universe. The Word of God reveals God as the ultimate Observer! "Nothing in all creation is hidden from God's sight. Everything is uncovered and laid bare before [His] eyes." (Hebrews 4:13) Nothing escapes God's all encompassing attention! We also understand that one of the defining attributes of this created universe is the wave-particle duality. So if we accept the fact of God's existence we can also accept the fact that God has created a universe where the wave-particle duality is part of the very fabric of reality. This is what has been called the "ghost-like" property of matter. We accept this fact from the scientific observation of the fabric of the cosmos at a quantum level. The wave-particle duality of quantum mechanics is an unbuilt feature of nature at a quantum level even under God's observation. This creates something of a paradox.

From these two simultaneous realities we can therefore accept that God's observation of the quantum world must in some way be relative in that it still allows for human observation to collapse the quantum superposition in an absolute and final manner. We could thus speak in terms of primary and secondary observation. Primary observation by God alters the fabric of nature by creating the quantum superposition whereby quantum "wavicles" are permitted to exist in two states simultaneously. This primary observation allows for the materialization of quantum waves in such a way that it brings forth a physical, material universe. Without God's observation, the quantum world would remain a universe of non-local waves that exist exclusively in a dematerialized state.

Secondary observation by the human observer collapses the wave function into an absolutized particle state where the quantum superposition no longer exists and the wave function is fully collapsed. This unbuilt mechanism of the quantum world is still intentionally discoverable, enabling humans to peer into the actual mechanism of the creation of the physical world. So there are two observers in the universe: God; the ultimate Observer and human beings as secondary observers. Without this unique feature of the ability of the human observer to collapse the wave function, we would never be able to understand the way that God has chosen to bring material realities into existence out of invisible non-local quantum waves.

GOD SAW AND GOD SAID

The Genesis creation narrative reveals that "God saw" and "God said." The creation came into existence because "God said..." But it is sustained because God, the Observer, continues to see. "In the beginning God created the heavens and the earth. The earth was without form, and void; and darkness was on the face of the deep. And the Spirit of God was hovering over the face of the waters. Then *God said*, "Let there be light;" and there was light. And *God saw* the light, that it was good." (Genesis 1:1-4)

Notice the sequence: first God *said*, and then God *saw*! "By faith we understand that the universe was formed at God's command." (Hebrews 11:3 NIV) After the initial phase of the creation process God looked at the heavens and the earth in a formless state and then He spoke again to the embryonic creation. Usually we speak to that which we behold. Remember the story of the cripple at the entrance to the temple and the apostles fixing their gaze upon him? "Peter and John looked at him intently, and Peter said, 'Look at us!'" (Acts 3:4 NLT) They looked and then they said! So God looked at what He had initially made and then He spoke again. Ten times in Genesis chapter one we read the words, "God said..." Each time He was speaking to the creation and expanding it until it was completed.

Six times the book of Genesis says, "And God saw that it was good." (Genesis 1:4,10,12,18,21,25) But the seventh time God saw that it was *very good*: "Then God saw everything that He had made, and indeed *it was very good*. So the evening and the morning were the sixth day. So the creation of the heavens and the earth and everything in them was completed. And on the seventh day God ended His work which He had done, and He rested on the seventh day from all His work which He had done. This is the history of the heavens and the earth when they were created, in the day that the Lord God made the earth and the heavens." (Genesis 1:31, 2:1-4)

God created the entire universe and "then God saw everything that He had made." The creation was made for God's own pleasure. The Hebrew word for "good" is *towb* and it means "beautiful" and "excellent." "Then God looked over all He had made, and He saw that it was *excellent in every way*." (Genesis 2:1 NLT) The pristine creation must surely have been more beautiful than anything we have seen on the fallen earth today. No wonder as God surveyed the beauty and majesty of all that He had made that He said that it was very good!

We take it for granted but those two short words "God saw..." convey a powerful world of theological and scientific significance! God is a watchful God who continually observes everything that He has made. "The eyes of the Lord are in every place, keeping watch on the evil and the good." (Proverbs 15:3) "The eyes of the Lord move to and fro throughout the whole earth." (2 Chronicles 16:9) "For He looked down from the height of His sanctuary; from heaven the Lord viewed the earth." (Psalm 102:19)

In the book of Zechariah the writer had an amazing prophetic encounter with an angel. "Now the angel who talked with me came back and wakened me, as a man who is wakened out of his sleep. And he said to me, 'What do you see?' So I said, 'I am looking, and there is a lamp stand of solid gold with a bowl on top of it, and on the stand seven lamps with seven pipes to the seven lamps.'" (Zechariah 4:1-2 NLT) A few verses later the angel interpreted the vision: "For these seven lamps represent the eyes of the Lord that search all around the world." (v.10) Seven is the number of perfection and these seven lamps represent the perfect and comprehensive vision of the Lord who sees everything throughout the entire universe. Nothing escapes His sight; His eyes are everywhere. David meditated upon the omniscience and the omnipresence of the Almighty, and his heart became overwhelmed:

"You have searched me, Lord, and you know me. You know when I sit and when I rise; you perceive my thoughts from afar. You discern my going out and my lying down; you are familiar with all my ways. Before a word is on my tongue you, Lord, know it completely. You hem me in behind and before, and you lay your hand upon me. Such knowledge is too wonderful for me, too lofty for me to attain. Where can I go from your Spirit? Where can I flee from your presence?... If I say, "Surely the darkness will hide me and the light become night around me," even the darkness will not be dark to you; the night will shine like the day, for darkness is as light to you... *Your eyes* saw my unformed body." (Psalm 139:1-7,11-12,16 NIV)

The "eyes of the Lord" speak to us of His constant watchfulness and care for all that He has made. His watchfulness speaks of His *sustaining* grace. "The Lord **watches over** the foreigner and **sustains** the fatherless and the widow." (Psalm 146:9 NIV) In the same way, God looks upon all that He has made and He sustains His entire creation with His watchful gaze and His powerful word. The watchfulness of the Lord also speaks of God's deep knowledge of His entire creation. "Known to God from eternity are all His works." (Acts 15:18) This revelation goes to the heart of His relationship with His creation. All that He has made is intimately known by God and sustained by the word of His power. "He **sustains** everything by the mighty power of his command." (Hebrews 1:3 NLT)

The biblical concept of the "fatherhood" of God highlights the "sustaining" dimension of God's relationship with His creation. The Hebrew concept of "Father" means one who brings forth and one who sustains that which He has brought forth. God does not create something and then just walk away. He is the Father of creation. His intimate, nurturing care extends to His entire creation, not just to human beings whom He loves as the "apple of His eye." "You are worthy, O Lord our God, to receive glory and honor and power. For You created all things, and they exist because You created what You pleased." (Revelation 4:11 NLT) "The Lord has made all for Himself." (Proverbs 16:4) God is not a casual observer of the work of His own hands, He is intimately engaged in His role as observer and sustainer, and He participates in the beauty of the universe by enjoying everything He has made.

God's creation is incredibly beautiful and clothed in immense glory. It arouses deep wonder and amazement. God said to Isaiah the prophet, "Be glad and rejoice forever in what I create!" (Isaiah 65:18) This is an invitation to participate in the supreme joy and delight that God finds as He rejoices over the works of His own hands. It is no wonder that the angels shouted for joy at the creation of the heavens and the earth. The Lord said to Job:

"Where were you when I laid the foundations of the earth? Tell me, if you know so much. Do you know how its dimensions were determined and who did the surveying? What supports its foundations, and who laid its cornerstone as the morning stars sang together and all the angels shouted for joy?" (Job 38:4-7 NLT) No wonder God stood back and surveyed everything that He had made and saw that it was very good! He rejoices over creation with unimaginable joy. As the intimate Observer, God is deeply engaged with the physical universe that He brought into being with His creative genius and His unlimited power.

Invisible quantum probability waves are an ocean of possibilities until they are observed by the Observer and are collapsed into new realities. How amazing is it that God has allowed quantum physicists the privilege of peeking into one of the secrets of the universe by discovering this incredible relationship between conscious observers and the quantum world and to discover the impact that conscious observers can have upon quantum possibilities! The properties of matter only come into existence through the interaction of the observer with the observed. The question is whether particles even exist without the effect of the observer. The Copenhagen Interpretation taught that quantum possibilities do not have an actual existence until they are observed. Quantum physicists stumbled by chance upon an extraordinary property of the quantum world, discovering that conscious observation of an electron determines the property of the electron. Prior to the interaction of the observer the electron is a probability wave but it is formless and empty. Once an observer interacts with a probability wave it collapses into a definite particle state and its behaviour is fundamentally altered. It is no longer formless.

Tohu, Bohu (Formless and Void)

This scientific discovery is entirely consistent with the Genesis creation account. The opening three verses of the Bible describe not only the *fact* of creation but also the *process* of creation in language that powerfully resonates with the recent discoveries of the mysterious nature of the quantum world. "In the beginning God created the heavens and the earth. The earth was *without form, and void*; and darkness was on the face of the deep. And the Spirit of God was hovering over the face of the waters. Then God said, "Let there be light;" and there was light." (Genesis 1:1-3) Genesis reveals that creation was a progressive process that was launched at the very beginning of time and was completed at the end of the "sixth day."

Once the creation process commenced, the Genesis narrative tells us that there was some kind of interim phase in which the heavens and the earth were initially described as being "without form" and "void." In this transitionary period there were as yet no stars or suns to emit light; therefore the entire embryonic universe was enveloped in complete darkness. "The earth was empty, a formless mass cloaked in darkness." (1:2 NLT) The earth had not yet taken any kind of physical form, nor had the stars or the galaxies been formed. The two Hebrew words for "without form" and "void" are *tohu* and *bohu*. These words were obviously placed together in part because they rhyme. *Tohu* means "empty space," "unformed" or "formless." It is interesting to note how the word *tohu* is translated in other places in the Old Testament. One interesting example is found in the book of Job: "God stretches the northern sky over ***empty space*** [*tohu*] and hangs the earth on nothing." (Job 26:7 NLT)

Tohu essentially means "formlessness" which is the perfect description of a universe consisting of probability waves that have not been collapsed into a materialised state through the interference of observation. String theorists suggest that immediately after the universe first exploded into existence it was a vast expanding mass of invisible strings of energy that existed in other invisible dimensions. As we learned from the book of Hebrews, God did not make the things that are seen (visible) from things that are visible. In other words, God made the visible world of matter from an invisible substance that eventually collapsed into matter. Therefore it would appear that in the first stage of creation God initially created the entire universe as an invisible super-massive field of energy that constituted the primordial "building blocks" or the sub-strata of the material universe.

"For this is what the Lord says – He who created the heavens, He is God; He who fashioned and made the earth, He established it; He did not create it to be ***empty*** [*tohu*], but ***formed*** it to be inhabited – He says: "I am the Lord, and there is no other!" (Isaiah 45:18 NIV) God did not create the earth to be *tohu* (unformed), therefore He "formed" it. *Tohu* was not the final state; it was only an interim state until God took the next step in the creation process. The word *formed* [*yatsar*] serves as the exact opposite of *unformed*. *Yatsar* means to "mould into a form." There was a time when the entire heavens and the earth were physically formless; then it was mysteriously transformed into the visible form that we now have the intense pleasure of observing.

The second word, *bohu*, is a close synonym of *tohu* and it is also used in Isaiah. "God will stretch out over Edom the measuring line of chaos [*tohu*] and the plumb line of desolation [*bohu*]." (Isaiah 34:11 NIV) *Bohu* means "emptiness" or a "vacuous space." This is also an intriguing description of the first developmental stage of the universe that was made up exclusively of super-heated invisible elements prior to congealing into matter. God said, "I looked at the earth, and it was empty [*tohu*] and formless [*bohu*]. I looked at the heavens, and there was no light." (Jeremiah 4:23 NLT) This fits perfectly with Genesis 1:2 which tells us that, "The earth was ***without form and void***; and darkness was on the face of the deep." As we compare Scripture with Scripture we discover that there really was this preliminary stage of creation where all that existed was invisible, un-collapsed probability waves of energy.

But as God continued to look and focus His attention upon the embryonic universe in its initial chaotic phase He spoke and as He spoke the heavens and the earth began to take shape and to form. Galaxies also began to form with billions of stars and their gravitational solar systems. The planets with their moons also began to form. As God said, "let there be light," streams of photons began to issue forth from the stars as they burst into unimaginably hot furnaces of atomic energy, illuminating the universe from one end to the other.

The universe could no longer be described as formless and void; it had taken on the unique attributes of marvellous design with each celestial and terrestrial body curiously taking on a perfect spherical shape. Each celestial body emitted a different measure of glory. "There are also celestial bodies and terrestrial bodies; but the glory of the celestial is one, and the glory of the terrestrial is another. There is one glory of the sun, another glory of the moon, and another glory of the stars; for one star differs from another star in glory." (1 Corinthians 15:40-41)

THE PROCESS OF QUANTUM CREATION

God's capacity to observe is intimately related to His capacity to speak. God first fixed His gaze upon the invisible elements of His initial creation whilst it was yet formless and empty, and as He looked He spoke to what He saw in the invisible quantum world. He called the things that were not as though they were! Through His observation and the power of His word, the invisible elements of creation took on form and shape, and the material universe began to come into existence, "So that the things which are seen [visible] were not made of things which are visible." (Hebrews 11:3) Invisible wave packets of energy collapsed into visible particles which formed the building blocks of larger physical objects that could eventually be viewed by the naked eye. Without this next level of intentional interaction the universe would still consist of a vast ocean of extra-dimensional, formless quantum energy that existed in a non-local state.

Why did God choose to create the heavens and the earth in these clearly defined stages? It is not for us to understand the mind of God in all of its complexity. "Who has known the mind of the Lord that he may instruct Him?" (1 Corinthians 2:16) But God has permitted humans to stumble into some of the deepest mysteries of the creative process as scientists probe the depths of the world of the quantum.

The wave/particle duality at the very heart of nature is a glimpse into the mystery of creation itself and it highlights the role of consciousness in the process of the formation of the universe at the sub-atomic level. Without observation the quantum world would remain a probability cloud of infinite possibilities, but these potentialities would never have been realised without the crucial role of the Observer of the entire creation. God saw...God said. God continues to see and God continues to speak. He holds the entire universe together with the word of His power. God speaks to what He sees.

The concept of the "observer effect" came into being in an attempt to describe the process of measuring the quantum. Before a quantum system has been interfered with through a conscious attempt to measure it, the quantum system is said to exist in a superposition of all possible states. When an observer consciously chooses to measure the exact location of an electron, the act of observation will determine the actual properties of that electron. When we are not looking, it will behave like a non-local wave of energy but when we are looking it behaves like a particle with a definite location. Look away again and it reverts to a wave function. The process of measurement actually forces an outcome upon the quantum system, thereby altering that system. One of the distinguishing features of quantum physics is that observation actually imposes certain properties upon that which is being observed. What an intriguing thought to meditate upon the fact that observation actually brings about the properties of nature.

God brought all of the building blocks of the physical universe into existence before He brought forth the actual universe of matter as we know it. When God intentionally looked at all He had made, the universe suddenly collapses into a materialised state. God continues to observe all that He has made and so the universe is maintained in a collapsed material state for as long as God continues to choose to intentionally observe the world. God measures the universe by observing it just like the quantum physicist who seeks to measure and probe the quantum world. God knows the exact number of stars and the exact number of galaxies because the Bible reveals that the universe is finite. God also knows the exact number of grains of sand in the earth. Nothing escapes His powerful observation of the entire universe.

QUANTUM FOUNDATIONS

Quantum physics reveals that the heavens and the earth are built upon an extraordinarily unique foundation. All that is visible is built from the world of invisible realities. The quantum world of invisible waves of energy constitutes the very *foundation* of heaven and earth. These realities are foundational in a number of ways. Firstly, quantum reality precedes material reality. Secondly, quantum reality undergirds the world. Ten times in the Old Testament we encounter the phrase: *the foundations of the earth*. But we also find that the Bible speaks of *"the foundations of heaven!"* (2 Samuel 22:8) Ten times in the New Testament we encounter the phrase: *the foundation of the world*, which is an inclusive term that encompasses the foundations of both the heavens and the earth. What an incredible thought that the *foundation of the universe* is something which is entirely invisible and non-local!

Language is a curious thing. The Bible has its own unique language because in the writing of the divinely inspired Scriptures the Holy Spirit carefully chose specific words to communicate specific thoughts and concepts. I see a remarkable convergence between the words that we see in the Bible that are used in relation to the creation of the universe and the words that are being used to convey concepts in quantum physics. Biblical concepts such as "formless" and "void" coupled with the idea of an intelligent Designer who observes and measures the universe – these are all ideas that powerfully converge to give us, as the community of faith, a language that helps us to understand *how* God created the heavens and the earth in the light of quantum mechanics.

In quantum physics, observation is the same as measurement. To measure quantum stuff it first has to be observed. Scientists seek to probe deeper and deeper into the heart of the quantum world but God alone is the one who can observe and measure the entire universe. "Who has *measured* the waters in the hollow of His hand, *measured* heaven with a span and calculated the dust of the earth in a *measure*? Weighed the mountains in scales and the hills in a balance?" (Isaiah 40:12)

"Where were you when I laid the *foundations* of the earth? Tell Me, if you have understanding. Who determined its *measurements*? Surely you know! Or who stretched the line upon it? To what were its *foundations* fastened? Or who laid its cornerstone, when the morning stars sang together, and all the sons of God shouted for joy?" (Job 38:4-7 NIV) God alone has observed or measured the entire universe. God knows that from our human perspective, "the host of heaven cannot be numbered, nor the sand of the sea measured." (Jeremiah 33:22) But our great omniscient God knows their exact number because of His capacity to observe and measure the entire universe with the blink of an eye.

Concerning the earth, God asked Job, "To what were its *foundations* fastened?" What an awesome scientific question. But God answers His own question in the book of Job: "God stretches the northern sky over empty space [*tohu*] and hangs the earth on nothing! (Job 26:7 NLT) Consider the progression of God's creation. The first step was to lay the invisible foundations of the visible world. The next step was to consciously observe it or to measure it because whatever God observes He automatically measures. The next step was for God to speak to His creation and as He exercised the mighty power of His word the visible world sprang into existence, being formed out of invisible yet powerfully real components that represented the foundation of the physical universe. "He stood and measured the earth." (Habakkuk 3:6) And as He measured the earth it stood up and was formed into its present physical form.

This is what the Lord Himself says that He did at the creation: "Indeed My hand has laid the *foundation* of the earth, and My right hand has stretched out the heavens; when I call to them, they **stand up** together." (Isaiah 48:13) What powerful imagery! This verse supports the idea presented in Genesis 1:2 that the creation of the universe occurred in two distinct stages. First God laid the invisible foundations of the heavens and the earth which were wave packets of invisible energy, and then He transformed the invisible world into the visible world. God spoke to that which was form-less and void, and the entire heavens and the earth simultaneously *stood up*! God looked and spoke and the entire universe underwent a profound metamorphosis from a formless state into a materialised state.

The Hebrew word for "stood up" in Isaiah 48:13 is *amad* and it means "to stand up,' "to arise" or "to raise up." It describes a transition and move-ment from one position to another. Prior to being "raised up" or "stood up," something would be described as being either in a seated or in a horizontal position. Something has to be in a different position before it can "stand up." When God spoke to His embryonic creation, it changed position. Quantum physicists tell us that without the interference of observation a quantum system exists in a *superposition* of two states. This is the wave/particle duality. Observation and measurement collapses the superposition so that a particle can be measured. An observed particle is now said to have a *position*, whereas prior to observation or measurement it existed in a *super-position* of all possible states.

Could it be that the Spirit-inspired Scriptures have been trying to tell us something about the actual process of creation for thousands of years, awaiting 20th and 21st century quantum physics to come along and shed light upon ancient revealed truth? All of this reminds me of that amazing verse in the book of Isaiah: "It is He who sits above the circle of the earth, and its inhabitants are like grasshoppers, who stretches out the heavens like a curtain, and spreads them out like a tent to dwell in." (Isaiah 40:22) For mil-lennia people thought that the earth was flat and some even lived in fear of falling off the edge of the earth. But, all along, the Scriptures were revealing that the earth was a giant circular sphere, just as the sun and the earth and the planets are spherical in shape.

WHEN DIVINE OBSERVATION CEASES

Just as the physical universe suddenly came into being, so shall it just as suddenly be dissolved at the end of the age. "It will happen in a moment, in the *blink* of an eye!" (1 Corinthians 15:52 NLT) At the twinkling of God's eye, in that moment when God blinks, when He removes His steady gaze from creation and withdraws His powerful voice, the creation shall all dissolve back into a formless void of invisible elements. And then He will create a new heavens and a new earth right before the delighted gaze of His redeemed sons and daughters, and perhaps He will even use the same invisible elements that He used to lay the foundations of the first heavens and earth! After all, the objects of His deepest love and affection were not there to rejoice over His greatest creative act at the first creation of the heavens and the earth. What a day that will be!

> The day of the Lord will come like a thief. The heavens will disappear with a roar; and the elements will melt with fervent heat; and the earth and everything in it will be laid bare. Since everything will be destroyed in this way, what kind of people ought you to be? You ought to live holy and godly lives as you look forward to the day of God and speed its coming. That day will bring about the destruction of the heavens by fire, and the elements will melt in the heat. But we are looking forward to the new heavens and new earth He has promised, a world where everyone is right with God. (2 Peter 3:10-13 NIV)

YOU ARE NOT GOD!

There is something unique about the observational capacities of the Divine Observer. God is more than an Observer of the entire universe; He is the Creator of the universe. The invisible elements of the universe respond uniquely to His creative voice so that when He observes and when He speaks, the creation literally stands up and is transformed into an entirely new form or position. God has allowed scientists to discover the "observer effect" and to discover the role that consciousness exercises upon the quantum world, but we must not blur the line between creature and Creator.

As conscious beings our human consciousness has the capacity to interfere with the quantum world, but this is nothing more than an extremely finite reflection of the infinite power of God's consciousness to create and maintain entirely new realities. Human beings are "creative" in a secondary sense. We are endowed with creative and imaginative abilities to manipulate and shape the world around us because we are made in the image and likeness of God. But God has not endowed human beings with ultimate creative power to speak things into existence in the way that only God can.

This is where the discovery of the so-called "observer effect" is carried beyond the pale of reality by New Age metaphysical speculators. The observer effect is invoked to assert that we humans have the God-like capacity to create our own reality. But this blurs the biblical line of demarcation between creature and Creator. New Age metaphysics asserts that you are God and that you are thus endowed with unlimited creative ability to create your own reality. Eager recipients of this inflated self-perception expend great emotional and mental energy seeking to merely create just one single day of harmony and bliss, only to discover that they are not God and they are not endowed with unlimited creative powers.

At the end of the day they discover that they are still mere mortals and that they are not God. If humanity were God there would not be so many disillusioned New Agers who are forced to face the reality that they are finite beings. Beyond all the hype of New Age speculation concerning the God-like status of humans, we are all faced with the limitations of humanity. This is what the Lord says about Himself: "I am God, and there is no other; I am God, and there is none like Me." (Isaiah 46:9)

Even though we humans are made in the image and likeness of God, we are nevertheless not God. We are not the "ultimate observer." We are the observed! We are not endowed with unlimited power. We are conscious beings and our consciousness interacts with the world around us, even at a quantum level, but we are not endowed with ultimate creative abilities to create entirely new realities out of nothing in the way that the Creator of the heavens and the earth can.

To assert that "you are God" as the New Age community wishfully asserts, is to send people forth on a journey that is doomed to end in frustration and despair. If you still cannot create your own day, let alone create your entire life, you can always tell yourself that you have not fully mastered the secret and you can always try a little harder. But we will always be humbled at the end of the day by our mortality and the limitations of our humanity.

We are dependent beings who need that gift of spiritual grace and power that only comes through the acknowledgement of our absolute dependency upon God to be the strength of our life. "My grace is sufficient for you, for my power is made perfect in weakness." (2 Corinthians 12:9 NIV) God's power is revealed in the context of the acknowledgement of our weakness.

What we believe determines what we practice. Right now at this period in Western history there are tens of millions of people buying into a theology that is being peddled to them that boldly declares that "you are God" and that you have the unlimited power to create reality. And, they are told, the discoveries of quantum physics prove that you create your own reality.

As human beings we intuitively realise that we were destined for greatness, but this greatness can only be realised through the path of humility and dependency on God, not through puffing ourselves up with over-inflated half truths that capitalise upon people's intuitive sense of the greatness of their destiny.

New Age practitioners are notorious for borrowing concepts that are true for those who are "in Christ" but are fundamentally false for those who are still "in Adam." The Bible reveals that for those who believe *in God* (as He is revealed in the Bible) "all things are possible for those who believe." (Mark 9:23) But the key is to put our faith *in God*, not in our own abilities and limited resources. In the next chapter we will delve a little deeper into the creative power of the Word of God that the true believers are given the unique privilege of participating in.

Chapter Six

SUPERNATURAL SOUND WAVES

Sound is of great significance to God. God thinks and His thoughts are spontaneously expressed as words and words are expressed as sounds. It is part of the very nature of God to communicate; God speaks and He hears. Speech is the vehicle through which God communicates His thoughts. His name is the "Word of God." The first verse of the gospel of John declares, "In the beginning was the Word!" As we might imagine, God has quite a lot to say! But communication is a two way street.

Because God is so passionate about communication He is also the most receptive being in the universe. He listens intently to the communication of others. "He who planted the ear, shall He not hear? He who formed the eye, shall He not see?" (Psalm 94:9) From cover to cover the Bible reveals a glorious God who is a personal being with eyes to see and ears to hear. "The eyes of the Lord are on the righteous, and His ears are open to their cry." (Psalm 34:15) You may never have thought about this, but do you realise that the reason you have two eyes and two ears is because God has eyes and ears?

When God chose to create the world He decided to make a very specific kind of world in which those who were made in His own image and likeness were uniquely endowed with the ability to speak and to hear. This is a fundamental aspect of what it means to be created in the image of God. God desired to have sons and daughters who were not only able to communicate with Him, they were also able to communicate with each other. We are all so accustomed to communicating from birth that we become a little bit jaded to the wonder and amazement of it all.

But every once in a while we are struck with a fresh sense of awe about who we are and of the extraordinary abilities we have been endowed with. Communication is an attribute of intelligence. As intelligent beings with a mind to think and a heart to feel we are naturally inclined toward communicating with one another. The capacity to speak and to hear are essential attributes of the image of God. We are relational beings because God is a relational being, and communication is fundamental to the whole nature of relationships.

So in the beginning God determined to make one very special planet that would be a fit habitation for human beings made in His own image and likeness. Whilst we cannot be completely sure, it is entirely possible that planet earth is the only planet in the entire universe with the capacity to sustain life. In fact, the more that astrophysicists study the physical attributes of the universe the more they are discovering just how extraordinarily fine-tuned the earth is for the existence of life. The level of fine-tuning is so precise in so many different aspects of the physics of the universe that the entire astrophysical community is awed by the realisation that the universe is full of these evidences for amazing fine-tuning. What an incredible thought just to contemplate the possibility that planet earth is completely unique in the entire universe!

The evidence of extraordinary fine-tuning is no secret amongst astrophysicists; they have been collectively inducted into a body of scientific knowledge that is neither challenged nor debated. Interpretations may vary, but the facts are indisputable. All of this evidence of the fine-tuning of the physics of the universe lends tremendous support to theistic creationism, but of course many secular astrophysicists are unwilling to draw theistic conclusions even in the face of the facts.

Evangelical believers who honour the concept of the inspiration and authority of Scripture recognise that the scientific evidence for amazing fine-tuning powerfully substantiates the biblical claim that God created the heavens and the earth. It appears as though God has designed the entire universe with one single objective: to create a perfect habitation for human beings. But there is an even higher purpose behind the creation of humans and that is the desire for intimate relationship with sons and daughters. Relationship necessitates communication and communication is entirely contingent upon the ability to speak and to hear. The idea that the universe was created for conscious human habitation is called the *anthropic principle*.

THE SCIENCE OF SOUND

In order to create the perfect environment that would enable human beings to be able to communicate with one another, it was necessary to create a biosphere with a specific atmosphere that would function as the ideal medium for sound waves to travel. God created intelligent human beings with the capacity to vocalise sounds and to project the sound of their voice in such a way that others could hear those sounds, so that intelligent communication could occur. The transmission of sound waves depends entirely upon the unique atmosphere that surrounds us. The atmosphere surrounding the earth is a relatively thin layer of gases consisting of 78% nitrogen, 21% oxygen, 0.04% carbon dioxide, 0.95% argon and water vapour which varies according to the level of humidity from place to place. This mixture of gaseous molecules fills the atmosphere that encases our beautiful biosphere and it is held in place through the force of gravity which causes the atmosphere of gases to "hug" the earth and not to float off into space.

The transmission of sound is a phenomenon of classical physics. Sound is a "mechanical wave" that is created through the disturbance of the molecules in our atmosphere. Without the medium of our atmosphere there would be no sound waves because sound can only be transmitted mechanically through a medium such as a gas or a liquid. Sound actually travels faster through liquid because it has a higher density than air. In dry air at a temperature of 70 degrees Fahrenheit[1] sound travels at 770 miles per hour.[2] The more humid the air the faster a sound wave travels because of the density of vaporised water molecules. The quality of the transmission of a mechanical sound wave depends upon a combination of factors such as humidity, air temperature, air pressure and altitude.

The atmospheric pressure at sea level is optimal for the transmission of mechanical sound waves. At sea level the average atmospheric pressure is 14.7 pounds per square inch[3] but air pressure decreases at higher altitudes, affecting the capacity of the atmosphere to transmit sound waves. Sound travels slower at a higher altitude because the atmosphere thins and the air pressure is much lower. The air pressure at the top of Mount Everest is so rarefied that it is only a third of the air pressure at sea level!

The speed of sound is also affected by the temperature of the air. Sound travels faster in hot air and slower in frigid air because heat expands the molecules of air, increasing air pressure and molecular density. The ideal conditions, therefore, for the transmission of mechanical sound waves are found at sea level in temperate and sub-tropical climates. It is hard to escape the conclusion that God created the atmosphere of the earth as the optimal medium for the transmission of sound waves.

We are all so accustomed to the presence of sound. Our ears are literally bombarded with a continual barrage of sound, some subtle and some not so subtle. I realised once how unusual it is to experience the complete absence of sound when I was on Mount Shasta in Northern California. We had journeyed above the tree line and there was no sign of life of any kind. A little bit higher up the mountain was the summer snow line, but for the majority of the year the place where I stood on the mountain was usually blanketed in snow with no sign of life. There were no trees, no birds and no crickets, just total silence. Standing in this barren place I was struck by the phenomenon of the complete absence of sound. It was a new experience for me but I am sure it would be a common experience for mountain climbers. Even at night time in remote locations our ears are still subjected to the ambient sounds of crickets chirping and other insect life. Total silence is a rare and eerie experience!

Sound requires a medium for the noise to be transmitted as a mechanical wave. Sound cannot be transmitted in a vacuum. If we were to take a piercingly loud siren and place it in an enclosed container such as a vacuum chamber in which the air has been completely removed, we would find that when we switch the siren on absolutely no sound would be heard because it is inside of a vacuum. There is no sound in space because space is a vacuum; it is almost completely devoid of the atoms that constitute physical matter.

Most atoms are drawn inexorably toward large masses because of the force of gravity, and these atoms inevitably clump together to form the molecules of gas and matter that are capable of mechanically transmitting sound waves. These clustered molecules must be densely packed together for the transmission of mechanical sound waves. Interstellar space is not a perfect vacuum because even in space there are a handful of atoms per cubic inch, but even in this virtual vacuum there are not enough atoms and molecules packed together to transmit sound waves. But unlike sound waves, electromagnetic waves can travel through a vacuum because they do not require a specific medium to transmit their energy.

It is only in an environment such as that found upon the earth that sound waves can be created and transmitted and as we have already observed, it is entirely possible that the life sustaining atmosphere of earth is completely unique in the universe. Within the atmosphere of earth, if we were to take a tuning fork and strike the tines physically, the fork would begin to vibrate. As the tines physically vibrate they begin to disturb the air molecules that are densely packed together. This disturbance is passed on to adjacent molecules as billions of molecules mechanically push one another in every direction.

When someone plucks a guitar string it causes a reverberation effect inside the wooden body of the guitar. The structure of the guitar with its carefully designed sound hole enhances the projection of the sound waves much like a megaphone enhances the projection of our voices.

The intensity of sound is measured in decibels [dB]. A quiet whisper registers approximately 20 dB whilst a jet engine at full thrust registers about 150 dB. A loud sound creates a greater disturbance in the atmosphere causing the molecules to push harder against one another. An exploding bomb creates such an intensely violent movement of air molecules that it can rupture somebody's ear drum if they are too close to the blast.

The loudest sound ever recorded in history was the eruption of Mount Krakatoa in August 1883. Mount Krakatoa is located between Java and Sumatra in Indonesia. The volcanic explosion was 13,000 times the size of the atomic blast that destroyed Hiroshima in 1945 and it was so intense that it was clearly heard in Perth, Australia, 1,930 miles away, and on the island of Mauritius, 3,000 miles away. The sound was estimated to exceed 180 dB up to 100 miles from the volcanic eruption. Can you imagine the force that would push air molecules a distance of 3,000 miles?

THE PHYSICS OF MUSIC

Different sounds vibrate at different frequencies. Physical objects that vibrate at only one cycle or one vibration per second are said to vibrate at 1 Hertz [Hz]. The slower the vibration, the lower the pitch or frequency that is produced. Conversely, the higher the vibration, the higher the pitch. The human ear can hear a range of 20 to 20,000 Hz. An elephant can hear a sound vibration as low as 5 Hz and a dolphin can hear up to 150,000 Hz. That is an extraordinarily high pitched frequency! But there are certain moths that can hear high pitch sounds all the way up to 240,000 Hz. The atmosphere of earth is capable of transmitting high frequency sounds that are way beyond our capacity to hear; nevertheless these are real "sounds" that can be detected with precision instruments.

All human beings love the sound of music. Music soothes the soul and uplifts the spirit. The love of music and the capacity to sing and make melody is something that reflects the very image and likeness of God. There are seven major keys in the musical scale, just as there are seven primary colours that constitute visible light. A pitch or a "note" represents the frequency of the sound we can hear. These are the seven letters in the musical alphabet: A "C" is 261.63 Hz (or 261.63 vibrations per second), a "D" is 293.66 Hz, an "E" is 329.63 Hz, an "F" is 349.23 Hz, a "G" is 392 Hz, an "A" is 440 Hz and a "B" is 493.88 Hz. Each of these seven primary notes can be played at a different octave which is a higher or lower note that vibrates at a higher or lower frequency within each of the seven major keys. There is a mathematical beauty behind the creation of music and, for those who are so inclined, all music can actually be figured out and expressed mathematically.

When different frequencies of sound are blended together, these notes form the fundamentals of music. A musical chord is a combination of three or more musical notes played at the same time to create a particular harmonic frequency. When chords are played in a specific rhythm and sequence, music is created. Music is not something that is unique to the earth. Music originated in the heart of God and all of heaven is filled with glorious music.

When God created the earth He determined to create a highly unique environment in the universe that could sustain the creation and transmission of the sound of music. Human beings are created by God to appreciate the delicate harmonies and blends of sound and music. It is a universal characteristic amongst human beings everywhere on the planet that we all enjoy music!

The apostle Paul was caught up into the third heaven. He said, "I was caught up into paradise and heard things so astounding that they cannot be told." (2 Corinthians 12:4 NLT) The apostle John was taken up into heaven and he recorded his prophetic encounters in the book of Revelation. When he was taken into heaven he heard heavenly sounds of music and singing that left an extraordinary impression upon him.

"And I heard a voice from heaven, like the voice of many waters, and like the voice of loud thunder. And I heard the sound of harpists playing their harps. They sang as it were a new song before the throne." (Revelation 14:2-3) The Greek word for "harp" is *kithara*. This was a seven stringed instrument used in ancient Greece. Interestingly, the kithara is the contemporary Greek name for the guitar. Both Paul and John heard all kinds of heavenly sounds that must have powerfully impacted their lives.

Heaven is filled with the music of harps and the songs of angelic choirs. There are also trumpets and sounds of thunder and the sounds of rushing waters. Heaven is filled with glorious sounds. It is also filled with the voice of God who sings over His creation. God is a supremely happy being who delights over His children with singing. "The Lord your God in your midst, the Mighty One, will save; He will rejoice over you with gladness, He will quiet you with His love, He will rejoice over you with singing." (Zephaniah 3:17) Heaven is filled with what John called "the song of the Lamb" (Revelation 15:3) which tells us a lot about the nature of God and His passion to sing over His creation.

Heaven overflows with music and these heavenly sounds communicate the glory of God. Because there is music in heaven, God determined that there should be music on earth just as there is in heaven. Music is just as much a vehicle of communication as the sound of a voice. Music is a language that transcends every human language. It conveys moods and feelings in the same way that we express our feelings, thoughts and moods through spoken language.

Our human voices can also be used melodically to sing in such a way that they can be blended with music. Singing is such an important part of every culture in human history. We sing because God sings! Some beautiful voices here on earth sound almost heavenly in their range and their quality. The voice is a wonderful musical instrument in itself!

LET HIM WHO HAS AN EAR...

The appreciation of sound is entirely dependent upon one small biomechanical instrument called the ear. God created the ear as a complex biological mechanism designed to receive mechanical sound waves and to decode those sounds into an intelligible signal and language. There would be no use in creating the optimum atmosphere for the transmission of sound waves without creating ears to appreciate these sound waves! The vocal chords and the ear are extraordinary symbiotic mechanisms that are designed to work in tandem with each other to facilitate intelligent communication.

We can make sounds and we can hear sounds! Imagine life without sound. Deafness is such a tragedy because it cuts people off from the pleasure of music and singing and it renders people unable to hear other people's voices. Jesus loves to open deaf ears to restore the wonder of the world of sound. Deafness is never God's will because it robs people of the enjoyment of an entire world of natural and aesthetic beauty that was created by God to be enjoyed.

The ear is a miracle of sensory perception. It has been intentionally designed and built by the creative genius of God to enable sound waves to be converted into electrical signals in the nervous system so that they can be decoded by the brain. This process is essential to facilitate audible communication and the perception of sound. Sound waves vibrating through the atmosphere are captured by the radar dish of the outer ear and funnelled into the ear canal so that these waves vibrate the eardrum (which is technically called the tympanic membrane). On the other side of the eardrum is the middle ear with three small highly sensitive bones called the hammer, the anvil and the stirrup. One of these three bones is the smallest bone in the human body.

The vibration of sound waves upon the eardrum are transmitted and amplified through these three tiny bones to the cochlea which is a coil-shaped hollow organ that is filled with fluid. The cochlea is the inner ear and once the sound waves pass into the cochlea they are transferred from an air to a liquid medium. It is within this liquid environment that microscopic hairs act as the mechanical receptors of sound waves. These receptors trigger a release of electrochemical signals which are carried through the main auditory nerve to the part of the cerebral cortex that is dedicated to the decoding of the electrical nerve signals into intelligible sound data.

The brain is processing sound data continuously and seamlessly 24 hours a day. The complex mechanism of hearing is nothing short of miraculous in its capacity to process an extremely broad spectrum of sound frequencies. It can process hundreds of frequencies simultaneously. An orchestra can create a vast range of different sounds from hundreds of instruments all being played in symphony, yet the ear can decode all of this complex data and provide us with an extremely pleasurable experience of stereophonic high fidelity sound.

Some people spend considerable amounts of money on expensive sound systems that are capable of reproducing the best possible sound quality in order to maximise the full capabilities of the sense of hearing. Most of the time we completely take for granted our capacity to hear sounds but it is important to pause and reflect upon the miracle of sound and hearing in the light of God's creative design.

SOUND AND MATTER

There is an increasing awareness that sound can be extremely powerful. Scientists have discovered numerous examples in nature of the power of natural sound waves to impact or reconfigure matter. The Swiss scientist, Dr. Hans Jenny, coined a term which he called "Cymatics" to describe the phenomena of the effect of sound waves upon matter. Cymatics is the study of sound wave phenomena. The term is derived from the Greek word *kyma* which means "waves." Dr. Hans Jenny discovered that various frequencies of sound waves created specific vibratory patterns in water and in fine particles like sand or salt. These experiments with sound can be scientifically repeated with identical outcomes.

Dr. Jenny would create various notes of sound using a tone generator, an instrument that can be programmed to emit a sound at a constant frequency, for example an "A" at 440 Hz. He would attach the tone generator to a flat metal plate and cause the metal plate to resonate at a predetermined pitch. Then he would place a layer of fine sand on the metal plate and observe the effect of the constant frequency in the pattern that would begin to form in the sand. As long as the tone was perfectly maintained the sand would begin to form extraordinary patterns almost resembling the beauty of Buddhist sand mandalas.[4]

Similarly, "Faraday Waves" also cause unusual patterns in highly viscous liquids, where the liquids actually begin to stand up with finger like protrusions when the liquid is attached to a tone generator set at 120 Hz. All of these experiments point to the fact that sound has a significant impact upon matter.[5]

We are all familiar with the experiment in which certain sound frequencies within the range of the human voice can shatter a wine glass.[6] Some of us would perhaps be familiar with the story of the collapse of the Tacoma Narrows suspension bridge in Washington in 1940 due to wind induced vibration. The bridge had only been open to traffic for a few months before its untimely collapse.

The investigation into the collapse of the bridge indicated that a phenomenon called "mechanical resonance" caused the entire bridge to begin vibrating and swaying at 0.2 Hz. At the time of the collapse there was a steady crosswind of 42 mph that set in motion a resonance effect that ultimately became so intense that the bridge completely collapsed.[7] The shattering wine glass and the collapsing bridge are both examples of the phenomenon of mechanical resonance.

All physical objects have a resonant frequency. Hi-fi enthusiasts are greatly irritated when something in their house begins to buzz at a certain pitch. Oftentimes a window pane or something structural in the room will begin to resonate at a certain frequency when music is played through speakers. Often the acoustics of a room will need to be adjusted to avoid objects vibrating when the frequency of the sound is near or below 100 Hz. Sometimes people find that their car will begin to vibrate at a certain speed. Other times a passing truck will cause windows to vibrate.

Thunder has the ability to shake the windows and the walls during a storm. These are all the effects of mechanical resonance. The inventor, Nikola Tesla [1856-1943] was fascinated by the concept of mechanical resonance. Tesla was a genius with over 700 patents to his name. He was the inventor of AC current electricity, triumphing over Thomas Edison's proposal to power great cities with DC electricity. This breakthrough in the transmission of electrical power made Tesla the "father of modern electricity."

Whilst living in New York City, Tesla set up a science laboratory in Manhattan in 1898 and experimented with a small electrical oscillator that created low frequency vibrations. In an experiment that went terribly wrong, he discovered that he could use his electrical resonance device to cause buildings on Houston Street, Manhattan, to begin to shake violently, simulating the effects of a man-made earthquake. Neighbours began to experience things falling off shelves, windows shattering and entire buildings beginning to shake.

Through the use of his oscillator Tesla set in motion a mechanical resonance both in his own building and in the adjacent buildings that would have led to the collapse of the buildings if he didn't hurriedly smash his own invention with a hammer. He had created a low frequency vibration that could potentially shake a building off its foundations! Years later Tesla described this incident to a reporter:

I was experimenting with vibrations. I had one of my machines going and I wanted to see if I could get it in tune with the vibration of the building. I put it up notch after notch. There was a peculiar cracking sound. I asked my assistants where the sound came from. They did not know. I put the machine up a few more notches. There was a louder cracking sound. I knew I was approaching the vibration of the steel building. I pushed the machine a little higher. Suddenly all the heavy machinery in the place was flying around. I grabbed a hammer and broke the machine. The building would have been about our ears in another few minutes. Outside in the street there was pandemonium. The police and ambulances arrived. I told my assistants to say nothing. We told the police it must have been an earthquake. That's all they ever knew about it.[8]

Tesla apparently continued experimenting with this device. Walking around New York City he found a half finished 10-story steel structure on Wall Street and he attached his battery powered frequency resonator to a steel girder. Apparently the device was only as big as a small clock. Within minutes the entire structure began to creak and shudder. Had he not switched it off the entire building would have collapsed. Tesla boasted that he could bring down the Empire State building with his small device. Tesla said, "Vibration will do anything. It would only be necessary to step up the vibrations of the machine to fit the natural vibration of the building and the building would come crashing down."[9] Tesla claimed that a larger device could split the earth in half by setting up a mechanical resonance with the earth.

Mechanical resonance is also used with great effect in the creation of music. Some musical instruments employ the principle of "sympathetic strings." The most notable example is the Indian sitar. Sympathetic strings are strings that are never played directly. Rather they are concealed beneath an upper layer of strings that are played by the musician. When an upper layer string hits a certain frequency this causes the sympathetic strings to begin vibrating without being touched physically. This creates a beautiful acoustic sound. When two identical tuning forks are place side by side and one of them is struck it will cause the other tuning fork to begin to vibrate and resonate at exactly the same frequency.

Mechanical resonance is also used with great success in the field of medicine. Sound waves are used by doctors to treat kidney stones. Lithotripsy is a non-surgical procedure that uses sound waves from a lithotripsy machine to disintegrate kidney stones. The stones are shattered by sound waves that resonate with the exact frequency of the kidney stones. The shattered particles of stone are then flushed out naturally by passing urine. This new technology that harnesses the power of mechanical resonance has rendered many surgical interventions unnecessary.

SOUND HEALING

The recognition of the impact of sound waves upon matter has captured the attention of the New Age community and has given rise to an ambitious industry that seeks to apply the power of sound to heal the emotions and the body. Sound healing is big business in New Age culture. If you go to a New Age fair or festival it is not an uncommon sight to see someone playing a didgeridoo over someone's body or to see someone else playing certain frequencies of sound with harmonic chimes or stringed instruments that are applied to different parts of the body.

Even the voice is used to seek to effect physical healing. The claims of the healing virtues of sound therapy are typically quite extravagant. It is claimed that these resonant frequencies applied to the body can slow down the brain waves and induce a deep meditative state of relaxation which will facilitate healing. It is also claimed that certain frequencies can heal dysfunctional organs of the body.

Sound waves are also allegedly capable of unblocking spiritual energy fields in and around the body, rebalancing the chakras and realigning the energy fields by bringing them into harmonic tuning with the tones that are generated by the instruments that are used. These "tone baths" allegedly resonate deeply into the organs and into the various parts of the body that they are applied to. Many instruments are used to immerse the patient in healing sounds. Some therapists use tuning forks, others use crystals or Tibetan singing bowls, all of which operate on the same principle of generating certain sound frequencies with the goal of effecting physical and spiritual healing.

It is proposed by sound therapists that each part of the body has its own natural vibratory frequency, and it is implied that these organs need to be "re-tuned" in order to restore harmony and health. This is a reworking of the thesis presented by acupuncturists that sickness occurs when the energy fields within the various organs of the body become imbalanced and that the insertion of acupuncture needles into highly specific points of the body will re-route the energy and will result in the restoration of harmony, balance and health. Some sound therapists apply different sound frequencies to the brain to seek to heal conditions like ADHD, stress headaches, insomnia and depression. The therapist will use headphones to apply one frequency into the left ear and another frequency into the right ear in order to create "binaural beats" that synchronise the two hemispheres of the brain. The goal is always to restore balance to something which has become dysfunctional because of alleged imbalance.

Sound therapists explain how the human body is in a constant vibratory state and, as it might be expected, the science of quantum physics is co-opted to explain that at a sub-atomic level the quantum field vibrates at certain frequencies. At this point sound therapists transition from the application of mechanical sound waves to matter, which is a phenomena of classical physics, to the application of mechanical sound waves to the vibratory field of the quantum world. In this cross over from the classical world to the quantum world it is proposed that mechanical sound waves have healing qualities that will transform the quantum world. Working with physical or emotional dysfunction at a quantum level allegedly results in healing at a classical or macroscopic level.

The New Age fascination with quantum physics is at an all time high. Many New Age healers invoke the word "quantum" into the title of their particular healing modality. It is not surprising that New Age healers would eventually make this "quantum leap" in claiming the "quantum benefits" of sound therapy, but it raises an interesting set of questions about the leap from the classical world to the quantum world. As we have seen, there is a huge gulf that exists between the nature of the quantum world and the nature of the classical world, and questions are automatically raised about the benefits of a mechanical sound wave upon a field that is so infinitesimally small that it is literally an entirely different world with its own set of quantum rules and laws.

THE IMAGINARIUM OF DOCTOR EMOTO

The New Age core belief that "consciousness creates reality" is a highly appealing idea to disempowered people. There are many who desperately want this belief to be proven true. But sometimes that desperation can cause people to be blinded to the truth. There is a scene in the *What the Bleep* movie where the central figure in the story, a deaf woman named Amanda, passes by an exhibition on a subway platform. The exhibition promotes the teachings of Dr. Masaru Emoto, a Japanese New Age practitioner who is the author of *The Hidden Messages of Water*, a New York Times bestseller. Dr. Emoto teaches that water that has been subjected to positive intentions and thoughts will form beautiful crystals when frozen whilst water subjected to negative messages will form ugly crystals.

The work of Dr. Emoto is included in the *What the Bleep* movie to add support to the assertion that consciousness creates reality. This is one of three appeals to alleged scientific research to strengthen their argument. The appeal to the Observer Effect in quantum physics is the first, the science of Dr. Emoto is the second and the capability of the brain to create new neuronal pathways in response to new stimuli is the third. As Amanda ponders the photographs of frozen water crystals, a man standing beside her comments that if 70% of the human body is made up of water it should make people think about what they are doing to their bodies by overloading them with negative messages. "If thoughts can do that to water, imagine what they can do to us!" The *What the Bleep* book also promotes the research of Dr. Emoto, hailing him as a brilliant scientist:

> Dr. Emoto put signs on bottles of water that expressed human emotions and ideas. Some of them were positive, such as "Thank You" and "Love." Others were negative, such as the sign that read "You make me sick, I will kill you." Contrary to the prevailing wisdom of science, the water responded to these expressions of consciousness, even though the words did not create a measureable physical action. The water with the positive messages formed beautiful crystals; the water with the negative messages became ugly and malformed. In response to this, a number of scientific researchers are busy replicating his work. Independent replication is part of the scientific method.[10]

The inclusion of Emoto's research in the *What the Bleep* film and subsequent book has stirred quite a controversy. Of course, there are many people who jump on the bandwagon and immediately quote Emoto as a leading authority on the subject of "mind over matter" but there are others who are more hesitant, asking if this is real science or pseudoscience. The issue became important to me when I began hearing a number of significant prophetic teachers in the church quoting the research of Dr. Emoto as though it was now a scientifically proven fact that our thoughts can change the molecular structure of water.

I became concerned that Christians were being swept along by a fad that had little or no scientific credibility. It is easy for a concept to take on a life of its own as it is passed from person to person as though it was absolutely true. If the church is indeed the "pillar and support of the truth" (1 Timothy 3:15 NLT) it is incumbent upon teachers to ascertain the integrity and veracity of a scientific truth claim before it is actively promoted amongst the people of God. Is Emoto adhering to the "scientific method," as the *What the Bleep* book claims?

As I began to probe a little deeper into the credibility of these outlandish claims, I became increasingly concerned that Dr. Emoto was promoting pseudoscience. The first red flag came when I discovered that the good doctor is not really a scientist at all. Emoto has said, "I believe in reincarnation. I believe that in my previous life I probably was a scientist working with water."[11]

This revelation may have prompted him at age 49 to obtain his "Doctorate of Alternative Medicine" [M.D.] in 1992 from the "Open International University for Alternative Medicine" in India for the up-front fee of US$750.[12] He has since acknowledged that he is not a real doctor or a scientist according to Western standards, which makes his "M.D." credentials nothing more than an embarrassing waste of $750! This alone ought to cast a shadow over his alleged scientific research.

But perhaps a greater shadow is cast by the fact that Emoto has admitted to deliberately selecting photographs that fit what he is hoping to find. An interviewer asked Emoto: "When you publish a water crystal photograph – how do you select the photograph? I imagine for any given word or piece of music, you take multiple samples and so have many images of the water from which to select." Emoto answered; "Good question. It is very important. I choose them for their goodness and their beauty. There is a phrase in Japanese, *shin zen be. Shin* means truth. *Zen* means goodness. *Be* means beautiful. I select photographs of crystals with all three elements combined."[13]

Emoto's biased selection of photographs reveals a significant flaw in his "scientific method." As a result, he has been widely criticised by the scientific community for his lack of peer review in the way he has conducted his experiments and posted his results. James Randi is a well known sceptic who challenges claims of paranormal activity. As a hobby he enjoys debunking pseudoscience. He is the founder of the *James Randi Educational Foundation* [JREF] and he has offered Emoto one million dollars if he can prove his experiments under scientifically rigorous double blind conditions. Randi said on his website:

> Dr. Emoto might very well believe that he's doing science. But he's not. He does no double-blind procedures, for one thing, which dooms these amateur efforts, right from the beginning. If he were to be blind to which words were being used to influence the water crystals, his search through the results looking for confirmation would be inconclusive. I'll risk the JREF million-dollar prize on that statement. If Dr. Emoto wants to win the prize, let him agree to perform his tests in a double-blind fashion, and I predict he'll get fuzzy results that prove nothing.[14]

So far, Masaru Emoto has not responded to the offer. Emoto certainly has some unorthodox "scientific" views on the origin and nature of water which ought to raise further questions about his scientific credibility. In a 2005 interview Emoto revealed his true beliefs about water:

> I believe water came from outside of this earth – from outer space. So, we cannot understand water with normal physics. I believe that water is a light, because water has many different kinds of shapes and forms. Maybe this universe is like water soup – a soup made of water! In my lectures, I talk about how water and water crystals are 10 percent goodness, 10 percent evil, and the rest – 80 percent – is opportunist. When the 10 percent that is goodness and the 10 percent that is badness in water crystals fight, then the 10 percent that is goodness wins and overpowers evilness. So, if the 10 percent of goodness would carry past that fight to the 80 percent that is opportunist, then the 80 percent will follow the goodness, not the badness.[15]

Emoto also believes that water has consciousness and is directly responsive to the vibrations of thoughts, words, music and images. He teaches that water molecules are sufficiently conscious to recognise the words of every single human language and to distinguish between pictures of Mother Theresa and Adolph Hitler. In one interview he was asked, "Would you tell us your philosophical thoughts about what you believe these water crystals really are?" He answered, "I came to the realization that these crystals are spirits."[16] That would explain why he believes that water is a *conscious* entity.

Emoto's pseudoscience is an excellent example of the wishful thinking and profound commitment of New Agers to marshal any scientific support that might potentially strengthen their assertion that consciousness creates reality. But if scientific credibility means anything to New Age teachers it would certainly help their cause to do some homework on who they are promoting in their attempt to strengthen their argument. The eagerness to promote Emoto and his unsubstantiated "scientific research" exposes a degree of desperation to locate any evidence from "science" to substantiate a predetermined spiritual dogma.

THE WORD OF GOD

Earlier in this chapter we examined the phenomena of mechanical resonance. Masaru Emoto's attempt to build a scientific case in support of the thesis that our words can alter reality at a molecular level falls into an entirely different category to the actual science of mechanical resonance. There is no comparison between true science and pseudoscience! There is sufficient scientific evidence to support the reality of the impact of sound waves upon matter. This is a scientifically proven feature of the macroscopic world of physics and the effect of these sound waves is something that can be observed macroscopically. But there is another level of reality in the universe that is revealed in the Bible. The Scriptures point to a different kind of sound wave that is non-local and non-mechanical.

Without natural sound waves we would not have a paradigm to understand the supernatural "sound" waves that come from the heavenly dimension. As we have already seen, there is a feast of sound, music, song and oration in heaven. One of the most powerful themes that runs through the Bible is the idea that the Scriptures are the written "Word of God." The Word of God is a different kind of sound that exists in, and issues from, the realm of heaven. Jesus explained this when He said, *"The words that I speak to you are Spirit,* and they are life." (John 6:63) The Word of God is a manifestation or an expression of the Spirit of God. God's words are actually "Spirit words." They are from another world.

The effect of mechanical sound waves upon physical matter mirrors a deeper reality that exists in the spiritual realm. I would like to propose that the impact of sound waves upon matter in the realm of classical physics is analogous to the impact of the waves of the Spirit upon non-local quanta in the realm of quantum physics. When God made the earth with its unique atmosphere capable of transmitting mechanical sound waves, it reflected a deeper level of reality that has always existed spiritually. God speaks and His words create a different kind of impact without the use of mechanical sound waves. There is something going on in the spiritual realm that occurs without the use of mechanical sound waves! The voice of the Lord is a non-local sound. It is a different kind of sound that is not a physical mechanical sound wave but it nevertheless is a wave of some kind.

The reality of the supernatural voice of the Lord is absolutely funda-mental to the whole biblical revelation. The Bible is a revelation of God to humanity and it takes the form of prophetic utterances through God-inspired prophets who heard the voice of the Lord and recorded what they heard. There is an underlying presupposition that the entire Bible is founded upon. This presupposition is that there is a personal God who seeks to com-municate His heart and mind to humanity through His word. This presup-position is never explained or defended; instead it is simply proclaimed as a self-evident fact. The Bible contains abundant proof that it is the Word of God for all those who humbly bow in reverential awe of God.

I have made some incredible discoveries about the Word of God on my spiritual journey. 27% of the Bible is predictive prophecy. The Bible contains 1,817 individual predictions concerning 737 separate subjects that appear in a total of 8,352 Bible verses. God revealed that He gave predic-tive prophecy as an internal proof that He was God. The Word of God has 100% accuracy in predictive prophecy. Some writers have called this element of predictive prophecy the "signature of God." "I am the Lord; that is My name!... Everything I prophesied has come true, and now I will prophesy again. I will tell you the future before it happens." (Isaiah 42:8-9 NLT)

God Himself says that when these prophecies come to pass, "then they shall know that I am the Lord their God." (Ezekiel 39:28) "And when that time comes, you will know that I am the Lord." (Ezekiel 24:24 NLT) If the Bible has anything less than 100% accuracy in predictive prophecy then it can be dismissed in its claim to be the Word of God. Many have set out to disprove the Bible but ended up turning to Christ when they realised that there is an internal proof embedded within the Scriptures that is an undeniable reality. Even the 61 major Messianic prophecies on their own have the power to convince the greatest sceptic!

The fulfilment of the predictive prophecies of the Bible is the most compelling argument in support of the fact that there is a trustworthy Voice that comes to us from another dimension. Over a thousand prophecies fulfilled with 100% accuracy convinces us that this Voice is thoroughly trustworthy. But if that is not enough proof, we are confronted by the additional fact that there is an extraordinary consistency of divine revelation that runs throughout this remarkable book. The 66 books of the Old and New Testaments were written by 40 different authors over a 1,500 year period, yet there is a seamless thread of revelation concerning the nature and character of God and of His unfolding redemptive purposes. This remarkable consistency is designed to bring us to the realisation that the Bible really has only one author! The Bible really is the written Word of God!

The consistency and prophetic accuracy of the Bible points to the reality of a different kind of Voice that comes forth to us from another dimension. This voice is supernatural in origin and it cannot be heard as a natural or mechanical sound wave. Jesus had a favourite saying. He would often make a profound statement and follow it up by saying, "He who has ears to hear, let him hear!" (Matthew 11:15) This saying was repeated eight times in the gospels of Matthew, Mark and Luke. In addition to that, seven times in the book of Revelation Jesus said, "He who has an ear, let him hear what the Spirit says to the churches."

Jesus revealed that there is a voice of the Spirit of God that can only be discerned by those who "have ears to hear." Paul taught that "The man without the Spirit does not accept the things that come from the Spirit of God, for they are foolishness to him, and he cannot understand them, because they are spiritually discerned." (1 Corinthians 2:14 NIV) Another translation says, "But people who aren't Christians can't understand these truths from God's Spirit. It all sounds foolish to them because only those who have the Spirit can understand what the Spirit means. We who have the Spirit understand these things, but others can't understand us at all." (1 Corinthians 2:14-15 NLT)

SUPERNATURAL SOUND WAVES

The Bible contrasts the reality of the supernatural Voice of God with the natural sounds of earth. We could use the language of "natural sound waves" versus "supernatural sound waves." One set of waves are mechanical waves that are transmitted through molecules of air pushing against one another until they reach our natural set of ears. The other kind of sound wave is completely supernatural.

These spiritual waves are not received by our natural ears. Rather they are received by a spiritual set of ears that are designed exclusively to pick up supernatural sound waves. These waves are just as real as mechanical sound waves and they have the unique property of exercising a profound effect upon the physics of the universe at a sub-atomic level. In fact, the Bible clearly reveals that it is this supernatural set of sound waves that created the universe and which continues to sustain the entire universe. The quantum world is highly responsive to these supernatural waves. God speaks and the quantum world responds to the voice of the Lord. There is something powerfully creative about the supernatural sound waves of heaven.

Jesus said that the words that He speaks are Spirit. In saying this He was actually making a clear distinction between the ordinary words spoken by human beings on earth and the words that proceed from the mouth of God. He was deliberately juxtaposing "the words that He speaks" with the words that everyone else on earth speaks! Mere human words do not have the capacity to release resurrection life.

Resurrection life can only be imparted supernaturally through the proclamation of the Word of God. That is because the Word of God *is* Spirit. There is an impartation of the invisible, yet supremely powerful, Holy Spirit that is communicated through the prophetic declaration of the Word of God. Jesus taught that there is incredible supernatural power released through the proclamation of the Word of God. The gospel is the power of God unto salvation. It is living and active and sharper than a two-edged sword.

On a natural level, sound waves definitely have the capacity to impact and reconfigure matter. But this is not a *creative* capacity; it is nothing more than the manipulation of physical realities through a mechanical sound wave. We make a sound with our voice or with a musical instrument and it has an impact upon someone's ear drum! A mechanical frequency causes something else to begin to vibrate at the same frequency. There is nothing magical about ordinary sound! But this mechanical effect reflects a deeper spiritual reality. Frequently natural things speak of invisible spiritual realities. Jesus used parables from nature to highlight and communicate spiritual things. Natural sound is the perfect analogy to help us understand the reality of supernatural sound.

We understand from Scripture that only the spoken Word of God has the unique capacity to *create* an entirely different reality in the material realm. The Word of God is clearly a different kind of sound. It has an auditory expression here on earth but it is a *creative word* that is spoken from another dimension. It is a "sound" within a sound. It has the capacity to create resurrection life, to perform miracles and to restructure matter at a quantum level. The contrast between the voice of God and ordinary human voices highlights the difference between a sound with creative power and the rather "ordinary" sounds that fill the earth.

This supernatural restructuring of the material world, exhibited in the ministry of Jesus, causes the sudden appearance of entirely new body parts that spontaneously appear out of nothing! Through the power of the Holy Spirit, Jesus could create a brand new eyeball out of nothing, which is an even greater creative miracle than the restoration of a dysfunctional eyeball! The supernatural healing ministry of Christ revealed a whole other level of creative power which was infinitely greater than anything that can be achieved through ordinary mechanical sound waves. Clearly there is a different level of reality in operation through the power of the Word of God.

The Word of God is the verbal expression of the Spirit of God. Jesus tells us that "God is Spirit." Paul puts it this way: "The Lord is the Spirit!" When God, who is Spirit, speaks, it is the voice of a being who exists in another dimension. God is an extra-dimensional spirit being. He exists independently of our physical universe. When God speaks, new material and spiritual realities are created out of nothing. God not only created physical human beings, He also created invisible angelic beings. The entire material universe came into existence out of nothing through the spoken Word of God. God said and there was!

This deeper reality reveals the vast superiority of Spirit over matter. Spirit is eternal whilst matter is temporal. In fact, the physical world is a product of the Spirit of God. God, who is a Spirit, spoke and the worlds were framed by the words that proceeded from His mouth. "In the beginning was the Word, and the Word was with God, and the Word was God. He was in the beginning with God. All things were made through Him, and without Him nothing was made that was made." (John 1:1-3) Biblical cosmogony teaches that the material universe has a supernatural origin derived exclusively from the realm of the Spirit and which sprang into existence through the creative voice of God. "In the beginning God created the heavens and the earth!" (Genesis 1:1) God said and there was!

"By faith we understand that the entire universe was formed at God's command, that what we now see did not come from anything that can be seen." (Hebrews 11:3 NIV) Another translation says that "the things which are seen were not made of things which are visible." As we saw in the previous chapter, the building blocks of the material world are non-local quantum realities.

The Bible doesn't teach "creation ex-nihilo," which is a Latin term that means "creation out of nothing." Rather, the Bible teaches that the physical creation is made of invisible quantum realities that cannot be seen. Remember the discussion in the previous chapter that revealed the two stages of creation. The first stage brought forward the foundational building blocks of the invisible quantum world and the second stage caused the material creation to spring forth from the quantum creation.

God formed the universe with the word of His power. In the same way, this physical universe, which was created by the Word of God, is similarly *sustained* by the Word of God. "He sustains the universe by the mighty power of His command." (Hebrews 1:3 NLT) "He existed before everything else began, and He holds all creation together." (Colossians 1:17 NLT) The Bibles teaches that the entire material universe was *created* by the Word of God and that it is likewise *sustained* by the Word of God.

The sustaining wave of God's power is distributed evenly throughout the entire universe! There is nowhere throughout the entire universe where these supernatural sound waves are not clearly heard! They do not need to "travel" like natural sound waves because they originate in another dimension, and this attribute of extra-dimensionality means that they reach all spatial locations in the universe simultaneously. This is the lesson of quantum non-locality.

Sound waves are an excellent analogy and prophetic illustration of the waves of energy that flow, metaphorically, from the mouth of God to sustain the universe. Of course, natural sound cannot sustain the entire universe. Natural sound can only travel through the earth's immediate atmosphere in the form of sound waves. Without our unique atmosphere there cannot be mechanical sound waves. These sound waves actually vibrate the molecules of our atmosphere and cannot travel any faster than 1,130 feet per second[17] under normal atmospheric conditions. But in the same way that sound waves travel through our immediate atmosphere, it is interesting to theorise that there are spiritual waves of energy that flow throughout the universe.

Remember that natural sound waves cannot travel through space, which is a virtual vacuum. However photons, or light waves, have the capacity to travel through space at the speed of light. Similarly, radio waves also have the capacity to travel through vast regions of space at the speed of light. Radio waves are a kind of electromagnetic radiation and, like photons, they can travel at almost 300,000 kilometres per second. That's seven times around the circumference of the earth per second!

What an extraordinary thought, that the mechanical sound waves that we are continuously immersed in inside of our biosphere possibly only occur in one place in the entire universe: here on earth! The rest of the universe is completely devoid of mechanical sound waves yet it is bathed in spiritual waves of energy that are released through the Word of God that sustains the universe.

RELEASING THE SUPERNATURAL SOUND

We have been considering the fact that the supernatural sound that goes forth from the mouth of the Lord is responsible for the creation of the heavens and the earth. This unique set of spiritual frequencies continues to resound over all creation, sustaining and upholding the universe. But it doesn't end there. Ever since the fall, the creation has been in bondage to corruption and decay. We are all very much aware that things are on a downhill slide into chaos. Our human bodies are slowly aging and we are all slowly dying!

The same majestic voice that sounds over creation also intervenes into our time/space world to arrest the descent into chaos and disorder by speaking order and life into the chaos and death. Every time Jesus healed the sick He was exercising the same power of the creative voice of God by restoring that which had descended into corruption and chaos. Sickness and disease is a degenerative condition that corrupts the perfection of God's creative design and beauty.

Whenever Jesus heals a sick person He is restoring something to its pristine state, and this is done through the same power of the spoken Word of God that created the world. The words that Jesus speaks are indeed "Spirit" and these spoken words continue to interrupt the downward descent into biological corruption, malfunction and chaos. The glorious ministry of Jesus demonstrated that the time had come for the creative voice of God to be heard once again upon the earth.

There is a God-ordained relationship between the spiritual sounds of heaven and the natural sounds of earth. Sound on earth was always intended to be in perfect harmony with sound in heaven. Natural sound was never intended to be devoid of the Spirit of God. Natural sound was designed by God to be a vehicle of expression for the voice and sounds of heaven.

God's intention has always been "on earth as it is in heaven!" The spiritual atmosphere of earth was always intended to be an outpost of the very atmosphere of heaven. This means that earthly sound waves were always designed to carry the atmosphere of heavenly glory.

There was never meant to be a disconnect between heaven and earth. The words that human beings were intended to speak on earth were the words that reflected the language of heaven. The language of Eden before the fall was the language of heaven. But ever since the fall there has been a profound disconnect between heaven and earth. Now there are sounds that are heard all over the earth that were never meant to be heard or to even have an existence. There are the cries of pain and oppression, the voices of blasphemy and obscenity, and the music of satanically inspired musicians. These are just some of the many sounds that are now completely out of harmony with heaven.

John the Baptist contrasted the words of Christ that were from heaven with the words of fallen humanity here on earth. "He who comes from above is above all; he who is of the earth is earthly and speaks of the earth." (John 3:31) Jesus said, "You are from beneath; I am from above. You are of this world; I am not of this world." (John 8:23) The apostle John contrasted the words of those who were of this fallen world with the words of those who were of God.

John was referring to the words of the false prophets when he wrote: "You are of God, little children, and have overcome *them*, because He who is in you is greater than he who is in the world. They are of the world. Therefore they speak as of the world, and the world hears them. We are of God. He who knows God hears us; he who is not of God does not hear us." (1 John 4:4-6) John virtually said that the citizens of heaven speak a different language to those who are of this fallen world. This passage of Scripture juxtaposes the reality of the sounds of this world with the sounds of heaven.

Our assignment as followers of Christ is to harness the power of sound and bring it back into harmony with heaven so that we can release it on earth. In John 17, Jesus prayed that we would be "one" even as He and the Father were one. The restoration of this spiritual unity between the Father in heaven and His sons and daughters on earth will result in the sounds of heaven being released once again through the body of Christ.

ON EARTH AS IT IS IN HEAVEN

We have the potential to bring our words into alignment with heaven and release the supernatural Word of God here on earth. We are called to preach the gospel on the earth and to speak the same word of authority that Jesus spoke in order to heal the sick and to cast out demons. When Christ comes to indwell a person He speaks through us and His words take on the expression of natural sound. This is the sound within the sound. We are called to release the supernatural sound of the preaching of the Word and we are also called to recover and release the supernatural sound of heavenly music on the earth.

As we have already seen, there is plenty of music and singing in heaven. There is a musical sound that is completely unique to heaven, but it can be captured on earth by the worshipping saints. "Blessed are the people who know the joyful sound!" (Psalm 89:15) This sound carries the glory of God and it releases the very atmosphere of heaven on earth. There is a strategic purpose in the divine calling of the saints to worship the Lord here on earth.

God's intention is that there should be a tipping point in our times of worship on earth when something supernatural begins to be released. The Bible calls this "the song of the Lord." (2 Chronicles 29:27) The writer of the book of Hebrews quotes a conversation between Jesus and the Father in which Jesus says, "I will declare Your name to My brethren; in the midst of the assembly *I will sing* praise to You." (Hebrews 2:12) Jesus loves to sing in the midst of the church. This is the song of the Lord being released on earth and He releases this new song through prophetically gifted worshippers.

David said to God, "You are my hiding place... You shall surround me with songs of deliverance." (Psalm 32:7) These "songs of deliverance" are prophetic sounds that are released from heaven that supernaturally set the captives free! They are so powerful that they can result in deliverance from demonic bondage. The church is challenged to capture that sound and release it through the power of songs accompanied by anointed music. God loves to breathe on the worship of His people and inhabit their praises with His supernatural presence.

When this happens the very sound of heaven penetrates the room and the atmosphere of heaven causes everything to change. As the church explores this dimension of releasing the supernatural sounds of heaven on earth there are many different aspects that need to be explored. This journey into releasing the music of heaven involves the unique combination of prophetic songs and the use of instruments to prophesy. David trained his musicians to "prophesy with harps, stringed instruments, and cymbals." (1 Chronicles 25:1)

In every generation the church has an opportunity to unify heaven and earth by capturing and expressing the sounds of heaven on earth. We are not told very much about the instruments of heaven. There are trumpets, harps, heavenly choirs and prophetic declarations. There are also some pretty awesome sound effects, such as thunder and the sound of many waters, all of which have their analogue here on earth. David placed a greater emphasis upon worship music than any other man in the Bible. He sought to capture the sounds of heaven here on earth.

The instruments employed by David were called "the musical instruments of God." (1 Chronicles 16:42) Some of these instruments were purposely built by David for worship in the house of the Lord. "The priests took their positions, as did the Levites with the *Lord's musical instruments,* which King David had made for praising the Lord and which were used when he gave thanks, saying, 'His love endures forever.' Opposite the Levites, the priests blew their trumpets." (2 Chronicles 7:6 NIV)

There is such a strong association between King David and the spiritual development of music in the Bible. "Then David and all the house of Israel played music before the Lord on all kinds of instruments of fir wood, on harps, on stringed instruments, on tambourines, on sistrums, and on cymbals." (2 Samuel 6:5) The *sistrum* was a percussion instrument similar to a castanet or a shaker. The Hebrew word for "tambourines" was *toph* which, by all accounts, was actually a percussion drum with an animal skin stretched over it.

Hand drums played an important role in the music of the Old Testament as did cymbals and bells. There were also wind instruments: the shophar and the trumpet and the pipes which were a kind of ancient flute. There were also stringed instruments such as the lyre and the harp. David was so in love with worshipping God that he ultimately established what came to be known as the Tabernacle of David which was a non-stop worship service with an orchestra of choirs, prophetic singers and an extraordinarily diverse range of instruments.

PROPHETIC DECREES

When the people of God are led by the Holy Spirit there can be a strong prophetic dimension to their actions on earth. Sometimes the Lord will direct His people to engage in a specific prophetic act as an expression of spiritual warfare. For example, the Lord said to Ezekiel, "You therefore, son of man, prophesy and clap your hands together." (Ezekiel 21:14) A couple of verses later the Lord says, "I will also clap My hands together, and I will appease My wrath; I, the Lord, have spoken." (Ezekiel 21:17)[18]

The idea is that when God's people clap their hands, the Lord will clap His hands with significant spiritual consequences. There are many exhortations to the people of God to raise their voices with a mighty shout. "Oh, clap your hands, all you peoples! *Shout to God* with the voice of triumph! For the Lord Most High is awesome; He is a great King over all the earth... God has gone up *with a shout*, the Lord with the sound of a trumpet." (Psalm 47:1-2,5) This psalm suggests that as the people on earth shout, the Lord will shout from heaven. This idea is even clearer in Isaiah 42.

Sing to the Lord a new song, and His praise from the ends of the earth... Let the wilderness and its cities lift up their voice... Let the inhabitants of Sela sing, **let them shout** from the top of the mountains. Let them give glory to the Lord, and declare His praise in the coastlands. The Lord shall go forth like a mighty man; He shall stir up His zeal like a man of war. **He shall cry out, yes, shout aloud**; He shall prevail against His enemies." (Isaiah 42:10-13)

Sometimes clapping and shouting can be a prophetic act and an expression of the unity between heaven and earth in making a certain sound. Music itself can be a prophetic declaration when it is led by the Holy Spirit. In the next verse we see the Lord exhorting His people to worship with the promise that He will conquer Israel's enemies.

> And you will sing as on the night you celebrate a holy festival; your hearts will rejoice as when people go up with flutes to the mountain of the Lord, to the Rock of Israel. The Lord will cause men to hear His glorious voice and will make them see His arm coming down with raging anger and consuming fire, with cloudburst, thunderstorm and hail. The voice of the Lord will shatter Assyria; with His sceptre He will strike them down. Every stroke the Lord lays on them with His punishing rod will be to the music of tambourines and harps, as He fights them in battle with the blows of His arm." (Isaiah 30:29-32 NIV)

As we have already seen, the Hebrew word for "tambourines" is *toph* which means a "hand drum." The idea is that the Lord will strike Assyria to the rhythm of the beat of the drum as the Israelites engage in warfare praise. The people of God were instructed to create the musical soundtrack for the conquest of their enemies![19] This is a powerful theme throughout the Old Testament.

Praise is presented as a weapon of warfare. "From the lips of children and infants you have ordained praise because of your enemies, to silence the foe and the avenger." (Psalm 8:2 NIV) "Let the saints be joyful in glory; let them sing aloud on their beds. Let the high praises of God be in their mouth, and a two-edged sword in their hand, to execute vengeance on the nations, and punishments on the peoples; to bind their kings with chains, and their nobles with fetters of iron; to execute on them the written judgment; this honour have all His saints. Praise the Lord!" (Psalm 149:5-9)

These are just a couple of examples of earth coming into unity with heaven through the vehicle of sound. God wants His people to harness the power of sound on earth to shift strongholds in the natural world. The triumphant shout released by the children of Israel as they surrounded the walls of Jericho is a tremendous illustration of this unified sound of heaven and earth.

It shall come to pass, when they make a long blast with the ram's horn, and when you hear the sound of the trumpet, that all the people shall shout with a great shout; then the wall of the city will fall down flat... So the people shouted when the priests blew the trumpets. And it happened when the people heard the sound of the trumpet, and the people shouted with a great shout, that the wall fell down flat. Then the people went up into the city, every man straight before him, and they took the city. (Joshua 6:5,20)

One of the greatest revelations of the New Testament is that Christ indwells His people who live on the earth. That is why they are called the body of Christ. Those who have received Christ as Lord become the hands and feet of Christ in the earth but they also become His mouth. God speaks prophetically through His people. "If anyone speaks, he should do it as one speaking the very words of God." (1 Peter 4:11 NIV)

Christ is like the invisible hand inside the glove. He is the One who speaks through His people to affect salvation, healing and deliverance. Human beings are uniquely fashioned to be the temple of God on earth. As we yield our vocal chords to the Lord that He might be glorified through us, He demonstrates His extraordinary wisdom and revelation by speaking through us to the nations.

This is the ultimate unification of heaven and earth as God unveils Christ in us and through us. Our voices actually become the sound of His voice on earth. In this way we become an expression of the prophetic voice of the Lord. His spiritual sound is expressed through our natural sound. We sing because He sings through us! Mechanical sound waves become the expression of another kind of supernatural sound wave that has the capacity to penetrate the entire universe.

This is the sound within the sound that shakes the wilderness. This is the voice crying in the wilderness. In the same way that mechanical sound waves at a certain low frequency can shake a building off its foundations, so the sound waves of heaven can shatter strongholds in our own lives and bring the walls crashing down like Jericho. We will revisit this theme in chapter twelve when we explore the relationship between the prophetic proclamation of the Word of God and the release of the glory of God on earth.

Chapter Seven

STRING THEORY AND THE VOICE OF GOD

We have been exploring the theme that Jesus Christ "sustains the universe by the Word of His power." (Hebrews 1:3) Remember that Jesus said, "The words that I speak to you are Spirit." (John 6:63) In the previous chapter we saw how our human words create natural sound but we contrasted this with the reality that the words of Christ are an expression of the supernatural sound of the Spirit. When Christ speaks, His words release the supernatural power of the Holy Spirit.

The word of God is living and active. Obviously it is not natural sound that sustains the universe. Instead, it is the energy of the Holy Spirit that sets in motion an invisible wave pattern that is everywhere present throughout the entire universal quantum field. It is a spiritual sound that is continually generated by the Spirit of God. This biblical revelation opens up some interesting ideas about the nature of the physical universe at the quantum level. From the revelation that the Word of God sustains the universe we can speculate about the relationship between the voice of God and the quantum building blocks of matter. This discussion inevitably leads us to interact with what some physicists call "string theory."

INTRODUCING STRING THEORY

String theory postulates the existence of unimaginably minute strings or loops of energy that are allegedly the constituent ingredients of the quantum world. Not all scientists embrace string theory but it is strongly advocated by some of the greatest minds in contemporary physics today. Of course, there is a question as to whether string theory can be either proved scientifically or disproved. It is certainly not something that will ever be observed even with the highest powered magnification.

These strings if they exist at all are way too tiny to be observed! The theory was developed as an attempt to unify the laws of physics on a macroscopic scale with the laws of the quantum world. This is quantum physics' Holy Grail, the discovery of the elusive "Theory of Everything." String theory was proposed as a means of reconciling the law of general relativity with the realities of quantum physics. This has been one of the great unresolved puzzles of contemporary physics. Where does the law of gravity fit within the picture of quantum mechanics?

How small is a string? Well, according to the theory, they are loops of vibrating energy that are a hundred billion, billion times smaller than a proton, so, as I have suggested, we won't be seeing them any time soon. The truth is we won't be seeing them, period! The "standard model" of particle physics asserts that the smallest elementary particles are zero dimensional point-like particles. String theory argues that they are loops of energy like minute elastic bands. One of the unique features of string theory is the proposal that these tiny loops of vibrating energy actually exist in other extra dimensions.

According to string theory, these strings are extra-dimensional fields of energy which are the building blocks of sub-atomic particles such as quarks, leptons, hadrons, bosons, gluons and neutrinos, etc. For many theoretical physicists the constituent ingredients of matter at a sub-atomic level are not zero dimensional point-like particles. Rather it is believed by some physicists that the most elementary building blocks of the quantum world are minute strings or filaments of vibrating energy. String theory first emerged in the 1970s but it has gained popularity and wider acceptance amongst some of the greatest minds in contemporary quantum physics. String theory is based upon solid mathematical equations that require additional hidden dimensions curled up within our familiar three dimensional spatial world.

There is an elegance and a beauty to string theory that makes it extremely attractive to theologians who are already accepting of the concept of the extra-dimensionality of the realm of the Spirit. Extra-dimensionality is the "stuff" of biblical theology! Brian Green wrote a book titled *The Elegant Universe*. Greene is one of the most articulate exponents of string theory in the world today. He titled his book *The Elegant Universe* because he theorises that there is an aesthetic and mathematical elegance at the smallest level of physical creation.

In the sub-atomic world proposed by string theorists, each string vibrates at a different frequency. The idea that every string vibrates differently is the factor which determines whether a particular string will result in the formation of a quark or a lepton, a meson or a hadron, a baryon or a neutrino. Don't be intimidated by these terms; they are building blocks of the more familiar sub-atomic particles (protons, neutrons and electrons) and according to string theory these particles are constituted by strings that vibrate at different frequencies.

String theory is immediately attractive to those whose minds are steeped in biblical revelation. As followers of Christ we are inducted into a realm of revelatory knowledge that enables us to view the world around us through the very eyes of the Creator. What we discover is a world of extraordinary elegance and beauty no matter where we turn our attention. From the sheer visual majesty of the universe with its staggering aesthetic beauty to the compelling evidence of extraordinary mathematical fine-tuning at every level of the physics of the cosmos, to the appearance of purpose and design in molecular biology and the mathematical brilliance of the genetic code and its role in the construction of the brain, no matter where we look as believers in God we are overwhelmed by the sense of awe and wonder generated by the elegance and beauty of nature.

It follows that this level of aesthetic beauty might continue right down to the smallest ingredients of the quantum world. Brian Greene is not a theologian but he is deeply aware that there is an elegance to every part of the universe, either macroscopic or microscopic. In adopting the motif of "elegance" in his development of string theory he is simply following a principle that is evident in every aspect of creation.

EXTRA DIMENSIONS

We are accustomed to thinking in terms of three or four familiar dimensions: the three spatial dimensions which describe the "whereabouts" of a material object and the fourth dimension of *time* which describes the "when" of an object or an event. We think in terms of "left and right," "back and forth," "up and down" and "when." But string theory postulates the existence of other hidden dimensions, a theory that is sustained and supported by scientific discoveries in the mysterious world of quantum physics. Discoveries such as quantum non-locality, quantum entanglement, quantum teleportation and quantum tunnelling point toward the existence of these other dimensions.

The scientifically and mathematically documented behaviour of the quantum world can only be explained if we allow for the existence of other dimensions. As we have seen, all of the discoveries of the quantum world are highly counterintuitive. That is, they contradict our understanding of physics at the macroscopic level we are accustomed to. One of the distinguishing features of quantum "weirdness" is the extra-dimensionality of the quantum world.

Extra-dimensionality is a powerful concept! Throughout this book we have proposed that the weird world of quantum physics represents the intersection between two worlds. It is the intersection between the world of spirit and the world of matter. It is like the buffer zone between spiritual realities and material realities. That is why the quantum world exhibits the attributes of both spirit and matter! The realm of spirit is by its very nature non-local. It transcends space and time, those four familiar dimensions that we are all accustomed to navigating in everyday life.

We have seen that when electrons and other sub-atomic particles are not being observed they are considered to exist in a dematerialised state. The rest of the time, scientists have discovered, the sub-atomic world exists in what can only be explained as some kind of extra-dimensional twilight zone. Terms such as "ghost-like" are adopted by quantum physicists to attempt to explain the weird attributes of the quantum world.

We recall the fact that Einstein described the counterintuitive behaviour of the quantum world as "spooky." String theorists are right at home with the idea of extra-dimensionality. They describe a universe in which as many as six other dimensions exist "curled up" within the four dimensions that we observe at a macroscopic level. The existence of other dimensions is the fundamental presupposition upon which string theory is established.

"Cosmogony" is the theory of the origins of the universe. Biblical cosmogony has always asserted the existence of other dimensions beyond space and time. The very concept of God presupposes the existence of something extra-dimensional or something outside of our four familiar dimensions. This other dimension is the dimension of spirit.

Those who have a firm belief in God do not struggle with the idea of the existence of other dimensions. The existence of God, and hence the existence of extra-dimensionality, explains the relationship between the sustaining Word of God and the vibrating strings of energy that some physicists believe constitute the "material" universe. That is why some theologians find string theory highly attractive. It substantiates something which is the very currency of biblical revelation.

If string theory is correct, God sustains the entire physical universe by vibrating the very strings of energy that He created by the word of His power. If the strings were to stop vibrating the entire universe would collapse because these strings of vibrating energy are the building blocks of sub-atomic particles and sub-atomic particles are the building blocks of matter. The one thing that string theorists never discuss is what causes the strings to vibrate! Why would a string just continue to vibrate forever unless it was being energised externally from another source of energy? This is one of the mysteries that emerge from string theory, but it is powerfully addressed by the revelation of the sustaining voice of God.

We saw in chapter five that if God were to withdraw His sustaining Word the entire physical universe would collapse and undergo a catastrophic nuclear meltdown. This is exactly what the Scriptures declare will occur at the end of the age when Christ returns. This revelation supports the thesis of the superiority of Spirit over matter. In the very moment that the sustaining Word of God is withdrawn over creation, the heavens and the earth will literally dissolve.

As we seek to reconcile the implications of string theory with the revelation of Scripture it would appear that we could propose that the extra-dimensional Holy Spirit sustains the material world by continually vibrating the minute extra-dimensional strings of energy that constitute the entire physical universe. What energizes and vibrates these tiny strings? This is one of the unsolved problems created by string theory. There must be some unlimited source of supernatural energy that causes these strings to continue to vibrate.

If all of matter is made up of protons, neutrons, electrons, etc., what excites and sustains these sub-atomic particles and keeps them in a state of perpetual motion no matter where they are in the universe? Eventually, according to the law of entropy, these sub-atomic particles would run out of energy and the atoms would simply decline into an inert state. With the inevitable deterioration of inertia, all of the particles that make up the universe would ultimately become completely inert. Something keeps the sub-atomic particles moving and vibrating. What could that possibly be?

God's Word Releases Energy

As we have already seen, according to Scripture it is the Word of God as the active vocal expression of the Spirit of God that sustains the material world. The Scriptures reveal that "the word of God is living and active." (Hebrews 4:12) The Greek word that is translated into the English word "active" is *energes* which is an adjectival form of the Greek noun *energeo*. It is elsewhere translated in the New Testament as "powerful, effective or effectual."

In the same way that the noun *energeo* can be transliterated into the English word *energy*, the Greek word *energes* can be transliterated into the English adjective, *energizing*. When we speak of something being "energized" we are indicating that there is an impartation of energy or spiritual power. The book of Hebrews not only reveals that Christ "sustains the universe by the mighty power of His command," (Hebrews 1:3 NLT) it also reveals that His word *energizes* the physical universe.

One way we can understand this is to theorise that at a sub-atomic level the continual vibration of these unimaginably minute strings of energy is occurring as the result of the Word of God being perpetually spoken over all of creation. The power source that sustains the universe is the power of the Holy Spirit. This is the invisible energy of the Holy Spirit that Paul called "His energy [*energeia*], which so powerfully works [*energeo*] in me." (Colossians 1:29 NIV)

In this text Paul used the Greek word *energeia* from which we derive the English word *energy*. This divine energy not only energizes the life of the believer, it also energizes the entire physical universe. Could it be that the acceptance of string theory amongst a number of quantum physicists converges with biblical revelation to provide evidence that this entire "physical" universe is actually energised by some kind of invisible spiritual energy?

Biblical revelation is dismissed by the vast majority of scientists as something which is beyond the scope of empirical science ,but the theory of an independent power source behind the physical universe is at least an interesting thesis that warrants further exploration. The acceptance of biblical revelation opens the door for significant advances in scientific knowledge through the proposal that the energy of the Holy Spirit is the hidden factor that sustains the very existence of this perpetual "cosmic dance" of the quantum world. Very little has been written on the possibility of a fundamental relationship between the energising power of the Spirit of God and the building blocks of the sub-atomic world, so let's explore this theme a bit further.

We are told in the Genesis creation narrative that the Spirit of God was "hovering over" creation. "The earth was without form, and void; and darkness was on the face of the deep. And the Spirit of God was *hovering over* the face of the waters." (Genesis 1:2) The Hebrew word for *hovering over* is *rachaph* which means to "move, to flutter or to shake."

Rachaph is only used in two other places in the Hebrew Old Testament. It appears in the book of Deuteronomy to describe the Lord overshadowing the nation of Israel. "He shielded him and cared for him; he guarded him as the apple of his eye, like an eagle that stirs up its nest and *hovers over* its young, that spreads its wings to catch them and carries them on its pinions." (Deuteronomy 32:10-11 NIV) Another translation describes the Lord as "*fluttering* over his young." (KJV) The third place where the Hebrew word *rachaph* appears is in Jeremiah 23:9 where we read, "My heart within me is broken because of the prophets; all my bones *shake*."

This idea of "shaking and fluttering" sheds light on the meaning of the word *rachaph*. It speaks of movement and motion and it describes an extra-dimensional source of spiritual energy that exercises a sustaining influence upon the entire created universe. Perhaps we could say the Spirit *vibrated* or *resonated* over the whole of creation.

Remember that the Spirit of God is presented in the Bible as the supreme source of supernatural energy. It is the energy of God that creates and sustains all things. The relationship between the role of the Spirit and the quantum world could be likened to the "sympathetic strings" on a musical instrument. This "resonance affect" illustrates the power of the Word of God to sustain the vibration of the minute strings of energy that conceivably constitute the elementary particles that constitute the world of matter.

If string theory turns out to be an accurate representation of quantum reality, then the whole physical universe is actually a manifestation of energy at a sub-atomic level, all of which is created and sustained by the creative Word of God. But as we begin to speak of the entire universe consisting of energy it must be asserted that from a biblical perspective this is a *created* energy and not the actual energy of the Holy Spirit. If we do not maintain a differentiation between the strings of energy that possibly constitute the material universe and the energy that flows from the sustaining Word of God we will end up in some kind of pantheism where, once again, it is asserted that the entire universe is God.

In order to be faithful to the biblical worldview we must always maintain a strong differentiation between the Creator and the creation whilst affirming the seamless relationship between the Creator and His creation. Perhaps we could say that the energy of the Holy Spirit is the power source that excites and energises these created strings that are themselves a manifestation of energy that exist within other dimensions.

Thousands of scientists have spent countless millions of hours studying and postulating various theories about the world of quantum physics. Some of the most complex mathematical equations ever conceived by the human mind have been developed in an attempt to crack the mysteries of quantum mechanics. As the world's greatest physicists and mathematicians have sought to plumb the depths of the mysteries of the quantum world, they have found themselves staring straight into the creative mind of God. Before the foundation of the world God conceived the vision to create the physical universe out of nothing.

The Scriptures reveal that "what we now see did not come from anything that can be seen." (Hebrews 11:3 NLT) Many extraordinarily brilliant quantum physicists believe that the "particles" that constitute the interior world of the atom are themselves created from invisible vibrating strings of energy in such a manner that they eventually coalesced into matter. All of this was conceived in the mind of God and brought to expression through the creative command of God. "God said, 'Let there be light and there was light!'" Light itself consists of waves of electromagnetic energy that "vibrate" at an extraordinarily high frequency.

If string theory is an accurate description of the smallest building blocks of matter, these vibrating strings of energy (and the sub-atomic particles they eventually constructed) were brought into being at the command of God as the foundational building blocks of matter. Because they were designed by God they could also be uniquely sustained by the Word of God through the energizing power of the Holy Spirit. The quantum world has been intentionally designed to obey the voice of God. When God speaks His creative word the entire quantum field can be rearranged, collapsed or restructured at His command.

There is a remarkable convergence between these theological concepts in the Bible and the emergence of string theory. To my mind, biblical theology powerfully supports string theory, not just because of the convergence of notions of extra-dimensionality or of elegance in design but because of the energising relationship between the Spirit of God and the strings that perhaps constitute nature at its very smallest scale. String theorists suggest that these strings vibrate at different frequencies to create a sub-atomic symphony of music.

THE MUSIC OF THE SPHERES

Pythagoras, the ancient Greek philosopher and mathematician (6th century BC) spoke of what he called the "Music of the Spheres." As a mathematician, Pythagoras was intrigued by music and the mathematical equations that undergirded the creation of music. He regarded the movement of the sun, the moon, the stars and the planets as a mystical expression of music. Because of his mystical and philosophical orientation he was inspired to explore the relationship between geometry, mathematics and music.

String theorists are now proposing that the elementary particles of the sub-atomic world are a form or music; a "music of the quantum world" if you like. Professor Edward Witten is one of the greatest physicists of our time. His scientific brilliance has been frequently likened to the brilliance of Einstein. Witten is one of the founders of string theory and he has proposed the idea that each string vibrates at a different frequency and that each unique frequency determines what sort of sub-atomic particle it becomes.

According to string theory, an elementary particle is not a point but a loop of vibrating string. Just like a violin or piano string, one of these "fundamental strings" has many different harmonics or forms of vibration. For a piano string, the harmonics consist of a basic note – such as middle C – and its higher overtones (one, two, or several octaves higher). The richness of music comes from the interplay of higher harmonics. Music played with a tuning fork, which produces only a basic note, sounds harsh to the human ear. In string theory, different harmonics correspond to different elementary particles. If string theory proves correct, all elementary particles – electrons, photons, neutrinos, quarks, and the rest – owe their existence to subtle differences in the vibrations of strings.[1]

If indeed all elementary sub-atomic particles are expressed uniquely because of the variation in the vibration of the strings, this creates an infinitely more complex understanding of the nature of the material world. To extend our speculation on the relationship between the Word of God and the sustaining power that it exercises over creation, we would be required to consider a higher level of complexity in the sounds and tones generated by the voice of God in order to vibrate the different strings of energy that constitute the material world.

This idea transcends any notion that there is a single "tone" that is generated by the Spirit of God that vibrates all of the strings of energy simultaneously. Rather, it would necessitate a multiplicity of unique "tones" that correspond to the different elementary particles. Brian Greene, one of the world's leading string theorists, expands upon this idea in his wonderful book, *The Elegant Universe:*

> Just as the different vibrational patterns of a violin string give rise to different musical notes, the different vibrational patterns of a fundamental string give rise to different masses and force charges. More frantic vibrational patterns have more energy, while less frantic ones have less energy. Thus, according to string theory, the mass of an elementary particle is determined by the energy of the vibrational pattern of its internal string. Heavier particles have internal strings that vibrate more energetically, while lighter particles have internal strings that vibrate less energetically.

> So we see that, according to string theory, the observed properties of each elementary particle arise because its internal string undergoes a particular resonant vibrational pattern. The "stuff" of all matter and all forces is the *same.* Each elementary particle is composed of a different string – that is, each particle is a different string – and all strings are absolutely identical. Differences between the particles arise because their respective strings undergo different vibrational

patterns. What appears to be different elementary particles are actually different "notes" on a fundamental string. The universe – being composed of an enormous number of these vibrating strings – is akin to a cosmic symphony.[2]

According to string theorists, these strings spontaneously vibrate at different frequencies or "notes" but, as we have seen, there is no speculation as to what causes these strings to continue to vibrate at their various consistent "notes." This is where the perspective of biblical theology adds greater light to the theory. Of course, there are a very limited number of elementary particles. There are three major sub-atomic particles: protons, electrons and neutrons.

These major particles are made up of six kinds of quarks, there are "gluons" which are particles that glue the quarks together, then there are photons, leptons, neutrinos, baryons, hadrons and mesons, all of which have a number of variations. There are also pions, muons and kaons which are mediator particles. Also, every particle has a corresponding "antiparticle" that has the same properties except for an opposite electrical charge. These antiparticles are sometimes called "antimatter." But in total there are probably no more than a few dozen elements that are the building blocks of the protons, neutrons and electrons.

Given what we know from the Scriptures, it is not farfetched to imagine that God continuously sustains each unique vibration of all the various strings that constitute the building blocks of matter. Perhaps there is a different set of "frequencies" that are continuously released from the invisible realm of heaven that sustain each individual note on every string simultaneously?

As we have already established, these are not ordinary sound waves as we are accustomed to on earth, because sound waves do not travel outside of earth's atmosphere. These are supernatural sounds that flow forth from the Spirit of God. Whilst it is purely speculative, it is possible that there indeed is a "cosmic symphony," (to borrow Brian Greene's terminology), of musical notes that continuously flow out of the throne of God in order to sustain the entire material universe. When this musical expression of the "song of the Lord" is ultimately withdrawn from creation the elementary particles will literally "melt with intense heat."

The Bible paints a glorious picture of the voice of God resounding over the whole creation. Not only did God speak the universe into existence with the power of His spoken Word, He also sustains the entire universe with the power of His voice. Both Ezekiel and the apostle John tell us that "His voice is like the sound of *many* waters." (Ezekiel 43:2, Revelation 1:15)

God's voice is not just a singular monotone; it is more like a tumultuous chorus of sounds and harmonies. Perhaps the voice of the Lord that sounds like "many waters" causes the frequencies of the "many waters" to begin to resonate and shake. "The voice of the Lord is over the waters; the God of glory thunders; the Lord is over *many waters*. The voice of the Lord is powerful; the voice of the Lord is full of majesty. The voice of the Lord *shakes* the wilderness." (Psalm 29:3-4,8)

The Bible reveals that Jesus Christ is the Lord of all creation and that all creation *trembles* at His mighty voice. His voice *shakes* or *vibrates* the very fabric of the earth at a sub-atomic level. The Hebrew word for "shake" is *chuwl* and it means to dance or to tremble. God makes the quantum world to *dance* and *tremble* at the sound of His voice. "He shakes the earth from its place and makes its pillars *tremble*." (Job 9:6 NIV)

God not only shakes the earth but He also shakes the heavens! "Therefore I will make the heavens *tremble*, and the earth will be *shaken* from its place." (Isaiah 13:13 NASB) "The Lord's voice will roar from Zion and thunder from Jerusalem and the earth and heavens will begin to *shake*." (Joel 3:16) "The pillars of heaven *tremble* and are amazed at his rebuke." (Job 26:11) God's voice resonates over all creation and all creation has been skilfully designed to respond to the resonance of the voice of Him who sounds like "many waters." I think it is significant that He whose voice "sounds like many waters" is revealed as being over the "many waters." Perhaps this is an ancient and pre-scientific way of saying that the harmonics and higher and lower octaves of His glorious voice actually vibrates the "many waters" at a quantum level.

The Song of the Lord

God reveals Himself as an intimate lover who sings over His beloved. "The Lord your God is with you, He is mighty to save. He will take great delight in you, He will quiet you with His love, He will rejoice over you with *singing*." (Zephaniah 3:17) If God sings over His people, it is also possible that He sings over His entire creation. God is the very creator of music and of every expression of aesthetic beauty. He is a musical God. He surrounds Himself with choirs of angels! He creates people in His own image who are endowed with extraordinary musical capabilities.

The "Song of the Lamb" (Revelation 15:3) is a redemptive song that is sung over God's creation. C.S. Lewis wrote *The Magician's Nephew* as part of his famous *Chronicles of Narnia* series. In chapters eight and nine there is a remarkable allegorical description of the creation event in which Lewis depicts Aslan singing Narnia into existence. The two key characters, Polly and Digory, are mysteriously transported into another time and place where they witness the creation of the universe. Suddenly Polly and Digory are catapulted into a formless void of absolute darkness and they have the privilege of witnessing something absolutely breathtaking.

> There were no stars. It was so dark that they couldn't see one another at all and it made no difference whether you kept your eyes shut or open. Under their feet there was a cool, flat something which might have been earth, and was certainly not grass or wood. The air was cold and dry and there was no wind. In the darkness something was happening at last. A voice had begun to sing. It was very far away and Digory found it hard to decide from what direction it was coming. Sometimes it seemed to come from all directions at once. Its lower notes were deep enough to be the voice of the earth herself. There were no words. There was hardly even a tune. But it was, beyond comparison, the most beautiful noise he had ever heard. It was so beautiful he could hardly bear it. Then two wonders happened at the same moment. One was that the voice was suddenly joined by other voices, more voices than you could possibly count. They were in harmony with it, but far higher up the scale: cold, tingling, silvery voices. The second wonder was that the blackness overhead, all at once, was blazing with stars. They didn't come out gently one by one, as they do on a summer evening. One moment there had been nothing but darkness; next moment a thousand, thousand points of light leaped out – single stars, constellations, and planets, brighter and bigger than any in our world. There were no clouds. The new stars and the new voices began at exactly the same time. If you had seen and heard it, as Digory did, you would have felt quite certain that it was the stars themselves which were singing, and that it was the First Voice, the deep one, which had made them appear and made them sing.[3]

Lewis is clearly recalling the fact that according to the Bible the initial creation event was accompanied by angelic singing and rejoicing at the marvellously skilful handiwork of the Creator. The Lord said to Job: "Where were you when I laid the earth's foundation? Tell me, if you understand. Who marked off its dimensions? Surely you know! Who stretched a measuring line across it? On what were its footings set, or who laid its cornerstone – *while the morning stars sang together and all the angels shouted for joy?*" (Job 38:4-7 NIV)

Did the angels initiate the songs or did they merely begin to sing in harmony with the Master Quantum Physicist as He sang creation into existence? The allegory continues in *The Magician's Nephew.*

> The Voice on the earth was now louder and more triumphant; but the voices in the sky, after singing loudly with it for a time, began to get fainter. And now something else was happening. Far away, and down near the horizon, the sky began to turn grey. A light wind, very fresh, began to stir. The sky, in that one place, grew slowly and steadily paler. You could see shapes of hills standing up dark against it. All the time the Voice went on singing. The eastern sky changed from white to pink and from pink to gold. The Voice rose and rose, till all the air was shaking with it. And just as it swelled to the mightiest and most glorious sound it had yet produced, the sun arose.

> Digory had never seen such a sun. You could imagine that it laughed for joy as it came up. And as its beams shot across the land the travellers could see for the first time what sort of place they were in. It was a valley through which a broad, swift river wound its way, flowing eastward towards the sun. Southward there were mountains, northward there were lower hills. But it was a valley of mere earth, rock and water; there was not a tree, not a bush, not a blade of grass to be seen. The earth was of many colours: they were fresh, hot and vivid. They made you feel excited, until you saw the Singer himself, and then you forgot everything else.

> It was a Lion. Huge, shaggy, and bright, it stood facing the risen sun. Its mouth was wide open in song and it was about three hundred yards away. The Lion was pacing to and fro about that empty land and singing his new song. It was softer and more lilting than the song by which he had called up the stars and the sun: a gentle,

rippling music. And as he walked and sang the valley grew green with grass. It spread out from the Lion like a pool. It ran up the sides of the little hills like a wave. In a few minutes it was creeping up the lower slopes of the distant mountains, making that young world every moment softer. The light wind could now be heard ruffling the grass. Soon there were other things besides grass. The higher slopes grew dark with heather. Patches of rougher and more bristling green appeared in the valley.

All this time the Lion's song, and his stately prowl, to and fro, backwards and forwards, was going on. Polly was finding the song more and more interesting because she thought she was beginning to see the connection between the music and the things that were happening. When a line of dark firs sprang up on a ridge about a hundred yards away she felt that they were connected with a series of deep, prolonged notes which the Lion had sung a second before. And when he burst into a rapid series of lighter notes she was not surprised to see primroses suddenly appearing in every direction. Thus, with an unspeakable thrill, she felt quite certain that all the things were coming (as she said) "out of the Lion's head." When you listened to his song you heard the things he was making up: when you looked round you, you saw them.[4]

In the beginning God said "Let there be light" (Genesis 1:3) but perhaps C.S. Lewis' fictional account is much closer to the truth than we might first think when he suggests that God sang these creative commands over the void rather than just speaking the words. Perhaps God continues to sing over all creation until the day that the heavens and the earth pass away with a great noise.

Remember that "sound" here on earth is a mere analogue or shadow of something that occurs in the invisible realm of the spirit. The words that Jesus speaks are Spirit. They may be clothed in an audible expression here on earth in order to communicate something to our ear drums that have been designed to pick up the mechanical vibrations of sound. But there is a higher reality that earthly sound points to. There is a sound beyond the sound. This higher reality is the communication of divine energy. It is a wave of the Holy Spirit that creates new realities at a quantum level and that continues to sustain the entire creation.

The Uni-Verse

It is indeed a compelling speculation to consider that the voice of God that resounds over the entire universe could actually sustain the material world at a quantum level by energising and vibrating the tiny strings that some theoretical physicists believe constitute the underlying fabric of the physical order. And what an equally fascinating thought that the entire physical universe is perhaps a mysterious dance of microscopic strings of energy that are perpetually vibrating to the multi-textured Voice that sounds like many waters!

The word "universe" actually means "one song." The universe is a direct product of the song of the Lord. What does God's song sound like? "The heavens declare the glory of God; the skies proclaim the work of His hands. Day after day they pour forth speech; night after night they display knowledge. There is no speech or language where their voice is not heard. Their voice goes out into all the earth, their words to the ends of the world." (Psalm 19:1-4 NIV) Consider the accumulation of verbs in this passage of Scripture: creation *declares* something, it *proclaims* something, it *pours forth speech*; creation has a *voice* and its *words* convey a coherent message that transcends the confusion of languages!

The universe is a song that God sung into being, and as a result the universe itself continues to resonate to the very song of the Lord at a sub-quantum level. The Bible reveals a creation that sings or resonates. "For you shall go out with joy, and be led out with peace; the mountains and the hills shall break forth into singing before you, and all the trees of the field shall clap their hands." (Isaiah 55:12)

"Let the heavens rejoice, let the earth be glad; let them say among the nations, 'The Lord reigns!' Let the sea resound, and all that is in it; let the fields be jubilant, and everything in them! Then the trees of the forest will sing, they will sing for joy before the Lord." (1 Chronicles 16:31-33 NIV) Luke records a story in the life of Jesus when His disciples began to praise Him, prompting the indignant rebuke of the religious leaders.

When Jesus came near the place where the road goes down the Mount of Olives, the whole crowd of disciples began joyfully to praise God in loud voices for all the miracles they had seen: "Blessed is the King who comes in the name of the Lord!" "Peace in heaven and glory in the highest!" Some of the Pharisees in the crowd said to Jesus, "Teacher, rebuke your disciples!" "I tell you," He replied, "If they keep quiet, the stones will cry out." (Luke 19:37-40 NIV)

Mountains and hills singing, the ocean resounding, trees clapping their hands, and rocks crying out in praise to God! Of course this is metaphorical language but it is a very real possibility that if scientists were able to create equipment that was powerful enough to record the sounds from the world of microscopic strings they could hypothetically decode the very frequencies of heaven.

In classical physics all material objects have their own unique resonant frequency. Similarly, if string theory is an accurate description of the sub-quantum world, then each string has its own length and its own resonant frequency. Brian Greene uses the analogy of a violin string.

To understand this, let's first think about more familiar strings, such as those on a violin. Each string can undergo a huge variety of different vibrational patterns known as resonances. These are the wave patterns whose peaks and troughs are evenly spaced and fit perfectly between the string's two fixed endpoints. Our ears sense these different resonant vibrational patterns as different musical notes. The strings in string theory have similar properties. There are resonant vibrational patterns that the string can support by virtue of their evenly spaced peaks and troughs exactly fitting along its special extent.[5]

> This leads us to the following realisation: If we can work out precisely the allowed resonant vibrational patterns of fundamental strings – the "notes," so to speak, that they can play – we should be able to explain the observed properties of the elementary particles. For the first time, therefore, string theory sets up a framework for *explaining* the properties of the particles observed in nature.[6]

Whilst scientists cannot penetrate the resonant frequencies of the strings that string theorists speculate about, there have nevertheless been breakthroughs in penetrating the sound signatures of molecules. In a November 2007 Internet article titled "Molecular Chords" we read:

> Researchers have for the first time analysed the frequency of molecular resonance, in the same way as musicians analyse the notes of a chord. Their results have even been made audible. In terms of physics, there

is hardly any difference between the resonance in a molecule and a musical chord. Both are created when vibrations with different frequencies overlap. In music, it is the notes that make up the chord. In molecules, these frequencies are also called quantum states. Molecular resonance usually consists of overlaid vibrations with different frequencies. The energy of these frequencies is equivalent to the energy which triggered the vibration.

A musical chord is created when notes, that is, sound waves, with different frequencies overlay each other. As the notes are part of a scale, they only have certain frequencies. In exactly the same way, atoms in a molecule can only vibrate at certain frequencies which then overlay each other and finally create the complete molecular resonance. By way of illustration, the researchers converted the resonance into an acoustic signal (sound waves) and made it audible, making the resonance into a musical chord. Variations in the loudness of the sound signals (beat) reflect the distance between the atomic nuclei resonating against each other. The audible beats are created by overlaying different pitches (frequencies), that is, the quantum states which make up the molecular resonance.[7]

In the same way that scientists have penetrated the sound signature of tiny molecules the phenomena is also occurring in the macroscopic world of galaxies, quasars and black holes. Astrophysicists have been able to convert the electromagnetic radio signals that are emitted from quasars and black holes into mechanical sound waves. These are the sounds that we would hear if sound could indeed travel through space.

We see the same phenomena in radio waves here on earth. We tune our radios into a coherent broadcast signal and the radio decodes the electromagnetic signal into audible sound waves. There are many websites that collect libraries of these "sounds" from space[8] and some of the sounds are quite eerie.[9] Even the earth emits a low hum,[10] far below the sound spectrum that is audible to human ears. If all the sounds could be heard simultaneously it would create an extraordinary symphony of the cosmic "music of the spheres."

Other scientists have discovered another way of detecting the sound signatures of black holes. They are learning how to "see sounds" from objects in space. A black hole attracts very dense clouds of gases and these gases are capable of transmitting sound waves. By studying the concentric ring patterns in the gases, astrophysicists have been able to discern that certain black holes emit a deep bass sound in B-flat but in octaves that are way below the threshold of human hearing.

In an article titled, "Black Hole Strikes Deepest Musical Note Ever Heard," we read, "Astronomers have detected the deepest note ever generated in the cosmos, a B-flat flying through space like a ripple on an invisible pond. No human will actually hear the note, because it is 57 octaves below the keys in the middle of a piano."[11]

Human beings love to design and create musical instruments for the sheer pleasure of enjoying the sounds that they can make. All of creation is God's musical instrument. It is his beautiful song! Could it be that the musical textures and intonations of His supernatural voice play the different strings that undergird matter which results in these strings theoretically emitting their own unique sound signature? Without deifying the creation as pantheists are prone to do, we could speculate that the whole of creation actually carries the diverse frequencies and sound signatures of heaven at the sub-quantum level.

Creation bears the fingerprints of the Creator. The evidence of intelligent design reveals the presence of an intelligent Designer. The fingerprints themselves are not God but they are the evidence that God has been there and has left His divine imprimatur upon His own creation. It is not so farfetched to imagine that the whole creation sings a song of praise to the Creator. David said, "Let heaven and earth praise Him, the seas and everything that moves in them." (Psalm 69:34) Psalm 148 is an exhortation to the whole of creation to Praise God.

Praise him, all his angels! Praise him, all the armies of heaven! Praise him, sun and moon! Praise him, all you twinkling stars! Praise him, skies above! Praise him, vapours high above the clouds! Let every created thing give praise to the Lord, for he issued his command, and they came into being. He established them forever and forever. His orders will never be revoked. Praise the Lord from the earth, you creatures of the ocean depths, fire and hail, snow and storm, wind and weather that obey him, mountains and all hills, fruit trees and all cedars, wild animals and all livestock, reptiles and birds, kings of the earth and all people, rulers and judges of the earth, young men and maidens, old men and children. Let them praise the name of the Lord, for His name alone is exalted; His glory is above the earth and heaven. (Psalm 148:2-13)[12]

How fascinating that we have come to a point in human history when scientists who probe nature at smaller and smaller scales are arriving at conclusions that correspond beautifully with the Scriptures that were written in an ancient pre-scientific age, yet which convey ideas and concepts that evoke similar feelings of awe and wonder as those that are stirred when we read the speculations of string theorists with their compelling analogies between the fabric of the sub-quantum world and the sounds of music that brings us so much pleasure!

We are living in fascinating times when there is a glorious convergence between biblical revelation and the speculative reaches of some of the greatest scientific minds on earth today. One thing is certain; there is a profound correspondence between the existence of the supernatural voice of God and the non-local quantum world that creation is built upon.

Chapter Eight

QUANTUM INFORMATION AND THE MIND OF GOD

In the previous chapter we began to explore the role of the Word of God in both creating and sustaining the universe at a quantum level. But now we would like to turn our attention to the role of *information* in the construction of the atoms and molecules of matter that constitute our physical universe. Information plays a crucial role in the creation of matter because, as it has been discovered, complex mathematical information is embedded within every expression of the physical world.

As we will learn in this chapter the quantum world carries complex information in the form of clearly defined mathematical properties. Heinz Pagels, the author of *The Cosmic Code: Quantum Physics as the Language of Nature*, says, "I think the universe is a message written in a code, and the scientists' job is to decipher that code."[1] The information within quantum systems is highly intelligible in that it can be formulated mathematically with accuracy, consistency and precision.

The language of quantum physics is clearly mathematical. Quantum theory has been hailed as the most successful theory of our time because it accurately predicts the behaviour of atoms and their quantum components. Christian physicist John Polkinghorne writes,

> It is no exaggeration to regard quantum theory as being one of the most outstanding intellectual achievements of the 20th century and its discovery as constituting a real revolution in our understanding of physical process. Although the full articulation of the theory

requires the use of its natural language, mathematics, many of its basic concepts can be made accessible to the general reader.[2]

INFORMATION IN NATURE

The Bible declares that "In the beginning was the Word, and the Word was with God, and the Word was God." (John 1:1) The "Word of God" is not just a mere sound; it is a vehicle that conveys both simple and complex information, and this information is expressed through language. Whilst information can be communicated through any human language so that it can be clearly understood by those who understand the code, it can also be expressed through the language of mathematics, as any trained physicist would be able to explain. It was Dr. Stephen Marquardt who declared that, "All physics is math."[3] There has always been an intimate relationship between quantum physics and mathematics. Mathematics is the unique scientific language that communicates a certain kind of complex information that describes the properties and processes of the physics of the universe.

Professor Werner Gitt of the German Federal Institute of Physics and Technology released a book in 1997 titled *In the Beginning Was Information*. The central thesis of the book is that information lies at the core of the entire universe and that all information is the product of divine intelligence which existed prior to the creation of the physical universe. In fact, all of creation points back to the existence of a divine consciousness that preceded creation. Professor Gitt convincingly argues that the information content of matter supports the theory of Intelligent Design because information is always the product of an intelligent Mind, not of pure random chance.

Professor Gitt uses the illustration of complex genetic information as a blueprint not only for the construction of life molecules but also as the source of the operational information that is programmed into every living molecule. It is one thing to create a specific molecule out of hundreds of smaller components (such as amino acids or ribonucleic acids) but it is an entirely different thing to create a functional molecule which repeatedly performs intelligent tasks, as do all of the molecules within the living cell. The key to the construction and programming of life molecules is always information, and that information is fundamentally mathematical.

It is worthwhile considering the degree of complexity in the information that is communicated through the human genetic code if only to expand our consciousness concerning the absolute marvel and wonder of creation and the strategic role that information plays in the construction of everything in the universe. Werner Gitt explains the basics of information through the lens of computer code:

> The **bit** (abbreviated from *binary digit*) is the unit for measuring information content. The number of bits is the same as the number of binary symbols. Binary states have the property that only one of the two binary symbols (1 or 0) can be involved at a certain moment. The bit is also the smallest unit of information that can be represented in a digital computer. When text is entered into a computer it is transformed into a pre-determined binary code and also stored in this form. One letter usually requires 8 binary storage positions, known as a **byte**. The information content of a text is then described in terms of the number of bits required.[4]

Now, let's apply that background information to the content of the genetic code. Jon W. Gordon explains just how vast the informational content of the genetic code really is:

> The genetic material, DNA, has only four subunits, which is more than the two numbers of the binary system. Therefore if DNA is going to write the instructions to produce a brain with tens of millions of interconnected neurons, a heart that pumps 100,000 times per day for up to 100 years without failing, a reproductive system that will initiate and support the development of a baby and the myriad other specialised structures and organ systems of a human, it is going to have to rely on length. How long is the DNA molecule? The number of subunits required to encode the development and function of a human is about three billion.
>
> If the genetic code were written out at 12 characters per inch, a size typical for a printout from a word processor, the total length of the printout would be about 47,000 miles. Even though the DNA bases are exceedingly small, the actual length of DNA required to encode a human is still about one metre. This metre of DNA is packaged into the nucleus of the cell, a structure only a few millionths of a metre across. The nucleus of a cell holds 6 gigabytes of genetic information (each nucleus actually has two complete copies of the 3 billion-base genetic code) in a structure far too small for the human eye to see![5]

The six gigabytes of information found in the nucleus of all 30 trillion cells in our body is *constructional* information. The genetic code is the blueprint for constructing complex molecules that are pre-programmed to function in a highly specific manner. Once the molecules are constructed they begin to "swing into action" and function the way they were designed to function. *Operational* information is of an entirely different order. Werner Gitt gives an estimate of the level of operational information generated in the human body on an average day.

> The amount of information streaming through the deliberate, as well as the involuntary activities of the human body is about 3 x 10^{24} bits per day. When this is compared with the total quantity of information stored in all of the libraries of the world – 10^{18} bits – we make an astounding discovery: The quantity of information processed in our bodies during the course of one day, is one million times greater than all the knowledge represented in the books of the world![6]

In part, this would be a reflection of the fact that the brain has such an unfathomable number of neuronal connections that are all continuously processing and exchanging complex information. The brain is unquestionably the crowning achievement of God's creative bio-engineering abilities. Michael Denton is a molecular biologist and he is the author of *Evolution: A Theory in Crisis*. He gives a staggering illustration to describe the power of one human brain.

> Each nerve cell puts out somewhere in the region of between 10,000 and 100,000 connecting fibres by which it makes contact with other nerve cells in the brain. Altogether the total number of connections in the human brain approaches 1,000,000,000,000,000. Numbers in the order of a thousand million, million are of course completely beyond comprehension. Imagine an area about half the size of the USA (one million square miles) covered in a forest of trees containing ten thousand trees per square mile. If each tree contained one hundred thousand leaves the total number of leaves in the forest would be 1000,000,000,000, equivalent to the number of connections in the human brain![7]

Richard Restak, author of *Brainscapes*, says, "Counting these connections at the rate of one connection per second would take 32 million years to complete. Even a section of the brain no bigger than a match head contains about a billion connections."[8] Michael Denton takes the illustration a step further.

> Despite the enormity of the number of connections, the ramifying forest of fibres is not a chaotic random tangle but a highly organised network in which a high proportion of the fibres are unique adaptive communication channels following their own specially ordained pathway through the brain. Even if only one hundredth of the connections in the brain were specifically organised, this would still represent a system containing a much greater number of specific connections than in the entire communications network on earth![9]

All information is ultimately quantum information because the building blocks of matter are quantum bits. It is not just in the assembly and function of biological life molecules that we discover this complex information. The geometric and symmetrical structures of non-living matter also exhibit definite mathematical properties that are consistent and measureable.

From the structure of galaxies to the structure of crystals and snowflakes there is evidence of mathematical information that gives rise to patterns that reflect visual beauty and elegance. We live in the midst of a world of extraordinary natural beauty where properties such as proportion and geometric symmetry render natural phenomena as beautiful and attractive.

When God spoke the universe into existence His word set in motion a cascading explosion of information all the way from quantum particles to the largest galaxies of space. Mathematical information is embedded in everything. Every aspect of classical physics and of quantum physics can be expressed mathematically and this language of mathematics is equally an expression of the Word of God.

Mathematics is clearly part of the language of God. When we study this mathematical signature at the core of every aspect of creation it becomes increasingly difficult to avoid the conclusion that there is a God and that this intelligent and all powerful being is an incomparably brilliant cosmic mathematician who has structured the universe on readily discernable patterns of precise mathematical formulas which enable scientists to describe the attributes and processes of the physical world.

THE QUANTUM COMPUTER UNIVERSE

Quantum physics has many different branches of study. One branch, quantum computing, has given rise to the proposition that the entire universe can actually be likened to a super massive quantum computer that is continually processing intelligent information. There are a number of fascinating books that have recently been written that explore this theme. Actual quantum computers are still in the developmental stage because there are significant challenges in harnessing and utilising the power of quantum information with reliability and accuracy. Nevertheless there is a continuing quest amongst quantum physicists to harness the power of the quantum world to build new generation computers that can process information at mind-blowing speeds with encrypted code that cannot possibly be cracked.

Back in 1959 Richard Feynman was the first to suggest that quantum mechanics could be harnessed to create "quantum computers." The original developers of binary computer code actually recognised that the simple "on/off" language of all computing mirrored attributes of the quantum world. New Age author, Gregg Braden, is one of a number of influential authors who has written on the theme of the universe as a massive quantum computer. He writes, "In the 1940s Konrad Zuse, the man credited with developing the first computers, had a flash of insight into the way the universe may work."[10]

In the 1970s Zuse wrote a book titled *Calculating Space* in which he reflected upon the insights he experienced in the 1940s in the development of the first computers. Zuse realised a connection between the machinery of the universe and the architecture of the earliest computer and its capacity to process information. He said, "It happened that in contemplating causality [the relationship between things that happen and what causes those things to happen]...I suddenly thought to interpret the cosmos as a gigantic calculating machine."[11]

John Archibald Wheeler noted in the 1980s that the wave-particle duality of quantum superposition worked on a binary system of two possible states. Conventional computers work on the principle of processing binary digits with only two possible states: 0's and 1's. Wheeler said; "Every *it* – every particle, every field of force, even the space-time continuum itself – derives its function, its meaning, its very existence entirely from binary choices: *bits*. What we call reality arises...from the posing of yes/no questions."[12]

In 1998 Wheeler said, "It is not unreasonable to imagine that information sits at the core of physics, just as it sits at the core of a computer."[13] These insights have contributed to a growing understanding that the universe actually processes information and that this information is carried by every atom and expressed through every part of creation. Gregg Braden develops this idea:

> Just as every computer uses binary language to get things done, it looks as if the computer of the universe uses bits as well. Rather than being made of 1's and 0's, however, the bits of creation appear to be the stuff everything is made from: **atoms**. The atoms of our reality either exist as matter or they don't. They're either here or not here, "on" or "off." When we think of the universe as a program, atoms represent "bits" of information that work just the way familiar computer bits do. They are either "on," as physical matter, or "off," as invisible waves."[14] All that we can see, feel, and touch in the universe, then, is the matter made of the atoms that are in the "on" state. The ones that we don't see, those that exist in the invisible (virtual) state, are in the "off" position.[15]

Seth Lloyd was the first person to design a functioning quantum computer. He is the author of *Programming the Universe* and he is professor of mechanical engineering at MIT. He boldly asserts that "the universe *is* a quantum computer!"[16] He doesn't suggest that the universe is *like* a quantum computer, he argues that it *is* a super-computer because it is always processing atomic information. He says, "The history of the universe is, in effect, a huge and ongoing quantum computation."[17]

Lloyd continues to build the prototype of a functional quantum computer based upon the blueprint of the discoveries of cutting edge quantum mechanics. He says that, "All interactions between particles in the universe convey not only energy but also information – in other words, particles not only collide, they compute. As the computation proceeds, reality unfolds."[18] Information is always the product of intelligence. It is never the product of pure random chance. The more our understanding of the complexity of the information embedded in nature grows, the more compelling the argument for Intelligent Design becomes.

The universe is ordered by divine intelligence right down to the sub-quantum level. Everything in the universe is the product of intelligence, causing it to have its own internal intelligibility that in turn causes it to be structured into a coherent expression of reality. This is where we see the beauty of mathematics and its intimate relationship to physics. It was Dr. Stephen Marquardt who said, "All life is biology. All biology is physiology. All physiology is chemistry. All chemistry is physics. All physics is math."[19]

When it comes to information, the language of the universe is unequivocally the language of mathematics. Many people never even catch a glimpse of the sheer beauty of mathematics. A lot of people develop an aversion to mathematics in school because it can be presented rather lifelessly by teachers who are themselves blinded to the beauty of this discipline. But the language of mathematics is as beautiful as any language except that it is somewhat impenetrable to the uninitiated.

The orderliness and beauty of mathematics is staggering, prompting Stephen Hawking to exclaim that "God Created the Integers!"[20] To contemplate the idea that God has ordered and built the universe on the foundation of mathematics is a profoundly mind-expanding exercise. According to some of the greatest mathematical minds in the world today, to penetrate the majesty of the mathematical universe is even more exhilarating.

The universe is a comprehensive mathematical miracle. There is an order that ascends all the way up the scale from the most fundamental building blocks of the material world to the highest expressions of material complexity. And within all of matter there is a mathematical precision that simply staggers the imagination.

Galileo said in 1623 that the universe "cannot be understood unless one first learns to comprehend the language and interpret the characters in which it is written. It is written in the language of mathematics and its characters are triangles, circles, and other geometric figures, without which it is humanly impossible to understand a single word of it."[21]

It was Galileo who reportedly said, "Mathematics is the language with which God wrote the universe." But often it is only the physicists with their complex mathematical skills and training who experience the exhilaration of penetrating and marvelling at the mysteries of the mathematical universe.

THE MATHEMATICAL ORDER OF NATURE

Before we explore the mathematical order of the quantum world any further, let's return briefly to the order of the molecular biological world. We have suggested that it is the mathematical order of the universe that gives rise to its *orderly function*. We see this extraordinary order in the interior world of the living cell. A protein molecule, for example, functions the way it has been designed and programmed to function. Our cells are full of countless millions of highly intelligent protein molecules that maneuver around the interior world of the cell with great purpose and mechanical dexterity.

These protein molecules have recently been likened to miniature molecular machines that behave exactly like advanced technological machines that have been programmed to perform numerous complex functions. "Wetware" is the term that has been coined to describe cellular and biological mechanisms that resemble the operational complexity of computer software. This unfathomable complexity has led scientist Dennis Bray to recently release a book titled *Wetware: A Computer in Every Living Cell*.

At the time of Charles Darwin, the earliest microscopes revealed a disappointing vision of the cell. It was nothing more than a tiny black dot that mysteriously self-replicated into two tiny black dots. But as technology has advanced, the interior world of the cell is beginning to be revealed in all of its glorious complexity. The new vision of the cell is nothing short of astonishing.

Michael Denton, a molecular biologist, is more familiar with the cell than most people, spending much of his life staring down an electron microscope. He suggests that the interior life of a single cell resembles the complexity of a city!

> To grasp the reality of life as it has been revealed by molecular biology, we must magnify a cell a thousand million times until it is twenty kilometres in diameter and resembles a giant airship large enough to cover a great city like London or New York. What we would then see would be an object of unparalleled complexity and adaptive design. On the surface of the cell we would see millions of openings, like the port holes of a vast space ship, opening and closing to allow a continual stream of materials to flow in and out. If we were to enter one of these openings we would find ourselves in a world of supreme technology and bewildering complexity. We would see endless highly organised corridors and conduits branching in every direction away from the perimeter of the cell, some leading to the central memory bank in the nucleus and others to assembly plants and processing units. The nucleus itself would be a vast spherical chamber more than a kilometre in diameter, resembling a geodesic dome inside of which we would see all neatly

stacked together in ordered arrays, the miles of coiled chains of the DNA molecules. A huge range of products and raw materials would shuttle along all the manifold conduits in a highly ordered fashion to and from all the various assembly plants in the outer regions of the cell.

We would wonder at the level of control implicit in the movement of so many objects down so many seemingly endless conduits, all in perfect unison. We would see all around us, in every direction we looked, all sorts of robot-like machines. We would notice the simplest of the functional components of the cell, the protein molecules, were astonishingly, complex pieces of molecular machinery, each one consisting of about three thousand atoms arranged in highly organised 3-D spatial conformation. We would wonder even more as we watched the strangely purposeful activities of these weird molecular machines. We would see that nearly every feature of our own advanced machines had its analogue in the cell: artificial languages and their decoding systems, memory banks for information storage and retrieval, elegant control systems regulating the automated assembly of parts and components, error fail-safe and proof-reading devices utilised for quality control, assembly processes involving the principle of prefabrication and modular construction. In fact, so deep would be the feeling of *deja-vu*, so persuasive the analogy, that much of the terminology we would use to describe this fascinating molecular reality would be borrowed from the world of late twentieth-century technology. What we would be witnessing would be an object resembling an immense automated factory, a factory larger than a city and carrying out almost as many unique functions as all the manufacturing activities of man on earth. However, it would be a factory which would have one capacity not equalled in any of our own most advanced machines, for it would be capable of replicating its entire structure within a matter of a few hours. To witness such an act at a magnification of one thousand million times would be an awe-inspiring spectacle."[22]

The orderliness of nature is nowhere more clearly revealed than in the complex function of the molecular machines inside the cell. There are two main kinds of molecules in the cell: the protein molecules and the nucleic acids that carry genetic information. Nucleic acids constitute both the DNA molecules and the messenger RNA molecules. Messenger RNA (mRNA) molecules functions with an extraordinary intelligence as they enter the nucleus of a cell in search of a highly specific section of DNA code somewhere amongst the six gigabytes of coherent genetic information.

Somehow this molecule knows exactly where it is going and exactly what it is looking for. It functions for all intents and purposes as a microcomputer that has been programmed to locate a specific section of code in order to make an exact "photocopy" of that piece of code. The mRNA then transports this strand of replica code to the ribosome where it is "read" and "translated" into the coherent assembly of a sequence of hundreds of amino acids that ultimately constructs a brand new protein molecule. This level of intelligent programming continues from a sub-cellular level right down to a quantum level. Because sub-atomic quanta are designed with a specific purpose and function, they also carry intelligible information in both the function and pattern of their own existence.

Cells are made of molecules and the molecules within the cell are composed primarily of oxygen, carbon, hydrogen and nitrogen. Water molecules (H_2O) make up approximately 65% of the cell. There are four major biopolymers in the cell: the proteins, the nucleotides, the carbohydrates and the lipids. The protein molecules are made of amino acids which in turn are made of oxygen, carbon, hydrogen and nitrogen plus a trace of sulphur. The nucleic acids, (the DNA and RNA molecules), are similarly made of the four same elements plus a trace of phosphorus. Carbohydrates are made of almost equal parts of carbon, hydrogen and oxygen whilst lipids (or fats) are made of carbon, hydrogen and a trace of oxygen. Most of what constitutes the cell consists of four different kinds of atoms.

Just as the protein molecules and the mRNA molecules within the cell function with an intelligent purpose and a specific goal, so do the atoms that constitute the molecules. Within the atom there is evidence of advanced intelligence in the complex construction of the atom and in the ability of these atoms to bond with certain other atoms to construct the molecules necessary for the fabrication of matter and life. An atom on its own is useless unless it bonds with other atoms to form matter, but why an atom bonds with specific atoms is a mystery. There is a direct parallel between the bonding of the nucleic acids and the amino acids in the cell and the bonding of atoms to form molecules.

Nucleic acids and amino acids are both biochemical compounds made up of a cluster of bonded atoms. The function of protein and DNA molecules are encoded into the molecules themselves so that they are intelligent molecules. The entire cell is full of countless millions of intelligent molecules all functioning exactly as they have been programmed by God to function and all interacting with one another with extraordinary grace and skill.

The interior life of the cell is a magnificent dance of divine order and meaning. Every molecule interacts with every other molecule as though each one knows exactly what it is supposed to do next. This same degree of sophistication and intelligent programming extends to the very atoms that make up the intelligent molecules.

No matter where we look in observing nature we see this same pattern of seemingly intelligent molecules and atoms behaving as though they know exactly what they are doing. If you were to interrupt them and ask them what they are doing they would not be able to explain their pre-programmed behaviour to you, but leave them to go on their merry way and you would observe them behaving with all the attributes of intelligence as they bond with their compatriots and function the way they are programmed to function.

It is extremely difficult to escape the conclusion that everything in the physical universe carries information in the form of programming so that it functions the way it was designed to function. This is why intelligent physicists describe the universe as a giant quantum computer at the sub-atomic level. It is no different to the argument that the cell behaves as a microcosmic super-computer complete with its information rich library of genetic material which functions as the blueprint for building every single living thing.

Max Planck was one of the greatest physicists of the 20th century. He is widely regarded as the founder of quantum mechanics. Because of his many contributions to the early development of quantum physics he was awarded the Nobel Prize for physics in 1918. In a speech titled "The Nature of Matter" presented in Florence, Italy, in 1944 he made a startling comment concerning the relationship between intelligence and matter:

> As a man who has devoted his whole life to the most clear headed science, to the study of matter, I can tell you this much as a result of my research about atoms: There is no matter as such. All matter originates and exists only by virtue of a force which brings the particle of an atom to vibration and holds this most minute solar

system of the atom together. We must assume behind this force the existence of a conscious and intelligent Mind. This Mind is the matrix of all matter.[23]

Planck was perhaps unwittingly pointing toward the reality of the mind of God who has mysteriously programmed all of the building blocks of matter to come together in a glorious symphony of extraordinary intelligence. Information is the product of mind, not of pure random chance. The billions of atoms that constitute the genetic code within the nucleus of the cell mysteriously come together to construct a highly sophisticated biological library of coherent, intelligent data.

Six gigabytes of genetic information self-replicates in the space of one and a half hours! It is estimated that the DNA double helix strands of just one cell are made of approximately 150 billion atoms all held together through the mystery of atomic bonding. Wherever we study life at a molecular level, we are confronted not only by intelligent design but also by pre-programmed intelligent, operational behaviour.

Max Planck suggested that the quantum world points toward the existence of a superior intelligent Mind in which "this Mind is the matrix of all matter." Lothar Schafer, the distinguished professor of physical chemistry at the University of Arkansas agrees. He says,

> In the quantum phenomena, we have discovered that reality is different from what we thought it was. Mental principles – numerical relations, mathematical forms, principles of symmetry – are the foundations of order in the universe, whose mind-like properties are further established by the fact that changes in information can act, without any direct physical intervention, as causal agents in observable changes in quantum states.[24]

Schafer is of course pointing to the "observer effect," which is the interference of consciousness upon the quantum wave, causing it to collapse into a materialised state. Schafer is the author of *In Search of Divine Reality*, in which he highlights the "mind-like" properties of the non-local quantum world. At the heart of this mind-like reality we discover the role of mathematics in ordering the material world all the way up from the very foundation of quantum reality. "At the foundation of reality, we find numerical relations – non-material principles – on which the order of the universe is based."[25]

Schafer continues, "The mind-like properties of the background of reality are also suggested by the fact that its order is determined by principles of symmetry, abstract mathematical patterns, to which the constituents of the material world have to conform."[26] Schafer confidently proposes that the quantum world, from which the material world exists, has distinct mathematical properties. "Probability waves are empty in that they carry no energy or mass. Numerical relations are their exclusive contents."[27] In order to draw out the fascinating properties of these quantum waves, Schafer contrasts the properties of electromagnetic waves with quantum waves:

> Light waves are electromagnetic waves, oscillating electric fields correlated with oscillating magnetic fields and they need no medium. They can travel through empty space. Quantum waves are not only non-material – needing no material medium to propagate – but in addition they are empty. Light waves can travel in empty space but they carry energy. Quantum waves also exist in empty space but carry no energy or any other mechanical quantity. They are simply numbers, numerical relations.[28]

The idea that quantum waves are nothing more than numbers or mathematical entities waiting to come into materialisation is a fascinating thought. Professor Schafer does not propose this idea lightly. The precise and consistent properties of quantum particles must be derived from some source. Charles Seife, in his book, *Decoding the Universe: How the New Science of Information Is Explaining Everything in the Cosmos,* writes, "The mysteries of quantum mechanics become much less mysterious – once you believe that information creates the structure of space and time."[29] Seife proposes that information is the key that gives definition to the mathematical properties of a quantum particle.

In his famous work called the *Timaeus*, Plato proposed that atoms are mathematical forms. He said, "Numbers are the highest degree of knowledge." Above the entrance to his academy was written, "Let no one ignorant of mathematics enter here." Plato taught that the material world was not the real world but a mere shadow of the real world.

He proposed that the world of matter reflected a deep mathematical order and beauty that was an expression of something transcendent and divine. He contrasted the "visible world" of nature with the "intelligible world" of "forms" that were unchanging and eternal. Plato linked the mind and "reason" with the "intelligible world" whilst the mortal body was linked to the visible world. Plato believed that mathematics was the purest link between the human soul and the world of the divine.

Throughout history many great philosophers and thinkers have concluded that there is a higher reality that is expressed through the universal perfection of mathematics which is an expression of some sort of consciousness that permeates the universe. Sir Arthur Stanley Eddington, the famous English astrophysicist, said, "To put the conclusion crudely – the stuff of the world is mind-stuff...and the substratum of everything is of mental character."[30]

Schafer concludes that "By every molecule in our body we are tuned to the mind-stuff of the universe."[31] From the perspective of biblical revelation we understand that the universe is ultimately a creation that emerges from the mind of God and that the entire creation can be understood through the language of mathematics. Schafer sought to develop the relationship between "mind-stuff" and matter in the light of quantum mechanics.

> The electrons in atoms are not tiny particles, little balls of matter, but they are standing waves, wave patterns or mathematical forms. We owe to Max Born the discovery that the nature of these waves is that of probability waves. Probabilities are dimensionless numbers. Probability waves are empty; they carry no mass or energy, just information on numerical relations. The basis of the order of the material world is non-material. In contemporary physics such conclusions were unexpected, but they are not new. Pythagoras already thought that "all things are numbers" and he claimed that "the harmony of the cosmos is based on the ratios of numbers." But what are probabilities? Ratios of numbers![32]

MATHEMATICS: DISCOVERED OR INVENTED?

For millennia there has been a debate over whether mathematics is discovered or invented. The platonic view of mathematics considers it to be something that is both objective, certain and true throughout the entire universe. This view maintains that pre-existent mathematical truths can be discovered through the skill and the intuition of the mathematician who is then able to explain the beauty of what he or she has discovered by writing it down in the form of complex formulas and equations.

The question as to whether mathematics is invented or discovered is the central philosophical issue surrounding the science of mathematics. The title of Stephen Hawking's brilliant history of mathematical thought, *God Created the Integers,* reflects the notion that mathematics is something which is discovered rather than invented. Mathematics is a product of nature. It occurs throughout the entire universe and it can be quantified and explained by the unique language of mathematics.

Many mathematicians are struck by the beauty of mathematics. Paul Erdos, the brilliant Hungarian mathematician once said, "Why are numbers beautiful? It's like asking why is Beethoven's Ninth Symphony beautiful. If you don't see why, someone can't tell you. I know numbers are beautiful. If they aren't beautiful, nothing is."[33] Ian Stewart, in his book, *Why Beauty is Truth,* argues that the discovery of mathematical attributes such as symmetry, which have been discovered to exist all the way down to the quantum world, point to an intrinsic beauty that reflects the *objective reality* of mathematics throughout the Universe.

It was John Keats who once wrote, "Beauty is truth; truth beauty." In the same vein the American poet, Edna St. Vincent Millay wrote, "Euclid alone has looked on Beauty bare." Euclid, of course was the famous Greek mathematician who is remembered as the "Father of Geometry." For over 2,000 years, Euclidean geometry was the only kind of geometry that existed. To look upon the geometry of the natural world is to look upon an exquisite form of beauty and, according to the philosophy of mathematical realism, it is to look upon discoverable truth. Mathematical realism maintains that mathematical entities exist independently from the human mind.

Einstein once said, "The human mind is not capable of grasping the Universe. We are like a little child entering a huge library.... The child knows that someone must have written those books. It does not know who or how. But the child notes a definite plan in the arrangement of the books – a mysterious order which it does not comprehend, but only dimly suspects."[34]

As we begin to explore the library it becomes evident that there are complex mathematical patterns that exist throughout the entire physical world. The universe is, in fact, a massive library of mathematical information that awaits our discovery. Sir Roger Penrose, the brilliant English mathematical physicist said, "There is something absolute and 'God-given' about mathematical truth....In my own mind, the absoluteness of mathematical truth and the Platonic existence of mathematical concepts are essentially the same thing."[35]

The proposal that all mathematics is merely an invention of the human mind is a reflection of the secular worldview that emerged at the Enlightenment. We live in a world of glorious natural beauty that conceals an equally elegant spectrum of precise mathematical properties. The more we discover about our universe the greater the awe and wonder that it inspires in our hearts. Calvin Clawson is a mathematician and the author of *Mathematical Mysteries: The Beauty and Magic of Numbers*. He speculates that if numbers are "purely objects of human thought, then why do they correspond so strikingly to the physical universe?"[36]

This is an excellent question! It is as though mathematics is the *discoverable* language of the universe. The universe can be decoded numerically and nature's numbers are descriptive of realities that have existed for aeons prior to the appearance of human beings who are uniquely endowed with the intellectual ability to measure and comprehend the mathematics of the Universe. As scientists have endeavoured to decode the universe, it has become evident that the mathematical fine tuning of the universe is so precise that it would appear that nature's numbers have been deliberately predetermined by a brilliant mathematical genius.

FINE-TUNING NATURE'S NUMBERS

The English astronomer, Sir Fred Hoyle, upon examining the evidence for the fine-tuning of the mathematics and the physics of the universe, famously commented that it appeared as though a "super-intellect has monkeyed with the physics"[37] of the universe. Professor Paul Davies said, "There is for me powerful evidence that there is something going on behind it all... It seems as though somebody has fine-tuned nature's numbers to make the Universe. The impression of design is overwhelming!"[38]

In *Nature's Numbers: the Unreal Reality of Mathematics*, author Ian Stewart writes, "The simplest mathematical objects are numbers, and the simplest of nature's patterns are numerical. In addition to numerical patterns, there are geometric ones. [And these] mathematical shapes can always be reduced to numbers."[39] The discovery of these mathematical patterns throughout nature is one thing; the discovery of the exquisite fine-tuning of these numbers is an entirely different phenomena.

The evidence for the fine tuning of the physics of the universe is absolutely overwhelming. Astrophysicists keep on discovering new features of the physics of the cosmos that strengthen the argument that we are living in the "just-right universe." The universe is extraordinarily fine-tuned mathematically and the attributes of the universe can be precisely measured by exact mathematical ratios and equations. In *The Creator and the Cosmos*, Christian author, Professor Hugh Ross documents in extraordinary detail the evidence for the mathematical fine-tuning of the Universe.

With the emergence of advanced technology, astrophysicists are now able to literally "measure the cosmos" and ascribe precise mathematical measurements to all of the physical constants of the universe. We will explore some of these constants in a moment, but first we need to define what we mean by "constants." In *The Constants of Nature*, Professor John D. Barrow, the English theoretical physicist, discusses what he calls "the numbers that encode the deepest secrets of the Universe." He says,

> There are aspects of the fabric of the Universe which are mysterious in their unshakeable *constancy*. There is a golden thread that weaves a continuity through nature. It leads us to expect that certain things elsewhere in space will be the same as they are here on earth. The constants of nature encode the deepest secrets of the Universe.[40]

These constants are everywhere throughout the Universe, but most notably they are discoverable in the constants inside the quantum field. There are constants in the four fundamental forces of physics: the strong nuclear force constant, the weak nuclear force constant, the gravitational force constant and the electromagnetic force constant. These constants are all mathematically determined. Similarly, there are constants in the mass of all sub-atomic particles just as there are constants in the mathematical relationship between these particles. These are called "coupling constants."

The quantum field exhibits an extraordinarily high degree of mathematical balance and harmony. If the four constants themselves were slightly weaker or slightly stronger the universe could not exist because even the slightest variation in one constant would have a cascading impact on the other constants so that their ratios would be thrown into chaos.

We would not be here to speculate on what an alternative mathematical universe would look like because, in all likelihood, there would not be a universe if it were not exactly as it is mathematically! Big bang cosmologists point out that our big bang was the just right big bang because if the mathematical and physical constants of the Universe were not precisely predetermined, the big bang would have immediately imploded in upon itself! It is as though the conditions of the laboratory were perfectly prepared before the scientific test was conducted.

Consider just how fine-tuned the physics of the universe really is. If the constant of the gravitational force were even minutely weaker or stronger by just 0.1 part per million, the universe would not exist! Because the ratio of one constant to another is even more fine-tuned, a slight variation in the gravitational constant would send a cascading effect throughout the fabric of the cosmos such that our universe could not possibly come into being!

For example, the ratio between the gravitational constant and the electromagnetic constant is fine-tuned to one part in 10^{40} which is an unimaginably fine degree of cosmic mathematical tuning! Professor Hugh Ross commented that, "The list of finely tuned characteristics for the universe continues to grow. The more accurately and extensively astronomers measure the universe, the more finely tuned they discover it to be. The degree of fine tuning is utterly amazing!"[41]

So far approximately three dozen unique mathematical parameters of the fine tuning of the universe have been discovered and, as we have pointed out, each of these constants exercise a profound influence upon the other constants. It seems as though the mathematics of the universe had to be perfectly balanced and figured out before the universe could even be created!

The astrophysical community has been inducted into a body of scientific knowledge concerning the fine tuning of the Universe that leaves little alternative to the viewpoint of intelligent design. Dr. Paul Davies, author of *God and the New Physics* wrote, "The laws of physics seem themselves to be the product of exceedingly ingenious design."[42]

As a further example of these constants within the quantum field we will consider what has been called the "fine structure constant." This is a fundamental physical constant that defines the strength of the electromagnetic interaction within the atom. It has been mathematically determined to be 1/137.035999070. In 1985 Richard Feynman made the following comments concerning the fine structure constant:

> It has been a mystery ever since it was discovered more than fifty years ago, and all good theoretical physicists put this number up on their wall and worry about it. Immediately you would like to know where this number for a coupling comes from: is it related to π or perhaps to the base of natural logarithms? Nobody knows.

It's one of the greatest damn mysteries of physics: a magic number that comes to us with no understanding by man. You might say the "hand of God" wrote that number, and "we don't know how He pushed His pencil."[43]

Hugh Ross makes the following observation about the exquisite precision of the electromagnetic force constant:

For life to be possible, more than forty different elements must be able to bond together to form molecules. Molecular bonding depends on two factors, the strength of the force of electromagnetism and the ratio of the mass of the electron to the mass of the proton. If the electromagnetic force were significantly larger, atoms would hang on to electrons so tightly no sharing of electrons with other atoms would be possible. But if the electromagnetic force were significantly weaker, atoms would not hang on to electrons at all, and again, the sharing of electrons among atoms, which makes molecules possible, would not take place. If more than just a few kinds of molecules are to exist, the electromagnetic force must be more delicately balanced yet.[44]

Another example of the fine-tuning of the constants within the quantum field is the precision of the measurement of the strong nuclear force constant. Again, Hugh Ross writes:

In the case of the strong nuclear force – the force governing the degree to which protons and neutrons stick together in atomic nuclei – the balance is easy to see. If this force were too weak, protons and neutrons would not stick together. In that case, only one element would exist in the universe, hydrogen, because the hydrogen atom has only one proton and no neutrons in its nucleus. On the other hand, if the strong nuclear force were of slightly greater strength than what we observe in the cosmos, protons and neutrons would have such an affinity for one another that not one would remain alone. They would all find themselves attached to many other protons and neutrons. In such a universe there would be no hydrogen, only heavy elements. Life chemistry is impossible without hydrogen; it is also impossible if hydrogen is the only element. How delicate is the balance for the strong nuclear force? If it were just 2% weaker or 0.3% stronger than it actually is, life would be impossible at any time and any place within the universe.[45]

For the universe to produce all the stars and planets necessary to explain the possibility of earth sustaining physical life, the value of the cosmic mass density must be fine-tuned to better than one part in 10^{60} and the value of the space energy density to better than one part in 10^{120}. In the words of Lawrence Krauss and many other astrophysicists, this one part in 10^{60} and 10^{120} is by far the most extreme fine-tuning yet discovered in physics.[46]

All astrophysicists are deeply aware of this exquisite fine-tuning of nature's numbers. It is the task of the astrophysical community to understand, to measure, and to attempt to explain the precise mathematical attributes and the laws of the universe. Hugh Ross makes the following observation:

> In all my conversations with those who do research on the characteristics of the universe, and in all my readings of articles or books on the subject, not one person denies the conclusion that somehow the cosmos has been crafted to make it a fit habitat for life. On the issue of the fine-tuning or careful crafting of the cosmos, the evidence is so compelling that I have yet to hear of any dissent.[47]

Hugh Ross also observes that, "The discovery of this degree of design in the universe is having a profound theological impact upon astronomers."[48] As we have already noted, Professor Paul Davies concedes that "the laws [of physics] ... seem themselves to be the product of exceedingly ingenious design."[49] The American physicist and cosmologist, Robert Jastrow explains the theological implications for the discovery of this degree of fine-tuning in the universe.

> For the scientist who has lived by his faith in the power of reason, the story ends like a bad dream. He has scaled the mountains of ignorance; he is about to conquer the highest peak; as he pulls himself over the final rock, he is greeted by a band of theologians who have been sitting there for centuries.[50]

Professor Robert Griffiths, the American physicist who in 1984 was awarded the Heinemann Prize in Mathematical Physics, once said, "If we need an atheist for a debate, I go to the philosophy department. The physics department isn't much use!"[51]

GOD IS THE ULTIMATE MATHEMATICIAN!

There are many compelling reasons for believing that there is a mathematical order to the universe that is imposed upon us by the divine mathematician who figured out all the precise mathematical formulas before He created the universe. The IBM mathematician, Clifford Pickover, writes in his book, *The Loom of God*, "I do not know if God is a mathematician, but mathematics is the loom upon which God weaves the fabric of the universe."[52]

The famous mathematician, Paul Erdos, idiosyncratically spoke of what he called *The Book*. In this metaphorical "book" God had written down the best and most elegant mathematical proofs. Whenever Erdos discovered a beautiful mathematical proof he would exclaim, "This one's from *The Book*!"[53]

From a biblical perspective there is compelling evidence that God did in fact create the integers. According to the Bible, nature is a revelation of God. Interestingly, God placed ten fingers on our two hands and ten toes on our two feet. That fact alone should tell us something about the mathematical mind of God and the origins of the base-ten decimal system, which is also evident throughout the Scriptures. As we turn to the Bible itself, which is a glorious revelation of the mind of God, we find a world of whole numbers,[54] ratios and fractions.[55] There are over 150 references to arithmetic and geometry in the Bible.

Both Noah's ark and the Ark of the Covenant were built according to the dimensions of the golden section or ϕ (phi).[56] Phi is an irrational number (1.6180...) We will talk more about this amazing number in the next chapter! Solomon made a bronze laver for his temple using the formula for π (pi). "He made the Sea of cast bronze, ten cubits from one brim to the other; it was completely round. Its height was five cubits, and a line of thirty cubits measured its circumference." (1 Kings 7:23) Pi is an irrational number (3.14159...) and is the ratio of a circle's circumference to its diameter.

God also seems to have some favourite numbers that occur frequently throughout the Bible, most notably 1, 3, 4, 7, 10, 12, 40, 50, 70, 120, 144, 400, 1,000, 1,290, 144,000, etc. God clearly loves numbers. He constructed the universe on sound mathematical principles so that we could experience the joy and wonder of discovering the complex mathematics that undergirds the very fabric of the cosmos. The Russian theoretical physicist, Alexander Polyakov, who was awarded the Heinemann Prize for Mathematical Physics in 1986, said,

> We know that nature is described by the best of all possible mathematics because God created it. So there is a possibility that the best of all possible mathematics will be created out of physicists' attempts to describe nature.[57]

It is the sheer elegance and the beauty of mathematics that inclines so many people toward the platonic idea that there is an order to nature that is both objective and discoverable and which reflects the perfection of something which is truly transcendental. The universe is indeed a message written in a code, and that code is unquestionably mathematics. It is indeed God who breathes "fire into the equations!"

The fact that we human beings can contemplate these realities is equally as staggering. When we consider the fact that the entire universe is the product of highly complex mathematical information, it is as though we are brought face to face with the reality of a supremely intelligent and all powerful God who smiles over human beings as they gaze into the mystery.

Gerald Schroeder, the Israeli physicist, released a book titled *The Hidden Face of God* in 2001. The thesis of his book is that the entire universe is undergirded by a mathematical beauty that points toward an intelligent designer whom he identifies as God. He skilfully argues that the essence of this mathematical quality behind our universe is, in fact, information which is, in turn, a property of the mind of God.

> That all existence may be the expression of information, an idea, a quantum wave function, is not fantasy and it is not some flaky idea. It's mainstream science coming from such universities as Princeton and M.I.T. There is the growing possibility that for all existence, we humans included, there's nothing, nothing as in "no thing," there. The world is more a thought than a thing.[58] It took humanity millennia before an Einstein discovered that, as bizarre as it may seem, the basis of matter is energy, that matter is actually condensed energy. It may take a while longer for us to discover that there is some non-thing even more fundamental than energy that forms the basis of energy, which in turn forms the basis of matter. John Archibald

Wheeler likened what underlies all existence to an idea, the "bit" (the binary digit) of information that gives rise to the "it," the substance of matter. If we can discover that underlying idea, we will have ascertained not only the basis for the unity that underlies all existence, but most important, the source of that unity. We will have encountered the hidden face of God![59]

The Copenhagen Interpretation of quantum mechanics proposes that unobserved quantum realities do not have any intrinsic attributes of their own. Advocates of this viewpoint propose that outside of the collapse of a wave function there is nothing that actually "exists." Nick Herbert tells us that "the Copenhagenists believe that when an electron is not being measured, it has no definite dynamic attributes. The Copenhagenists claim, not that such attributes are meaningless but that they are non-existent!"[60]

However, whenever a quantum reality is observed or measured, it collapses the wave function and materialises with consistently observable mathematical properties. This single fact ought to compel us toward the idea that unobserved quantum realities do have an independent existence, but that their properties are more akin to mathematical ideas that carry information. Schroeder suggests that "Every particle...appears to be an expression of information."[61]

The mathematical beauty embedded throughout nature has profound metaphysical implications, leading many metaphysicists to incorporate the ubiquitous presence of mathematics, or what they sometimes call "Sacred Geometry" into their spiritual worldview, as we will see in the next chapter. New Agers in particular, gaze wistfully into the mathematical mysteries of Sacred Geometry, seeking answers to the meaning and significance of the universe and our place in it.

Chapter Nine

GOLDEN PHYSICS AND QUANTUM GEOMETRY

We concluded the previous chapter with a brief introduction to the hottest issue in the philosophy of mathematics. Is mathematics discovered or invented? This is a debate that has raged for thousands of years. There are two opposing schools of thought in this debate, and both viewpoints appear ultimately to be shaped by opinions about God.

Those of an atheistic persuasion gravitate toward the view that mathematics is purely an invention of the human mind as mathematicians seek to create a language and rules to explain the structure of the universe. This is not to say that atheistic mathematicians do not see an extraordinary order and beauty to mathematics. Bertrand Russell [1872-1970] is an excellent example of a mathematician and a philosopher who appreciated the beauty of mathematics. Russell was a devout atheist and the author of *Why I am not a Christian*. Nevertheless he could say,

> Mathematics, rightly viewed, possesses not only truth but supreme beauty – a beauty cold and austere, like that of sculpture, without appeal to any part of our weaker nature, without the gorgeous trappings of painting or music, yet sublimely pure, and capable of a stern perfection such as only the greatest art can show. The true spirit of delight, the exaltation, the sense of being more than Man, which is the touchstone of the highest excellence, is to be found in mathematics as surely as poetry.[1]

Even the most devout atheist and secularist can still appreciate the beauty of mathematics without reaching any specific ontological conclusions. However, there are many who see in nature some kind of veiled signpost that points inexorably to an intelligence or consciousness that undergirds and gives shape to the entire mathematical structure of the universe.

This camp obviously includes monotheists who believe in the existence of a personal God but it also includes agnostic scientists like Stephen Hawking who speak of the "mind of God" and New Age metaphysicists who reject the notion of a personal God yet embrace the idea of a mysterious "divine consciousness" that inexplicably permeates the whole of creation. As a thoroughly convinced theist, there is no doubt which camp I fall into. I am fully persuaded that there is compelling evidence to support the existence of God and this is clearly the thesis that permeates this entire book. Definite mathematical patterns can be uncovered throughout the whole of nature and these patterns are a powerfully compelling evidence for the mathematical brilliance of the mind of God.

The goal of this chapter is to trace one specific mathematical pattern that has been detected from the quantum field all the way up to the spiral galaxies that are sprinkled throughout the universe. This specific pattern has been called the "Divine Proportion," the "Golden Section," the "Golden Mean" or the "Golden Ratio." Wherever we look in the developmental transitions from quarks all the way up to macroscopic objects we can discern the role that this unique mathematical pattern plays in the building blocks of nature.

The building blocks of complex living beings are cells; the building blocks of cells are molecules. The building blocks of molecules are atoms and the building blocks of atoms are protons, neutrons and electrons. However as we study matter at smaller and smaller scales we find that the building blocks of protons, neutrons and electrons are things such as quarks and leptons. Anything smaller than this scale is purely theoretical, but the most popular contender in the quest for a "theory of everything" has been string theory. As we journey through a survey of matter from the smallest scale to the largest conceivable scale we continually run into the Divine Proportion! This ought to be front page news but, regrettably, it is a fact understood by very few people.

Quantum Physics and the Divine Proportion

We have seen that there is a mathematical beauty that interpenetrates all of nature and this phenomenon deepens the mystery of intelligent self-ordering matter. Some readers may already be familiar with the "Golden Section" and the Fibonacci numbers which reveal a staggering mathematical harmony in nature's geometry that is deeply embedded throughout the construction of all matter. For millennia some of the greatest mathematicians and philosophers have marvelled at the mathematical patterns that permeate all of nature.

How is it that atoms can mysteriously come together to build molecules and molecules can come together to build matter with these same mathematical patterns that exist all the way up from quarks to solar systems? Why is there a mysterious mathematical relationship between the sub-atomic "parts" and the "whole" of the human body? There is such an intrinsic aesthetic beauty in the ratios and proportions found in nature that the mathematical monk, Luca Pacioli, first used the term *Divine Proportion* in the 15th century to describe this phenomenon. He wrote a book under the same title that was beautifully illustrated by Leonardo Da Vinci, who is credited with the conception of the term *Golden Section*.

The exact mathematical proportion of the Golden Section has a specific number and that is ϕ, pronounced "fye." Mario Livio, the author of *The Golden Ratio*, considers ϕ to be the "world's most astonishing number." In his fascinating book he has a chapter titled, "Is God a Mathematician?" Livio is inclined toward the view that "God is indeed a Mathematician."[2] He is compelled toward this conclusion because there are certain mathematical miracles that have been *discovered* that clearly exist independently of the human mind. He writes,

> To claim that mathematics is purely a human invention...ignores some important facts in the nature of mathematics. First, while the mathematical rules (e.g., the axioms of geometry or of set theory) are indeed creations of the human mind, once those rules are specified, we lose our freedom. The definition of the Golden Ratio emerged originally from the axioms of Euclidean geometry; the definition of the Fibonacci sequence from the axioms of the theory of numbers. Yet the fact that the ratio of successive Fibonacci numbers converge

to the Golden Ratio was *imposed* upon us – humans had no choice in the matter. Therefore, mathematical objects, albeit imaginary do have *real* properties.[3]

As we explore this divine pattern in nature it strengthens the conviction that God is the author of nature and that His mathematical signature can be found everywhere in His creation. Remember that nature itself is a revelation of God and that all of nature declares the glory of God. King Solomon was fascinated by the wisdom of God embedded in nature. He said, "It is the glory of God to conceal a matter, but the glory of kings is to search out a matter." (Proverbs 25:2) "He composed some 3,000 proverbs and wrote 1,005 songs. He could speak with authority about all kinds of plants...He could also speak about animals, birds, reptiles, and fish." (1 Kings 4:32-33 NLT)

Solomon was intrigued by the revelation of God in nature! If he were alive today we might speculate that he would be fascinated by the divine proportion in nature. There are deep mysteries concealed in the heart of matter that only highly advanced technologies are capable of probing at the deepest level. We are living in an era when scientists are discovering nature's secrets all the way down to the quarks and the leptons that make the sub-atomic particles within the atom and, amazingly, the same mathematical patterns are emerging within the quantum field!

The Golden Section describes a ratio or geometric proportion that reveals a definite mathematical pattern in nature. Plato revelled in this mathematical beauty. He showed his students that there were many points along the line that would result in even ratios that would produce a simple fraction. But there was a certain uneven point along that line where the ratio of the whole line to the longer proportion equals the ratio of the longer proportion to the shorter proportion. This point on the line produces a Golden Section. The uneven ratio is the same at 3:5, 5:8, 8:13, 13:21, etc.

Mathematically, this irrational golden number is 1.6180339...which is called "phi" and is symbolised by the Greek letter ϕ. Its inverse number is 0.6180339...which is $1/\phi$. Phi is $(1 + \sqrt{5})/2$. Plato demonstrated that this seemingly random "golden" proportion appears ubiquitously throughout nature as a naturally recurring mathematical phenomenon.

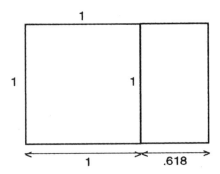

This golden number is not something contrived by bored mathematicians. It occurs not only in linear lines but also in geometric shapes. The Golden Ratio is an expression of mathematical beauty that has been discovered in the proportions and angles within squares, rectangles, triangles, pentagons, pentagrams and spirals that are all based on φ and this pattern is readily discoverable in all sorts of natural phenomena from nautilus shells to pine cones to the arrangement of sunflower seeds.

Wherever we look in nature, this golden number magically appears. This same ratio occurs in the so-called "Fibonacci numbers" that reveal a curious numerical sequence that has been discovered by mathematicians. These numbers were known to the ancient Egyptians and the ancient Greeks. Scott Olsen, in his enlightening book, *The Golden Section: Nature's Greatest Secret*, describes this mysterious sequence of numbers.

> Nature widely expresses the Golden Section through a very simple sequence of whole numbers. The astounding Fibonacci number series, 0, 1, 1, 2, 3, 5, 8, 13, 21, 34, 55, 89, 144, 233, 377…is both additive, as each number is the sum of the previous two, and multiplicative, as each number approximates the previous number multiplied by the Golden Section. The ratio becomes more accurate as the numbers increase. Inversely, any number divided by its smaller neighbour approximates φ. Each Fibonacci number is the approximate geometric mean of its two adjacent numbers.[4]

The Golden Section and the Bible

This numerical and geometric pattern is not contrived. It is readily discoverable in nature. It was called the "Divine Proportion" precisely because it appears to be a trademark of God's handiwork in nature. Its ubiquity in nature suggests that it is God's mathematical signature. A study of the Bible reveals that this number was definitely not unknown to God. The Golden Ratio is evident in God's instructions to Noah to build the Ark in a 3:5 ratio. "And this is how you shall make it: The length of the ark shall be three hundred cubits, its width fifty cubits, and its height thirty cubits." (Genesis 6:15) All in perfect divine proportion!

The Ark of the Covenant, which was intended to host the localised presence of God on earth, was also designed according to the Golden Ratio. "You shall make a mercy seat of pure gold; two and a half cubits shall be its length and a cubit and a half its width." (Exodus 25:17) Similarly the altar of the tabernacle was designed on the same 3:5 ratio. "You shall make an altar of acacia wood, five cubits long and five cubits wide – the altar shall be square – and its height shall be three cubits." (Exodus 27:1) As further evidence of divine design the proportion of the Old Testament to the New Testament is also an approximate 3:5 ratio.[5] In addition to this, the dimensions of the New Jerusalem in the book of Revelation reveal a perfect ϕ ratio.

> One of the seven angels...said to me, "Come, I will show you the bride, the wife of the Lamb." And he carried me away in the Spirit to a mountain great and high, and showed me the Holy City, Jerusalem, coming down out of heaven from God. It shone with the glory of God, and its brilliance was like that of a very precious jewel, like a jasper, clear as crystal. It had a great, high wall with twelve gates, and with twelve angels at the gates. On the gates were written the names of the twelve tribes of Israel. There were three gates on the east, three on the north, three on the south and three on the west. The wall of the city had twelve foundations, and on them were the names of the twelve apostles of the Lamb. The angel who talked with me had a measuring rod of gold to measure the city, its gates and its walls. The city was laid out like a square, as long as it was wide. He measured the city with the rod and found it to be 12,000 stadia in length, and as wide and high as it is long. He measured its wall and it was 144 cubits thick, by man's measurement, which the angel was using." (Revelation 21:9-17 NIV)

The total area of the New Jerusalem is 12,000 x 12,000 stadia[6] = 144,000,000 square stadia. The thickness of the walls of the New Jerusalem was 144 cubits. 144 is the 12th Fibonacci number in the Fibonacci sequence. 144 is the only square number in the entire sequence. 144 is a product of phi: $\phi^{12} / \phi + 2$. The total area of the city was $\phi^{12} / [\phi + 2] \times 10^6$.

Interestingly, the angel measured the city with a *measuring rod of gold*. Could this golden measuring rod be a divine measure? One thing is certain; God is the author of the Golden Ratio and this mathematical signature appears not only in His written Word but also in the revelation of God throughout nature. This biblical fact coupled with the revelation of the Golden Ratio throughout nature ought to arrest our attention!

We are all familiar with the first verse of John's gospel: "In the beginning was the Word..." (John 1:1) The Greek word "Logos" is translated as "Word," however in ancient Greek culture the word "logos" was also closely associated with the concepts of "logic" and "ratio,"[7] both of which are related to mathematics.

The ancient Greeks practiced "Isopsephy" which is a Greek word to describe the practice of adding up the numerical values of the individual letters in a Greek word to give a single number. Each Greek letter was attributed a numerical value. Scott Olsen points out that "By the science of Gematria,[8] the name Jesus sums to 888,[9] Christ is 1480,[10] and the two together = 2368. These are in the Golden proportion 3:5:8, with Christ the Golden Mean."[11]

Even the name "Jesus Christ" is a perfect Golden Ratio of the "Word." Some might think this is stretching things too far, but remember that God Himself revealed to the apostle John that the "number of the beast" was "666." This lends credibility to the Hebrew practice of Gematria and the Greek practice of Isopsephy which attributed numerical values to both Hebrew and Greek letters.

> "He also forced everyone, small and great, rich and poor, free and slave, to receive a mark on his right hand or on his forehead, so that no one could buy or sell unless he had the mark, which is the name of the beast or the number of his name. This calls for wisdom. If anyone has insight, let him calculate the number of the beast, for it is man's number. His number is 666." (Revelation 13:16-18 NIV)

GOLDEN PHYSICS

Part of the mystery of the Golden Section is the relationship of the lesser parts to the whole. Nature doesn't occur randomly. There is an internal structure to nature that can be detected on every level. Frequently the smaller parts mirror the whole. David Bohm, one of the great physicists of the 20th century, was preoccupied with the relationship between what he called the hidden "implicate order" and the outer "explicate order" which revealed the way in which matter made explicit something which is already implicit in the quantum realm.

"Bohmian mechanics" reflects Plato's concept of the two worlds: as above, so below. Commenting on this relationship Bohm said, "The essential feature of quantum interconnectedness is that the whole universe is enfolded in everything and that each thing is enfolded in the whole."[12] According to Bohm, matter is nothing more than the "excitation on the virtual sea of the implicate order."[13]

Perhaps more than any other 20th century physicist, Bohm ventured deeply into metaphysics in his personal quest to understand the very essence of physical reality. As matter comes into existence it reveals a pre-existent intelligence and order that has always existed as the *optimum mathematical formulae* for the structure of the atom and for the building of complex molecules.

We are about to delve into some complex mathematical concepts which may not appeal to every reader. Even if you are not particularly fond of mathematics, I would like to take the opportunity to strongly encourage you to read this section carefully. The additional effort required to grasp these concepts is highly rewarding. My own opinion is that this material is an absolutely mind-blowing revelation of God's creative genius! As we noted earlier, Dr. Stephen Marquardt points out that, "All physics is math."[14]

Many of the greatest physicists have also been some of the world's greatest mathematicians. Few of them are ignorant of the significance of the Golden Section. Dating right back to Plato, Euclid and Pythagoras, even the ancient mathematicians marvelled at the Golden Section. Alexey Losev, the brilliant Russian philosopher said, "From Plato's point of view, and generally from the point of view of all antique cosmology, the universe is a certain proportional whole that is subordinated to the law of harmonious division; the Golden Section."[15] Staring into the rabbit hole of the Golden Section is so extraordinary that each new discovery invites us to go even deeper. Referring specifically to what he called the "Golden Proportion of the Ancient Greeks," Richard Feynman exclaimed, "What miracles exist in mathematics!"[16] What miracles indeed!

Now, this is where the real fun begins. As scientists continue to probe the heart of the quantum world the mysterious golden ϕ proportion seems to reappear again and again. In fact, the "Golden Section" has yielded significant discoveries when it has been used as a tool to explore the mathematics of the quantum world. Alexey Stakhov and Boris Rozin argue that, "It is impossible to imagine future progress in physical and cosmological research without a consideration of the Golden Section."[17] They point to a string of recent extraordinary scientific breakthroughs that have occurred as a result of probing nature through the prism of the Golden Section. They conclude that,

> These discoveries give reason to suppose that the Golden Section may be a kind of "metaphysical knowledge" or "universal code of nature," which could become the foundation for the future development of science, in particular, mathematics, theoretical physics, genetics, and computer science. It seems that the dramatic history of the Golden Section, which has continued over several millennia, may conclude with a great triumph for the Golden Section in the beginning of the 21st century.[18]

Remember the words of Heinz Pagels, the author of *The Cosmic Code: Quantum Physics as the Language of Nature,* who said, "I think the universe is a message written in a code, and the scientists' job is to decipher that code."[19] All current cutting edge scientific research points in the direction of the Golden Section being a major part of this universal code of nature. In previous decades mathematicians and quantum physicists have arrived at theoretical approximations of the mass, weight and size of sub-atomic particles through rigorous proofs and mathematical equations. However, many of these calculations are undergoing revision by a number of quantum physicists as they re-evaluate these calculations in the light of the Golden Section.

One example is the estimate of what is called the "Planck length." This is the smallest measurable length in quantum physics and has been determined as 1.6160×10^{-35}m. According to Brian Greene this is the "size of a typical string in string theory."[20] Some scientists are now re-calculating the Planck length as 1.6180×10^{-35}m and allowing all subsequent calculations to be based on this figure as a more accurate representation of the actual Planck length.[21] This, of course, is $\phi \times 10^{-35}$m.

But that is just the tip of the iceberg. The adoption of the Golden Mean as an interpretative model for measurements within the quantum field is beginning to yield some extraordinary discoveries. Some of the discoveries are nothing short of remarkable, leading a number of excited physicists to declare that traditional quantum field theory needs to be replaced with a new "Quantum Golden Field Theory." So let's explore the field of "quantum geometry" to see what mathematical marvels it reveals.

QUANTUM GOLDEN FIELD THEORY

Professor Mohammad El Naschie, a brilliant Egyptian theoretical physicist, made an extraordinary scientific breakthrough when he discovered the role of ϕ in determining the actual mass of sub-atomic particles. He noted that his theoretical values [see chart], determined as a direct product of ϕ, were almost identical to the experimental values previously determined by quantum physicists. According to Scott Olsen, in his discussion of what he calls "Golden Physics," El Naschie has provided "a profound theoretical basis for the central role the Golden Section plays as the 'winding number' in the harmonic manifestation of quark and sub-atomic particle masses."[22]

According to El Naschie, when particle physics is seen through the eyes of ϕ it becomes "a cosmic symphony" wherein the particles themselves "are a rather non-complex function of the Golden Mean and its derivatives."[23] In his own words, his recalculation of electron, neutron, proton and quark masses in light of ϕ is "in excellent agreement with the majority of the scarce and difficult to obtain data about the mass of quarks. It takes only one look at these values for anyone to realise that they form a harmonic musical ladder."[24] "Seen through the eyes of the golden mean renormalization groups, the mass spectrum of high energy particles resembles a non-linear dynamical symphony where everything fits with everything else. We could start virtually anywhere and derive everything from everything else."[25]

Sub-Atomic Particle	Φ Value	Theoretical Value
Electron	$\sqrt{(10\phi^2)}/10$	0.51166 *MeV*
Neutron	$20\phi^8$	939.574 *MeV*
Proton	$20\phi^8\cos(\pi/60)$	938.28 *MeV*
Up Quark	$2\phi^2$	5.236 *MeV*
Down Quark	$2\phi^3$	8.472 MeV
Strange Quark	$10\phi^6$	179.442 *MeV*
Charm Quark	$300\phi^3$	1,260.82 *MeV*
Beauty Quark	$10^3\phi^3$	4,236.067 *MeV*
Truth Quark	$10^4\phi^3$	2,360.679 *MeV* [26]

The most important thing to note in the table above is that each sub-atomic particle exhibits attributes of the Divine Proportion or the Golden Section. El Naschie explains that "the appearance of the Golden Mean... indicates that it is the simplest realistic unit from which [we] can start developing a highly complex structure."[27] According to El Naschie, inside the quantum field, "The Golden Mean plays a decisive role!"[28] El Naschie published his initial discoveries in a 1994 paper titled *Is Quantum Space a Random Cantor Set with a Golden Mean Dimension at its Core?*

El Naschie proposes that the quantum field is actually structured upon the mathematics of the Golden Section and that this optimum mathematical formula is the key to unlocking the deeper mathematics of the quantum field. The miracle of his discovery is that all of his ϕ-based mathematical equations actually predict precise values of sub-atomic particles that converge upon the values that have already been determined by physicists through other scientific experiments and calculations without reference to the Golden Mean! El Naschie calls his new theoretical paradigm the "E-infinity theory."

In a 2008 research paper titled "An Outline for a Quantum Golden Field Theory," El Naschie proposed that "Conventional quantum field theory may be advantageously reformulated in terms of a Golden Mean based number system."[29] It is becoming increasingly apparent that this so-called "Golden Mean number system" which is so pervasive throughout nature, appearing all the way from the sub-atomic world to the structure of our solar system and even to the structure of spiral galaxies, is in fact the number system that God has used to build the entire structure of the material universe. El Naschie discusses the significance of this newly emerging number system.

> Mathematics in some views is nothing but a good system of notations. Somewhat analogously, physics is highly affected by a good or lucky choice of physical units. If all this is true and it is to a large extent true, so what about the role played by "number systems" in mathematical physics? The answer is really simple as it is definite: if notations and units are important, the number system we are using is crucial. In fact it is almost everything.[30] It is virtually impossible to imagine our modern scientific achievement and the resulting vast technological progress if we would not have had the good sense of

replacing the Roman number system by our present decimal system based on Arabic numbers.[31]

At the commencement of the 21st century, physicists and mathematicians are discovering the fundamental role the Golden Mean plays in the structure of matter and this suggests the emergence of an entirely new number system that proposes a new fundamental unit of measurement because of its ubiquitous appearance throughout the world of physics.

According to El Naschie, "The remarkable success of E-infinity Cantorian space-time theory in solving many highly complicated problems in high energy physics may be traced back to the fact that the theory unconsciously has introduced a new number system to physics."[32] This new number system, of course, is the Golden Mean number system which represents what El Naschie describes as "the beginning of what Scott Olsen has called 'Golden Physics.'"[33] El Naschie continues,

> The Golden Mean and the Golden Mean based number system upon which Quantum Golden Field Theory is based is anything but mystical. Looking at organic forms for instance as well as many mathematical facts, one finds the Golden Mean because a Golden Mean based theory is simply the simplest and most perfect. This is visible everywhere on the macroscopic level. For the micro cosmos on the other hand, and in an even more profound way, the Golden Mean seems to dominate in every rational mathematical modelling because it is the very principle upon which nature has constructed itself.[34]

Professor El Naschie bases his proposal for the existence of a "Quantum Golden Field Theory" upon rigorous mathematical calculations. All the mathematics is laid out in paper after paper. "Quantum Golden Field Theory possesses an ultra-high degree of symmetry which is manifest in various ways. This is particularly clear in the coupling constants as well as the mass spectrum."[35]

The convergence of El Naschie's theoretical outcomes with existing experimental data concerning the known mass of sub-atomic particles and the coupling constants of particles within the quantum field are so precise that El Naschie gives the following challenge: "The result is exact and the reader is strongly advised to follow the standard analysis and perform the detailed calculations to judge and ascertain for himself what a Golden Mean harmonization could do."[36]

All of the mathematical computations are laid out for his readers to compare the conventional theoretical outcomes with the new outcomes of the Quantum Golden Field Theory. "Before giving our exact Quantum Golden Field Theory result, we reproduce first the result obtained using conventional quantum field theory. Nothing could speak for the simplicity and exactness of our theory more than to contrast the [conventional] computation with ours using the Quantum Golden Field Theory."[37]

I am not a mathematician but it is evident through a survey of the calculations that the results are indeed compelling, especially when the original approximations are renormalised using the Golden Mean based number system. The conclusion is staggering! The Golden Mean is the mathematical formula that the entire quantum field is structured upon! Mario Livio, author of *The Golden Ratio*, calls φ the "world's most astonishing number!" He made this observation before any of these facts concerning the Quantum Golden Field Theory had come to light. These newest discoveries make this number even more astonishing!

The Ukrainian mathematician, Professor Alexey Stakhov, is a world authority on the subject of the Golden Section. He is the author of *Mathematics of Harmony* which is the product of over four decades of study of the Golden Section. In a paper titled "Fundamentals of a New Kind of Mathematics," he said, "Feynman expressed his admiration of the Golden Proportion in the following words: "What miracles exist in mathematics!"[38]

Stakhov's many papers document the development of what he calls "Harmony Mathematics" from Plato, Euclid and Pythagoras all the way to El Naschie. He notes the contribution of the American mathematician, George Bergman, who at the age of 12 published a paper in 1957 titled "A Number System with an Irrational Base." Bergman said, "I have developed a system that is based, not on an integer, or even a rational number but on the irrational number otherwise known as the Golden Section."[39] Little did Bergman know that this new number system would be the key to unlocking the mathematics of the quantum world!

The unfolding marvels of Quantum Golden Field Theory do not end with a new number system. This new model of the quantum field even proposes to resolve the mystery of the quantum interference pattern in the double-slit experiment. According to Stakhov, "Prominent theoretical physicist Mohamed El Naschie is a world leader in the field of the Golden Mean applications to theoretical physics, in particular, quantum physics. El Naschie's discovery of the Golden Mean in the famous physical two-slit experiment – which underlies quantum physics – became a source of many important discoveries in this area, in particular, the E-infinity theory."[40]

E-infinity theory is an emerging model of quantum space-time, based specifically upon the mathematics of the Golden Mean. I have included an explanation of El Naschie's E-infinity Cantorian space-time model in the **Appendix** for readers with an appetite to explore how this new model has evolved and exactly how it is founded upon Golden Ratio mathematics. The **Appendix** also expands upon the relationship between the Golden Mean and the famous double-slit experiment and the wave/particle duality.

SACRED GEOMETRY

Some readers may already be aware that certain sectors of the New Age community take tremendous interest in the metaphysical implications of the extraordinary mathematical patterns that exist throughout the entire universe. "Sacred Geometry" is the name given to a field of study where science and spirituality powerfully intersects in Western culture. Not all New Agers are attracted to the sciences but those who are inevitably become fascinated by nature's numbers and the unique geometry and "Divine Proportions" found throughout nature.

Sacred Geometry is really a spiritual expression of mathematics and geometry that delights in every single geometric and mathematical pattern found in nature. As we might anticipate, the Golden Section is centre stage in every book and every piece of literature on the theme of the geometry of nature. New Agers are absolutely fascinated by the Golden Section. Sacred Geometry seeks to plumb the depths of the Divine Proportion throughout nature and it inevitably leaves an indelible impression of intelligent design.

Sacred Geometry venerates every kind of pattern that exists in nature. The New Age community claims to be the sole authority on the theme of Sacred Geometry. They claim the exclusive right to interpret nature to the world because they have spent more time than anybody else exploring the wonders of these seemingly "divine" patterns. As seekers of the truth they are moving toward an awareness of a strong element of design in nature but, as long as they doggedly adhere to a pantheistic worldview, they consistently fail to see even the most compelling evidences of mathematical and geometric design in nature as the evidence of the fingerprints of a personal God.

Instead they postulate the existence of a Universal Mind wherein the element of design is a reflection of some sort of expression of ambiguous universal consciousness. In spite of their pantheistic interpretation, those who have explored the wonders of Sacred Geometry have done us all a great service in bringing to light what is really a powerful argument for the existence of an Intelligent Designer.

Not all who are aware of Sacred Geometry are inclined toward the conclusions that a Christian would arrive at when exposed to the amazing discoveries of the geometry of the natural world. In fact, Sacred Geometry has traditionally been the domain of the occult. Freemasonry places a significant emphasis upon geometry and numbers. The famous symbol of Freemasonry is a compass and a square. The architecture of Freemasonry reveals their fascination with the mystical power of symbols and geometric structure.

Similarly the wider occult community shares this fascination with Sacred Geometry. Both satanists and neo-pagans have adopted the symbol of the pentagram. The five-pointed star is regarded as a symbol of magical or occultic power. The pentagram is built upon the Golden Ratio and was once used by the early Christian community until it was adopted by the occult community and infused with occult significance.

The iconic status of Sacred Geometry in the occult community has caused many within the Christian community to reject the discipline altogether rather than seeing it as a reflection of God's creative genius within nature. However, there is a strong revelatory thread woven into the science of Sacred Geometry that greatly glorifies the Creator. So let's continue our exploration of God's geometry.

MOLECULAR GEOMETRY

Beyond the field of quantum geometry another area of study in the broader field of Sacred Geometry is the geometry of the atomic and the molecular world. Atoms and their sub-atomic particles are the building blocks of molecules. When atoms bond with each other they bond at precise geometric angles to form a molecule. It is this complex three-dimensional geometric assembly of atoms that gives rise to the "mass" that constitutes matter. A complex material object is nothing more than the assembly of billions of atoms all arranged geometrically in an interlocking assembly of atoms.

The study of the geometric structure of molecules is called "Molecular Geometry." Carbon, hydrogen, nitrogen and oxygen are the four most common atoms in the human body. The atoms of a water molecule, for example, (which consists of two atoms of hydrogen and one atom of oxygen) bond at approximately 108° in relation to one another. According to Olsen, the bonding of the atoms that constitute the building blocks of life "all have internal bond angles which approximate the internal 108° angle of a penta-gon."[41] Olsen notes that "The prevalence of natural pentagonal forms may result from the symphony of golden relationships in the pentagon."[42] These golden relationships reveal the role that ϕ exercises in atomic bonding.

Olsen observes that "The Golden Section plays a fundamental role in the structure of 3-D space."[43] As we have already noted, a molecule is an ordered geometric assembly of atoms. Atoms bond together with other atoms through either *ionic* (electrostatic) bonds or *covalent* bonds in which the electrons that orbit the atomic nuclei are shared between atoms. In complex molecules, large numbers of atoms bond together to form complex geometric configurations. For example, carbon, one of the most common constituents of life molecules, can bond with many other carbon atoms.

C_{60} forms a perfect icosahedron which is a geometric structure with 20 faces and is structured as a direct product of ϕ.[44] The icosahedron is one of the five Platonic Solids where all angles are the same, where all faces are identical and all sides are equal. Three Platonic Solids, in particular, exhibit extraordinary ϕ ratios. The octahedron (8 faces), the dodecahedron (12 faces) and the icosahedron (20 faces) all exhibit compelling properties of the Golden Section.

The geometric structure of a molecule ultimately determines the function of the molecule. Atoms often bond with one another according to the Fibonacci sequence. A good example of this pattern is seen in uranium oxide compounds: U_2O_5, U_3O_8, U_5O_{13}, U_8O_{21} and $U_{13}O_{34}$.[45] A similar pattern exists in chromium oxide: Cr_2O_5, Cr_3O_8, Cr_5O_{13}, Cr_8O_{21}. These are all

Fibonacci sequences that, of course, are the product of φ. Even in the order of molecular sequencing we find the Golden Section!

The most significant molecules are life molecules because they are the building blocks of all living things. One of the most fascinating features of these microscopic molecules is their ordered complexity. How do they carry out such complex biological processes? No-one really knows. Much of the activity within the cell revolves around the interaction between the nucleic acids (DNA molecules) and the amino acids (protein molecules). I was absolutely fascinating to discover that φ plays an important role in the structure of both DNA and protein molecules. Like the many atoms that they are made of, DNA nucleotides are also structured upon the same golden ratio![46]

DNA is a helical or spiral structure based upon the unique chemical sequencing of self-organising nucleic acids. There are four basic nucleic acids that form into long chain molecules: adenine (A), guanine (G), cytosine (C) and thymine (T). The genetic code is based upon the bonding between these four chemical compounds and the sequence in which they appear. The actual geometric structure of DNA measures 34 angstroms long by 21 angstroms wide for each full cycle of its double helix spiral and again, these are Fibonacci numbers. [34/21 = φ].

A cross sectional view of the double helix viewed from the top forms a decagon which is, in essence two pentagons. "Each spiral of the double helix must trace out the shape of a pentagon."[47] God has designed this self-replicating pattern for carrying many gigabytes of critical genetic information. Encoded within the DNA molecule is the blueprint for the construction of countless protein molecules and their complex function within the cell.

Professor M. Rakocevic, the author of *The Genetic Code as a Golden Mean Determined System,* explains how the Fibonacci sequence is found throughout DNA. "For the first time it is shown that the genetic code, as a binary code, is determined by the Golden Mean through the unity of the binary-code tree and the Farey tree."[48] It has now also been firmly established that the Golden Mean ratio is responsible for the construction of amino acids into protein molecules.[49] Professor Chi Ming Yang writes,

> The majority of the 20 amino acids selected in the genetic code are naturally selected by a double-Golden Mean. A pronounced similarity exists between the Lucas series (a numerical basis of the

Golden Mean) and amino-acid side-chain carbon-atom numbers, presumably suggesting that the amino acids selected into the genetic code system seems to follow the natural Golden Mean by the Lucas series, when the 20 amino acids in the genetic code system are viewed as a whole.[50]

An additional feature of protein molecules is the role that φ plays in the molecular geometry of amino acid chains. As protein molecules are built from a specific sequence of amino acids the backbone of their geometric structure is built on what are known as "phi (φ) and psi (Ψ) bonds."[51] These terms indicate the mathematical angles at which amino acids bond and once again φ plays a critical role. It is now evident that from the sub-atomic scale to the molecular scale there is a definite mathematical relationship wherein the Divine Proportion fractalises throughout the atomic and molecular world. A "fractal" is a fraction of the whole where an attribute of the whole is retained in every part.

THE GOLDEN RATIO IN THE HUMAN BODY

Further up the scale there is evidence of the Divine Proportion in all of nature from countless plants, to shells, to insects, to the human body, to the solar system all the way up to spiral galaxies! The Golden Section is ubiquitous throughout the universe. Large volumes have been written on this subject and space does not allow us to explore this theme in any depth. We will focus exclusively on the human body as our example of the way in which the Golden Section is evident in the proportions of nature.

Our bodies are full of the Divine Proportion. The length of the forearm from the elbow to the tip of the finger exhibits φ [5:13] proportions divided at the wrist.[52] Scott Olsen notes that "The three bones of each of your fingers are in golden relationship."[53] We have two hands with five fingers with three sections in each finger [2:3:5]. This is a Fibonacci sequence. The shape of our ear is designed on a perfect φ spiral just like the nautilus shell. The side view of the human head and the frontal view of the human face all exhibit φ proportions. Good proportion is essential to the perception of beauty. The "perfect" face has perfect φ values. The sheer mathematical beauty of the quantum world ultimately manifests in the beauty of nature throughout all of creation.

The Golden Section can also be readily detected in the dimensions and proportions of the teeth, the lips and the mouth. Perfect φ dimensions have now become the template for orthodontic corrections just as φ is the template for cosmetic surgery to the face.[54] The structure of the entire human body is based on the Golden Section,[55] famously illustrated by Da Vinci in the *The Divine Proportion*. Scott Olsen observes that, "The journey from child to adult also contains another surprise: a baby's navel is at its midpoint and its genitals occur at the golden point, but when fully grown these reverse, as an adult's midpoint is at the genitals with the navel approximating the Golden Section."[56] It seems as though the Golden Section shows up everywhere in the human body.

These extraordinary patterns, (such as φ) are all an expression of quantum information. Scientists who are pioneering the development of quantum computers are convinced that atoms function as carriers of information with each atom behaving like a "bit" of conventional computer information. Quantum bits are called "qubits." Because they contain information they also communicate information. "As the computation proceeds, reality unfolds," says Seth Lloyd. As the reality of our universe unfolds through atoms, molecules and ultimately complex expressions of matter like you and I, we see that equally complex mathematical patterns persist at every level of reality. Seth Lloyd writes,

> The universe is the biggest thing there is and the bit is the smallest possible chunk of information. The universe is made of bits. Every molecule, atom, and elementary particle registers bits of information. Every interaction between those pieces of the universe processes that information by altering those bits. That is, the universe computes, and because the universe is governed by the laws of quantum mechanics, it computes in an intrinsically quantum-mechanical fashion; its bits are quantum bits. The history of the universe is, in effect, a huge and ongoing quantum computation. The universe is a quantum computer. As it computes, the universe effortlessly spins out intricate and complex structures.[57]

The intricate and complex structures that the quantum universe effortlessly spins out are none other than the mathematical attributes of the Golden Mean. How else can we find any rational explanation for the ubiquity of the Golden Mean from the sub-atomic world to the macroscopic world of nautilus shells, pine cones, sunflower seeds all the way through to the human body? Seth Lloyd points out that mathematical information has a distinct physical expression.

Harald Weiss and Volkmar Weiss are the authors of a brilliant paper titled, *The Golden Mean as Clock Cycle of Brain Waves*. Their research reveals that:

> The principle of information coding by the brain seems to be based on the Golden Mean. This insight that the measurement of any physical quantity and quality is based on repetitions of the Golden Mean, opens an astounding variety of possibilities to encode and decode information in the most efficient way. With this property the brain can use simultaneously the powers of the Golden Mean and the infinite Fibonacci word (synonymously called the golden string, the golden sequence for coding and classifying.) Every positive integer can be a sum of Fibonacci numbers; it can also be understood as a finite sum of positive and negative powers of the Golden Mean. There can be no doubt that our brain uses for computing, inherent and inborn properties of the physical universe.[58]

Harald Weiss and Volkmar Weiss have discovered that brainwaves have a fundamental harmonic of 2ϕ. Their research implies that "all other harmonics are infinitesimals or multiples of ϕ, including the resonant frequencies which are powers of $2\phi/2$. Even more, the brain can use powers of the Golden Section or the infinite Fibonacci word for its coding."[59] This discovery has profound implications for information theory. Already, computer scientists use the Fibonacci sequence for complex programming. "Computer Scientists like the Fibonacci sequence because it is a good example of something that can be programmed easily using what is known as *recursion*. Recursion just means you define something using a simpler version of itself."[60]

These natural ϕ recursions are God's signature throughout all of nature. God has written ϕ into the code of the physical universe and we are living in a time when the knowledge of the Golden Section throughout nature is exploding. Scott Olsen calls the Golden Section "Nature's greatest secret" but really it is God's greatest secret encoded into the entire universe as a compelling evidence of divine design. Remember the words of Heinz Pagels, the author of *The Cosmic Code: Quantum Physics as the Language of Nature.* "I think the universe is a message written in a code, and the scientists' job is to decipher that code."[61] The code has been deciphered, and it is $\phi = 1.61803398875$.

We have only touched the surface in exploring the Golden Section in nature. A deeper study is a tremendously rewarding experience. The concept of fractals is helpful to understand the mathematical relationship found at the core of all matter. The term "fractal" was coined by Benoit Mandelbrot in 1975 to define the property of *self-similarity* in geometry. Studying nature through the lens of fractals helps us to see how the mathematical properties of the human body can fractalise into cells, how cells can fractalise into molecules, how molecules fractalise into atoms and how atoms fractalise into quantum particles with the same mathematical ϕ proportions expressed throughout.

What is so remarkable is that these complex mathematical patterns are discernable from the sub-atomic level all the way up to our macroscopic level of existence and beyond into the cosmic scale so that these mathematical patterns continually illustrate the relationship between the whole of reality and its lesser parts. The Golden Mean has fractal properties that continue infinitely. These properties are revealed in the Golden Rectangle which forms a perfect Golden Spiral that spirals in upon itself infinitely. [See images].

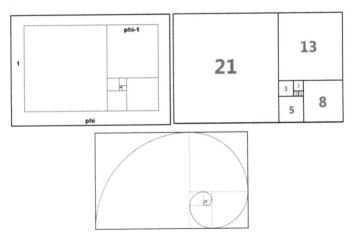

How is it that a non-local quantum wave can materialise into a solid particle with perfect ϕ proportions and this same mathematical signature ascends the scale of matter all the way from the micro cosmos to the macro cosmos? As we focus upon one of the great mysteries of the universe we are brought face to face with the revelation of the mathematical mind of God as it manifests in His creation.

The Scriptures reveal that nature itself is a revelation of God and that nature is the visible manifestation of the very mind of God. "For since the creation of the world God's invisible qualities – His eternal power and divine nature – have been clearly seen, being understood from what has been made, so that men are without excuse." (Romans 1:20 NIV)

The discovery of the role of φ in the quantum field brings us one step closer to a "unified field theory" which has been the holy grail of physics. We are privileged in the 21st century to gaze into a deep and enduring mystery. The human mind is not only *capable*, it is also *designed* to contemplate the mind of God. We were created to contemplate the mystery of our own creation and to discover the evidence for the mind of God that permeates all of creation. This continuing quest explains the enduring fascination of Sacred Geometry. It is indeed "sacred" because it points us to God.

QUANTUM "MIND-STUFF"

If anything, the ubiquity of the Golden Mean throughout nature helps us to come to terms with the mind-like nature of ultimate reality. In the previous chapter we quoted Sir Arthur Stanley Eddington, the famous English astrophysicist, who said, "To put the conclusion crudely – the stuff of the world is *mind-stuff*... and the substratum of everything is of mental character."[62]

Lothar Shafer highlights the mystical convergence between what he calls the "mind-like background of the universe"[63] and the human mind. This "mind-like background" is expressed mathematically and its beauty can only be fully appreciated by intelligent beings who have been endowed with the intellectual capacity to understand the complex mathematical equations that describe the fabric of the cosmos. According to Lothar Shafer:

> That the basis of the material world is non-material is a transcription of the fact that the properties of things are determined by quantum waves, – probability amplitudes which carry *numerical relations*, but are devoid of mass and energy. In the quantum phenomena we have discovered that reality is different than we thought. Mental principles – *numerical relations, mathematical forms, principles*

of symmetry are the foundations of order in the universe.[64] In the quantum phenomena, mind turns into matter.[65] By every molecule in our body we are tuned to the mind-stuff of the universe.[66]

Quantum physicists are driven by a quest to discover the ultimate nature of physical reality. As they continue to probe the atom and its sub-atomic building blocks they are stumbling upon deeply compelling evidence for divine design even at a quantum level. For millennia, scientists and mathematicians have marvelled at the miracle of the Divine Proportion appearing throughout creation on a macro scale.

That the Golden Mean should now be discovered at the very heart of the atomic world ought not to surprise us. It is further evidence that we live in a universe laden with metaphysical signposts that inexorably point us to the very source of creation itself: an omniscient, omnipresent, and omnipotent Divine Being who has left His fingerprints and His signature all over creation so that those with an inquisitive mind may stumble upon the glorious evidences of His intelligent design and turn to Him in awe and worship.

New Age metaphysicists gaze into the mystery of the sacred geometric structure of nature at the macro level and at the quantum level, but even their greatest thinkers and exponents of the marriage between quantum physics and New Age mysticism lack a penetrating understanding and explanation of the actual mechanism of the creation of the universe.

The rejection of a personal Creator has left them in a twilight zone where they have a consciousness of the mystery without an understanding of the cause or the means through which the mystery came into being. Their answer is that the universe just exists and we can now study it in greater scientific detail than ever before, yet we have absolutely no idea how it actually came to be the way it is! It just is!

Biblical creationism, on the other hand, gives a solid explanation of the very cause and the means through which the universe came into existence and it all points to a profoundly intelligent, omniscient and omnipotent being who crafted the cosmos in His mind before bringing it into existence through His power. "It is the glory of God to conceal a matter, but the glory of kings is to search out a matter." (Proverbs 25:2)

Through the unfolding revelations of quantum mechanics some scientists are beginning to accept the idea that the ultimate source of the quantum world points toward the existence of a brilliant "mind!" That "mind" is no less than the glorious omniscient mind of the Creator! "Who has known the mind of the Lord?" asks Paul. The precision fine-tuning of nature's numbers, even at the quantum level, reveals the existence of the mind of God.

As we follow the signposts of the greatest discoveries of quantum physics over the past century, they all point inexorably toward the existence of a conscious transcendent Being who has unfathomable intelligence and unimaginable power and who has designed the universe on the solid principles of precision tuned mathematics and physics before bringing it all into existence through His power. The fact that it is all so wonderfully finetuned and that we can study and appreciate the marvel and the wonder of it all causes us to bow down in worship before this awesome Being who created the heavens and the earth as a fit habitation for human beings.

We have been made in the very image and likeness of God and as glorious "image-bearers" we are subsequently endowed with the ability to study and ponder the reason for it all and, in so doing, hopefully find our way back to God. The apostle Paul pointed his audience to the rudimentary evidences of intelligent design 2,000 years ago. He said that God "has not left Himself without testimony." (Acts 14:17 NIV)

The entire creation reveals and displays the glory of God, and the mysterious world of the quantum is a vital part of this divine testimony. The question is: will we read the signposts and humble ourselves before Him or will we exalt our own understanding and become fools? Paul warned that there would be those who recognised the evidence of design but who would nevertheless reject it.

For since the creation of the world God's invisible qualities – His eternal power and divine nature – have been clearly seen, being understood from what has been made, so that men are without excuse. For although they knew God, they neither glorified Him as God nor gave thanks to Him, but their thinking became futile and their foolish hearts were darkened. Although they claimed to be wise, they became fools! (Romans 1:20-22 NIV)

From a biblical perspective the ultimate expression of this descent into foolishness is the rejection of the knowledge of God. "The fool has said in his heart, 'There is no God.'" (Psalm 14:1) God's glory is powerfully revealed in the discoveries of quantum physics. The most up to date discoveries suggest that the consistently perfect mathematical properties of the quantum field reveal the glorious mind of God in His intricate design of nature at the sub-atomic level. The science of quantum physics brings us face to face with the mind of God. If we reject the revelation of divine design that lies at the heart of every single atom we descend into foolishness and futility. The mathematical perfection exhibited in the golden quantum field is one of the most compelling revelations of the glory of God in our physical universe.

There are millions of people in the world who read the same signposts that followers of Christ also read, yet they refuse to take the next step of humility in acknowledging the handiwork of God. Some of them are molecular biologists, some are quantum physicists, some are astrophysicists, some are teachers of Sacred Geometry and some of them are New Age seekers. I would like to encourage everyone who reads this book to take the next step. King David pondered the revelation of the glory of God's creation and said, "Oh, taste and see that the Lord is good; blessed is the man who trusts in Him!" (Psalm 34:8)

Part Two

RESTRUCTURING THE QUANTUM UNIVERSE

In the first part of the book, titled **Mapping the Quantum Universe**, we explored the revelation of the quantum world through the lens of biblical theology. As with the rest of creation, everything that has been discovered in the world of quantum mechanics is, according to the Bible, a revelation of the glory of God. "The heavens declare the glory of God; the skies proclaim the work of His hands. Day after day they pour forth speech; night after night they display knowledge. There is no speech or language where their voice is not heard. Their voice goes out into all the earth, their words to the ends of the world." (Psalm 19:1-4 NIV) Every aspect of creation is ultimately a revelation of the transcendent nature and power of God. This is especially true of the unfolding revelation of the microcosmic quantum world over the past 100 years. "For since the creation of the world His invisible attributes are clearly seen, being understood by the things that are made, even His eternal power and divine nature." (Romans 1:20) The more we learn about the quantum world the clearer the glory of God comes into focus.

Now, as we embark upon the second part of this book, **Restructuring the Quantum Universe**, we will explore the way in which the quantum world can be fundamentally restructured through the supernatural intervention of God. First we will examine how the quantum universe has actually been designed in such a way that it can be hacked into and re-structured through the mind and power of God. We will also explore the vain attempts of humanity to seek to shape the quantum world apart from the power of God. We will conclude this section with a call to recover the biblical mandate to become co-workers together with Christ. Those who are "in Christ" are given the mandate to bring heaven to earth by doing the very works of Christ in supernaturally restructuring the quantum world! In the same vein it is also the mandate of the people of God to accurately interpret the revelation of quantum physics to the world in the light of the integration of this field of science with everything that God has revealed in His Word concerning His authority and power over the quantum universe.

Chapter Ten

QUANTUM PHYSICS AND THE SUPERNATURAL

I am personally fascinated by the supernatural realm. I actually became a follower of Christ as a result of seeing the supernatural power of God manifested in a remarkable healing. I was still a teenager when a handful of friends who had become followers of Christ came over to my house to tell me and my friends about their experience of the love and power of God.

While we were all sitting in the living room a friend who lived in our house had a major seizure whilst taking LSD. He was in the kitchen and he collapsed after a sudden, violent convulsion that resulted in the overturning of tables and chairs. The sound of crashing furniture sent us running into the kitchen to discover that our friend's face had turned completely blue as he lay motionless on the floor. He appeared to have swallowed his own tongue and his airways were blocked. From all appearances he appeared to be dead!

Immediately the visiting Christians did what seemed totally natural to do. They laid hands on the motionless man and commanded him to be healed in the name of Jesus. Within minutes our friend was supernaturally restored. To this day I am still not sure if he had died, but it is entirely possible that my friends and I had witnessed a resurrection from the dead! His recovery was so dramatic that he was no longer tripping on LSD! Instead he was sitting there in his right mind as though nothing had happened. Within minutes the ambulance arrived and the paramedics checked him out but could not find anything wrong with him.

This event took place in 1979. Since that extraordinary experience I have often wondered what the outcome would have been had not a group of supernaturally attuned believers been in our house in this moment of crisis. This event speaks as powerfully to me today about the reality of God as it did three decades ago! I had been sensing the call of God upon my life for many months and the conviction of the Holy Spirit had been intensifying in my heart. This display of raw supernatural power was the tipping point that resulted in me giving my life to Christ at the age of nineteen.

Both the Old and New Testaments are full of remarkable stories just like this that describe the supernatural power of God invading our physical world. Even after God supernaturally created the heavens and the earth, He was still revealed in Scripture as being powerfully active on planet earth. The stories of Old Testament supernatural intervention in human affairs are too numerous to recount. Virtually every book in the Old Testament describes some level of supernatural intervention by God.

Many of the miracles in the Bible contradict the known laws of physics. It would seem that God enjoys overriding conventional laws of physics to reveal His absolute authority over nature and to surprise humans with His supernatural power. In the book of Genesis we read of Enoch, who "enjoyed a close relationship with God throughout his life. Then suddenly, he disappeared because God took him." (Genesis 5:24 NLT) One moment Enoch was present on the earth, the next moment he completely dematerialised!

One of the most striking stories of the violation of physical laws appears in the book of Exodus. "The Israelites went through the sea on dry ground, with a wall of water on their right and on their left." (Exodus 14:22 NIV) Elijah was instantaneously translated into heaven in a fiery chariot that caused him to suddenly disappear from the face of the earth. We are told that Elisha his servant "saw him no more." (2 Kings 2:11-12) There is another story in Second Kings where Elisha the prophet caused an iron axe-head to float to the surface of the Jordan River. (2 Kings 6:5-6)

MATERIALISATION AND DEMATERIALISATION

In addition to the thousands of supernatural healings that Jesus did, there were certain events in the life of Jesus that clearly violated the laws of classical physics. On two occasions in the gospel of John the Jews sought to stone Jesus, but He mysteriously escaped the angry crowd. "Then they took up stones to throw at Him; but Jesus hid Himself and went out of the temple, going through the midst of them, and so passed by." (John 8:59)

The way John describes this event seems to indicate that Jesus *passed through their midst* as though He somehow dematerialised. The second occurrence seems to suggest that the very same thing happened. "Then the Jews took up stones again to stone Him ... they sought again to seize Him, but He *escaped out of their hand.*" (John 10:31,39)

When Jesus preached in His own home town of Nazareth He so infuriated the people in the synagogue that they attempted to murder Him. "So all those in the synagogue, when they heard these things, were filled with wrath, and rose up and thrust Him out of the city; and they led Him to the brow of the hill on which their city was built, that they might throw Him down over the cliff. Then *passing through the midst of them*, He went His way." (Luke 4:28-30)

In each of these events, facing certain death, Jesus literally dematerialised and escaped out of the hand of His adversaries, enabling Him to continue His ministry. God had appointed Jesus to die on the cross; not to be stoned to death by an angry mob. In each instance His life was genuinely threatened by murderous men who were not inclined to let Him slip out of their hands.

Many other events that defied the known laws of physics occurred throughout the life of Jesus. Jesus walked on water and invited Peter to come to Him on the water. "When the disciples saw him, they screamed in terror, thinking he was a *ghost*." (Matthew 14:26 NLT) They did not have a grid for this event. The Greek word they used to describe Jesus was a *phantasma,* from which we derive the English word "phantom."

There are only a handful of possible explanations for the walking on water miracle. One possibility is that Jesus and Peter mysteriously dematerialised so as to appear to be physical beings though weighing nothing so that they could walk on the water. Alternatively, the water was transformed into a solid state so as to be able to sustain two men walking upon its surface. Or, the third possibility was that the water remained a liquid; Jesus and Peter's bodies remained solid, and they experienced a levitation miracle in which they temporarily defied gravity. Whatever occurred that night upon the lake, the laws of classical physics were mysteriously defied!

On a number of occasions Jesus dematerialised His physical body and passed through walls so that He appeared inside rooms with locked doors. There is no doubt that Jesus was resurrected in a physical body. He ate fish with the disciples and Thomas stuck his hands in Jesus' wounds. The disciples told Thomas that they had seen the resurrected Christ, to which he said;

> "I won't believe it unless I see the nail wounds in his hands, put my fingers into them, and place my hand into the wound in his side." Eight days later the disciples were together again, and this time Thomas was with them. The doors were locked; but suddenly, as before, Jesus was standing among them. He said, "Peace be with you." Then he said to Thomas, "Put your finger here and see my hands. Put your hand into the wound in my side. Don't be faithless any longer. Believe!" "My Lord and my God!" Thomas exclaimed. Then Jesus told him, "You believe because you have seen me. Blessed are those who haven't seen Me and believe anyway." (John 20:25-29 NLT)

In this story Jesus clearly dematerialised as He passed through either the locked door or through the walls, and then He rematerialised within the room. One moment He could walk through the walls, the next He was a solid physical being whom Thomas physically handled and felt. Because Jesus is the Lord of the universe He has the capacity to consciously collapse quantum realities into a material state or to instantaneously reverse the process and dematerialise quantum realities back into a superposition so that the quantum realities can tunnel through a wall or a material barrier. We see this divine ability demonstrated, not only in walking through walls but also in many of the miracles that Jesus performed which involved some kind of materialisation or dematerialisation.

In the book of Acts we continue to see miraculous events that defy the laws of physics. Jesus appeared to His disciples for forty days after His resurrection. At the close of this period He was addressing His disciples for the last time.

> It was not long after He said this that He was taken up into the sky while they were watching, and He disappeared into a cloud. As they were straining their eyes to see Him, two white-robed men suddenly stood there among them. They said, "Men of Galilee, why are you standing here staring at the sky? Jesus has been taken away

from you into heaven. And someday, just as you saw Him go, He will return! (Acts 1:9-11 NLT)

This was a levitation miracle that carried Jesus physically into another dimension! Whilst He could have just dematerialised before the disciples' eyes, He chose to exit the planet by physically ascending into the heavenly dimension until He was out of sight; defying the law of gravity and ultimately dematerialising out of the physical plane of existence! In another story that would cause the authors of Star Trek to be green with envy, Philip the evangelist was literally transported from one geographical location to another.

Philip and the eunuch went down into the water and Philip baptized him. When they came up out of the water, the Spirit of the Lord suddenly took Philip away, and the eunuch did not see him again, but went on his way rejoicing. Philip, however, appeared at Azotus and travelled about, preaching the gospel in all the towns until he reached Caesarea. (Acts 8:38-40 NIV)

We are not exactly told whether this was a large scale quantum teleportation miracle or whether Philip was physically carried from one geographical location to another, but the narrative appears to suggest that Philip was instantaneously quantum teleported from one place to another. This would imply that if the Ethiopian eunuch was actually observing Philip at the moment of the miracle he would have seen his body dematerialise right before his eyes. In like manner, someone on the streets of Azotus may have seen Philip suddenly rematerialise. These kinds of strange occurrences were not isolated instances in the lives of the first century people of God. The supernatural powerfully intersected the lives of the early followers of Christ.

Throughout the New Testament we are confronted with a massive upsurge in supernatural activity. The supernatural was continually being released for three years through Christ, who healed thousands upon thousands of people from all sorts of extreme "incurable" physical conditions. In addition to His remarkable authority over disease, Jesus exhibited extraordinary power over nature. He calmed the storm, He walked on water, He turned water into wine, He raised the dead and, on at least one occasion, He commanded healing over a considerable geographical distance when He healed the Centurion's servant. (Luke 7:7) That was quantum non-locality at its best! The Centurion said, "Just say the word from where you are, and my servant will be healed." (Luke 7:7 NLT)

THE DESTRUCTION OF BEAUTY

In Part One of this book we journeyed together through the quantum maze to arrive at a point of clarity concerning the glory that is revealed through the quantum world. Each chapter brought us closer to the realisation that God is the architect of the quantum world and that it is a microcosmic world of elegance, beauty and exquisite fine-tuning for the sustaining of matter and ultimately of life. The Scriptures declare that "He has made everything beautiful in its time." (Ecclesiastes 3:11)

God only makes beautiful things, and the beauty of His creation corresponds to the truth of who God is. Beauty indeed corresponds to truth! We read in the Genesis creation account that "God saw everything that He had made, and indeed it was *very good*." (Genesis 1:31) The Hebrew word for "good" is *towb* and one of the nuances of this Hebrew word is "beautiful."

As God figuratively stepped back from the canvas of creation at the end of the "sixth day," He looked at all that He had made and soaked up the sheer aesthetic beauty of the entire creation. Think of the most glorious high definition image taken by the Hubble Space Telescope and you might catch a fleeting glimpse of the vision of the glory of God's creation that God Himself beheld when He finished creating the heavens and the earth.

In the last book of the Bible, the apostle John was taken into heaven and saw the twenty four elders bowing down in worship declaring, "You are worthy, O Lord our God, to receive glory and honour and power. For you created everything, and it is *for your pleasure* that they exist and were created." (Revelation 4:11 NLT) The incomparable beauty of creation was ultimately brought forth for the pleasure and the enjoyment of God. The angels of God shouted for joy at the creation as they entered into the pure exhilaration and ecstasy of the creative power and mind of God. (Job 38:7)

The beauty of creation is but a dim reflection of the beauty and the glory of the Creator. God is the most beautiful and perfect being in the entire universe. The Bible speaks glowingly of the "beauty of the Lord." (Psalm 27:4, 90:17) God is absolutely beautiful because He is perfect and resplendent in glory. Because God is beautiful, everything He has made is also beautiful because beauty is the trademark of God's creative handiwork. That is why the whole of creation declares and reveals the glory of God. There was a brief season after the initial creation where beauty and perfection characterised everything that God had made. Even Lucifer, the glorious light-bearer appointed as the "covering cherub" over the Garden of Eden was *perfect in beauty* until he fell into the sin of pride.

> You were the perfection of wisdom and beauty. You were in Eden, the garden of God. Your clothing was adorned with every precious stone – red carnelian, chrysolite, white moonstone, beryl, onyx, jasper, sapphire, turquoise, and emerald – all beautifully crafted for you and set in the finest gold. They were given to you on the day you were created. I ordained and anointed you as the mighty angelic guardian. You had access to the holy mountain of God and walked among the stones of fire. You were blameless in all you did from the day you were created until the day evil was found in you. Your great wealth filled you with violence, and you sinned. So I banished you from the mountain of God. I expelled you, O mighty guardian, from your place among the stones of fire. Your heart was filled with pride because of ***all your beauty***. You corrupted your wisdom for the sake of your splendour. So I threw you to the earth and exposed you to the curious gaze of kings. (Ezekiel 28:12-17 NLT)

This once perfect angelic being was so beautiful that he fell into sinful pride, and so began the descent of God's creation into the abyss of death and destruction with all of its attendant ugliness. Lucifer, the resplendent angel who once reflected the glory and beauty of the Lord, had become Satan who is now identified as the Destroyer. His name in Greek is Apollyon, which literally means "the one who destroys." (Revelation 9:11) His self-appointed assignment, according to Jesus, is to "steal, and to kill, and to *destroy*." (John 10:10) This once perfect fallen being is now hell-bent on destroying everything that is beautiful in God's creation. His first mission in the Garden of God was to win the allegiance of Adam and Eve and to convert them to the dark side. The moment Adam and Eve rebelled against God the human race descended into an abyss of sin and destruction.

If Lucifer was in the Garden of Eden before he rebelled against the Lord, we could speculate that there was something about the glorious creation of Adam and Eve in the very image and likeness of God that provoked rebellion in Lucifer. Perhaps it was jealousy because Adam and Eve enjoyed an elevated status above the angelic order of creation. Whatever it was that incited pride and rebellion in the heart of this majestic angel, we understand that he exalted himself and sought to occupy a position that exceeded his divinely ordained status.

How you are fallen from heaven, O Lucifer, son of the morning! You have been thrown down to the earth, you who destroyed the nations of the world. For you said to yourself, "I will ascend to heaven; I will raise my throne above the stars of God; I will sit enthroned on the mount of assembly, on the utmost heights of the sacred mountain. I will climb to the highest heavens and be like the Most High." But instead, you will be brought down to the place of the dead, down to its lowest depths. Everyone there will stare at you and ask, "Can this be the one who shook the earth and the kingdoms of the world? Is this the one who destroyed the world and made it into a wilderness? (Isaiah 14:12-17)[1]

The fall of Lucifer and the subsequent fall of mankind into sin and depravity gave rise to the sudden appearance of an entirely new phenomenon in the universe: *ugliness*. Ugliness is the very antithesis of beauty. Beauty is attractive, it awakens something within us and it entices us, whereas ugliness is repulsive; it repels and drives us away.

We were made to be fundamentally attracted to that which is beautiful and to recoil at that which is deformed and distorted. Satan seeks to destroy everything that is beautiful because it reminds him of God. He has reserved his greatest wrath for human beings because they are the only part of creation that explicitly bear the very image and likeness of God. Everything Satan touches is rendered ugly. His agenda is to render the entire creation ugly, to bring it into agreement with the ugliness that now characterises this tragic dark figure.

Thomas Dubay is the author of *The Evidential Power of Beauty*. His book is a theological reflection on the aesthetics of beauty in science and nature and the intimate relationship between beauty and truth. Because beauty is in some way a reflection of God, it always points us toward the truth. Dubay quotes Richard Feynman who said, "You can recognise truth by its beauty."

Satan seeks to destroy that which is beautiful in order to wipe out the very memory of God from the human heart and to lock humanity into chains of darkness and deception. To do this he must eradicate everything that is beautiful and distort it until it becomes ugly. Thomas Dubay defines beauty as that which has a radiant and splendorous *form* resulting in its aesthetic appeal and loveliness. He contrasts ugliness with beauty:

Strange as it may seem, ugliness can contribute to our appreciation of beauty. Because the "ugly" lacks the unity, proportion and wholeness that radiates splendour, it is, by definition deformed. That is why it is unsightly, twisted, disfigured, even perverted and grotesque. This in turn explains why we find the ugly displeasing, repulsive, hideous, loathsome, all in differing degrees according to the extent of the deformation. The ugly is largely negation; a deprivation of due truth and goodness.[2]

Satan chose to make the physical body one of the major arenas of battle because the human body is the crowning achievement of God's creative power and genius. There are attributes of the human body, such as the brain and its relationship to the mind, that reveal the glory of God in such a way that it staggers the imagination. The organs of the body such as the eyes and the ears are a reminder to the powers of darkness that God sees and hears. So the devil seeks to literally render humanity blind and deaf.

The power of human reproduction is so filled with the glory of God that the devil seeks to render humanity infertile. Every system in the human body reflects the glory of God in a manner that exceeds the glory of every other aspect of creation, because human beings are made in the image and likeness of God. Jesus dignified the human body even further by becoming incarnate in a physical body of flesh and blood.

There is considerable biblical evidence that sickness and disease is regarded as the work of the devil. "For this purpose the Son of God was manifested, that He might destroy the works of the devil." (1 John 3:8) "God anointed Jesus of Nazareth with the Holy Spirit and with power, [and He] went about doing good and healing all who were oppressed by the devil, for God was with Him." (Acts 10:38)

Jesus came to earth and literally declared war on sickness and disease, seeking to overthrow the curse of infirmity wherever He encountered it. Satan had made the physical body an arena of battle by causing disease to enter the human race. Therefore Jesus responded, while He was on earth, by seeking to destroy all of the devil's works. It is part of the very nature of God to heal the sick, and Jesus displayed the Father's heart perfectly in His relentless war upon sickness and disease.

QUANTUM PHYSICS AND THE POWERS OF DARKNESS

At this point we should ask what capacity the devil has to interact with the sub-atomic world. The broader question probes the relationship between the powers of darkness and the material world of nature. Any infiltration into the world of matter is inevitably an infiltration into the world of the quantum, because the quantum realm is the foundation of all physical matter. The satanic kingdom is an invisible spiritual kingdom inhabited by millions, perhaps even billions, of dark spirit beings. Satan is the ruler of this realm of spiritual darkness. Immediately under him are "principalities and powers" and under them are what Paul calls "the spiritual hosts of wickedness in the heavenly realms." (Ephesians 6:12)

The satanic kingdom is an extra-dimensional kingdom that exists in the spirit realm, so this immediately raises the question about Satan's capacity to manipulate the material world. The Scriptures reveal a considerable amount of information about the relationship between Satan and the material realm. God wants us to understand the extent and the boundaries of Satan's capacity to infiltrate and to rule over nature so that we can develop a strategic response to overthrow the works of darkness. We must know our enemy and his capabilities concerning the extent of his supernatural ability to exercise an impact upon the material world.

From the outset we need to establish some biblical truths about God and His relationship to the physical world that He created. From a biblical perspective it must be firmly established that God alone is the Creator. Satan and his demonic hordes **do not** have the capacity to **create** in the quantum world, but they do have the capacity to manipulate, to interfere with and to corrupt matter at a biological level. As we have already seen, Satan is revealed as the "destroyer." Jesus revealed that, "The thief does not come except to steal, and to kill, and to **destroy**." (John 10:10) From what God has revealed in Scripture, it would appear that the powers of darkness have considerable abilities to manipulate matter at a molecular or biological level. But they do not have the ability to create anything.

There is only one being in the entire universe that can actually create new material realities at a quantum level and, of course, that is God. When God speaks His creative word over nature, the quantum world immediately responds and new realities spring into being! But we must acknowledge, on the basis of biblical revelation, that because the devil is an extra-dimensional spirit being he has been granted a limited capacity to manipulate matter at a biological level because he actually exists in another dimension from which the material world can be manipulated. The spirit world has the capacity to impose itself upon the material world but the material world does not have the capacity to impose itself upon the world of spirit, because the dimension of spirit is clearly superior to the dimension of matter. Satan is a spirit being and as such he has the capacity to infiltrate nature and work all manner of counterfeit miracles.

I do not believe that Satan is ultimately capable of violating the integrity of the quantum world. He cannot upset the perfect mathematical equilibrium within the quantum field; otherwise he would have the capacity to destroy the entire fabric of the cosmos. However, as we progress up the scale from the quantum world to the molecular world there is evidence that the powers of darkness do have the capacity to re-configure the molecular building blocks of matter in order to create chaos and disease in biological systems. The biblical revelation of the existence of spirits of infirmity, or what another Bible translation calls "a sickness caused by a spirit," (Luke 13:11 NASB) reveals the capacity of the devil to break down order at the molecular and cellular level.

As long as a spirit of infirmity is present in a person's body, disease or sickness continues to exercise authority over flesh and blood. But as soon as a spirit of infirmity is cast out by a higher spiritual authority the physical body begins to return to its normal functionality at a molecular level and at a macroscopic level. Jesus delighted in casting out spirits of infirmity as a means of healing those who in some situations were being *physically* "oppressed by the devil." (Acts 10:38)

In all cases, when a spirit of infirmity was cast out, the person returned to good health. Of course, not all disease is directly caused by the satanic kingdom but those of us who respect the authority of Scripture need to acknowledge that the Bible certainly attributes some disease to the powers of darkness and that ought to be instructive to us concerning the capabilities of the demonic world of spirit beings.

From this we learn that demons are extra-dimensional beings that have the capacity to hack into the material world and to wreak havoc and ultimately death through disease and the breakdown of physical order. The dark world of evil spirits has the capacity to inflict disease and disorder all the way down to the molecular level, precisely because they are *spirit* beings. Job's boils were attributed directly to satanic power. Whilst the powers of darkness cannot violate the integrity of atoms and their sub-atomic components, they can, however, *restructure* nature at a molecular level to bring forth disease and physiological dysfunction.

Diseased cells and organs take on a different structure that is deprived of the original beauty that characterises life at a cellular and organic level. Cancer is widely believed amongst charismatic Christians to be caused, in some instances, by spirits of infirmity that trigger chaotic growth of cancerous cells. Humanity *was* protected from this world of spiritual darkness up until the fall, but once Adam and Eve came under the authority of spiritual darkness all hell broke loose in the physical world.

Satan seeks to eliminate every trace of beauty that would point humanity back toward the truth. Remember that there is a divine relationship between beauty and truth. The presence of beauty in the physical world is a signpost that reveals the truth about God's creative handiwork. It is therefore Satan's number one agenda to stamp out beauty and distort the whole of creation until it is rendered ugly. Sin makes everything ugly as it obliterates all that is holy and pure. In the same way, every disease causes the breakdown of the beauty and the divinely programmed functionality of the human body.

BEAUTY FOR ASHES

Jesus heals from a parallel universe! There is only one other universe or world that is parallel to our own physical universe and that is the realm of heaven. In Jesus' world there is no question about issues of possibility or impossibility. That is why when Jesus came to our world He said, "With God all things are possible!" (Matthew 19:26) If there is a God, then all things are possible. If there is no God, then many things ought to legitimately be deemed *impossible*.

However, Jesus only used the word *impossible* when He was on earth, in order to juxtapose His world against ours. Things that are impossible from the finite perspective of humanity are entirely possible because there is a God who is limitless in His power and His capabilities. So Jesus' world invaded our world and He demonstrated that all things were now possible with God. The invasion of God's world into our world is described as the coming of the Kingdom of Heaven. God's will is for His Kingdom to come on earth just as it is in heaven!

The coming of the Kingdom in the person of Christ signalled the restoration of the beauty that once characterised the pristine creation before the fall. If something is beautiful it reminds Satan of God and has the potential to point humanity back toward God. Therefore the kingdom of darkness is on a mission to destroy every aspect of the beauty of God's creation.

We suggested that one of the major arenas of battle in this agenda to uglify creation was the battle that is now being waged over the human body and the issue of the presence of sickness and disease in our lives. Jesus has come and has declared full scale war on sickness and disease because God is good. It is God's very nature to overthrow every legacy of the fall and to restore all things to their pristine beauty. Every time Jesus healed the sick He was beautifying His creation one person at a time.

When Jesus came into the synagogue in Nazareth and read from the Isaiah scroll, he turned to Isaiah 61 and publicly read what some have called the *Kingdom Mandate*. "The Spirit of the Lord is upon Me, because He has anointed Me to preach the gospel to the poor; He has sent Me to heal the brokenhearted, to proclaim liberty to the captives and recovery of sight to the blind, to set at liberty those who are oppressed and to proclaim the year of the Lord's favour." (Luke 4:18-19)[3]

It is highly improbable that Jesus stopped reading the scroll after this verse. It is more probable that He continued to read the rest of the passage, which included these words from the original text in Isaiah: "To console those who mourn in Zion, to give them *beauty for ashes*, the oil of joy for mourning, the garment of praise for the spirit of heaviness; that they may be called trees of righteousness, the planting of the Lord, that He may be glorified." (Isaiah 61:3) Beauty for ashes! These are powerful words and a glorious description of the Kingdom ministry of Jesus.

Jesus came to explicitly restore the beauty of creation. His glorious Kingdom ministry paved the way for the restoration of beauty on every level of human existence. He came to overthrow the power of sin in the human heart through the free gift of His righteousness. He came to heal every wound in every heart. He came to heal every disease and sickness and to cast out demons from every person who needed deliverance.

"For the Lord takes pleasure in His people; He will beautify the humble with salvation." (Psalm 149:4) What wonderful words: *"He will beautify..."* This is a glorious description of God's plan of redemption. He will not rest until every single human being is beautified by His salvation, until every soul is freed from the power of sin, until every broken and damaged body is healed, and every demon is cast out of the people who are made in His image and likeness.

King David said, "Let the beauty of the Lord our God be upon us." (Psalm 90:17) In the beginning human beings were crowned with the glory and the beauty of the Lord. This beauty was robbed and marred by the devil. But everything God touches becomes beautiful again. "He has made everything beautiful in its time." (Ecclesiastes 3:11) We could actually describe God's plan of redemption as a mission to beautify the whole of creation once again.

Jesus steps onto the world stage from another world and demonstrates that in His world everything is beautiful and that He has come to impose the realities of His world upon our world until everything, once again, is made beautiful. At the climax of the ages, when Jesus returns again He will destroy the present heavens and the earth and will make a new heavens and a new earth that will be just as beautiful as the first creation when He said, "It is very good!" Or as the Hebrew word *towb* suggests, "It is very beautiful!"

SUPERNATURAL MINISTRY

Every time Jesus healed the sick or raised the dead He was demonstrating the absolute authority of God over the sub-atomic quantum world. Jesus confidently declared, "All authority has been given to Me in heaven and on earth!" (Matthew 28:18) This same authority that was conferred by the Father upon the Son has in turn been conferred upon the church by the Son of God. God has chosen to share this extraordinary privilege with all those who are *in Christ*. Those who have faith in Christ have the opportunity to participate in the very works of Christ and to become co-workers together with Him to minister in the miraculous, but it is still Christ who does the works through His disciples.

Paul had the right perspective when he said, "For I will not presume to speak of anything except what Christ has accomplished through me, resulting in the obedience of the Gentiles by word and deed, in the power of signs and wonders, in the power of the Spirit." (Romans 15:18-19) All the glory belongs to Christ alone who continues to minister through His church which He identifies as His "body," that unique company of people who are called to manifest the fullness of Christ in the earth.

Jesus trained His disciples to do the same miraculous works that He did. Part of their heavenly calling was to be miracle workers just like their Master. They were called by God to be releasers of the glory realm of heaven. The words that Jesus spoke were Spirit and life and they had the power to recreate matter at the quantum level. Jesus taught His disciples how to speak just as He spoke. He taught them how to speak words that were a manifestation of the Spirit: words that were born of the Spirit and inspired by the Father in heaven. Just as Jesus did not speak on His own authority, so the disciples were trained to speak only what they heard the Father speak. They were trained by Christ to speak directly to diseases and infirmities and to command them to leave. They were trained to perform creative miracles through the power of the Holy Spirit.

The world had never seen discipleship like this before! At the heart of this specialised training of the disciples was the capacity to do miracles just like Christ. Jesus said that the essence of this unique form of discipleship was the replication of His own supernatural ministry through His disciples. "It is enough for a disciple that he becomes like his Teacher and a servant like his Master." (Matthew 10:25)

Christ's goal in discipleship was to reproduce every aspect of His own life and ministry in every disciple so that they became like Him in the world. "As He is, so are we in this world." (1 John 4:17) Jesus was sent by the Father and His disciples were sent by Christ. "As the Father has sent Me, I also send you." (John 20:21) The first disciples were thoroughly equipped to work miracles because they had been trained by Christ. "I tell you the truth, anyone who has faith in me will do what I have been doing. He will do even greater things than these, because I am going to the Father." (John 14:12)

Physical healing is the direct result of the creative Word of God spoken by the Lord Jesus Christ. When Jesus speaks the word of healing it releases the power or energy of the Holy Spirit to transform the physical body at the quantum level. To witness such a miracle at extreme magnification would be an extraordinary experience, for we would see entire cells and even organs being instantaneously restructured at a sub-atomic level right before our eyes. Whenever Jesus healed a disease or a physical affliction, it was a miniature replication of the creation event described in the book of Genesis.

The power to heal and to restore is actually the same creative power that God displayed when He materialised the heavens and the earth in the beginning. The supernatural power of God can cause something to materialise, to dematerialise or to undergo a complete metamorphosis from one form to another. God can make missing body parts materialise with a word. He can make cancerous tumours and cells dematerialise instantaneously and He can transform a dysfunctional eyeball into a fully functional eyeball through the power of His Word. "He sent His word and healed them." (Psalm 107:20)

MIRACLES IN THE NEW AGE MARKETPLACE

I am the director of a healing ministry that takes the glory of God into New Age festivals. New Agers are completely awake to the supernatural. They have a magical view of the universe and they are deeply aware of the existence of spiritual power. They are so open to the supernatural that we always see hundreds of miracles every time we go into these events. There is no greater joy than seeing someone come into our healing booth with some sort of severe pain in their body and leaving totally free of pain. The look on their faces is absolutely priceless!

I remember one gentleman coming into the booth with severe pain in his foot. He had a congenital deformity from birth and he had an operation on his foot when he was a boy. The surgeons had placed steel pins in his bones to hold the foot in its proper place, but whenever this man walked he experienced increasing pain. He had walked far too much at the festival that day and fortunately he came to the right place. We laid our hands upon his ankle and the pain that he had experienced his whole life completely disappeared. When he finally got up to leave he walked away completely healed and with the most astonished look on his face. That was fun!

At a recent festival we witnessed a miracle of "quantum tunnelling" where God caused a physical object to dematerialise and rematerialise in a completely new location. An elderly woman limped past our booth and one of the girls on our team asked the woman if she would be willing to receive prayer for her foot. She was eager to receive prayer because she had stepped on a chunk of glass and it had been embedded in her foot. The doctors had recently operated on her foot but could not remove the piece of shattered windshield glass without risking nerve damage so they stitched the foot back up in the hope that the glass would move by itself so that it could be removed at a later date.

The woman had her foot bandaged with a dressing from the recent operation. Her bandaged foot was inside her shoe to protect it. Stephanie placed her hand on the injured foot and commanded the piece of glass to be removed by the power of God. Instantly a chunk of windshield glass appeared on the floor next to the shoe. Stephanie picked it up and said to the woman, "Is this your piece of glass?" Both the woman and Stephanie were astonished as the woman explained she recognised the shape of the glass from a recent X-ray of her foot.

The woman proceeded to remove her shoe and carefully remove the bandage and the dressing. By this time a small crowd gathered because of the sound of the reaction of those involved. I was personally observing as the bandage was finally removed. The woman nearly passed out when she saw that the stitches from the X-shaped incision had completely disappeared! All that remained was a grey blister. The woman pressed down where the glass had been and she realised that it had been completely removed. The chunk of glass had passed through the bandage, through the shoe and onto the carpet. This was quantum tunnelling at its best!

This miracle was documented in photographs and the woman was so impacted that she wrote down the healing testimony. She was already a nominal believer but this event revealed that God loved her and that He cared about her well-being enough to remove both the chunk of glass and the fresh stitches in her foot. This story has since spread around the world and has been a source of astonishment and wonder. Throughout the gospels people were "astonished" by the miracles of Christ and were left with a sense of deep awe and wonder at the supernatural works of God.

When we go into these festivals, we have tremendous favour with the festival organisers. We are given the opportunity to minister the glory of God from the main performance stage. After building an atmosphere of the glory of God through releasing the supernatural sounds of heaven, we begin to call out various medical conditions by word of knowledge. On one occasion God spoke to me about a person who had just suffered whiplash in a car accident. There were only about 100 people in the audience so I stepped out in faith and released the word. Fortunately a woman quickly identified herself in the crowd, and as I released the creative word of healing in the name of Christ she was instantly healed right in front of the crowd.

The same day I had another word about severely deteriorating eyesight, and another woman identified herself and stepped out of the crowd. She wore glasses and my wife ministered to her. She removed her glasses and my wife laid her hands upon her eyes and commanded them to be healed. Immediately her eyes became hot and she was instantly healed. To check that she was fully healed, she reached into her bag to read the fine print in the footnotes of her book and discovered that her eyes were 100% healed and that she could read clearly without pain.

We have seen deaf people healed as a result of words of knowledge in these festivals. We have seen metal removed from a woman's leg! One moment she could feel the metal plate and the screws near her knee, but the next moment all of the metal had been removed. As a result the woman was able to run up and down the aisle in the festival. We have seen chronic arthritis instantly healed! In our most recent outreaches to these festivals we are seeing upwards of 400 miracles occurring over four days. God loves to display His glory in the marketplace!

The elderly woman who had the glass removed from her foot was so impacted by our ministry that she brought her friends back to the next festival and sat eagerly with them in the audience as we ministered from the main stage. I had two significant words of knowledge about a frozen shoulder and a deaf ear, and both people turned out to be friends of the woman who had experienced the glass miracle. As we are settling into the rhythm of ministry from the stage our confidence is increasing, so I decided to have some fun with the woman with the frozen shoulder.

In front of a large audience, I asked her to show everybody how far she could lift her arm before she experienced excruciating pain. Of course, she was only able to lift her arm a small distance. I commanded her shoulder to be healed in the name of Christ and then asked her to show everyone how far she could now lift her arm. There was a collective gasp as she raised it significantly into the air! But she was not completely healed, so I commanded the shoulder to be completely "un-frozen" and the woman was then able to swing her arm around in the air completely free of pain. The audience burst into spontaneous applause, and the woman with the shoulder was in a state of complete astonishment!

This public miracle built the platform for the woman with the deaf ear. I asked a couple of our team members to gather around the woman and to release the power of Christ. Within a minute or two the woman's deaf ear was completely opened and she was astonished, along with the rest of the crowd who witnessed the miracle. Needless to say, the woman who experienced the glass miracle was thrilled that she brought her friends along to both witness and experience firsthand the supernatural power of God.

We always see deaf ears opened every time we go into these festivals! There is nothing more beautiful than seeing someone holding their hearing aids with a sense of bewilderment and joy as they walk out of the festival, genuinely wondering what just happened to them. Of course we always tell people who it was who just healed them, and as a result we see dozens of people give their lives to Christ on the spot because God just revealed Himself to them!

Our sessions on the main stage are turning into a tremendous opportunity to release the supernatural power of Jesus. At every festival we are given a minimum of three sessions and we have up to one and a half hours per session to minister to the audience. Such is the favour we have at these events that our session times are three times longer than any other stage performer!

In recent festivals we have been releasing what we call "healing tunnels" where, on some occasions, we have had over 100 people pass through the tunnel formed by our healing team. Recently we saw almost every person healed as they passed through the tunnel. My wife was at the end of the tunnel with a microphone announcing the healings one by one to an astonished crowd of onlookers. This is consistently becoming one of the most exhilarating experiences that we have ever experienced in our lives!

MIRACLES IN THE HEALING ROOMS

I am also the local director of a healing room, and we are a part of the International Association of Healing Rooms. There are approximately 1,000 healing rooms scattered all over the world. Each week we run a local healing room on the main street of a predominantly New Age town and we see people regularly healed. We have had all sorts of chronic conditions instantly healed by the power of Christ. The glory of the Lord rests over the healing room and everyone who enters the room gets powerfully impacted by the presence of the glory of God.

In 2009 we had a couple come to the healing room who just three months previously had been in a motorbike accident and they were both thrown from the bike, suffering significant injuries. The woman's ankle was severely fractured but the doctors failed to properly diagnose the fracture. She had just had an X-ray the day before she hobbled into the healing room. Her foot was completely healed, followed by her neck, and then God lengthened her injured arm by about 2 to 3 centimetres because it came out of the cast shorter than her other arm. Meanwhile her boyfriend experienced healing in the other healing room, and when they came together they compared healing stories. Neither of these people were followers of Christ but they were so shocked by the goodness of God that they eagerly received a Bible and went away powerfully impacted by the love and power of God.

In recent times we are seeing people visiting the healing room who receive their healing while they are still in the waiting room. By the time it is their turn to come into the healing room they are already healed! In recent years there have been far too many healings to remember. In the past year we have seen an explosion of healings, not only in the healing rooms and the New Age marketplace but also on the streets of our town. Our prophetic teams go out on "treasure hunts" and find their treasure and heal them!

We conduct a street level outreach every Friday night with a collection of crazy hand drummers and fire twirlers, and we give away hundreds of cups of free chai tea. These events always draw a good crowd. Recently I met a couple of men who were soaking up the vibe and enjoying a cup of chai. I asked one of the men if he was experiencing pain and he told me he was in chronic back pain with titanium inserted into one of his vertebrae. We prayed for this guy and he was instantly healed! All the pain left his upper spine! He then asked us to pray for him to be delivered from nicotine addiction.

His friend, who observed the back healing said, "Can I have some, too?" He didn't need any physical healing so we offered to lead him into a supernatural encounter with Christ. We ministered to him and he fell into a deep trance accompanied by intense sobbing. He later attested to having the most wonderful experience of his life as his heart was healed of some deep emotional pain. One of the most memorable aspects of this healing encounter was the look of astonishment on the faces of these two men. They asked us with all sincerity who we were, questioning if we were really angels!

I recently met the fellow who experienced the back healing and he was still enjoying his new back but he was even more astonished by the fact that he had not touched a cigarette since the night we prayed for him. His nicotine addiction was completely healed along with his back! This is the power of the Kingdom of Heaven invading the earth and this explosion of healings and words of knowledge is taking place all over the earth, where dedicated followers of Jesus are experiencing the very things that Jesus promised His disciples that they would see if they were willing to forsake everything to follow Him. "These signs will follow those who believe...they will lay hands on the sick and they will recover." (Mark 16:17-18) We have embraced the call to discipleship and found these words to be gloriously true!

Chapter Eleven

JESUS' KEY TO QUANTUM MIRACLES

Every time Jesus healed the sick, the quantum field was being either totally re-created or restructured to come into perfect divine order. When God heals a cancer sufferer, the multiple billions of sub-atomic particles that constituted cancerous cells are instantly dematerialised or dissolved through the power of His Word. These quantum realities are actually *taken out of existence*! When Jesus gave a blind man totally new eyeballs he was performing a glorious quantum miracle! In this quantum miracle the billions of sub-atomic particles that constitute the construction of a brand new eyeball *come into existence* in an instant, perfectly structured and made complete at the voice of His command.

Jesus exercised perfect authority over nature at a quantum level. Through the power of the Holy Spirit His voice was the very voice of God on earth. It was the same creative voice that spoke at the dawn of creation when all the morning stars sang for joy. Jesus said, "The words that I speak to you I do not speak on My own authority; but the Father who dwells in Me does the works." (John 14:10) The works of the kingdom – healing the sick, casting out demons, cleansing the lepers and raising the dead – were all done at the command of the voice of the Lord.

John the Baptist said concerning Jesus that, "He whom God has sent *speaks the words of God*, for God does not give the Spirit by measure." (John 3:34) God poured out the Holy Spirit upon Jesus and this enabled Jesus to speak the words of God into the lives of people in all kinds of situations of extreme need. The Word of God is the verbal expression of the Spirit of God. All that Jesus said and did on earth He did as a man, not as God. He demonstrated what a human life filled completely with the Holy Spirit looked like. "I tell you the truth, the Son can do nothing by Himself; He can do only what He sees His Father doing, because whatever the Father does the Son also does." (John 5:19)

Jesus said, "For I have not spoken on My own authority; but the Father who sent Me gave Me a command, what I should say and what I should speak. Therefore, whatever I speak, just as the Father has told Me, so I speak." (John 12:49-50) Of course, this was a seamless process. Jesus didn't parrot the words that were dictated to Him by the Father with a five second delay. Jesus gives us a clue as to how this seamless prophetic utterance works when He said to His disciples, "At that time you will be given what to say, for it will not be you speaking, but the Spirit of your Father speaking through you." (Matthew 10:19-20 NIV)

Jesus could command instant supernatural healing and even the resurrection of a dead man whose sixty trillion cells had all been decomposing in the summer heat for four days. Resurrection from the dead is the most extreme creative miracle! Lazarus was so dead that he was seriously decomposing. "When Jesus came, He found that he had already been in the tomb four days." "Lord, by this time there is a stench, for he has been dead four days!" (John 11:17,39) All sixty trillion cells in Lazarus' body were truly dead. Do you realise what an extraordinary miracle it is to raise a decomposing body back to life? This is the extreme resurrection power of God!

I have met a man who has raised many people from the dead. His name is Surprise Sithole from Africa and he is the International Director of Iris Ministries, which was founded by Rolland and Heidi Baker in Mozambique. He has preached in my spiritual community, New Earth Tribe in Byron Bay, Australia, on two occasions in 2009 and 2010. The first time he was with us he told a story that filled us all with astonishment and awe. He told us about visiting a hospital in Africa where the doctors and nurses had gone on strike because of the appalling conditions. Inside the hospital was the stench of death, decaying flesh and human excrement. Many were near death and the conditions were appalling.

Surprise and his team began healing the sick and raising the dead. He told us of one woman who had been dead for at least two or three days.

She had maggots crawling in and out of her mouth which was agape with rotten food still inside. Together, Surprise and his team commanded this long dead woman back to life. She recovered and spat the rotten food out of her mouth. The team were ecstatic with joy and wonder. They proceeded to heal every single person in the hospital and then to clean the entire hospital. When the doctors and nurses returned they found a spotlessly clean hospital with no more patients. Surprise has raised many other people from the dead in Africa! He is like a man who stepped out of the book of Acts into the 21st century!

Jesus was anointed by the Holy Spirit to speak the very words of God and to effect supernatural transformation at a quantum level. Whenever He spoke the words that were directed and inspired by the Spirit it resulted in extraordinary miracles. No ordinary human being could affect such miracles that resulted in the transformation of the quantum field. Ordinary human voices cannot affect such a profound transformation of matter at a quantum level. Ten thousand ordinary voices could speak in perfect unison to sickness and disease and nothing would happen! Unless someone was to speak the creative word of God under the inspiration and direction of the Holy Spirit, nothing whatsoever would happen.

It is only the creative word of God that spoke creation into existence in the beginning that can also create order out of chaos in the quantum world of atomic particles. Jesus said, "The words that I speak to you are Spirit, and they are life." (John 6:63) Only the power of the Holy Spirit can create life and recreate damaged or missing organs. God loves to display His power over nature by speaking into that which is "formless and void" to create something orderly and perfect. (See Genesis 1:2)

In those sectors of the Christian community that embrace and pursue the supernatural ministry of Christ there is a tendency to distinguish between an ordinary miracle and a "creative miracle." A creative miracle is identified as a miracle that results in the appearance of a new organ or a new limb, such as in the healing of a blind eye or the cleansing of a leper. But really, every miracle is in fact a "creative miracle," because the creative power of the Word of God has created an entirely new reality at a quantum level.

Even the healing of a headache is an expression of God's creative power to trigger a sudden reduction in the swelling of vascular blood vessels and veins in the outer layer of the brain that cause pressure and pain. The most common cause of headaches is the swelling of these veins. Tension type headaches are experienced by up to 80% of the population and are extremely common. These types of headaches result from a spike in nerve signals sent to the brain from the dilated blood vessels.

If we were able to watch the miracle of the healing of a headache at a scale that was visible to the naked eye, we would witness a sudden visible reduction in the dilation of these vessels resulting in a change in the electrochemical signals flowing through the trigeminal nerve that causes the "sensation" of an aching brain. Every supernatural intervention of God could effectively be defined as a creative miracle because some act of divine creation always occurs.

ONLY DO WHAT YOU SEE JESUS DOING!

Jesus trained His disciples to do the very same things that He Himself had been doing. As part of this training He explained to them the unique nature of His interior relationship with His Father, in the understanding that His relationship with the Father would become the pattern for the unique relationship that the disciples were about to enter into with the Father. Jesus told His disciples that He only ever did what He saw His Father doing. I'm not sure how comforting this statement was to the disciples because they were definitely having trouble identifying what the Father was doing on most occasions. Let's look at this passage in the gospel of John.

> "I tell you the truth, the Son can do nothing by Himself; He can do only what He sees His Father doing, because whatever the Father does the Son also does. For the Father loves the Son and shows Him all He does. Yes, to your amazement He will show Him even greater things than these." (John 5:19-20 NIV)

Embedded in this text is a powerful key to supernatural ministry which I will endeavour to unpack. Everything Jesus did was merely a reflection of what His Father in heaven was doing, because Jesus enjoyed a perfect intimate relationship with His Father. He was always in touch with what His Father was doing in any given situation. That's great for Jesus and we rejoice in everything Jesus did when He was upon the earth because it was a powerful revelation of the will of His Father in heaven.

However, it's not necessarily that helpful for us when we feel like we are fumbling around on earth perpetually wondering what the Father is up to in heaven. But here is the key: Jesus was modelling a life of intimacy with the Father to open up to us the reality of the potential for each of us, as sons and daughters, to enter into the same kind of intimacy with Jesus that He enjoyed with His Father.

Everything Jesus did was a reflection of the will and desire of His Father. The Father was healing the sick, therefore Jesus was healing the sick! The Father was raising the dead; Jesus was raising the dead! Jesus explained that apart from the Father He could do nothing. But Jesus went on to say our new relationship with the Son was now to become a reflection of the Son's relationship to His Father.

He said, "I am the vine, you are the branches. He who abides in Me, and I in him, bears much fruit; for **without Me you can do nothing**." (John 15:5) I'm not sure if you caught the significance of this statement, so I will rephrase it to drive home the reality of what Jesus is saying. He begins in John 5 by saying that the Son can "do nothing by Himself," He is utterly dependent upon the Father. Then in John 15, Jesus said that we can do nothing without Him, in the same way that He could do nothing apart from the Father.

Because Jesus was the perfect image of the Father on earth we are no longer left wondering what the Father is doing. Philip said to Jesus, "Show us the Father!" Jesus answered by saying, "He who has seen Me has seen the Father; so how can you say, "Show us the Father?" (John 14:9) Everything Jesus did, in dependency upon the Father, was a revelation of the Father.

This revelation was driven home to me one time when I was healing the sick in a public setting. I was ministering on stage at a New Age festival, releasing the healing power of Jesus. I had a word of knowledge for a specific medical condition. I felt that the Lord had impressed upon me that there was someone present who was suffering from a severe earache in one ear. Fortunately a man with a severe earache responded from the back row. From the performance stage I commanded his ear to be healed, but nothing seemed to shift.

I work in a team, so I handed the microphone to the next team member to release words of knowledge, and I walked down the back of the audience to lay hands on the man with the chronic earache. While I was standing there with my hand on the man's ear, conscious that all eyes were upon me, the Lord spoke to me and said, "Only do what you see Jesus doing!"

Suddenly I had faith to see this man's earache supernaturally healed, so I spoke to the ear and commanded the pain to leave.

He was instantly healed (much to my relief) and I was left to ponder this powerful revelation. Of course, the words of Jesus in John 5 suddenly made perfect sense. Jesus did what He saw His Father doing and we are now called to do what we see Jesus doing which, as it turns out, is exactly what the Father is doing! We now know exactly what the Father is doing because we have Jesus as the visible image of the invisible God! If we know what Jesus would do in a given situation we also know exactly what our Father would do.

SUPERNATURAL TRAINING

Jesus plunged His disciples into an intensive training program to equip them to do the supernatural works of God. He explained to His disciples that the words that He spoke were "Spirit." This was a "third heaven" healing modality that Jesus trained His disciples to operate in. At the centre of this specialised spiritual training was the power of the proclamation of the Word of God to affect miracles. The disciples were trained by Jesus to proclaim the Word of God.

The "Word" was to become their weapon of warfare against all the works of the enemy. Paul called the Word of God the "sword of the Spirit." Jesus taught the disciples how to speak the Word of God into situations of need. He said, "Have faith in God. For assuredly, I say to you, whoever *says* to this mountain, 'Be removed and be cast into the sea,' and does not doubt in his heart, but believes that those things he says will be done, he will have whatever he says." (Mark 11:22-23)

Jesus taught His disciples to speak to the mountains that needed to be removed. He said, "Whoever *says* to this mountain..." He didn't teach His disciples to pray to God for the mountain to be removed. He taught them to *say* to the mountain! He exhorted them to "believe that those things he *says* will be done," promising the disciple that he will have "whatever he *says*." The key in this extraordinary third heaven model of training was to actually speak the Word of God to the mountain under the inspiration of the Holy Spirit.

This was exactly how Jesus ministered healing and deliverance. He didn't pray to the Father for the mountains of disease and demonic bondage to be removed. He spoke directly to the mountains and they were removed! This man, who was filled with the Holy Spirit, spoke the words of God, and the material world around Him obeyed. Jesus used this same approach whether He was commanding a demon to leave, or a disease to be healed, or a dead body to be raised to life. No matter what the problem, He always spoke to the problem. He even spoke to the wind and the waves and commanded them to be still.

> That day when evening came, Jesus said to His disciples, "Let us go over to the other side." Leaving the crowd behind, they took Him along, just as He was, in the boat. There were also other boats with Him. A furious squall came up, and the waves broke over the boat, so that it was nearly swamped. Jesus was in the stern, sleeping on a cushion. The disciples woke Him and said to Him, "Teacher, don't you care if we drown?" He got up, rebuked the wind and said to the waves, "Quiet! Be still!" Then the wind died down and it was completely calm. He said to His disciples, "Why are you so afraid? Do you still have no faith?" They were terrified and asked each other, "Who is this? Even the wind and the waves obey Him!" (Mark 4: 35-41 NIV)

Did Jesus calm the storm as God or as a man anointed by the Holy Spirit? It is hard to escape the conclusion that Jesus rebuked the disciples for their lack of faith in this particular situation because He expected them to be able to speak to the storm themselves rather than having to ask Jesus to do it for them. After all, they had been with Jesus for some time now and had been subjected to this same lesson over and over again. There is such a large body of material in the four gospels related to this approach to ministry that it becomes extremely difficult to argue with the fact that Jesus both modelled a particular kind of ministry to the disciples and expected them to adopt the very approach that He Himself used.

At the centre of this never before seen approach to doing ministry was the role of speaking the Word of God to the mountain that needed to be removed. Jesus rebuked demons, He rebuked fevers and He rebuked the wind, all rebukes issuing from His mouth. A significant component of this supernatural training program included a series of lessons in how to exercise power over the natural world. On one occasion Jesus cursed a fig tree to teach the disciples this lesson.

Early in the morning, as he was on his way back to the city, he was hungry. Seeing a fig tree by the road, he went up to it but found nothing on it except leaves. Then he said to it, "May you never bear fruit again!" Immediately the tree withered. When the disciples saw this, they were amazed. "How did the fig tree wither so quickly?" they asked. Jesus replied, "I tell you the truth, if you have faith and do not doubt, not only can you do what was done to the fig tree, but also you can say to this mountain, "Be removed and be cast into the sea," and it will be done. If you believe, you will receive whatever you ask for in prayer." (Matthew 21:18-22)

Wherever Jesus went, the people were continually astonished at the level of authority He exercised when He spoke. "They were astonished at His teaching, for His word was with authority. Amazed, the people exclaimed, "What authority and power this man's words possess! Even evil spirits obey Him and flee at his command!" (Luke 4:32,36) Jesus walked in perfect spiritual authority. He continually released the glory of God on earth through the power of His words. This was the "third heaven" healing modality modelled on earth for everyone to see. Jesus lived and breathed those famous words: "On earth as it is in heaven!" He exercised the power of the keys of the Kingdom of Heaven and then He passed on to the disciples the very same set of keys.

The critical issue in third heaven healing is *who* is speaking the Word of God. Jesus taught His disciples how to speak words that are imbued with the power of the Holy Spirit and the glory of God. He assured the disciples that their words would achieve the same results, but the most important key to this unique healing modality is staring us in the face. Jesus only gave this authority and power to those who were in right relationship with Him. He gave His ***disciples*** authority and power to heal the sick and to cast out demons. He didn't give this authority to just anybody. He only gave the keys of the Kingdom of Heaven to bind and loose to His disciples, to those who were living directly under His authority and who were filled with His Spirit.

The disciples had authority to bind and loose because they were becoming men and women *under* authority. The Centurion understood this principle and he was applauded by Jesus for his exceptional faith in perceiving the nature of Jesus' relationship to His Father! Jesus said, "If you abide in Me, and My words abide in you, you will ask whatever you desire, and it shall be done for you." (John 15:7) Answered prayer and fruitful Kingdom ministry flows exclusively out of that "John 15" abiding relationship of intimacy with the Father and the Son. The unique mystical relationship outlined in John 15 therefore becomes the pattern for radical Kingdom fruitfulness.

INTIMACY AND KINGDOM FRUITFULNESS

Jesus modelled this unparalleled intimacy with the Father and He revealed that Kingdom fruitfulness is proportionate to Kingdom intimacy. Jesus said, "I and My Father are one." (John 10:30) Jesus perfectly executed the Father's will on earth in relation to healing the sick because of the depth of His intimacy with the Father. He was exceedingly fruitful in the works of the kingdom because of his intimate fellowship with the Father. There was absolutely nothing that came between the Father and the Son. When Jesus lived on earth He walked in the fullness of uninterrupted fellowship with the Father. This deep oneness of spiritual union and intimacy with the Father was the solid foundation for the extreme fruitfulness of Jesus ministry. Jesus was powerfully established in the love of His Father as a precursor to supernatural ministry.

Because Jesus lived as a man upon the earth in complete dependency upon the anointing of the Holy Spirit, He had to walk in faith in His Father. He was not exempt from the necessity of walking by faith just because He was the Son of God. He walked by faith as a man on earth as an example to His followers that they too must have complete faith in God, just as He continually displayed through His own personal life. Jesus displayed perfect faith in God when He lived on earth. Faith is both confident belief and unwavering trust. Jesus believed in the Father and He implicitly trusted in Him even when He had to walk through the valley of the shadow of death in the Garden of Gethsemane. His faith did not waver, because He was secure in the Father's love.

Jesus let His disciples in on a powerful spiritual secret. It was the secret of intimacy in relation to Kingdom fruitfulness. We were just examining the profound secret of Jesus' relationship with His Father in John 5. But this statement leads us into an even more thrilling prophetic insight into the nature of supernatural ministry. "I tell you the truth, the Son can do nothing by Himself; He can do only what He sees His Father doing, because whatever the Father does the Son also does. For the Father *loves* the Son, and shows Him all things that He Himself does." (John 5:19-20) This statement opens up the specific nature of Jesus' relationship to His Father – an intimate love relationship! The Greek word for *loves* in this verse is *phileo*. This was the love of intimate friendship.

In every other instance where Jesus spoke of the love of the Father He customarily used the word *agape*. But there was one other exception to this tradition. In the Upper Room discourse, Jesus said to His disciples, "For the Father Himself *loves* you, [*phileo*] because you have loved Me, and have believed that I came forth from God." (John 16:27) Jesus sought to bring the disciples into the same dimension of intimate friendship with the Father that He had eternally enjoyed. "No longer do I call you servants, for a servant does not know what his master is doing; but I have called you friends [*philos*], for all things that I heard from My Father I have made known to you." (John 15:15)

Jesus had effectively transitioned the disciples through the pathway of servanthood into the intimacy of friendship with God. They had become the friends of God because they believed. James described the faith-filled actions of Abraham, the father of faith. He said, "And the Scripture was fulfilled which says, 'Abraham believed God, and it was accounted to him for righteousness.' And he was called the friend [*philos*] of God." (James 2:23)

Intimate friendship fuels deeper faith. Paul put it this way: "The only thing that counts is faith expressing itself through love." (Galatians 5:6 NIV) The NKJV describes this relationship as "faith working through love." The Greek word for *working* is *energeo*. Paul taught that faith is energised by love. Authentic biblical faith is the outflow of intimacy with God. As God pours the experience of His love into the core of our being it energises true faith. The deeper we experience the unconditional love of the Father, the deeper will be our faith. Jesus experienced the fullness of the Father's love and it produced extreme kingdom fruitfulness.

Faith was never intended to be a formula to obtain spiritual results. It was not something that we were intended to attain outside of the context of deep intimacy with God. Paul said, "Though I have the gift of prophecy, and understand all mysteries and all knowledge, and though I have all faith, so that I could remove mountains, but have not love, I am nothing." (1 Corinthians 13:2) Love must always precede faith, otherwise faith is reduced to a formula. "And now these three remain: faith, hope and love. But the greatest of these is love." (1 Corinthians 13:13 NIV) Certain aspects of the early "word of faith" movement in the mid-20th century represented an "Ishmael movement" that preceded the fulfilment of the true prophetic promise concerning healing. Some "word of faith" teachers defined faith as a "force." It was not uncommon to hear preachers speaking of the "force of faith" as though it was a technique or a formula.

Jesus said, "Have faith in God." (Mark 11:22) Faith is not a commodity. It is a *relational* expression of confident belief and absolute trust that is powerfully energised by the intimate love that flows from the Father. It is faith *in* God, not faith in faith. Jesus modelled this intimate relationship perfectly and He sought to lead His disciples into the same kind of fruitfulness that flowed exclusively out of an intimate love relationship with the Father. He said, "Abide in Me, and I in you. As the branch cannot bear fruit of itself, unless it abides in the vine, neither can you, unless you abide in Me. I am the vine, you are the branches. He who abides in Me, and I in him, bears much fruit; for without Me you can do nothing." (John 15:4-5) Jesus was seeking to draw His disciples into the very pattern of intimacy with the Father that He displayed throughout His personal life and ministry. "I tell you the truth, the Son can do nothing by Himself!" (John 15:19) In the same way, He said, "For without Me you can do nothing." (John 15:4)

Right after Jesus said that He could do nothing by Himself in John 5, He introduced the concept of intimacy with the Father: "For the Father *loves* the Son, and shows Him all things that He Himself does." (John 5:20) This is the only foundation of fruitfulness. Jesus could now call His disciples "intimate friends" who had also entered into the experience of the *phileo* love of the Father just as He had. "As the branch cannot bear fruit of itself, unless it abides in the vine, neither can you, unless you abide in Me." "Abiding" speaks of intimate fellowship. After Jesus said, "I have called you friends" (John 15:15), He said, "You did not choose Me, but I chose you and appointed you that you should go and bear fruit, and that your fruit should remain, that whatever you ask the Father in My name He may give you." (John 15:16) Can you see the connection? The fruit flows out of the intimacy.

The works of faith that produce radical kingdom fruitfulness are energised by the experience of the Father's intimate love and affection. This was the secret to the success of Jesus' Kingdom ministry, and it is the hidden key to the success of the fruitfulness of our ministry as sons and daughters who are intimately loved by our Father. Intimacy precedes fruitfulness just as love precedes authentic faith. Faith is nurtured in the context of the deepening revelation of the Father's love. "So then faith comes by hearing, and hearing by the word of God." (Romans 10:17)

Jesus said, "He who received seed on the good ground is he who hears the word and understands it, who indeed bears fruit and produces: some a hundredfold, some sixty, some thirty." (Matthew 13:23) The highest yields of Kingdom fruitfulness come out of the context of hearing the Father affirm His love to us over and over until we enter into the experience of His love just as Jesus enjoyed the endless experience of His Father's love. The Father speaks a specific word over His adopted sons and daughters, and it is the same word the Father spoke over the Son: "You are My beloved Son, in whom I am well pleased." (Mark 1:11) This heavenly proclamation of the intense intimacy and love that flows out of being *in* the Beloved Son is the key to energising radical faith.

THE SPIRIT OF FAITH

There is a dimension of radical kingdom faith that many believers fail to appropriate. We have just explored the reality that Jesus lived by faith when He was upon the earth. Could it be that this same quality of faith, energised by the Father's love, could be appropriated in the hearts of His disciples? Paul moved in a supernatural dimension of faith which he identified as the "gift of faith" in his catalogue of the gifts of the Spirit.

> The manifestation of the Spirit is given to each one for the profit of all: for to one is given the word of wisdom through the Spirit, to another the word of knowledge through the same Spirit, *to another faith* by the same Spirit, to another gifts of healings by the same Spirit, to another the working of miracles, to another prophecy, to another discerning of spirits, to another different kinds of tongues, to another the interpretation of tongues. (1 Corinthians 12:7-10)

The gift of faith is a supernatural expression of faith that reflects the very same faith that Jesus displayed when He lived as a man on earth. This is clearly what Paul taught in his second epistle to the Corinthians when he explained what it meant to have the very life of Jesus indwelling our mortal bodies.

> For we do not preach ourselves, but Christ Jesus the Lord, and ourselves your bondservants for Jesus' sake. For it is the God who commanded light to shine out of darkness, who has shone in our hearts to give the light of the knowledge of the glory of God in the face of Jesus Christ. But we have this treasure in earthen vessels that

the excellence of the power may be of God and not of us. Always carrying about in the body the dying of the Lord Jesus, that the life of Jesus also may be manifested in our body. For we who live are always delivered to death for Jesus' sake, that the life of Jesus also may be manifested in our mortal flesh. So then death is working in us, but life in you. And *since we have the same spirit of faith*, according to what is written, "I believed and therefore I spoke," we also believe and therefore speak! (2 Corinthians 4:5-7,10-13)

There are significant supernatural benefits of the life of Jesus manifested in us as we embrace the power of the cross. Paul said that "we have the same spirit of faith." Who do we have the same spirit of faith as? The theme of the passage is unquestionably the person of Christ. Paul is therefore saying that because Christ is in us, we also have the same "spirit of faith" as Jesus. This is similar to Paul's assertion that "we have the mind of Christ." (1 Corinthians 2:16) Every Christian has the mind of Christ, but not every Christian appropriates it and walks in it. It is the same with the "spirit of faith." Every Christian has it but not that many appropriate it and walk in it.

Christ Himself is the "author and perfector of our faith." (Hebrews 12:2) He has initiated this supernatural quality of faith in our hearts and He is committed to the perfecting or maturing of the faith of every one single believer until we all come to the "full assurance of faith." (Hebrews 10:22) Luke told us about Stephen whom he described as "a man full of faith and the Holy Spirit." (Acts 6:5) Because he was "full of faith and power, he did great wonders and signs among the people." (Acts 6:8) How did Stephen transition from an immature believer to a man who was living in such faith that he was able to work awesome signs and wonders? He simply allowed the Holy Spirit to establish the fullness of the life of Jesus in his heart and to act upon his confidence and trust in the nature of God to heal the sick.

Paul had entered into this same dimension of supernatural faith and he longed for this same spirit of faith to be replicated in the life of every believer. "My little children, for whom I labour in birth again until Christ is formed in you." (Galatians 4:19) Another translation says: "Oh, my dear children! I feel as if I am going through labour pains for you again, and they will continue until Christ is fully developed in your lives." (NLT) As the life of Christ is fully "formed" in us, His faith is activated in our personal lives.

Paul put it this way: "I am crucified with Christ: nevertheless I live; yet not I, but Christ lives in me: and the life which I now live in the flesh I live

by *the faith of the Son of God*, who loved me, and gave Himself for me."
(Galatians 2:20 KJV) Paul proclaimed, "Christ Jesus our Lord: in whom we
have boldness and access with confidence by *the faith of Him*." (Ephesians
3:12 KJV) The faith of Christ is a heavenly expression of absolute confidence and boldness that flows out of intimate fellowship with the Father.
The deeper the oneness, the deeper the confidence!

Those who are "in Christ" have been blessed "with every spiritual blessing in the heavenly places in Christ." (Ephesians 1:3) Part of this package
of heavenly blessings is a supernatural expression of faith that produces the
same Kingdom fruitfulness that Jesus produced. As we are established in
love and energised by the gift of intimacy bestowed upon us by the Father's
love, we begin to enter into the same spirit of faith that Jesus exhibited in the
working of extraordinary miracles. This sheds new light on the exhortation
of Jude to the church. "I found it necessary to write to you exhorting you to
contend earnestly for *the faith* which was once for all delivered to the saints."
(Jude 3 NKJV)

The very faith of Christ is established in us, but only as we learn to
exercise that supernatural faith. Faith requires an action. "Faith by itself, if
it is not accompanied by action, is dead." (James 2:17 NIV) We must open
our mouth and speak the word of faith. Paul understood the power that was
released through addressing the mountains with the Word of God. He said,
"And *since we have the same spirit of faith*, according to what is written,
"I believed and therefore I spoke," we also believe and therefore speak!" (2
Corinthians 4:13) Jesus said, "I tell you the truth, *if you have faith* and do
not doubt, not only can you do what was done to the fig tree, but also you
can say to this mountain, 'Be removed and be cast into the sea,' and it will be
done." (Matthew 21:22)

It is not enough just to believe in God. James tells us that even the
demons believe and tremble. (James 2:19) We who believe must also learn
how to speak to sickness and disease in the power of the Holy Spirit until we
see the same results that Jesus saw. Paul called this the proclamation of the
"word of faith." "The word is near you, in your mouth and in your heart"
(that is, the *word of faith* which we preach)." (Romans 10:8) Paul's point is
that if we believe in the power of God then we must speak to the mountains
of opposition until they are removed. Paul is wrestling out loud with this
extraordinary "third heaven" model of Kingdom ministry that Jesus trained
His disciples to operate in.

Nothing will happen if we do not open our mouth and speak words that flow from a heart filled with the spirit of faith. "Whoever **says** to this mountain...will have whatever he **says**!" If we will allow Christ to apprentice us so that we become authentic disciples, we must learn to prophesy to the mountains and the strongholds until they are fully removed. Those who have been endued with the spirit of faith are called to speak to every kind of sickness and disease, to speak to demons and command them to leave, to speak to the wind and the waves, and even to speak to dead bodies to command them to live. All of the works of faith hinge upon the cultivation of the exercise of the word of faith that flows from a heart that is bathed in the love of the Father.

GLORY AND ONENESS WITH THE FATHER

There is a crucial issue here that we cannot afford to overlook, and this is the relationship of each disciple to the glory of God. Jesus' intent is that all of His disciples come into such a deep encounter with the glory of God that they literally become bathed in the glory of heaven. Jesus is seeking to draw every disciple into the "glory zone" that surrounds the Father and the Son so that they live under an open heaven and minister out of the context of heavenly glory, just as Jesus Himself ministered.

> I do not pray for these alone, but also for those who will believe in Me through their word; that they all may be one, as You, Father, are in Me, and I in You; that they also may be one in Us, that the world may believe that You sent Me. And *the glory which You gave Me I have given them*, that they may be one just as We are one: I in them, and You in Me; that they may be made perfect in one, and that the world may know that You have sent Me, and have loved them as You have loved Me. Father, I desire that they also whom You gave Me may be with Me where I am, *that they may behold My glory* which You have given Me; for You loved Me before the foundation of the world. (John 17:20-24)

Jesus' prayer is that "they all may be one, as You, Father, are in Me, and I in You; that they also may be one in Us." This is the prayer of Jesus concerning His disciples, but after He expressed His heart's desire to His Father He then proceeded to explain the means through which this prayer would be answered. He said, "The glory which You gave Me I have given them, **that they may be one** just as We are one: I in them, and You in Me; that they may be made perfect in one." This intimate prayer of Jesus to His Father reveals that the impartation of His glory to the saints is the key to bringing us into the depths of oneness that Christ has purposed for His disciples. We can automatically assume that the depth and intensity of spiritual oneness that Jesus envisaged in His high priestly prayer is infinitely greater and deeper than we could ever understand.

Paul had entered into a measure of this deep mystical union with the glory of Christ, and this became the chief objective of his ministry into the life of every disciple that was entrusted to his pastoral care. Paul understood that Jesus' mission was to bring "many sons to glory." (Hebrews 2:12) "He called you by our gospel, for the obtaining of the glory of our Lord Jesus Christ." (2 Thessalonians 2:14) Peter also understood this same prophetic objective: "He has called us to receive His own glory and goodness!" (2 Peter 1:3 NLT)

Unless the Holy Spirit establishes our hearts in this deep and intimate oneness with Christ and the Father, we will never enter into the level of supernatural ministry that Jesus has prepared for His followers to walk in. There are many glorious kingdom works "which God prepared in advance for us to do." (Ephesians 2:10 NIV) Our destiny is to be clothed in supernatural glory so that we can minister out of that heavenly glory. It is imperative that we understand by revelation that the spirit of faith is only activated in the glory realm.

Just as Jesus spoke out of the context of being immersed in His Father's glory, now His disciples have the privilege of obtaining the glory of Christ so that they are fully immersed in His glory. Then they can also minister out of the context of the glory of heaven. Jesus lived in two realms simultaneously. His body was on earth but His spirit was in heaven. He said, "No one has ascended to heaven but He who came down from heaven, that is, the Son of Man who is in heaven." (John 3:13) Because His disciples are in Him and He is in them, they too are seated in heavenly places in Christ. Paul said "we are citizens of heaven, where the Lord Jesus Christ lives." (Philippians 3:20 NLT)

When we are fully baptized in the glory of Christ we enter into a dimension of deep oneness with Christ, so that when we speak on earth our voice also proceeds out of the context of being immersed in the glory just as the voice of Jesus proceeded out of the glory. The words that Jesus spoke on earth were Spirit and they carried the very atmosphere of the glory of God. According to Peter, the Holy Spirit is called the "Spirit of Glory." (1 Peter 4:14) It is the role of the Holy Spirit to communicate and impart the glory of Christ on earth. Jesus is the pattern of supernatural ministry and He always spoke out of the glory realm.

God calls us to worship Him as the primary means of becoming immersed in the atmosphere of heaven. Glory encounters prepare the disciples of Jesus for supernatural ministry. As we ascend in worship into the presence of the Father and the Son we become marinated in the presence of His glory. Peter was so immersed in the glory that after his baptism into the Spirit of Glory even his shadow healed the sick. Or was it his shadow? Perhaps it was a glory zone that was established around him as he ministered under an open heaven.

RELEASING THE GLORY OF HEAVEN

God wants the voice of His disciples to speak out of the atmosphere of the glory of heaven! That is why He imparts His glory to the church. The disciples in Acts were so immersed in the glory cloud of heaven that supernatural miracles were continually manifesting around them. Jesus had effectively trained the twelve to minister out of the glory realm. They received the glory so they could give it away. We will develop this theme in greater detail in chapter thirteen.

Glory now defines the ministry of the saints on earth just as it defined the ministry of Christ. Paul understood the relationship between glory and supernatural ministry. He said, "Therefore, since we have *this ministry*, as we have received mercy, we do not lose heart." (2 Corinthians 4:1) What is *this ministry?* Paul also wrote, "We all, with unveiled face, beholding as in a mirror the glory of the Lord, are being transformed into the same image from glory to glory, just as by the Spirit of the Lord." (2 Corinthians 3:18) This is our ministry; to obtain the glory of God on earth and display the glory of God's heavenly kingdom.

Every disciple of Jesus has been ordained to be a healing revivalist and a releaser of the glory of God, just as Jesus released the glory. God's will has never changed. His desire is to display his glory on earth in the 21st century to the same extent that it was displayed 2,000 years ago in Christ. Oh, how the church has fallen away from the faith whenever Christianity has been reduced to nothing more than the weekly attendance of a boring meeting in a dead, backslidden church.

Authentic kingdom ministry is a prophetic declaration of the glory of the Kingdom of God that is accompanied by demonstrations of the glorious riches of heaven. "All you have made will praise you, O Lord; your saints will extol you. They shall speak of the glory of Your kingdom and talk of Your power; so that all men may know of Your mighty acts and the glorious splendour of Your kingdom." (Psalm 145:10-12) These powerful biblical themes of glory, power and the kingdom belong together in the Scriptures. Jesus prayed, "For Yours is the kingdom and the power and the glory forever." (Matthew 6:13) Paul exhorted the disciples to "walk worthy of God who calls you into His own kingdom and glory." (1 Thessalonians 2:12) The Kingdom of Heaven is indistinguishable from the glory of God.

The kingdom is the realm of God's glory. One Bible translator[1] chose to use the word "realm" everywhere the Greek word *basileia* [kingdom] appeared in the Greek New Testament. From this perspective, Jesus came preaching the realm of heaven and tangibly demonstrating the inbreaking of the realm of heaven. That's a really helpful way to think about the reality of the kingdom! There is such an intimate relationship between the kingdom and the glory that whenever the kingdom comes in power the glory of God is made tangible on the earth. Jesus caused the glory of God to become tangible and visible through the miracles and signs and wonders he displayed when He was upon earth. Jesus revealed that God is deeply passionate about revealing His glory on the earth. That is why He is looking for a company of people who will embrace the calling to become apprentices of Jesus and learn how to minister out of the glory.

Radical kingdom ministry begins with the revelation that God wants His glory to be *seen* upon the earth! "Arise, shine; For your light has come! And the glory of the Lord is risen upon you. For behold, the darkness shall cover the earth, and deep darkness the people; But the Lord will arise over you, and His glory **will be seen** upon you. All nations will come to your light. Mighty kings will come to **see your radiance**." (Isaiah 61:1-3) Christ Himself was full of the glory of God. "And the Word became flesh and dwelt among us, and we beheld His glory." (John 1:14)

Jesus was the revelation of the glory of the Father, yet the miracles of Christ make the glory of God even more visible upon the earth. Jesus said, concerning the resurrection of Lazarus, "Did I not say to you that if you would believe you would *see the glory of God*?" (John 11:40) Isaiah prophesied about the coming of John the Baptist, describing him as the voice of one crying in the wilderness saying, "Prepare the way of the Lord." (Isaiah 40:3) John's ministry was the prelude to the glorious appearance of the Christ through whom it was said, "The glory of the Lord shall be revealed, and all flesh *shall see it* together; for the mouth of the Lord has spoken." (Isaiah 40:5) Whenever the glory of God shows up on the earth it always becomes visible in some tangible way.

As the glory of God is being poured out all over the earth with increasing intensity, there are extraordinary miracles occurring. Those believers who are pressing into the glory realm are witnessing a major upsurge in the manifestation of miracles. The church is longing for a restoration of the miraculous ministry of Christ, but Christ is longing for a people who will seek first the glory of His kingdom. Miracles will automatically follow.

As the church presses into the glory realm there will be a corresponding spike in the miraculous. But to press into the glory realm necessitates a shift in focus for the church. God wants His people to get totally blasted with His awesome glory, but the prerequisite for this experience is that we embrace the invitation to deep intimacy and oneness with Christ and the Father.

When this kind of oneness is released in the church, Jesus said that it will have global ramifications. "The glory which You gave Me I have given them, that they may be one just as We are one: I in them, and You in Me; that they may be made perfect in one, and that *the world may know* that You have sent Me, and have loved them as You have loved Me." (John 17:22-23) The world will surely know that Christ is risen from the dead when the church embraces the intimacy paradigm that Christ is seeking to establish in the church.

Until then Jesus continues to make intercession for the church, "that they all may be one, as You, Father, are in Me, and I in You; that they also may be one in Us, that *the world may believe* that You sent Me." (John 17:21) Christians desperately want the world to believe in Christ, but Christ tells us that the path to this global revolution is for the church to embrace the call to deep level intimacy and to begin the journey into the Father's heart.

FORMULA OR INTIMACY?

The world is looking for formulas to create their own reality and shape their own destiny. Jesus does not promote magical formulas. He is calling us to intimate relationship with the Father, and He has promised that the establishment of this kind of deep level spiritual intimacy will have global ramifications. This is not a theological theory. It was proven in the early church. Remember that it was the enemies of the church, not the believers, who said, "These who have turned the world upside down have come here too!" (Acts 17:6)

Intimacy with God will again turn the world upside down in the 21ˢᵗ century. That is why Jesus, who ever lives to make intercession for the saints, continues to pray fervently that His disciples will enter into the fullness of the experience of the Father's love. Jesus is the perfector of our faith! He perfects our faith by establishing us in the intimacy of the Father's love so that the same spirit of faith may be powerfully activated in our lives. Rolland Baker regards intimacy with God as the key to Surprise Sithole's supernatural ministry. He says, "Surprise is blessed by an extraordinary intimacy with Jesus that few even imagine, but in his ministry he spurs many on to that same love affair he has with his Lover and Maker. God's method is a person and Surprise is a person who carries His glory to a rare degree."[2]

Jesus' prayer is that "the world may know that You have sent Me, *and have loved them as You have loved Me.*" (John 17:23) Pause for a moment to reflect upon this mind-blowing concept and to allow the Spirit of revelation to breathe upon this sacred truth! Jesus wants the world to know that the Father loves His sons and daughters exactly as He loves His own Beloved Son. Sons and daughters who enter into the transformational experience of the Father's love become giants of faith. "The people who know their God shall be strong, and carry out great exploits." (Daniel 11:32) They will not be known for their words alone. If words could win a lost world it would have been accomplished by now, for the church is full of words.

Jesus understood that words alone were not sufficient to convince the world of the reality of God. He said, "Believe me when I say that I am in the Father and the Father is in me; or at least believe on the evidence of the miracles themselves." (John 14:11 NIV) Jesus said to the doubters, "Do not believe me unless I do what my Father does. But if I do it, even though you do not believe me, believe the miracles, that you may know and understand that the Father is in me, and I in the Father." (John 10:38) Miracles are an essential part of the equation, and the necessity of the supernatural is implicit to the prayer that Jesus prayed in John 17. The world will truly know when the church is established in the true spirit of faith!

Jesus concludes this extraordinary prayer by saying, "O righteous Father! The world has not known You, but I have known You; and these have known that You sent Me. And I have declared to them Your name, and will declare it, that *the love with which You loved Me may be in them*, and I in them." (John 17:25-26) Jesus finishes His prayer by personally committing Himself to the continual unveiling of the nature of the Father to those whom the Father has given Him out of the world. He will continue to reveal the love of the Father until His disciples are so deeply established in the experience of the Father's love that a true community of radical faith emerges once again in the earth.

Jesus asked the question, "When I, the Son of Man, return, how many will I find who have faith?" (Luke 18:8 NLT) This is still an open question but, as you are reading this, I urge you to decide that you will be numbered amongst the company of those who press in to the full assurance of faith. This is the prerequisite for the restoration of the ministry of the glory of God on the earth, and there are many forerunners who are pressing violently into the fullness of the kingdom to show us the true path of kingdom faith and power.

I have deliberately laboured the point concerning the necessity of intimacy with God in order to participate in the supernatural works of Jesus. I have done this for a specific reason and that is to prepare the way to contrast the unique healing modality of Jesus and His disciples with the healing modality that lies at the core of New Age spirituality. In later chapters one of our goals will be to draw an even clearer delineation between these two approaches to healing as we juxtapose the "formula approach" against the "intimacy approach" outlined by the historical Jesus. But before we get there, we want to go a little deeper into an exploration of the glory realm and the relationship between the unveiling of the glory of God and the flow of signs and wonders.

Chapter Twelve

QUANTUM PHYSICS AND THE GLORY OF GOD

Everything we have discussed up to this point has been foundational to bring us to the subject that we are about to explore in this chapter. I called this book *Quantum Glory,* not only because the quantum world is a revelation of the glory of God but also because the quantum world has been designed to be comprehensively restructured through the invasion of the glory of God from heaven.

In Part One we sought to come to terms with a number of important scientific concepts that are uniquely associated with the quantum world. These concepts, which include quantum non-locality, the wave/particle duality, quantum entanglement and extra-dimensionality, help to shed greater light upon the mysterious nature of the world we live in. We have explored these themes, many of which are at the frontier of quantum research, in order to bring into focus the relationship between God and His creation at a quantum level.

Throughout this book I have proceeded on the premise of the certainty of the existence of God and the reality of His glorious voice and His unlimited power. We have sought to reconcile everything in biblical revelation with the discoveries of quantum physics in order to develop a penetrating insight into the nature of quantum reality in the light of revealed truth.

Now we want to turn our attention toward an aspect of God that brings into even greater focus the exact nature of these supernatural "waves" that we have introduced and discussed in the previous two chapters. I want to introduce a concept that I will identify throughout this chapter as "glory waves." I would like to suggest that these "waves" of heaven's glory are just as real and as tangible as any other "waves" known to physicists, even though they will never be acknowledged by secular quantum physicists.

There are light waves, there are electromagnetic waves, there are quantum waves, there are sound waves, and there are also glory waves! The supernatural energy of the Holy Spirit that flows from the throne of God is actually expressed as a wave of divine glory that issues from the presence of God. At times this glory realm becomes tangible in and through the people of God.

The Bible is full of references to the reality of the glory of God. It is important that we are clear about what the glory of God actually is. We will look at the context in which the glory of the Lord was tangibly manifested in the Bible. Perhaps the best way to come to terms with the nature of the glory is to read the historical narratives of the invasion of the glory realm into human experience.

There are four key concepts closely associated with the manifestation of the glory of God on earth. The first is the glory *cloud*, the second is the appearance of *smoke* as a manifestation of the fire of His glory, the third concept is the *light* of the glory of God and the fourth is the intimate relationship between the *power* and the glory of God. Let's explore these four concepts, beginning with the glory cloud.

THE GLORY CLOUD

The first time the glory cloud appeared on earth was in Exodus 16. God had just led the children of Israel out of Egypt and had brought them into the wilderness. "Moses and Aaron said to all the children of Israel, 'At evening you shall know that the Lord has brought you out of the land of Egypt. And in the morning you shall see the glory of the Lord!'" (Exodus 16:6-7) Just as they had prophesied the day before, "It came to pass, as Aaron spoke to the whole congregation of the children of Israel, that they looked toward the wilderness, and behold, the glory of the Lord appeared in the cloud." (Exodus 16:10) This mysterious cloud kept reappearing in the Old Testament. The next time, it appeared on Mount Sinai.

The glory of the Lord settled on Mount Sinai. For six days the cloud covered the mountain, and on the seventh day the Lord called to Moses from within the cloud. To the Israelites the glory of the Lord looked like a consuming fire on top of the mountain. Then Moses entered the cloud as he went on up the mountain. And he stayed on the mountain forty days and forty nights. (Exodus 24:16-18)

The next time the glory cloud appeared was upon the completion of the building of the Tabernacle in the wilderness. "Then the cloud covered the tabernacle of meeting, and the glory of the Lord filled the tabernacle. And Moses was not able to enter the tabernacle of meeting, because the cloud rested above it, and the glory of the Lord filled the tabernacle." (Exodus 40:34-35) The fourth time the glory cloud appeared was over the Tabernacle again. "They turned toward the Tabernacle of meeting and suddenly the cloud covered it and the glory of the Lord appeared." (Numbers 16:42) The next time this glory cloud visibly appeared was at the opening ceremony of Solomon's Temple:

> The Levites who were the singers...stood at the east end of the altar, clothed in white linen, having cymbals, stringed instruments and harps, and with them one hundred and twenty priests sounding with trumpets; indeed it came to pass, when the trumpeters and singers were as one, to make one sound to be heard in praising and thanking the Lord, and when they lifted up their voice with the trumpets and cymbals and instruments of music, and praised the Lord, saying: "For He is good, For His mercy endures forever," that the house, the house of the Lord, was filled with a cloud so that the priests could not continue ministering because of the cloud; for the glory of the Lord filled the house of God. (2 Chronicles 5:12-14)

This cloud of glory was the same cloud that descended upon the Mount of Transfiguration when Peter, James and John had the privilege of seeing Jesus in His glorious splendour discussing His impending crucifixion with Moses and Elijah. This was the sixth time the glory cloud descended visibly upon the earth. "While Jesus was still speaking, behold, a bright cloud over-shadowed them; and suddenly a voice came out of the cloud, saying, 'This is My beloved Son, in whom I am well pleased. Hear Him!'" (Matthew 17:5)

Throughout church history there have been many accounts of the glory of the Lord appearing in meetings like a thick cloud or mist. I personally witnessed this on one occasion in Arizona in 2008. But perhaps the most significant appearance of the glory occurred in the Azusa Street revival in Los Angeles at the beginning of the 20th century. Many people who were a part of this extraordinary revival have independently corroborated reports of the glory cloud as a regular feature of the revival in Los Angeles. In a remarkable book titled, *They Told Me their Stories*, young people who were present in these meetings recalled their experiences. One young man named Brother Anderson was just 15 years old when the revival broke out in 1906. He described this amazing epiphany.

> Anderson told me that the Shekinah Glory was hard to explain because it could only be described, but not understood. At times he would come into the building and there would be kind of a glow. There were times when God would start moving and working and a smoke-like substance would begin to glow even brighter. People could walk through it and sometimes it would sort of roll. You couldn't take a fan and blow it out, nor was it something you could pick up. Brother Anderson confessed that he tried because it looked so tangible. He remembered that at times the mist would get so thick that it would fill the whole building. Anderson noted that at times even [William] Seymour was fascinated with the heavy mist that filled the room. In fact, there were times that Seymour would take his feet and kind of play with the thick Shekinah Glory. Brother Anderson was awed by the Glory and described it as part of heaven coming down. You could walk in it, sit down in it, run your hands through it and breathe it into your lungs but you couldn't capture it.[1]

Another youth, Ralph Riggs, was just 12 years old when the revival broke out. He recalled the Shekinah Glory as it would come into the building in Azusa Street.

> Most of the time the Shekinah Glory was spoken of with reverence but there was one time that Brother Riggs shared revealing a lighter side. He told me that when Seymour would get down there, the Shekinah Glory would get so thick that you could hardly see the ground. With a smile he confessed that there were times when it was so thick that he and Ward [his friend] would get in the back of the room and play hide-and-go-seek in the mist. I asked him to talk seriously about the Shekinah Glory. Brother Riggs explained the experience: "I tasted a bit of heaven. Ward and I would talk and share that Azusa Street must have been what heaven was like. God must have sent some part of heaven down here."[2]

THE SMOKE OF THE GLORY

Sometimes the glory of the Lord appeared in the Bible as smoke and fire. When God gave the law to the children of Israel, the Lord descended upon Mount Sinai in a cloud of smoke. It is hard to imagine that this was literal smoke because Moses went up into the mountain to meet with the Lord. Rather, it was a cloud so thick that it appeared like smoke. It is more probable that the glory appeared as a thick mist. I have been in meetings where the glory cloud entered the building as a smoky mist. God is revealed metaphorically as a Consuming Fire and, to quote the famous saying: Where there is smoke there is fire!

> It came to pass on the third day, in the morning, that there were thundering and lightnings, and a thick cloud on the mountain; and the sound of the trumpet was very loud, so that all the people who were in the camp trembled. And Moses brought the people out of the camp to meet with God, and they stood at the foot of the mountain. Now Mount Sinai was completely in smoke, because the Lord descended upon it in fire. Its smoke ascended like the smoke of a furnace, and the whole mountain quaked greatly. And when the blast of the trumpet sounded long and became louder and louder, Moses spoke, and God answered him by voice. Then the Lord came down upon Mount Sinai, on the top of the mountain. And the Lord called Moses to the top of the mountain, and Moses went up. (Exodus 19:16-20)

There are two references to the cloud of smoke in the book of Isaiah. The first reference appears to be in the context of a Messianic prophecy concerning the restoration and purification of the people of God. "The Lord will create over all of Mount Zion and over those who assemble there *a cloud of smoke* by day and a glow of flaming fire by night; over all the glory will be a canopy." (Isaiah 4:5 NIV)

The second reference to the cloud of smoke appears when Isaiah saw the Lord. He heard the Seraphim crying out, "Holy, holy, holy is the Lord of hosts; the whole earth is full of His glory!" And the posts of the door were shaken by the voice of him who cried out, and *the temple was filled with smoke*." (Isaiah 6:3-4) In the book of Revelation we are told that this smoke is the appearance of the glory of the Lord. "The temple was *filled with smoke from the glory of God* and from His power." (Revelation 15:8)

On that great day of Pentecost, fire visibly appeared over the heads of the early disciples symbolizing the descent of the glory of God from heaven upon the early church. "What looked like flames or tongues of fire appeared and settled on each of them." (Acts 2:3 NLT) Another unique feature of the Azusa Street revival was the manifestation of the fire of God descending visibly upon the building. Sister Carney was a significant figure from the very beginning of the revival. She was just 17 years old when the revival broke out in 1906. She has vivid recollections of seeing with her own eyes the fire come down from heaven. This epiphany was so intense that on some occasions the fire department was called to the building because onlookers were convinced the building was on fire.

> When I asked Sister Carney to describe the Shekinah Glory fire reported by many, she told her story. She recalled the fire department coming because of a call that the building was on fire. When they arrived, they didn't smell any smoke or see any evidence of fire. Sister Carney asked John Lake why the fire department kept coming and looking for the fire. He explained that the fire was coming down from heaven into the building and fire was going up from the building and meeting the fire coming down. Fascinated, Sister Carney went out, walked about a half a block, and saw the awesome sight for herself. To her, this divine connection of fire coming down from heaven and going up to heaven was just further evidence of God's mighty presence in that place. Whenever this connection was present, the power of God was even more intense within the meeting.[3]

This awesome manifestation of both fire and a cloud, reminiscent of the experience of the children of Israel in the wilderness, was seen by many at Azusa Street. Brother Anderson corroborated the story of the fire coming down upon the church.

> I pressed Brother Anderson to tell me about the "fire." Although he was not one of the first to go out and witness the event, he told me that he had seen it. He said it looked like flames about fifty feet in the air coming down and was also going up out of the roof to meet, merge, and go on through the flame coming down. Young Anderson would just stand there with his mouth open. He didn't know how to explain it, but it was real. He told me the burning bush described by Moses now made sense.[4]

The Light of the Glory

We began this study by observing that the glory of the Lord appeared in the Bible in four unique ways: first as a cloud, secondly as smoke and thirdly as a bright and shining light. On a number of occasions when the glory of the Lord appeared visibly it came with the appearance of brilliant light. Whenever we think of the glory of the Lord in the New Testament, we most often associate it with the appearance of intense light. On the Mount of Transfiguration the glory of the Lord descended both as a cloud and as a bright light.

> Jesus took Peter, John and James with him and went up onto a mountain to pray. As He was praying, the appearance of his face changed, and his clothes became as *bright as a flash of lightning*. Two men, Moses and Elijah, appeared in *glorious splendour*, talking with Jesus. They spoke about his departure, which he was about to bring to fulfilment at Jerusalem. Peter and his companions were very sleepy, but when they became fully awake, *they saw His glory* and the two men standing with Him. (Luke 9:28-32 NIV)

The light of the glory of the Lord was so intense that Mark said, "His clothes became dazzling white, whiter than anyone in the world could bleach them." (Mark 9:3 NIV) Matthew tells us that Jesus "was transfigured before them. His face *shone like the sun*, and his clothes became as white as the light." (Matthew 17:2 NIV) This intense light is reminiscent of Ezekiel's heavenly encounter with the King of Glory.

> Above the expanse...was what looked like a throne of sapphire, and high above on the throne was a figure like that of a man. I saw that from what appeared to be his waist up he looked like glowing metal, as if full of fire, and that from there down he looked like fire; and *brilliant light surrounded him*. Like the appearance of a rainbow in the clouds on a rainy day, so was the *radiance around him*. This was the appearance of the likeness of the *glory of the Lord*. When I saw it, I fell face down, and I heard the voice of one speaking. (Ezekiel 1:26-28 NIV)

The glory of the Lord shines with a glorious and intense light. "And behold, the glory of the God of Israel came from the way of the east. His voice was like the sound of many waters; and the earth *shone with His glory*."

(Ezekiel 43:2) When Jesus confronted Saul of Tarsus on the Damascus road, Saul was surrounded by the blazing light of the glory of God.

> "Now it happened, as I journeyed and came near Damascus at about noon, suddenly *a great light from heaven shone around me*. And I fell to the ground and heard a voice saying to me, 'Saul, Saul, why are you persecuting Me?' And those who were with me indeed saw the light and were afraid, but they did not hear the voice of Him who spoke to me. And since I could not see for *the glory of that light*, being led by the hand of those who were with me, I came into Damascus." (Acts 22:6-7,9,11)

Paul was literally blinded by the intensity of the light of the glory of God. Later he went on to talk about the relationship between the light and the glory of God. "For it is the God who commanded light to shine out of darkness, who has shone into our hearts to give the light of the knowledge of the glory of God in the face of Jesus Christ." (2 Corinthians 4:6) The light of the glory of God is a heavenly reality that is even brighter than the light of the sun. It has illuminative properties just as the light of the stars that illuminate the entire universe. We are told in the book of Revelation that the city of God, the New Jerusalem, "had no need of the sun or of the moon to shine in it, for the glory of God illuminated it. The Lamb is its light." (Revelation 21:23) Jesus described Himself as the "light of the world." The light of the glory of God is a real light, but it emanates out of the being of God. Natural light is merely a prophetic picture of the greater reality of the supernatural light of heaven.

THE PHYSICS OF GLORY

Heaven is filled with the light of the glory of God, but it isn't a natural light; it is a supernatural form of light. Bright "natural" sunlight consists of a stream of countless billions of photons. Photons are a wave form of electromagnetic radiation. They have zero mass so they can travel through a vacuum at the speed of light. Each day the earth is bombarded with this stream of electromagnetic radiation from the sun. Visible light falls within a narrow range of the spectrum of electromagnetic radiation. We call it "visible light" because it can be detected by the human eye.

There are other wavelengths of electromagnetic radiation that are completely invisible to the human eye. These include ultraviolet light, infrared light, gamma rays, X-rays, microwaves and radio waves. These waves of energy are all on either a higher or lower frequency that cannot be detected by our eyes. White light refracts into the seven colours of the rainbow, and each colour has a different frequency. Red light has the longest wavelength and violet has the shortest wavelength. Infrared and ultraviolet light are just outside the fringes of the visible light spectrum. When the seven primary colours of the rainbow are seen together, these seven wavelengths appear as "white light."

Natural light is merely an analogue of the supernatural light of the glory of God, even as natural sound is an analogue of supernatural sound. Which came first, natural light or supernatural light? Of course, the supernatural light of God preceded the creation of natural light. John said, "This is the message which we have heard from Him and declare to you, that **God is light** and in Him is no darkness at all." (1 John 1:5) God is supernatural light, and this being who is Himself light is the one who spoke into the darkness and created natural light.

"God said, 'Let there be light!' and there was light. And God saw the light that it was good; and God divided the light from the darkness. God called the light Day, and the darkness He called Night." (Genesis 1:3-5) God created natural light as a prophetic picture of supernatural light. In Chapter Six we saw how natural sound echoes the supernatural sound that exists in the heavenly dimension. We understand the concept of God as light because we are all so accustomed to the existence of natural light. Even a child can understand the concept of darkness as the absence of light. In the same way, spiritual darkness is the absence of the illumination that comes from the supernatural light of God.

There is a fundamental relationship between the supernatural light of heaven and natural light here the earth. In an earlier chapter we explored the relationship between the supernatural sounds of heaven and the natural sound waves of earth. We saw how the supernatural sound can manifest itself seamlessly through earthly sounds. All the words that Jesus spoke were in fact the supernatural voice of God expressed through natural sound waves here on earth. In the same way, the supernatural light of heaven can express itself through natural photons which are quantum waves. Suddenly the glorious light of heaven can invade earth and manifest as an explosion of natural photons that are energised by the glory realm of heaven.

This is particularly spectacular when it happens at night! Peter was in prison in the book of Acts. "Suddenly, there was a bright light in the cell, and an angel of the Lord stood before Peter." (Acts 12:7 NLT) Angels carry the glory of heaven and whenever they appear the entire room can be filled with light. At the birth of Jesus, angels appeared at night to the shepherds, and the night sky was illumined! "Now there were in the same country shepherds living out in the fields, keeping watch over their flock by night. And behold, an angel of the Lord stood before them, and the glory of the Lord shone around them, and they were greatly afraid." (Luke 2:8-9) In the book of Revelation John saw an angel coming down from heaven and "the earth was illuminated with his glory." (Revelation 18:1)

When the supernatural light of heaven shines on earth during the daytime, there is an even greater intensification of light that exceeds natural sunlight. Saul was marching to Damascus to kill the Christians when "suddenly a light shone around him from heaven." (Acts 9:3) Paul revealed what had happened to him on the Damascus road when he testified to King Agrippa. "At midday, O king, along the road I saw a light from heaven, **brighter than the sun**, shining around me and those who journeyed with me." (Acts 26:13) The face of Jesus on the Mount of Transfiguration shone in broad daylight "**like the sun**" (Matthew 17:2) and "His clothes became dazzling white, whiter than anyone in the world could bleach them." (Mark 9:3 NIV) The supernatural light of the glory of God is even brighter than sunlight in its strength.

Natural sunlight is extremely bright, but the supernatural light of heaven can eclipse the intensity of the sun to the extent that Saul was actually blinded by the brightness of the light of God's glory. On occasions when the glory of God is manifested as bright light the natural photons are in some way eclipsed by supernatural photons that shine brighter than any light that can be created by the sun. This is like the effect of a supernova. But because the glory is manifested on earth as natural photons within the visible light spectrum, they must be clothed in some sort of natural quantum phenomena in order to be detected by the human eye. In the same way that supernatural sound can be manifested as natural sound, so supernatural light can be manifested as natural light. We could use the language of light within light and sound within sound.

The intensity of natural light is measured in "lumens." Lumens measure the total power of light that is emitted from a light source. One lumen equals the amount of light emitted by one candle that falls on an area of one square foot. This is called a "foot-candle" which is the standard measurement in the United States. Light is always measured in relation to the area that it illuminates. The international standard of measurement is now the "lux." One lux is equal to one lumen per square metre. "1000 lumens concentrated into an area of one square metre lights up that area with an illuminance of 1,000 lux. The same 1000 lumens spread out over ten square metres produces a dimmer illuminance of only 100 lux."[5]

One lux is the equivalent of the light of the full moon shining in full intensity at night. A clear moonless night only registers 0.001 lux, as the earth is dimly illumined by the light of the stars. An average room illumined by an incandescent bulb is approximately 50 lux. A brightly lit office can be as great as 400 lux. The maximum intensity of full sunlight on a clear day is 10,000 lux. The light that Saul of Tarsus saw on the Damascus road was "brighter than the sun!"

Whilst it is purely speculative, we could estimate that the full intensity of the glory of God exceeds 100,000 lux! The light that Saul experienced was so bright that it blinded him until he was supernaturally healed three days later. Saul must have felt like he had just witnessed a giant supernova in the daytime! A supernova is a stellar explosion that can radiate as much energy in a short interval as our sun could release over its entire lifetime. The supernova is an awesome prophetic picture of the explosion of God's glory.

Paul tells us that God "lives in *unapproachable light*." (1 Timothy 6:16 NIV) The light of the glory of God is so intense that no human being can endure the full intensity of this light. Moses asked God to show him His glory but God refused because the full intensity of the glory of God would have killed him. God said that no-one could see His full glory and survive! Only a select handful of people in the history of the Bible have had experiences where they saw the throne of God, and even then they must have been supernaturally shielded from the full intensity of the light of God so that they could live to tell the story. God accommodates the frailty of human flesh by turning the intensity of the light down low. The glory of God that illuminates heaven has properties that are deliberately replicated by natural light here on earth. One of those properties is the appearance of a rainbow around the throne.

Ezekiel and the apostle John were both taken into heaven and stood before the throne. Both of them tell us that the unapproachable light of

God that proceeds from the throne of God was refracted as a rainbow that encircled the throne. A rainbow is an optical phenomenon where light is refracted through a mist of fine water droplets in the atmosphere. John tells us that "there was a rainbow around the throne." (Revelation 4:3) Ezekiel also saw it. He said, "Like the appearance of a rainbow in the clouds on a rainy day, so was the radiance around Him. This was the appearance of the likeness of the glory of the Lord." (Ezekiel 1:28 NIV) The supernatural glory of God is refracted from the throne into the seven colours of the rainbow.

The glory cloud that sometimes appears on earth is actually a heavenly phenomenon that on rare occasions descends upon the earth. It is possible that the brilliant light of God is refracted through a visible glory cloud that surrounds the throne. When God made natural light to shine upon earth He modelled it upon the supernatural light of His presence by making visible natural light to refract into the seven primary colours of the rainbow. Whenever we shine pure white light through a prism it refracts into seven beautiful colours and this reflects the quality of the supernatural light of God in heaven.

The Power and the Glory

The fourth concept associated with the glory of God is "power." The relationship between the light of the glory of God and the power of God is paralleled in nature through the relationship between natural light and electricity. Individual quanta of natural light travel as a wave of electromagnetic radiation. A photon leaves the sun as a particle, it travels through space as a wave, but it arrives at its destination as a particle. The wave-particle duality of photons is a property of all quanta, including electrons. Nikola Tesla discovered what he called the "photoelectric effect" in 1901 and patented the first invention to harness photoelectric power.

Photons actually carry electrical charge so that when a photon collides with a metallic surface such as in a solar panel the energy of the photon is absorbed by the electrons and an electrical current is created as electrons break away from atoms. That is why solar panels can convert photons into electrical power. In a similar manner the supernatural light of God energises those who are radiated by the glory of God. God's glory is extremely powerful. It is not an inert substance; it actually imparts spiritual power or energy. That is why the concept of the glory of God is so closely associated with the power of God.

King David said, "Yours, O Lord, is the greatness, the *power* and the *glory*, the victory and the majesty!" (1 Chronicles 29:11) David wanted to experience the power and the glory of God. He said, "I have looked for You in the sanctuary, to see Your **power** and Your **glory**." (Psalm 63:2) He said, "Your saints shall bless You. They shall speak of the *glory* of Your kingdom, and talk of Your **power**, to make known to the sons of men His mighty acts, and the *glorious majesty* of His kingdom." (Psalm 145:10-12) In the New Testament there is an even more explicit relationship between the power and the glory of God. Jesus linked these two concepts in the prayer He taught His disciples: "For Yours is the kingdom and the *power* and the *glory* forever." (Matthew 6:13) Paul referred to "the *glory of His power.*" (2 Thessalonians 1:9) He prayed that his disciples would be "strengthened with all might, according to *His glorious power.*" (Colossians 1:11) In the book of Revelation, "The temple was filled with smoke from the *glory* of God and from His *power.*" (Revelation 15:8)

David said, "For the Lord God is *a sun* and shield; The Lord will give grace and *glory.*" (Psalm 84:11) God's grace is His empowering presence. David likened the Lord to a sun. The sun that energises planet earth is a powerful prophetic picture of the very nature of God. Our sun is a super massive ball of gaseous fire that emits unimaginable heat, energy and light. Similarly, the God of the Bible is revealed as a glorious fire. "For the Lord your God is a *consuming fire.*" (Deuteronomy 4:24) "The sight of the glory of the Lord was like a *consuming fire* on the top of the mountain in the eyes of the children of Israel." (Exodus 24:17)

The glory of the Lord is always closely associated with the presence of fire. In the book of Leviticus, Moses and Aaron had prepared an offering before the Lord on the altar and suddenly "the glory of the Lord appeared to all the people. Fire came out from the presence of the Lord and consumed the burnt offering. And when all the people saw it, they shouted for joy and fell facedown." (Exodus 9:23-24 NIV) Daniel saw the throne of God and the one thing that impacted him was the presence of fire. "The Ancient of Days took His seat. His clothing was as white as snow; the hair of His head was white like wool. His throne was *flaming with fire*, and its wheels were all ablaze. A *river of fire* was flowing, coming out from before Him. Thousands upon thousands attended Him; ten thousand times ten thousand stood before him." (Daniel 7:9-10 NIV) This "river of fire" represents a stream of the energy of the Spirit that emanates from the throne of God. Paul said, "Do not put out the Spirit's fire." (1 Thessalonians 5:19 NIV)

Daniel continued to gaze upon the vision of the throne of God. "I was watching in the night visions and behold, *one like the Son of Man* coming with the clouds of heaven! He came to the Ancient of Days and they brought Him near before Him." (Daniel 7:13) John experienced the great privilege of gazing into the eyes of the Son of Man. "I turned to see the voice that spoke with me. And having turned I saw seven golden lampstands, and in the midst of the seven lampstands *one like the Son of Man*, clothed with a garment down to the feet and girded about the chest with a golden band. His head and hair were white like wool, as white as snow, and *His eyes like a flame of fire*; His feet were like fine brass, as if refined in a furnace, and His voice as the sound of many waters; He had in His right hand seven stars, out of His mouth went a sharp two-edged sword, and His countenance was *like the sun shining in its strength*." (Revelation 1:12-16)

I have always thought it to be a strange irony within the English language that we call Jesus the *Son* and we also call the star that our planet orbits, the *sun*. In so many ways the natural sun is a prophetic picture of the Son of God, not least of which is the fact that the sun is the light of the world. The sun is also a burning fire that energises and empowers the earth.

THE GLORY THRESHOLD

The concept of "thresholds" is important in every aspect of physics. As we have already seen, there is a certain threshold at which the world of classical physics crosses over into the world of quantum physics. That precise threshold can be somewhat elusive, but there is a certainty that it does exist. There is a threshold at which water molecules begin to freeze. This is 32° F.[6] There is a threshold at which water molecules vaporise into steam, which is 212° F.[7] All elements have different boiling points and freezing points. For example, nitrogen, which makes up 78% of the earth's atmosphere, occurs naturally as a gas. It freezes at -346.0° F.[8] and it boils at -320.5° F.[9], which means it only occurs as a liquid between freezing point and boiling point which is a very narrow range. Nitrogen vaporises into a gas at a temperature threshold above -320.5° F.

Just as there are thresholds in all aspects of physics, so there are thresholds in the spiritual realm as well. Consider the theme of the presence of the Lord. It is universally understood amongst theologians that God is an omnipresent being. Omnipresence means that God is everywhere present throughout the entire universe. David said, "Where can I go from Your Spirit? Or where can I flee from Your presence? If I ascend into heaven, You are there; If I make my bed in hell, behold, You are there." (Psalm 139:7-8)

Even though God is omnipresent, this does not guarantee that someone might discern His presence at the extremities of the universe. There is another threshold of the presence of the Lord and this is called the manifest presence of God. At a certain point the omnipresence of God crosses over to the manifest presence. The Lord said to Moses, "My Presence will go with you, and I will give you rest." (Exodus 33:14) The manifest presence describes the subjective conscious awareness that God is intentionally revealing His presence to us. This is something that is subjectively and spiritually discerned. Many Christians have felt the presence of the Lord, but fewer have encountered the glory of God.

Moses understood that there was a difference between the presence of God and the glory of God. Whist I am sure he appreciated the fact that God had promised him that His presence would accompany him, nevertheless Moses was not satisfied with God's manifest presence. Moses said to God, "Please, show me Your glory." (Exodus 33:18) Moses made this request between his first ascension to the top of Mount Sinai in Exodus 19 and his second ascension in Exodus 34.

He had already encountered the thick glory cloud on the top of the mountain, where God revealed Himself as a consuming fire. Moses was not satisfied merely with His presence, as wonderful as that was. There is a threshold at which the presence of the Lord crosses over into the glory of the Lord. To use a spatial illustration, if someone was a long way away from God, living in the world and engaging in an evil lifestyle, that person would be a complete stranger to the presence of the Lord even though the reality of the omnipresence of God guarantees that God is present even where someone is living a hellish existence.

However, if that person came to full repentance upon hearing the gospel message, the Holy Spirit would come to dwell in that person's heart. As her spiritual senses were developed and cultivated she would soon come to discern the presence of the Lord around her. Because she is now indwelt by the Holy Spirit, the presence of the Lord actually dwells within her because her "spirit" has been joined to the Holy Spirit. At times she may even become acutely aware of a strong sense of the presence of the Lord, for example, when she gathers together with the saints to worship the Lord and the presence of the Lord falls upon the meeting. But if she was to purpose in her heart to seek the Lord she can be assured that the Lord is the rewarder of those who diligently seek Him. As she draws near with a sincere heart she may even have some encounters with the presence of the Lord that leave her quite overcome by the experience of God's nearness.

The Bible says, "Draw near to God and He will draw near to you." (James 4:8) Moses experienced a definite threshold between the manifest presence and the glory realm as he contended for a deeper experience of God. God says, "You will seek Me and find Me, when you search for Me with all your heart." (Jeremiah 29:13) David said, "I have looked for You in the sanctuary, to see Your power and Your glory." (Psalm 63:2) Those who seek to encounter the fullness of the glory of God shall find it when they seek for it with all their heart. When we cross the threshold from the presence realm to the glory realm, things really begin to shift. Paul talked about the danger of being shut out from "the presence of the Lord and from the glory of His power." (2 Thessalonians 1:9) Jude talked about entering "the presence of His glory with exceeding joy." (Jude 1:24) The Bible differentiates between the presence of the Lord and the presence of His glory.

To borrow from the imagery of the Tabernacle, the threshold is experienced as we transition through the Holy Place into the Holy of Holies. Even within the Holy Place the priest would have experienced a strong sense of the presence of the Lord. The three pieces of furniture in the Holy Place were the lampstand, the golden altar of incense and the table of shewbread. Each day the priest would refill the oil in the lampstand, refill the incense on the altar and replace the loaves of bread. The lampstand actually represented the presence of the Lord and the illumination that the Spirit brings. The high priest only entered the Holy of Holies once a year on Yom Kippur, and on this rare occasion he entered a room that was supernaturally illuminated by the "Shekinah Glory" of God.

When the Tabernacle was completed, the glory of the Lord descended upon the Tabernacle and it filled the Holy of Holies with an abiding glory. The word *shekinah* means "to dwell, to rest, to abide or to make a habitation." "Moses was not able to enter the tabernacle of meeting, because the cloud **rested** [*shekinah*] above it, and the glory of the Lord **filled** the tabernacle." (Exodus 40:35) The Holy of Holies is the inner temple, and it was filled with a visible light that shone with the glory of the Lord. The Holy Place was illuminated by the lampstand, but the Most Holy Place was illuminated by the Shekinah. In Ezekiel's vision of the temple, the glory of the Lord spilled out from the Most Holy Place into the outer court. "A cloud filled the inner court. Then the glory of the Lord rose from above the cherubim and moved to the threshold of the temple. The cloud filled the temple, and the court was full of the radiance of the glory of the Lord." (Ezekiel 10:3-4 NIV) There is a threshold between the inner court or the Holy of Holies and the Holy Place. This threshold is represented by a veil. Believers are invited to "enter within the veil" (Hebrews 6:19) and experience the Shekinah Glory.

CROSSING THE THRESHOLD

Bob Sorge attempts to explain the distinction between the presence realm and the glory realm by charting the levels of intensity of the presence of God as it crosses over into the glory realm. As a means of illustrating the threshold points, he created a chart. The vertical axis represented the degree of intensity. On the horizontal axis he assigns 1–10 on the presence scale followed by 11–25 on the glory scale. 10 was the threshold that represented a distinct transition from the experience of the presence of the Lord as it crossed the threshold into the experience of the glory. 20 was the upper threshold of the ability of a human being to withstand the growing intensity of the glory without being consumed. The chart continued beyond 20 because there is no limit to the degrees of intensity to the glory of the Lord.

Even as there are degrees of intensity in the sphere of Presence, in a similar way there are degrees of intensity in the sphere of Glory. I see Presence and Glory as comprising a continuum. Presence can become so strong that God crosses the divide and manifests His glory in a tangible way. There is no end to the chart because the intensities of God's glory are limitless. God's omnipresence (the level where 95% of earth lives most of the time) might register around a zero or a one in the Presence realm. His manifest Presence in a corporate time of high worship might register around a nine or a ten. And then we enter that sphere where we move from Presence to Glory – where we cross the sensory threshold. When God heals a sick person we're talking about a Glory manifestation that might register around a twelve in the Glory realm. The survival threshold is that point where God's Glory becomes so intense that a person in this body of flesh would be killed if exposed to that level of glory.[10]

Moses said to God, "Please show me Your glory!" And God said, "You cannot see My face; for no man shall see Me, and live. And the Lord said, "Here is a place by Me, and you shall stand on the rock. So it shall be, while My glory passes by, that I will put you in the cleft of the rock, and will cover you with My hand while I pass by. Then I will take away My hand, and you shall see My back; but My face shall not be seen." (Exodus 33:20-23) It was God's mercy to shield Moses from the full intensity of His glory.

"Chabod" means weight, and when God's glory intensifies there is a supernatural heaviness that presses down physically upon the people of God. In Solomon's Temple, "the house of the Lord was filled with a cloud so that the priests could not continue ministering because of the cloud, for the glory of the Lord filled the house of God." (2 Chronicles 5:12-14) We can imagine the priests lying incapacitated on the ground because of the intensity of the glory explosion! In the book of Revelation there is a description of the glory becoming so intense that no-one could enter the temple. "The temple was filled with smoke from the glory of God and from His power, and no one was able to enter the temple." (Revelation 15:8) Bob Sorge writes:

> God's glory filled the heavenly temple with such intensity that no-one – no angel, no elder, no cherub, no living creature, no-one – was able to enter that Glory. This intensity of Glory would be "off the chart." It's amazing to consider that the holy ones who inhabit the very throne of God and who dwell among the fiery stones are not able to sustain the fullness of God's glory when it is manifest![11]

What a terrifying thought that there is a survival threshold in our capacity to experience the glory of God. John saw the glorified risen Christ in Revelation, chapter one, and said, "When I saw Him, I fell at His feet as dead. But He laid His right hand on me, saying to me, 'Do not be afraid; I am the First and the Last.'" (Revelation 1:17) There is a threshold at which the experience of God's presence transitions into glory. All who draw nearer and nearer to God will inevitably cross this invisible threshold. At this point the experience of glory moves beyond something that is spiritually discerned. It becomes physical!

> Presence is subjective. Glory is objective. In the Presence realm what various people experience becomes a very subjective, individualized thing. One person receives one thing, another person feels something totally different. One person is super-blessed, another

feels totally bypassed; one person is blitzed, another person is falling asleep. When God visits us with His Presence, everyone responds or receives differently based upon their faith level, intensity of concentration, and how God chooses to touch them in the uniqueness of their own personal challenges and needs. But the Glory realm is objective. By "objective" I mean that everybody experiences the same thing in the same way because God has moved past spiritual impressions into physical manifestations. The Glory realm was what happened when the cloud filled Solomon's temple during its dedication ceremonies. Everyone saw the cloud, none of the priests were able to stand to perform their service. The Glory became an objective reality in the physical realm. When Glory comes, "all flesh shall see it together!" (Isaiah 40:5)[12]

The kingdom ministry of Jesus resulted in powerful physical experiences everywhere He went. Every single healing was a powerful physical event. But it was not uncommon to see people shaking violently, trembling and weeping at Jesus' feet. The most common phenomenon when the glory showed up was for people to fall facedown. Peter, James and John heard the audible voice of God and "they *fell on their faces* and were greatly afraid." (Matthew 17:6) A woman reached out and touched the hem of Jesus garment and was instantly healed. "Then the woman, knowing what had happened to her, came and *fell at his feet, trembling with fear*." (Mark 5:33 NIV)

Intense physical effects were the hallmark of Jesus' kingdom ministry. A demonised boy was brought to Jesus to be healed. When the boy saw Jesus, "immediately the spirit convulsed him, and he *fell on the ground* and wallowed, foaming at the mouth." (Mark 9:20) One of the ten lepers who were healed by Jesus "returned, and with a loud voice glorified God, and *fell down on his face* at His feet, giving Him thanks." (Luke 17:15-16) When the soldiers came to arrest Jesus, He said to them, "Whom are you seeking?" They answered Him, "Jesus of Nazareth." Jesus said to them, "I am!" Now when He said to them, "I am!" they drew back and *fell to the ground*." (John 18:4-6) We could imagine Jesus travelling the countryside, moving from village to village, leaving a pile of bodies on the ground weeping and trembling because they had just encountered the glorious power of God.

When the glory of God is revealed, there are always physical manifestations. The glory becomes visible as physical infirmities and deformities are instantly healed. Withered hands suddenly grow back! New eyeballs appear! Deaf ears are physically opened! The cripples stand up and walk! Leprosy instantly disappears! The dead are raised up from their graves! This is spectacular stuff! There is no greater pleasure than participating in the kingdom works of Jesus. Every miracle is a glory encounter that carries the reality of heaven. Whenever the glory falls, there is objective physical evidence that God has brought heaven to earth. When the church crosses the threshold into the glory realm God crosses the threshold and recreates matter at a quantum level! The glory spills out of heaven onto earth.

The appreciation of the physical implications of this ministry of glory brings us to the point where we can begin to understand the consequences at a quantum level of this kind of supernatural invasion. When the glory comes, it brings a sudden transformation in the quantum field as entirely new body parts are created. This is why the glorious ministry of Jesus caused matter on some occasions to suddenly "materialise" at a quantum level all the way up to the macroscopic level. On other occasions He caused matter to completely "dematerialise," and on yet other occasions he caused matter to undergo a comprehensive metamorphosis from one form into another.

At the centre of the quantum healing ministry of Jesus is the concept of materialisation and dematerialisation. Virtually everything that Jesus did in the gospel narratives that constituted a miracle involved either some kind of materialisation or dematerialisation. Similarly, in the book of Acts the disciples of Jesus caused body parts to either materialise or dematerialise. In the book of Acts God caused His own people to sometimes dematerialise and rematerialise in another location. This quantum phenomena lies at the heart of biblical miracles. But it is not just in the arena of physical healing that we see this effect. Turning 180 gallons of water into the best quality wine also qualifies as a quantum miracle, as does the daily appearance of manna in the wilderness. And these kinds of miracles are also occurring today in churches that are focused upon experiencing the glory realm of heaven on earth.

I have been present in gatherings where copious amounts of oil have begun pouring from people's hands. I have even experienced this phenomenon myself at the same time it happened to others. People in my own church have experienced oil running down the walls in gatherings where the glory of God fell upon them. I have seen a fine gold dust begin to appear all over people's bodies and their clothing as the glory increased.

I have also personally experienced these things happen to me at times when the glory realm began to manifest. These kinds of supernatural occurrences have been reported with increasing frequency all over the earth. The miracle of the manna is not restricted to Old Testament times. Many people have experienced manna supernaturally appearing in Christian gatherings or inside their Bibles. Critics and sceptics can mock and ridicule these kinds of things, but I have seen them with my own eyes!

Others have experienced water turning into top quality wine and still others have experienced priceless gemstones appearing supernaturally in their midst. Credible testimonies abound of feathers falling in meetings and rain falling inside a building. I have even been present in gatherings where these feathers began to fall, and I have seen them with my own eyes. Similarly, I have been present in gatherings where the glory of the Lord appeared as a smoky mist accompanied with the strong smell of smoke.

I had the privilege of being in one gathering of thousands of believers in Kansas City in 1994 where a glory explosion took place. I physically smelled the fragrance of the Lord. It was like beautiful fresh roses and the fragrance exploded over us like a bomb. Simultaneously dozens of people were instantly healed without anyone even laying hands upon them. Outside the conference centre I saw a visible rose-coloured glow of a "glory cloud" resting upon the building.

Dozens of people lay all over the parking lot, some draped over the hood of their cars, others on the ground. People were being carried out of the building. Inside the building hundreds of people were lying on the floor, some in a deep spiritual trance, some experiencing visions, some laughing uncontrollably, others were weeping intensely. Simultaneously the fire alarm was set off in the building because the manifestation of the glory of God became so intense.

This is what happens in a glory explosion. It crosses the threshold of subjectivity into a powerful physical experience of the glory and the power of God. These are some examples of the manifestations that accompany the outpouring of the glory of the Lord.

Chapter Thirteen

Ministering out of the Glory Cloud

s we have seen in the previous chapter, the glory of God is the very substance of the non-local realm of heaven. It tangibly manifests upon the earth as either a cloud, as smoke, as visible extra-dimensional light or as supernatural power. Whenever the glory shows up on the earth there is a shift in the very quantum fabric of the universe at a local level. Jesus carried this atmosphere of the glory of God, and when He spoke He affected quantum miracles as heaven invaded earth. Wherever He went He carried the atmosphere of glory. Subsequently His words were imbued with the glory of the Father and they affected the transformation or the re-creation of the quantum field.

Jesus healed the sick either with a word of authority or with "the touch of His hand." Luke highlighted the fact that when Jesus healed the sick He did it either with a word or through physical touch. We see these two approaches to releasing the glory in the following passage:

> After leaving the synagogue that day, Jesus went to Simon's home, where He found Simon's mother-in-law very sick with a high fever. "Please heal her," everyone begged. Standing at her bedside, He spoke to the fever, rebuking it, and immediately her temperature returned to normal. She got up at once and prepared a meal for them. As the sun went down that evening, people throughout the village brought sick family members to Jesus. No matter what their diseases were, the touch of his hand healed every one. (Luke 4:38-40 NLT)

As the people observed the healing ministry of Jesus they quickly figured out that this principle of touch seemed to release the healing power of God. Many of us would be familiar with the story of the woman with the issue of blood.

> A woman who had had a hemorrhage for twelve years came up behind him. She touched the fringe of his robe, for she thought, "If I can just touch his robe, I will be healed." Jesus turned around and said to her, "Daughter, be encouraged! Your faith has made you well." And the woman was healed at that moment. (Matthew 9:20-22 NLT)

When Jesus and the disciples arrived at Gennesaret, "The news of their arrival spread quickly throughout the whole surrounding area, and soon people were bringing all their sick to be healed. The sick begged Him to let them touch even the fringe of His robe, and all who touched it were healed." (Matthew 14:35-36 NLT) In other places in the gospel narratives we are told that "many sick people were crowding around Him, trying to touch Him." (Mark 3:10 NLT) What an amazing reality! Jesus was so energised by the glory of God that people pressed in around Him to receive their healing. Jesus could even feel the glory flowing out of Him! When the woman with the issue of blood crept up on Jesus to touch the hem of His garment, Jesus felt the glory flow out of His body and into the sick woman.

> Jesus said, "Who touched Me?" When all denied it, Peter and those with Him said, "Master, the multitudes throng and press You, and You say, "Who touched Me?" But Jesus said, "Somebody touched Me, for I perceived power going out from Me." Now when the woman saw that she was not hidden, she came trembling; and falling down before Him, she declared to Him in the presence of all the people the reason she had touched Him and how she was healed immediately. (Luke 8:45,47)

As we have already seen, there is a powerful convergence between the idea of the quantum world as a buffer zone between the material world and the spiritual world and the revelation of the supernatural glory waves of heaven that are capable of restructuring the sub-atomic world from the other side of the quantum looking glass. Glory waves are designed to create entirely new quantum realities. These two realms were made for each other! On the one hand we have the material world that, according to the latest research in quantum physics, is really a manifestation of extra-dimensional energy at a sub-atomic level. And then, on the other side of the looking glass we have the intense glory of God which has the capacity to restructure and re-create this reality at a sub-atomic level.

These two realms: the glory realm of heaven and the quantum realm of matter came into dramatic collision in the coming of Jesus Christ. Jesus was sent into the world to display the glory of God and to demonstrate the supernatural capacity of the glory realm to impact and transform the quantum world of nature. "And the Word became flesh and dwelt among us, and *we beheld His glory*, the glory of the One and Only, who came from the Father, full of grace and truth." (John 1:14 NIV)

His glory was pre-eminently displayed in His power over nature that He demonstrated through the ministry of the Spirit of Glory. When Jesus turned water into wine (an extraordinary display of His power over the quantum world) we read that "This miraculous sign at Cana in Galilee was Jesus' first *display of His glory*. And His disciples believed in Him." (John 2:11 NLT) Turning water into wine was Jesus' very first miracle. Every subsequent miracle was a further display of His glory, culminating in His glorious resurrection from the dead, "Just as Christ was raised from the dead by the glory of the Father!" (Romans 6:4)

There was a dramatic prophecy about the impending appearance of the supernatural ministry of Christ in the book of Isaiah. The coming of the Lord would be heralded by the coming of John the Baptist.

> The voice of one crying in the wilderness: "Prepare the way of the Lord; make straight in the desert a highway for our God. Every valley shall be exalted and every mountain and hill brought low; the crooked places shall be made straight and the rough places smooth; and the glory of the Lord shall be revealed, and all flesh shall see it together; for the mouth of the Lord has spoken. (Isaiah 40:3-5)

The ultimate purpose of the coming of Christ was to reveal the glory of God to all flesh. But the coming of Jesus was just the beginning. He commissioned His disciples to perpetuate the ministry of the Father's glory to the ends of the earth. The same glory that the Father imparted to Jesus was imparted to His disciples. In John 17 Jesus prayed to the Father, "The glory which You gave Me *I have given them*, that they may be one just as We are one." (John 17:22) Paul said, "He called you by our gospel for the obtaining of the glory of our Lord Jesus Christ." (2 Thessalonians 2:14) The Father was continually lavishing His own glory upon His Son so that Jesus reflected His Father's glory upon the earth.

In the same way, Jesus continues to lavish His glory upon His disciples so that they can continue to release and reflect His glory in the earth. The ministry of the church is a ministry of heaven's glory. When Jesus trained His disciples He was training them how to release high level realms of glory on the earth, which is exactly what they continued to do in the book of Acts. Peter had such a glory zone around him that even his shadow healed the sick. Was it his shadow or was it an atmosphere of glory that extended beyond his physical body?

> Through the hands of the apostles many signs and wonders were done among the people. And believers were increasingly added to the Lord, multitudes of both men and women, so that they brought the sick out into the streets and laid them on beds and couches, that at least the shadow of Peter passing by might fall on some of them. Also a multitude gathered from the surrounding cities to Jerusalem, bringing sick people and those who were tormented by unclean spirits, and they were all healed. (Acts 5:12,14-16)

Did you catch that? "They were *all* healed!" The disciples were moving in such high level glory that everyone was being healed just as when Jesus ministered. "With *great power* the apostles gave witness to the resurrection of the Lord Jesus and great grace was upon them all." (Acts 4:33) Great power is *mega dunamis* in the Greek language. As time progressed after the initial explosion of Pentecost, much of the church had all but forgotten the intensity of the glory realm that was poured out upon the church in those early days. It was with great sadness that Jesus said to one of the churches in the book of Revelation, "You have a *little power*." (Revelation 3:8 NASB) This was *micro dunamis* in the Greek!

In less than 60 years the church had transitioned from *mega dunamis* to *micro dunamis* and the glory had departed from the church. The church had become "Ichabod!" "Chabod" is the Hebrew word for glory and it means the "weighty" presence of God. "Ichabod" meant the glory had departed! Eli the priest had two sons, Phinehas and Hophni. In a great military defeat the Ark of the Covenant was captured by the Philistines. Phinehas and Hophni were killed and soon after Phinehas' wife gave birth to a son. "Then she named the child Ichabod, saying, 'The glory has departed from Israel!' because the ark of God had been captured." (1 Samuel 4:21) The church without the glory of God is likewise Ichabod!

THE MINISTRY OF THE GLORY

There is something that remains for us to lay hold of! "He called you by our gospel for the obtaining of the glory of our Lord Jesus Christ." (2 Thessalonians 2:14) Paul regarded the "riches of His glory" as the true inheritance of the saints. (Ephesians 1:18) In 2 Corinthians 3 Paul begins to contrast the ministry of the Old Covenant with the ministry of the New Covenant. He describes the ministry of the Old Covenant as a ministry of condemnation and of death. This revelatory chapter reveals that the true ministry of the New Covenant is a ministry of the Spirit of Glory. This is our inheritance in Christ.

> Our sufficiency is from God who also made us sufficient as min-isters of the New Covenant, not of the letter but of the Spirit, for the letter kills but the Spirit gives life. But if the ministry of death, written and engraved on stones, was glorious, so that the children of Israel could not look steadily at the face of Moses because of the glory of his countenance, which glory was passing away, *how will the ministry of the Spirit not be more glorious*? For if the ministry of condemnation had glory, the ministry of righteousness *exceeds much more in glory*. For even what was made glorious had no glory in this respect, because of *the glory that excels*. For if what is pass-ing away was glorious, what remains is *much more glorious*. There-fore, since we have such hope, we use great boldness of speech, un-like Moses, who put a veil over his face so that the children of Israel could not look steadily at the end of what was passing away. But their minds were blinded. For until this day the same veil remains unlifted in the reading of the Old Testament, because the veil is taken away in Christ. But even to this day, when Moses is read, a veil lies on their heart. Nevertheless when one turns to the Lord, the veil is taken away. Now the Lord is the Spirit; and where the Spirit of the Lord is, there is liberty. But we all, with unveiled face, be-holding as in a mirror the glory of the Lord, are being transformed into the same image *from glory to glory*, just as by the Spirit of the Lord. Therefore, since we have this ministry, as we have received mercy, we do not lose heart. (2 Corinthians 3:5–4:1)

The theme of this passage of Scripture is the ministry of the Spirit of Glory. It begins by talking about the ministry of the New Covenant and it ends by talking about the ministry of the New Covenant which is clearly a ministry of glory. The key to being transformed from glory to glory is in beholding the glory of the Lord. Remember that Jesus prayed that His disciples would "be with Me where I am, that they may **behold My glory** which You have given Me; for **You loved Me** before the foundation of the world." (John 17:24) We have seen how the glory of God is revealed pre-eminently in the revelation and the experience of the love of the Father.

Jesus had enjoyed this ministry of the Father's love through all eternity past, but now through His death on the cross the veil has been torn and the way into the Holy of Holies has been made accessible through the shed blood of Christ. The outpouring of the Spirit upon the saints now mediates the experience of the love of the Father that Jesus has eternally enjoyed. The glory of Jesus is the intense love of His Father. "For the Father loves the Son and shows Him everything He is doing." (John 5:20) It is because the Father loves the Son that Jesus is so filled with the Father's glory. The hope of glory is the transformational experience of the love of God.

Therefore, having been justified by faith, we have peace with God through our Lord Jesus Christ, through whom also we have access by faith into this grace in which we stand, and rejoice **in hope of the glory of God**. Now hope does not disappoint, because the love of God has been poured out in our hearts by the Holy Spirit who was given to us. (Romans 5:1-2,5)

The glorious hope of the saints is found in the riches of the experience of the love of the Father. Jesus' prayer to the Father was, "That the love with which You loved Me may be in them." (John 17:26) His mission was not complete until He brought us back into the intimate experience of the love of the Father. This is the ultimate glory encounter. There is the encounter with the glory of His light and with the glory of His power, but the supreme encounter is with the glory of His love. This is what it means to "behold His glory" and this is the continuing prayer of Jesus. He will not be satisfied until we enter into the fullness of the tangible experience of the love of the Father!

Using the lens of Jesus' experience on the Mount of Transfiguration, we can gain insight into the glorious hope of the saints. The Father lavished the experience of His love upon His Son by declaring over Him, "This is My Son whom I love!" (Matthew 17:5 NIV) This was the substance of the Voice that came from the Majestic Glory. Jesus looked up into the loving eyes of His Father and experienced an upgrade of glory. In the same way, as we, (with an unveiled face), behold the glory of the Father's love, we are "transformed into the same image from glory to glory, just as by the Spirit of the Lord." (2 Corinthians 3:18) The more we experience the glory of His love, the more we will be equipped to minister His supernatural power and His love.

It is so profound that the next verse speaks of this supernatural ministry: "Therefore, since we have this ministry, as we have received mercy, we do not lose heart." (2 Corinthians 4:1) We do not become discouraged because we live in the hope (or the confident expectation) of the experience of the glory of God. The very same word used to describe the experience of Jesus on the mountain is the word that Paul uses to describe this transformation from glory to glory. The word is *metamorphoo* and it means to undergo a profound metamorphosis from one form to another. God intends to take His beloved disciples to the mountain top again and again to experience the depths of His intimate love so that they are changed from one degree of glory to another.

It is this series of glory encounters that qualifies and equips the saints to participate with Jesus in the ministry of glory. All we need to do is to ascend the mountain of the Lord in worship, stand under the cloud of His radiant glory, and receive that divine radiation that demolishes the stranglehold of the flesh and releases the life of Christ within us. Christ in us is the confident expectation of glory! (Colossians 1:27)

The disciples of Jesus went from one profound glory encounter to another over a period of three years. They constantly experienced the revelation of the glory of God in Christ. "We beheld His glory; the glory of the One and Only who came from the Father." (John 1:14) As the disciples journeyed with Jesus, it ultimately produced in them a ministry of glory that matched that of their Master. "A disciple is not above his teacher, nor a servant above his master. But it is enough for a disciple that he be like his teacher, and a servant like his master." (Matthew 10:24-25) The early disciples were conformed to the image of Christ. They were transformed into the same image from glory to glory.

We are living in a time when the glory of God is beginning to become manifest in a way that has not been seen since the days of the early church. As the people of God seek the face of Christ together, they are beginning to experience the glory realm of heaven touching earth. As we purpose in our hearts to experientially draw near to God, we inevitably cross a threshold where we begin to enter the glory zone.

"Therefore, brothers, since we have confidence to enter the Most Holy Place by the blood of Jesus...*let us draw near to God* with a sincere heart in full assurance of faith." (Hebrews 10:19,22 NIV) We are invited to experientially enter the Most Holy Place that is filled with the Shekinah Glory of God. The glory of God is much greater than a powerful theological concept. It is a powerful spiritual reality that God desires His people to experience. As we experience that heavenly glory here on earth, we literally become one with God just as Jesus and the Father were one. The experience of the glory of God is the catalytic factor that catapults us into a deep spiritual oneness with God. This oneness cannot be achieved any other way than through a series of glory encounters. Jesus ministered out of the glory realm, but He never resorted to formulas or techniques. The ministry of glory flows out of one thing and one thing alone, and that is the realm of intimate relationship. There is no room for formulas or magical techniques in the glorious ministry of the Kingdom. It only flows out of intimate knowing. "This is eternal life, that they may know You, the only true God, and Jesus Christ whom You have sent." (John 17:3)

As we enter "within the veil" we are crossing the threshold and entering into the realm of intense glory that emanates from the intimate friendship of the King of Glory. When we experientially cross this threshold, the glory begins to manifest and to overshadow the people of God on the earth. In this glory zone the supernatural power of God begins to manifest with greater intensity. Miracles increase in frequency and in quality in the thick glory of God. Creative miracles and unusual signs and wonders begin to occur.

The veil between the material world and the invisible realm of heaven becomes so thin that all sorts of glory manifestations begin to appear. Water literally turns into wine. The anointing oil of God begins to appear upon people's hands, faces and feet. People become covered in fine gold dust. The saints begin to see angelic beings and to experience visions and heavenly visitations. The prophetic anointing goes to new levels as people begin to fall into trances and have powerful revelatory encounters. These are the kinds of supernatural phenomena that occur when the glory of God overshadows His people.

THE MATRIX OF THE SUPERNATURAL

Throughout the Old Testament the glory cloud occasionally became visible upon the earth. These manifestations of the glory cloud were a prophetic prelude to the coming of the cloud upon Jesus at His baptism and upon the people of God on the Day of Pentecost. I want to turn our attention toward the relationship between Jesus and the cloud of glory. There is something about this revelation of the glory cloud that surrounded Jesus on earth that is designed to unlock this dimension for the church, because it points toward God's intent for the church to be clothed in the same glory cloud in order to bring forth the same supernatural fruitfulness. "As He is, so also are we in this world!" (1 John 4:17 NASB) The church is now invited to re-present Christ to the world in the fullness of His supernatural love and power, and God has purposed that will only be achieved as we enter into the fullness of the mystery of what it means to be "in Christ."

We begin this journey by considering Jesus before He was clothed in this heavenly cloud. For thirty years Jesus lived upon the earth unaccompanied by the cloud. Then, suddenly, at His baptism at the River Jordan the heavens were opened and the supernatural cloud descended and overshadowed Jesus for the remainder of His time on earth. For three years Jesus ministered under an open heaven.

What actually took place for Jesus in this moment to transform Him into a man who now carried the very atmosphere of heaven? Was Jesus suddenly filled with the Holy Spirit at the River Jordan? If so, what was His former spiritual state? If John the Baptist was filled with the Holy Spirit from his mother's womb (Luke 1:15) could we ever conceive that Jesus' experience of the Spirit was in some way inferior to that of John's? Would not Jesus have been perfectly filled with the Spirit from His mother's womb? After all, He was the perfect Son of God! I would like to suggest to you that Jesus was already full of the Holy Spirit, just like John, prior to His baptism at the River Jordan.

What really came upon Jesus at the River Jordan was an *external* overshadowing of the Spirit of Glory, and this overshadowing presence accompanied Jesus for the rest of His days upon the earth. The Holy Spirit was already indwelling Jesus in fullness before His baptism, but now the anointing of the Spirit had come *upon Him* for the purpose of supernatural ministry. Right after the coming of this heavenly anointing Jesus was launched into ministry, so there is an indisputable link between the external anointing of the Spirit and supernatural ministry. Jesus preached His first public sermon after this inaugural event in the synagogue in Nazareth. His opening words were,

> The Spirit of the Lord is upon Me because He has anointed Me to preach the gospel to the poor; He has sent Me to heal the broken-hearted, to proclaim liberty to the captives and recovery of sight to the blind, to set at liberty those who are oppressed; and to proclaim the year of the Lord's favour. (Luke 4:18-19)[1]

From heaven's perspective this event at the River Jordan was a public coronation of the King. Jesus was not recognised by man as the King, but He was certainly recognised by His Father. The Spirit descended in a visible manner and came and overshadowed Jesus, and the voice of the Father made the following pronouncement: "This is My beloved Son, in whom I am well pleased." (Matthew 3:17) At this precise moment Jesus was "clothed" with supernatural power from on high as He stepped into His kingly calling and ministry. His kingly garments were robes of the power and the glory of His Kingdom. From this moment onward Jesus was supernaturally clothed in glory! From heaven's perspective the Father made the pronouncement,

> I have installed my King on Zion, my holy hill. I will proclaim the decree of the Lord: He said to me, "You are my Son; today I have become your Father. Ask of me, and I will make the nations your inheritance, the ends of the earth your possession. You will rule them with an iron sceptre; you will dash them to pieces like pottery." Therefore, you kings, be wise; be warned, you rulers of the earth. Serve the Lord with fear and rejoice with trembling. Kiss the Son, lest he be angry and you be destroyed in your way, for his wrath can flare up in a moment. (Psalm 2:6-12 NIV)

I have suggested that Jesus was already filled with the Holy Spirit before His baptism. This idea is reinforced by Paul who said, "For it pleased the Father that in Him all the fullness should dwell." (Colossians 1:19) "For in Him dwells all the fullness of the Godhead bodily." (Colossians 2:9) As the one and only Son of God, Jesus was already indwelt by the fullness of the Father and the Spirit prior to His baptism. If Jesus wasn't filled with the Holy Spirit prior to His baptism, what was He filled with?

Can we conceive of the sinless Son of God needing to fill some kind of spiritual void in His interior life? There was clearly an abiding anointing of the Spirit indwelling the Messiah before He was baptized at the River

Jordan. But in addition to this abiding anointing of fullness, Jesus was now also anointed by the Holy Spirit for ministry by His Father. His coronation resulted in the Spirit now overshadowing Him by coming *upon Him* for the purpose of kingly ministry. This was the prophetic promise of the sign of the unveiling of the Messiah: the Spirit will not only be in Him, it will also be resting *upon Him* in a unique manner.

> Behold, My Servant, whom I uphold; My chosen one in whom My soul delights. I have put My Spirit *upon Him*; He will bring forth justice to the nations. He will not cry out or raise His voice, nor make His voice heard in the street. A bruised reed He will not break and a dimly burning wick He will not extinguish; He will faithfully bring forth justice. (Isaiah 42:1-3 NASB)

> The Spirit of the Lord will rest *upon Him* – the Spirit of wisdom and of understanding, the Spirit of counsel and of power, the Spirit of knowledge and of the fear of the Lord. (Isaiah 11:2)

Bill Johnson highlights the distinction between the indwelling anointing of the Spirit and the Spirit coming upon us for ministry.

> Anointing means "smeared" – it is God covering us with His power-filled presence. Supernatural things happen when we walk in the anointing! For the most part, the anointing has been hoarded by the church for the church. Many have misunderstood why God has covered us with Himself, thinking it is for our enjoyment only. Perhaps this phrase will help clarify this point: ***He is in me for my sake, but He's upon me for yours!*** The anointing equips us to bring the world into an encounter with God.[2]

The purpose of the Spirit coming upon us as believers is exactly the same as the purpose of the Spirit coming upon Jesus: it is to equip us for supernatural ministry. "***God anointed Jesus*** of Nazareth with the Holy Spirit and with power, who went about doing good and healing all who were oppressed by the devil, for God was with Him." (Acts 10:38) This anointing for ministry only comes upon the ***servants*** of the Lord. He comes powerfully upon those who have purposed in their heart to minister to the needs of others. "Behold My ***Servant***: I will put My Spirit *upon* Him." Another word for "servant" is "minister." The Greek word *diakonos* can be translated as either a *servant* or as a *minister*. The Spirit does not come upon self-centred Christians who have no interest in ministering to others!

God anointed Jesus specifically for the purpose of empowered super-natural ministry. Notice that Jesus didn't minister before He was anointed by the Spirit. But when the Spirit came "upon" Jesus, suddenly His ministry was **turbo-charged**. This "anointing" is a supernatural empowerment that comes from above. It comes **upon us**, whereas the abiding anointing resides **within us**. This empowering anointing remained in its fullness upon Jesus from the moment of His baptism, and He consistently moved in the full-ness of the anointing of the Spirit for ministry. Jesus was clothed in the Spirit of wisdom, the Spirit of prophecy, the Spirit of knowledge, the Spirit of counsel and the Spirit of might. There was a supernatural overshadowing over the life of Jesus that clothed Him in the very atmosphere of heaven. As a result, the supernatural exploded through His life and signs and wonders followed Him because He brought the very atmosphere of heaven to earth!

The overshadowing Spirit of God is the key to releasing creative miracles. It's all about the atmosphere that it releases! This unique spiritual environ-ment that is created whenever a child of God is enveloped in the glory cloud actually becomes the matrix of the supernatural! The term "matrix" is a Latin word that means "womb." It is "a situation or surrounding substance within which something else originates or develops." It is also defined as "an environment in which something develops." Jesus was supernaturally "con-ceived" in the womb of Mary through the overshadowing glory. The angel Gabriel said to Mary, "The Holy Spirit will come **upon you**, and the power of the Most High will **overshadow** you." (Luke 1:35) The Spirit coming "upon" people is always described as an "overshadowing." The English word "overshadowing" is translated from the Greek word *episkiazo*. Without this divine overshadowing, there are no miracles! But whenever we see this over-shadowing coming upon either Jesus or His disciples it always results in an explosion of the supernatural.

At Jesus' baptism, the Spirit of Glory came and rested upon and com-pletely enveloped Him! Jesus was surrounded by a zone of heavenly glory that extended beyond His physical body. From the moment of His heavenly coronation Jesus ministered under the glory cloud. He was literally "bap-tized into the cloud," to borrow the phrase from Paul. "For I do not want you to be ignorant of the fact, brothers, that our forefathers were all under the cloud and that they all passed through the sea. They were all baptized into Moses in the cloud and in the sea." (1 Corinthians 10:1-2 NIV) The Greek word "baptized" means to be "immersed." To be baptized in the "sea" speaks of the children of Israel passing through the Red Sea, whereas being baptized into the cloud speaks of the glory coming upon the people of God in the wilderness. As Jesus passed through the "sea" of the River Jordan, He was baptized into the cloud and from that moment onwards He remained "under the cloud."

> When all the people were baptized, it came to pass that Jesus also was baptized; and while He prayed, the heaven was opened. And the Holy Spirit descended *in bodily form like a dove* upon Him, and a voice came from heaven which said, "You are My beloved Son; in You I am well pleased. (Luke 3:21-22)

We are told that the Holy Spirit descended "*in bodily form like a dove* upon Him." Note that the Scriptures do not say an actual dove came down and landed on Jesus' shoulder, as some paintings and movies seem to suggest. The way the words are constructed, it is more likely that the Spirit came *in bodily appearance as if He were a dove*. A friend of mine, Del Marie McAlister, saw a vision that helps explain what happened at the baptism of Jesus. "I saw a vision of a human-sized dove descending on Jesus and enfolding Him in His wings. I cannot find the words to explain what I saw next, except to say that the two merged into one."[3]

Gerhard F. Hasel, professor of Old Testament and biblical theology, says, "The comparison of the Holy Spirit to a dove seems to reflect Genesis 1:2, where the Spirit of God broods over the waters. 'The earth was without form, and void; and darkness was on the face of the deep. And the Spirit of God was hovering over the face of the waters.'" Rabbi Ben Zoma, a younger contemporary of the apostles, quotes the rabbinical tradition that "the Spirit of God was brooding on the face of the waters *like a dove* which broods over her young but does not touch them."[4]

Jesus was fully enfolded in the Spirit so that He was literally clothed in the Spirit of power and glory from above. The heavens were now fully opened to Jesus and He was completely overshadowed and enveloped in the atmosphere of heaven. This tangible glory extended beyond His physical body. The "halo" was first used in religious art in the 4th century to depict the glory of Christ that extended beyond His physical body. The imagery was later extended to the saints in acknowledgement that they were now clothed in the same glory. A "halo" is a circle of light drawn by artists to depict the glory of the Lord.

There were two other terms that were used historically to describe the radiance of divine glory. The first term was a "nimbus." In religious artwork, a nimbus was "an indication of radiant light drawn around the head of a saint," or "a splendid atmosphere that surrounds a person." Artists spoke of the "nimbus" of Christ or of a saint. "Nimbus" is also a more familiar term used in meteorology to describe a dense rain-bearing cloud. The second term was an "aureola," which is essentially identical to a nimbus. This was a Latin term meaning "golden," which was later abbreviated to "aura." The New Age movement eventually adopted the term "aura" to describe a field of divine energy surrounding a person.

Jesus lived for 30 years on earth without attracting any great attention to Himself. But as soon as He was clothed with the glory He turned the world upside down! In the book of Revelation John saw an angel clothed in the glory of heaven. "I saw still another mighty angel coming down from heaven, *clothed with a cloud*. And a rainbow was on his head, his face was like the sun, and his feet like pillars of fire." (Revelation 10:1) If a mighty angel could be "clothed with a cloud" when he came to earth, how much more was Jesus "clothed with a cloud" after His baptism? Jesus was the first man to be clothed in the glory of heaven since Adam. Adam was clothed in the glory of Christ until he sinned and fell short of the glory of God. The moment Adam sinned, the glory cloud departed.

As soon as Adam fell into sin he automatically felt naked because he was no longer clothed in the glory of heaven. He said, "I was afraid because I was naked; and I hid myself." (Genesis 3:10) Four thousand years passed before another man walked the earth who was once again fully clothed in the power and the glory of heaven. Jesus also promised His disciples that they too would be "clothed with power from on high" when the Day of Pentecost had fully come. The Father is preparing a bride for His Son, but the bride is naked until she is clothed in this cloud of glory.

Jesus said, "I counsel you to buy from Me...white garments, that you may be clothed, that the shame of your nakedness may not be revealed." (Revelation 3:18) This was an invitation to join the company of "overcomers," those saints who have laid hold of their inheritance. "He who overcomes shall be clothed in white garments!" (Revelation 3:5) These white garments that Jesus counsels His disciples to put on are reminiscent of the glory that came upon Jesus on the Mount of Transfiguration. "As he was praying, the appearance of his face changed, and his clothing became dazzling white." (Luke 9:29 NLT)

The Glory on the Mount of Transfiguration

The overshadowing anointing of the Spirit that came upon Jesus at His baptism reminds us of the cloud of glory that enfolded Jesus on the Mount of Transfiguration! In both instances the Father spoke from heaven: "This is My Beloved Son in whom I am well pleased!" This cloud was also the manifest presence of the Father of Glory who overshadowed His Beloved Son while He was on earth. The Father proclaimed His love for His Son at His baptism but He reaffirmed it audibly on Mount Tabor when the disciples' eyes were opened to spiritual realities that had already been established back at the River Jordan. The Mount of Transfiguration event gives us an even deeper glimpse into the nature of the relationship between the Father and the Son, because it was here that the disciples saw heaven open with their natural eyes.

> Jesus took Peter, James, and John his brother, and led them up on a high mountain by themselves; and He was transfigured before them. His face shone like the sun, and His clothes became as white as the light. And behold, Moses and Elijah appeared to them, talking with Him. Then Peter answered and said to Jesus, "Lord, it is good for us to be here; if You wish, let us make here three tabernacles: one for You, one for Moses, and one for Elijah." While he was still speaking, behold, *a bright cloud overshadowed them*; and suddenly *a voice came out of the cloud*, saying, "This is My beloved Son, in whom I am well pleased. Hear Him!" (Matthew 17:1-5)

This was the same glory that descended upon Jesus at His baptism, only now the cloud was made visible to Peter, James and John. Notice also that it was the voice of the Father that proceeded out of the glory cloud. This insight gives us an additional key to manifesting miracles upon the earth. The glory cloud is a *relational reality* shared intimately between the Father and the Son and all those who are in the Son. The Father is bringing many sons to glory! His intention is to have an entirely new breed of intimate sons and daughters who are "in the Beloved Son" and who manifest the glory of their Father. Jesus always comes "in the glory of His Father" (Matthew 16:27) and He is raising up a company of Father-pleasers who cannot live apart from the glory of their Father. Their one desire is to host the glory cloud and release the supernatural!

Paul said, "For I consider that the sufferings of this present time are not worthy to be compared with the glory that is to be revealed to us. For the anxious longing of the creation waits eagerly for the revealing of the sons of God." (Romans 8:18-19 NASB) The old King James Version called this "the manifestation of the sons of God." Paul used the Greek word "apokalupsis" which means the revelation, the manifestation, or the unveiling. The sons of God are revealed on earth whenever they stand by faith in the finished work of Christ, stand in the power of the new creation, and embrace the glory of the Father which now belongs to the sons and daughters of God as part of their spiritual birthright.

Jesus imparts this glory realm to His brethren whenever they embrace the invitation to an intimate relationship with the Father. Jesus said, "The glory which You [Father] gave Me I have given them." (John 17:22) The "manifestation of the sons of God" is really the manifestation of the Father's intimate love poured out upon the hearts of His sons and daughters. "How great is the love the Father has lavished on us, that we should be called children of God! And that is what we are!" (1 John 3:1 NIV) The children of God find their true identity in relationship to their Father, who longs to lavish the identity of sonship upon all of His children. He gives us a new name! The glory cloud gathers heavily around the sons and daughters who lay hold of their new identity in Christ. We must not overlook the relational dimensions of the cloud. It only comes upon those who fall in love with the Father just as Jesus loved His Father. The Father simply cannot stay away from those who love Him freely in the midst of the darkness and widespread rebellion of humanity. The Spirit falls upon anyone who loves God.

THE VOICE THAT COMES FROM THE CLOUD

Matthew, Mark, Luke and Peter all record the Mount of Transfiguration event. The one overwhelming thing that struck them in recording this glorious epiphany was the voice that spoke out of the cloud. It was the very voice of God that spoke out of the midst of the glory cloud! This Voice that speaks out of the cloud has the power to create, to sustain, to destroy and to instantly heal all sicknesses and disease. In order to understand the properties of this glorious Voice, we need to explore its unique attributes. We find a particularly interesting clue in the writings of Peter. Peter was recalling the extraordinary glory encounter he had with James and John when he was with Jesus on the Mount of Transfiguration.

We did not follow cleverly invented stories when we told you about the power and coming of our Lord Jesus Christ, but we were eyewitnesses of His majesty. For he received honour and glory from God the Father when the Voice came to him from the Majestic Glory, saying, "This is my Son, whom I love; with him I am well pleased." We ourselves heard this Voice that came from heaven when we were with him on the sacred mountain. (2 Peter 1:16-18)

The particular aspect of this passage that I want to focus upon concerns the *quality* of this Voice that came out of the realm of "Majestic Glory." There is something about the quality of this Voice that actually carries the atmosphere of heavenly glory. Peter focuses upon two realities: the person of Christ and the Voice of the Father, and he explores the relationship between these two realities. Concerning Jesus, he said, "We were eyewitnesses of His majesty." The Greek word Peter used for "majesty" is *megaleiotes* and it actually means "majestic glory and splendour." The New Living Translation says, "We have seen His *majestic splendour* with our own eyes." Peter was referring to his own experience on the Mount of Transfiguration, where he saw the true essence of the person of Christ. The three disciples saw His majestic glory shining like the sun. "His face **shone like the sun**, and his clothes became as white as the light." (Matthew 17:2 NIV)

This glorious majesty of Christ is closely linked to the manifestation of His divine power. In Luke 9, the word *megaleiotes* is translated as **mighty power**. Jesus performed a spectacular healing on a demonised boy: "And they were all amazed at the **mighty power** of God." (Luke 9:43 KJV) Another version says, "Awe gripped the people as they saw this display of God's power." (NLT) With this insight, let's return to Peter's comment. He was saying, "We were eyewitnesses of His mighty power and His glorious splendour!" This power and splendour was bestowed upon Christ by His Father in heaven: "For He received honour and glory from God the Father."

The way this glory was imparted was through the Voice that spoke out of the Majestic Glory! Jesus chose to reflect the Father's glory upon the earth. He acknowledged that it was the Father who bestowed this glory upon Him. In John 17 Jesus spoke of "the glory which You gave Me." (John 17:22) He prayed, "Father, I desire that they also whom You gave Me may be with Me where I am, that they may behold My glory which You have given Me; for You loved Me before the foundation of the world." (John 17:24) The Father's glory and majesty was displayed every time Jesus performed miracles and supernatural demonstrations of His power.

There are those rare moments in the history of the people of God where the glory cloud of God descended visibly upon the earth. We have already noted those occasions in the Old Testament. But it happened again when Jesus went up on the Mount of Transfiguration. On this glorious occasion the cloud descended, not upon a building or a mountain, but upon a person. "For he [Christ] received honour and glory from God the Father when the voice came to him from the *Majestic Glory*."

The term for "Majestic Glory" in Greek is *megaloprepes doxa*. Like *megaleiotes* it means "magnificent glory" or "excellent glory." What happened when the Father lavished this extreme glory upon His Son? Every time the story is recounted by Matthew, Mark or Luke we are told the glory of God became visible and tangible upon the Lord Jesus. "He was transfigured before them. His face shone like the sun, and His clothes became as white as the light." (Matthew 17:2)

Can you see the relationship between the Voice speaking from the Majestic Glory and the upgrade of glory experienced by Jesus? There was a profound transference of divine glory from heaven upon the Son of God. Jesus was literally transfigured before the disciples. The Greek word for "transfigured" is *metamorphoo* and it means to be changed from one form into another. Only the glory of God from heaven has the power to bring such an extraordinary metamorphosis. It was as though the disciples were peering into the eternal relationship that has always existed between the Father and the Son.

Jesus even referred to that quality of relationship that He had enjoyed with the Father before the foundation of the world. The fullness of this glorious relationship was expressed in the love between the Father and the Son. Jesus spoke of the disciples beholding "My glory which You have given Me; for You loved Me before the foundation of the world." (John 17:24) It was on the Mount of Transfiguration that the Father said, "This is My Beloved Son, in whom I am well pleased." (Matthew 17:5)

As the Father spoke these words over His Son, something happened to the very sub-atomic structure of Jesus' physical body. Supernatural glory waves from heaven mysteriously energised the natural photons, causing brilliant natural light to stream forth from His face and from His body; all because the Father spoke over the Son out of the Majestic Glory. This is the point of Peter's commentary. This voice issued forth from the supernatural realm of glory. It came out of a particular *context*. It was not just a voice that came out of nowhere. It was the voice of God that came out of the majestic glory realm of heaven. Because it was a voice that came out of this supernatural realm of glory, it carried an impartation of the glory and power of God. This was not just any old voice. It was the audible voice of a loving Father speaking from heaven over His Beloved Son.

The only incident in human history that comes anywhere close to what happened to Jesus was the experience of Moses on Mount Sinai. Moses had been in the presence of the Majestic Glory for forty days, and he became so saturated in the glory of God that it caused the skin of his face to begin to radiate heavenly glory. "It came about when Moses was coming down from Mount Sinai that Moses did not know that the skin of his face shone because of his speaking with Him. So when Aaron and all the sons of Israel saw Moses, behold, the skin of his face shone, and they were afraid to come near him." (Exodus 34:29-30 NASB) But the glory of the New Covenant is infinitely greater than the glory of the Old Covenant, and to mark the advent of this New Covenant the Father lavished His glory upon His Son so that all who believe and who are "in Christ" get to luxuriate in the sheer ecstasy of the Father's love.

God communicates His glory in a number of ways. One of the primary ways that the glory of God is communicated is through the spoken Word of God. When God speaks, His glory is powerfully released. Paul called it "His glorious power" because the power of God is a manifestation of the glory of God. It is a power that is full of God's glory! Whenever the glory of God shows up, there is always a release of supernatural power. Jesus demonstrated the power of God over disease and sickness, and every time He healed someone God's glory was increasingly revealed. We have already noted the biblical relationship between the power and the glory of God.

At this point I would like to turn our attention toward the relationship between the supernatural sound waves of God's voice and the glory of God. In the book of Isaiah we read, "The Lord will cause **His glorious voice** to be heard." (Isaiah 30:30) There is a "glorious" quality to the voice of God because His voice is saturated in the atmosphere of heaven which is filled with His glory.

> The voice of the Lord is over the waters; the **God of glory** thunders; the Lord is over many waters. The voice of the Lord is **powerful**; the voice of the Lord is **full of majesty**. The voice of the Lord shakes the wilderness. (Psalm 29:3-8)

The Hebrew word for "majesty" is *hadar* and it means "magnificence, beauty, glory and splendour." The voice of God is full of glory and splendour. There is an aesthetic beauty to the sound of His voice. Jesus displayed the glory of God whenever He ministered healing. He either spoke the Word and healing was released or His glorious presence spontaneously released His healing power without a word even being spoken because Jesus was saturated in the atmosphere of heaven. Because Jesus was surrounded in the thick glory cloud of heaven, His voice released this same glorious power.

Let's not overlook the context out of which Jesus spoke. Even when Jesus spoke on the earth, He was "the Son of Man who is in heaven." (John 3:13) John the Baptist said concerning Jesus: "For He whom God has sent speaks the words that the Father gave Him to speak." (John 3:34) Jesus acknowledged that the words He spoke were actually the words of God. "These words you hear are not my own; they belong to the Father who sent me." (John 14:24) "The words that I speak to you I do not speak on My own authority; but the Father who dwells in Me does the works." (John 14:10)

Jesus was in full and perfect alignment with the Father; that is why He said, "I and My Father are one." (John 10:30) Jesus opened His mouth and the Father spoke straight through Him to heal sicknesses and to raise the dead, and this was the pattern for the new breed of spiritual sons and daughters who were emerging in the earth. "Do not worry about how or what you should speak. For it will be given to you in that hour what you should speak; for it is not you who speak, but ***the Spirit of your Father*** who speaks in you." (Matthew 10:19-20) This is the voice of healing that speaks out of the Majestic Glory!

This revelation adds even greater weight to the fact that the words that Jesus spoke on earth were "Spirit." His words were thoroughly impregnated and saturated with the power of the Holy Spirit, who is called the "Spirit of Glory." (1 Peter 4:14) The Spirit has been sent to communicate the glory realm of heaven and to bring the reality of heaven to earth. Jesus was transfigured (*metamorphoo*) by the Spirit of Glory on the Mount of Transfiguration, and the saints are also transformed from one degree of glory to another by the Spirit of the Lord. "But we all, with unveiled face, beholding as in a mirror the glory of the Lord, are being transformed (*metamorphoo*) into the same image from glory to glory, just as by the Spirit of the Lord." (2 Corinthians 3:18) The Spirit of Glory has been sent to impart the fullness of the glory realm of heaven to the saints on the earth, and out of this lifestyle of glory encounters the glory realm will be revealed through the saints in the same manner that it was revealed through Jesus.

There were a couple of other occasions in the Bible when this Voice spoke out of the glory cloud. Recalling the events on Mount Sinai, Moses said, "Surely the Lord our God has shown us His glory and His greatness, and we have *heard His voice* from the midst of the fire." (Deuteronomy 5:24) Moses actually used this phrase about the voice of the Lord speaking out of the midst of the fire ten times in the book of Deuteronomy! The Mount of Transfiguration event actually came as the climax on earth of a number of glorious epiphanies where God descended and spoke audibly out of the cloud. According to J.P. Heil in his book, *The Transfiguration of Jesus*, "The cloud serves as the medium out of which the 'voice of God' speaks. Based on the background provided primarily by the cloud that overshadowed the Tent of Meeting, the overshadowing cloud of the transfiguration epiphany functions as an *oracular cloud*."[5]

Ezekiel experienced the glorious Voice when he was taken into heaven: "Like the appearance of a rainbow in the clouds on a rainy day, so was the *radiance around him*. This was the appearance of the likeness of the *glory of the Lord*. When I saw it, I fell facedown, and *I heard the Voice* of one speaking." (Ezekiel 1:26-28 NIV) It also happened to Saul of Tarsus. "Now it happened, as I journeyed and came near Damascus at about noon, suddenly *a great light from heaven shone around me*. And I fell to the ground and *heard a voice* saying to me, 'Saul, Saul, why are you persecuting Me?'" (Acts 22:6-7) Peter, James and John had exactly the same experience when they heard the Voice from the Majestic Glory. What transcendent realms of glory that beautiful Voice carries! What peace it imparts, what power it releases!

It is only the voice that is spoken out of this realm of Majestic Glory that has the capacity to restructure reality at a quantum level. This is what Jesus was talking about when He said, "The words that I speak to you are Spirit and they are life." (John 6:63) The words that He spoke were bathed in the glory of heaven that is communicated and imparted through the person of the Holy Spirit. Creative miracles follow wherever the words that are bathed in the Spirit of Glory are spoken. Jesus demonstrated on earth the capacity to speak to hideous diseases and to see them dissolved by the power of His words. Every person He ministered to was completely healed.

Behind the prophetic declarations of Jesus was the entire realm of heavenly glory that gave power to the words that He spoke.

THE MIRACLE OF BILOCATION

As we have seen, one of the unique properties of the quantum world is the capacity of a quantum particle to be in two places at one time. In the famous double-slit experiment we saw that a single electron fired at a double-slit screen actually passes through both slits at the same time! The electron literally "bilocates" so it spreads out as a wave and passes through the two slits, creating an interference pattern. Jesus Himself was actually in two places at the same time. He was standing on the earth as a physical man, yet through His spirit He was simultaneously in heaven enjoying uninterrupted fellowship with the Father. It was this supernatural oneness that Jesus shared with the Father that set the context for the explosion of the glory of God through His ministry on the earth.

The regenerated human spirit, supernaturally joined [or entangled] with the Spirit of God, is similarly in two places at one time. "He who is joined to the Lord is one spirit with Him." (1 Corinthians 6:17) As a result of the miraculous new birth, my human spirit, which is the real me, is now in heaven just as Jesus was in heaven even when He was on the earth. Paul says that, "Our citizenship is in heaven." (Philippians 3:20) Jesus said, "To him who overcomes I will grant to sit with Me on My throne, as I also overcame and sat down with My Father on His throne." (Revelation 3:21) The overcomers are those who appropriate by faith the heavenly realities that belong to them as heirs of God and joint heirs with Christ. As we lay hold of the fullness of the new creation and begin to live out of that new reality, we manifest a supernatural lifestyle and bring forth supernatural fruit.

The calling of the sons and daughters of God is to lay hold of that for which God has laid hold of them. We are called to host the glory cloud here on earth just as Jesus hosted the very atmosphere of heaven on earth. As Bill Johnson puts it: "We are brokers of another world." There is no greater adventure than for born again sons and daughters to step into their heavenly calling and learn to bring heaven down to earth.

Even when He was on earth, Jesus lives in a continuous face to face encounter with the Father in heaven. Moses prayed to God and said, "They have heard that You, Lord, are among these people; that You, Lord, *are seen face to face and Your cloud stands above them*, and You go before them in a pillar of cloud by day and in a pillar of fire by night." (Numbers 14:14) If we want to be a people who host the fullness of the overshadowing glory cloud, we must learn how to live in a face to face encounter with the Lord. "In the light of the King's face is life and his favour is like a cloud of the latter rain." (Proverbs 16:15) "If My people who are called by My name will humble themselves, and pray and *seek My face*, and turn from their wicked ways, then I will hear from heaven, and will forgive their sin and heal their land." (2 Chronicles 7:14) "When You said, *Seek My face*, my heart said to You, "Your face, Lord, I will seek." (Psalm 27:8)

"For it is the God who commanded light to shine out of darkness, who has shone in our hearts to give *the light of the knowledge of the glory of God in the face of Jesus Christ*." (2 Corinthians 4:6) We are now called to look steadily at the face of Jesus. The inward transformation that comes through a face to face encounter with the glory of God facilitates a greater overshadowing of the glory cloud. "All of us have had that veil removed so that we can be mirrors that brightly reflect the glory of the Lord. And as the Spirit of the Lord works within us, we become more and more like Him and reflect His glory even more." (2 Corinthians 3:18 NLT)

Hosting the glory cloud necessitates living face to face with God. We can't have the fullness of the overshadowing cloud unless we seek His face! His eyes are fixed on you! Therefore, "Let us fix our eyes on Jesus, the author and perfecter of our faith." (Hebrews 12:2 NIV) Face to face means eye to eye! His eyes are like burning fire. The great men and women of the Bible and from church history were people who dedicated themselves to live in a face to face encounter with the eyes of fire in order to release the fullness of heaven on earth.

We are called to minister **under the cloud** because Jesus ministered **under the cloud**. There cannot be any true Kingdom ministry without the presence of the cloud. Jesus called this overshadowing cloud of glory "the promise of the Father" for all of the sons and daughters! "Behold, I send the promise of My Father *upon you*; but tarry in the city of Jerusalem until you are clothed with power from on high." (Luke 24:49)

The cloud of the Father's glory is part of the inheritance of the sons of God, but not all sons and daughters press into the place where they lay hold of this overshadowing presence and learn how to minister under the cloud. Sometimes only a handful of believers in a local church lay hold of this inheritance and learn how to flow in releasing the glory. Whole generations have come and gone where not one single disciple discovered the exhilaration of ministering under the cloud.

When Jesus ministered, He continually spoke about His Father who gave Him the words to speak and the miracles to perform. For Jesus, as the one and only Son of God who came down from heaven, the precious anointing from on high was, in fact, the Father enveloping the Son and expressing Himself through Him. Jesus promised that the day would come when this same Spirit would be poured out upon the disciples.

> I will ask the Father, and He will give you another Helper, that He may be with you forever; that is the Spirit of truth, whom the world cannot receive, because it does not see Him or know Him, but you know Him because He abides with you and will be in you... I will not leave you as orphans; I will come to you. In that day you will know that I am in My Father! (John 14:16-20 NASB)

To Jesus, the Holy Spirit was the Spirit of His Father. Ever since His baptism He enjoyed the intimate closeness of His Father who enveloped Him in the cloud of His presence. The anointing of the Spirit that overshadowed Jesus continually communicated the nearness of the Father to the Son. Why did Jesus call the gift of the Spirit the "Promise of the Father"? Simply because the Holy Spirit is the "Spirit of adoption" (Romans 8:14) who delivers us from our orphan identity. "I will not leave you as orphans; I will come to you."

Jesus was so intimately clothed with the promise of the Father that He was *in the Father*. When the Spirit of adoption came upon the disciples they were comprehensively freed from the orphan identity and it was in that moment that they understood, just as Jesus had prophetically promised, that Jesus had always been "in the Father." This orphan/adoption paradigm sheds fresh insight upon the words of Jesus who said: "Behold, I send the promise of My Father *upon you*." The question we need to ask is whether the Holy Spirit is the "Father's promise" or is He the promise of "the Father"? We cannot forget that Jesus also called Him, "the Spirit of your Father." (Matthew 10:20)

> Do you not believe that *I am in the Father*, and the Father in Me? The words that I speak to you I do not speak on My own authority; but the Father who dwells in Me does the works. Believe Me that *I am in the Father* and the Father in Me, or else believe Me for the sake of the works themselves. (John 14:10-11)

The Holy Spirit is the active agent of both the Father and the Son. He communicates the intimacy of the Father to the sons and daughters, but He also communicates and imparts the Spirit of Sonship to us so that we cry "Abba Father!" (Romans 8:15) When the Father looks down upon us, He sees the Spirit of His Son indwelling every adopted son and daughter. Christ is now in us and He is the hope of glory. We have the anointing of the Spirit abiding permanently in each of us who are born of the Spirit. The appearance of the glory of the Son in us is so powerfully attractive to the Father of Glory. Glory attracts glory! The Father loves to cover His sons in glory! *Mega dunamis* is released when the hearts of the sons and daughters of God on earth are turned to the Father of Glory, and the Father lovingly overshadows them in the cloud of His presence. "The Spirit of Glory and of God rests **upon you.**" (1 Peter 4:14) Isaiah prophesied that the glory cloud would come **upon** us!

> Arise, shine; For your light has come! And the glory of the Lord is risen **upon you.** See, darkness covers the earth and thick darkness is over the peoples, but the Lord rises **upon you** and His glory appears **over you.** (Isaiah 60:1-2)

God doesn't change! He deeply desires to have a people through whom He can display His glory. In the ideal world, every believer should seek to live a life that is fully overshadowed by the glory of the Father. It fascinates and thrills me to meditate upon the fierce intentionality of the Lord to display His glory through His people. He is just as intentional about displaying His glory today through His church in the 21st century as He was to display His glory 20 centuries ago through His Beloved Son. The fulfilment of this divine desire depends not upon God but upon the intentionality of His people. He is waiting for a company of people to arise in the earth who will not be content with anything less than a full scale revival of the glory of God covering the earth as the waters cover the sea. The secret work of the Spirit amongst the people of God to shift their vision and their degree of intentionality toward a commitment to the full recovery of the ministry of glory continues deep within the heart of the church.

THE DOUBLE PORTION

God is seeking to release the double portion of His anointing. "Instead of their shame My people will receive a double portion." (Isaiah 61:7 NIV) Did you know there are two different anointings in the New Testament?

According to both Paul and John, every born again believer has the anointing of the Spirit abiding within them. This is the first anointing. "You have an anointing from the Holy One...The anointing which you have received from Him abides in you." (1 John 2:20,27) There are only two kinds of people in the world: those who have received the gift of the Holy Spirit and those who have not. Paul said, "If anyone does not have the Spirit of Christ, he does not belong to Christ." (Romans 8:9) According to Paul, the leading pneumatologist of the New Testament, every born again believer has had the Holy Spirit poured out upon them at the new birth. This may contradict many popular second blessing pneumatologies, but Paul was clearly at pains to avoid anything that leaned toward a two-stage initiation into the realm of the Spirit.

> He saved us through the washing of rebirth and renewal by the Holy Spirit, whom He ***poured out*** on us generously through Jesus Christ our Savior, so that, having been justified by His grace, we might become heirs having the hope of eternal life. (Titus 3:5-7 NIV)

In Paul's theology the rebirth of the Spirit was unequivocally synonymous with the outpouring of the gift of the Holy Spirit.

> Therefore, since we have been justified through faith, we have peace with God through our Lord Jesus Christ, through whom we have gained access by faith into this grace in which we now stand... because God has ***poured out*** his love into our hearts by the Holy Spirit, whom he has given us. (Romans 5:1-5)

Paul taught that we have all been baptized in one Spirit into one body and have all been made to drink of one Spirit! "For we were all baptized by one Spirit into one body – whether Jews or Greeks, slave or free – and we were all given the one Spirit to drink." (1 Corinthians 12:13 NIV) Gordon Fee, a Pentecostal theologian and perhaps one of the world's greatest authorities on Pauline pneumatology, translates this verse this way, "For indeed, we were all baptized in one Spirit so as to form one body, whether Jews or Greeks, slave or free and we were all given one Spirit to drink to the fill." The Greek preposition *en* is translated "in/with/by." Therefore the Spirit is the element into which all believers have been baptized! Try as you will, you will not be able to find any hint of a two stage initiation into the realm of the Spirit in Paul's theology. This "level playing field" is supported by other non-Pauline authors of the New Testament.

When we receive the Holy Spirit at conversion we receive all of Him, not just part of Him. The Holy Spirit is a person! How do we receive part of a person? Did you receive part of Christ at conversion? We either receive the gift of the Holy Spirit or we do not! According to John, "God does not give His Spirit by measure!" (John 3:34) "For God gives the Spirit without limit." (NIV) "God does not give His Spirit sparingly or by measure, but boundless is the gift God makes of His Spirit." (Amplified) "Don't think He (God) rations out the Spirit in bits and pieces!" (MSG) The word "measure" is *metron* in the Greek and it means "by degree" or "by limited portion." If we "receive the Spirit," we receive Him in fullness. There is an impartation of the fullness of God to every born again believer! "For in Christ all the fullness of the Deity lives in bodily form, and you have been given fullness in Christ." (Colossians 2:9-10) John agrees: "Of His fullness we have **all** received and grace for grace." (John 1:16) When God gives the gift of the Spirit He pours Him out in fullness.

The issue is not one of God's generosity but of our capacity to walk in the fullness of the gift of the Holy Spirit. Our problem is that we leak! We are leaky and broken vessels. Who except for Jesus can walk in the absolute fullness of the Spirit anyway? Paul highlighted the necessity of frequent experiential infillings with the Holy Spirit. "Do not get drunk on wine, which leads to debauchery. Instead, be filled with the Spirit." (Ephesians 4:18) The Greek tense of this verb is "*Be being filled...*" Paul urged believers to be continuously filled with the Spirit. "Don't drink too much wine. Drink the Spirit of God; huge draughts of Him!" (MSG) Even in the book of Acts there was the initial infilling of the Holy Spirit followed by subsequent infillings. "All of them were filled with the Holy Spirit and began to speak in other tongues as the Spirit enabled them." (Acts 2:4) But only a couple of chapters later we read: "After they prayed, the place where they were meeting was shaken. And they were all filled with the Holy Spirit and spoke the word of God boldly." (Acts 4:31)

Paul taught that God had already imparted the fullness of the Spirit. His vision for believers was that they could be brought to the place where they could live experientially in the fullness of the Spirit. He prayed specifically "that you may be filled to the measure of all the fullness of God." (Ephesians 3:19) In effect Paul was saying that every believer may be experientially "filled to the measure of all the fullness of the Spirit of God." This experiential state of fullness indicates the Holy Spirit ruling over our entire being and bringing every area of the soul (mind, will and emotions) under the influence and control of the Holy Spirit. In this state, the love, the joy and the peace of the Holy Spirit rules over our mind and our emotions. "May the God of hope fill you with all joy and peace as you trust in Him, so that you may *overflow* with hope by the power of the Holy Spirit." (Romans 15:13 NIV)

This is where the double portion comes into clearer focus. There is yet another anointing which comes upon the saints for the purpose of engaging in the ministry of the Kingdom. God speaks to His anointed and promises "to open before him the double doors so that the gates will not be shut." (Isaiah 45:1) Jesus spoke of the Spirit of the Lord coming *upon Him* in order to engage in certain expressions of supernatural Kingdom ministry. (Luke 4:18-19) A believer can live in this state of personal fullness without any reference to a participation in the ministry of the Kingdom to others. The indwelling of the fullness of the Spirit results in deep personal edification and an engagement in the bliss and ecstasy of knowing and loving God.

The anointing that abides within you is for your own edification and personal empowering to live in the fullness of the new creation in Christ. Paul made a clear differentiation between self-edification and the ministry of edifying others. "He who speaks in a tongue *edifies himself,* but he who prophesies *edifies the church.*" (1 Corinthians 14:4) "But you, dear friends, *build yourselves up* in your most holy faith and pray in the Holy Spirit." (Jude 20) There is nothing wrong with self-edification. "David strengthened himself in the Lord his God." (1 Samuel 30:6) We would all benefit in learning how to strengthen and build ourselves up in the Lord.

The anointing of the Spirit of Glory that comes upon the believer when they step into an intentional place of engaging in the ministry of edifying and building up others is clearly distinguished in the New Testament from the personal dimensions of an intimate relationship with the Father. Plenty of the great mystics experienced the heights of intimacy and ecstasy in their relationship with the Father without ministering to others. They lived in and enjoyed the fullness of the anointing that abides within every believer. But in contrast, the anointing of the Spirit of Glory resting *upon* the believer is to be distinguished from the anointing of the Spirit indwelling and filling the believer. Walking in the fullness of both anointings is the double portion. Remember the words of Bill Johnson: *He is in me for my sake, but He's upon me for yours!* God has already imparted the fullness of His Spirit to every believer for their own sake, but a much smaller percentage of the church enter into the experience of the additional anointing that comes to empower us to release the supernatural realm of miracles.

The state of the believer who is indwelt by the fullness of the third person of the Holy Spirit parallels that of Jesus before His baptism at the River Jordan. Jesus was filled with the Holy Spirit before the Spirit came upon Him to overshadow Him for the purpose of ministry. Similarly, every believer can enjoy the fullness of the indwelling Spirit without the overshadowing glory. We have significantly cheapened the anointing by attributing the experience of the Spirit anointing us for the purpose of Kingdom ministry to a one-time event in our collection of past spiritual experiences. The overshadowing glory cloud is a dynamic reality that can come in various degrees of intensity. It is not a static state but an intensely dynamic realm that comes in proportion to the development of a skill set that revolves around learning to engage in supernatural ministry.

All true Kingdom ministry is "'gift-based ministry": it flows through us as we learn how to operate in the gifts of the Spirit. The Greek word for "anointing" is *chrisma*. The Greek word for "gifts" is *charisma*. The gifts of the Spirit are actually diverse ***anointings*** that come upon us specifically for the purpose of Kingdom ministry. They are unique supernatural *empowerments* of the grace of God to minister in the supernatural abilities of Jesus. Grace is God's empowering presence. The gifts are expressions or manifestations of the Spirit. Paul taught that the gifts of the Spirit were empowerments that come ***upon*** believers for the purpose of ministry.

There are diversities of anointings in the body of Christ. These anointings rest upon us when we step out to minister to others. Moving in the anointing of the overshadowing glory demands the development of the gifts of the Holy Spirit as disciples step out to do the supernatural works of Jesus. We greatly diminish this glorious supernatural charismatic anointing for releasing the healing and prophetic abilities of Christ by reducing the experience of the Spirit coming powerfully upon us to a single past experience that we add to our repertoire of past experiences.

As I have pressed into greater prophetic insight into the nature of the overshadowing glory cloud, my entire paradigm of the Christian life has been massively upgraded and shifted. I now understand this dimension of the Spirit coming upon us for the purpose of engaging in gift-based ministry as a dynamic dimension of intense spiritual encounter whereby a follower of Christ is comprehensively clothed in supernatural abilities to release miracles. This supernatural overshadowing releases extreme creative miracles! It is the matrix of the miraculous! "The Holy Spirit will come **upon you**, and the power of the Most High will **overshadow** you." (Luke 1:35) The same Greek word for overshadowing [*episkiazo*] is used in reference to Peter's shadow. "They brought forth the sick into the streets, and laid them on beds and couches, that at the least the **shadow** of Peter passing by might **overshadow** [*episkiazo*] some of them." (Acts 5:15)

Peter was so intensely overshadowed by the glory cloud of heaven that people who came anywhere within his immediate proximity were completely healed. This was clearly one of the "greater works" that Jesus promised His disciples that they would do. "I tell you the truth, anyone who has faith in me will do what I have been doing. He will do even greater things than these, because I am going to the Father." (John 14:12 NIV) Paul's experience of the overshadowing glory led him into realms of supernatural ministry that also fall within the category of "greater works." "God did extraordinary miracles through Paul, so that even handkerchiefs and aprons that had touched him were taken to the sick, and their illnesses were cured and the evil spirits left them." (Acts 19:11-12 NIV) That is a heavy realm of supernatural glory!

There is a dimension of life in the Spirit where this overshadowing suddenly comes upon the disciple of Christ. In order to step into this supernatural dimension, the saint must already be living internally in the fullness of the Spirit. As he or she steps intentionally into a place of engaging in the ministry of the Kingdom, that which is already inside the believer suddenly jumps to the outside and the double portion anointing kicks in. Now he or she has both a strong internal and external anointing and is restored to that state of existence that preceded the fall. Suddenly the saint is clothed in an invisible though tangible cloud that extends considerably beyond the physical parameters of his or her body. A good father always wants his own son or daughter to exceed him. In the same way, Jesus reserved dimensions of Spirit ministry that were to eclipse anything He ever did Himself. There is no record of Jesus releasing healing without either the spoken word or through physical contact, yet the disciples in the book of Acts were so clothed in this glory anointing they were releasing healing merely through their presence.

THE GATHERING STORM CLOUD

Tremendous spiritual power is released through the overshadowing cloud of glory. In nature, certain kinds of clouds produce thunder and lightning! The natural things speak of the invisible things! The supernatural lightning of heaven bursts forth from the overshadowing glory cloud, releasing great spiritual power. Lightning is an atmospheric discharge of electrical energy that issues from the base of an overshadowing thundercloud striking the ground beneath. A bolt of lightning can reach temperatures of 30,000 degrees Celsius, which is more than six times the temperature of the surface of the sun! Lightning is accompanied by thunder as the extreme heat of the lightning bolt produces a rapid outward expansion of the air, releasing a loud sonic shock wave. Phenomenal power is released through lightning strikes. A typical lightning bolt releases a billion volts and over 40,000 amps of electricity, enough to light up 150,000,000 light bulbs simultaneously!

God designed lightning on earth to speak prophetically of heavenly things! Natural lighting is a prophetic picture of the lightning and thunder of heaven that surrounds the throne of God. "And from the throne proceeded lightning, thundering, and voices. Seven lamps of fire were burning before the throne, which are the seven Spirits of God." (Revelation 4:5) The throne of God is an atmosphere of intense power and glory. "The God of Glory thunders!" (Psalm 29:3) "He fills His hands with lightning and commands it to strike its mark." (Job 36:32 NIV) "His glory covers the heavens and the earth is full of His praise. His radiance is like the sunlight; rays of brilliant light flash from His hands where His power was hidden." (Habakkuk 3:3-4) "His splendour covers the skies, His glory fills the earth. He is as bright as lightning; a two-pronged lightning bolt flashes from His hand. This is the outward display of His power." (NET Bible) Once Jesus came under the overshadowing cloud, He repeatedly released the lightning of heaven through His hands so that whenever He laid hands upon people they literally felt the fire and the power of God go through them like electricity!

We cheapen this supernatural endowment of the lightning anointing of heaven by reducing it to a second stage of initiation into life in the Spirit. The anointing for supernatural ministry needs to become a **present dynamic experience** of the glory of the Lord resting powerfully upon us for the purpose of high level Kingdom ministry. God wants to cut through the trite religious formulas and traditions of the church in order to impart a real overshadowing of *mega dunamis*. "And with **great power** the apostles gave witness to the resurrection of the Lord Jesus. And **great grace** was upon them all." (Acts 4:33) This dimension of spiritual empowerment is available to all who earnestly seek it!

Followers of Christ need to be trained in both the theology and the practical dynamics of radical gift-based ministry in order to prepare the way to receive a mighty impartation of the glory anointing from heaven in order to do the very works that Jesus did. Jesus devoted Himself to train a small band of men to release the glory just as He continually modelled to them for three years. But for many in the contemporary church scene, Christianity has been reduced to a lifestyle of weekly church attendance that is frequently oriented around the consumption of excellent Christian entertainment. How many churches see themselves as outposts of heaven designed to raise up healing revivalists and ministers of the glory realm who learn how to minister under an open heaven?

God is training a faithful remnant to minister under the cloud. Whenever the disciples go out to minister, they should determine that they will only ever minister under the cloud of glory. Too many Christians have been content to try to minister without an open heaven! We must follow the cloud, just as the children of Israel followed the cloud in the wilderness. The cloud always leads us out into the marketplace. We lay hold of the cloud in the secret place so that we can follow the cloud out into the marketplace. When we minister under the cloud, we are fully clothed in the seven-fold Spirit of wisdom, revelation, knowledge, counsel and power.

God gave Patricia King a vision of saints ministering under an open heaven.

In a vision, I saw portals opened in heaven over individuals on earth. Glory streams from the throne room that appeared like columns of light poured out revelation, blessing, power, and favour through the heavenly portals into the lives of these individuals. Everywhere these believers went, the open heaven followed them. There was a continual flow of the glory through the portals. Columns of glory, bounty, and blessing enveloped their lives. As the vision continued, I saw many believers standing under these columns of heavenly glory. They were calling out to the Lord saying, "Let Your Kingdom come, let Your will be done, on earth as it is in heaven." I could hear them repeating this in unity and with intense passion over and over again. As they continued to call out, more portals were opened. The Lord is opening up portals of His presence and blessing over individuals who are seeking Him with all their heart, those whose minds and hearts are fixed on the things above and not on the things that are of the earth. These believers will realize an increase in heavenly and divine encounters and focus. Increased revelation of the Kingdom, increased sense of the Lord's presence and a realization of angelic visitation will be experienced in addition to a greater release of power and favour in their lives. Finally, I saw the Lord's arm opened wide as a sign of invitation for all His people to live under an open heaven.[6]

There is no limit to the degree of intensity of the manifestation of the glory cloud of heaven. Sometimes the cloud even becomes visible and tangible. It is time for the church to enter the cloud! We are living in the greatest season in the history of the church. The book of Acts was localised to one geographical region of the earth. The first century move of God never expanded beyond the borders of the Roman Empire. This emerging move of God is global and it will result in the knowledge of the glory of the Lord covering the earth as the waters cover the sea!

This is the season for the faithful remnant to draw near to God in worship and reverential awe! "Therefore, since we are receiving a kingdom that cannot be shaken, let us be thankful, and so worship God acceptably with reverence and awe, for our God is a consuming fire." (Hebrews 12:28-29 NIV) God has promised to have a people who are covered in His glory. The people of God know they are on the right track toward the fullness of the manifestation of the cloud when they begin to experience the "Spirit of burning" as a preparation to walk in the holiness and purity of the Lord. Isaiah prophesied of a day when the Lord would raise up an army of Kingdom warriors who would not allow anything to stand in their way of fulfilling their prophetic destiny.

> In that day the Branch of the Lord shall be beautiful and glorious; and the fruit of the earth shall be excellent and appealing for those of Israel who have escaped. And it shall come to pass that he who is left in Zion and remains in Jerusalem will be called holy; everyone who is recorded among the living in Jerusalem. When the Lord has washed away the filth of the daughters of Zion...by the Spirit of judgment and by the Spirit of burning, then the Lord will create above every dwelling place of Mount Zion, and above her assemblies, a cloud and smoke by day and the shining of a flaming fire by night. For glory will be a covering over all. (Isaiah 4:2-5)

Chapter Fourteen

SCIENTIA GLORIAM: THE KNOWLEDGE OF THE GLORY

Not long after the Lord brought the children of Israel out of Israel, He sent twelve spies into the Promised Land to report to the people what this land was like. Two spies brought back a good report but ten spies brought back a bad report and discouraged the people of God. As a result of this bad report, the people rebelled and refused to obey the Lord. This was a crucial moment in the life of the children of Israel because the Lord decreed that this unbelieving generation would not enter the Promised Land.

But it was there in the Wilderness of Paran that the Lord gave a prophetic promise that a day would come when God would indeed raise up an obedient people who would fulfil His purposes in the earth. God said to the children of Israel, "But truly, as I live, all the earth shall be filled with the glory of the Lord." (Numbers 14:21) He issues a prophetic decree that there would come a day under a new covenant where the same glory that was revealed through Jesus would be revealed to the ends of the earth through His glory filled church!

THE KNOWLEDGE OF THE GLORY

There is another prophetic promise in the book of Habakkuk that is very similar to the promise in Numbers 14, but it adds a different element. The Lord said through the prophet, "For the earth will be filled with the *knowledge of the glory* of the Lord as the waters cover the sea." (Habakkuk

2:14) Why might the Lord include this idea of the *knowledge* of the glory in addition to the *reality* of His glory filling the earth? We encounter exactly the same phrase: the **knowledge of the glory** in the New Testament.

Paul said, "For it is the God who commanded light to shine out of darkness, who has shone into our hearts to give the light of the **knowledge of the glory** of God in the face of Jesus Christ." (2 Corinthians 4:6) There is the reality of the glory of the Lord and, in addition, there is the knowledge of the glory of the Lord. I want to suggest that the knowledge of the glory of God poured out on the people of God represents the key to the reality of the glory of God being fully released throughout the earth.

There is a body of prophetic wisdom released from heaven that represents the very keys to unlocking heaven. Jesus wants His church to possess the keys to the Kingdom of Heaven. The Moffatt Translation always translates the Greek word for kingdom [*basileia*] as "realm." "I will give you the keys of the realm of heaven." (Matthew 16:19 Moffatt) Fortunately, God doesn't seek to withhold these keys! But religion always takes away the keys to the glory realm. God said that His people "are destroyed for lack of knowledge." (Hosea 4:6) There is a lost body of prophetic wisdom and knowledge that God is seeking to restore to His people. This is the lost art of releasing revival glory.

Jesus confronted the religious spirit in His day which sought to rob the people of God of an encounter with Him. "Woe to you experts in the law, because you have taken away the **key of knowledge**. You yourselves have not entered, and you have hindered those who were entering." (Luke 11:52) This theme is also recorded in Matthew's gospel. "Woe to you, you impious scribes and Pharisees! You shut the Realm of heaven in men's faces; you neither enter yourselves, nor will you let those enter who are on the point of entering!" (Matthew 23:13 Moffatt)

The key to the door of heaven is the knowledge of the glory. It is the **key** of knowledge, the loss of which results in the destruction of the people of God through the devastation of religion. The Greek word for *shut* is *kleio* whilst the Greek word for "key" (as in the "key of knowledge") is *kleis* which comes from the root word *kleio,* meaning to lock or to unlock a door. Jesus is handing His people invisible keys [kleis] to the realm of heaven's glory, and these keys are crucial revelations which unlock heaven and usher the people of God into a face to face encounter with the King of Glory.

The "knowledge of the glory" in Hebrew is *yada kabowd. Yada* is a word that implies a deep and intimate knowledge of someone or something. *Kabowd* is the tangible glory of the Lord. In the Hebrew language it is something *weighty,* which is why Paul uses the phrase the "*weight* of glory." (2 Corinthians 4:17) In Latin, the "knowledge of the glory" is the *scientia gloriam. Scientia* is the Latin word for knowledge and it is the same word from which we derive the English word "science." We could actually speak of the *science of the glory.* Science is, in its broadest sense, any systematic body of knowledge that is capable of producing a scientific prediction or a predictable outcome. Accurate prediction is central to good science. There is a body of knowledge in the Kingdom concerning the nature of the glory realm and the necessary factors that will release the glory of the Lord in the earth.

Paul specifically prayed "that the God of our Lord Jesus Christ, the **Father of glory**, may give to you the Spirit of wisdom and revelation in the **knowledge of Him**. I pray also that the eyes of your heart may be enlightened in order that you **may know**..." (Ephesians 1:17-18) God forbid that we should reduce the knowledge of the glory realm of heaven to a scientific formula. The "knowledge of the glory" cannot be reduced to a formula because it is always **relational**; nevertheless it is, in a sense, a unique science.

As we have seen in previous chapters, it is really the "science" of intimacy and we would do well to become students of the intimacy realm! According to Paul, this knowledge that God seeks to impart is an intimate knowledge of the Father of glory. The Greek word Paul used for *knowledge* was *epignosis.* This is one my absolute favourite Greek words. It describes a unique revelatory knowledge that only comes through the activity of the Spirit of revelation. *Epi* is a prefix meaning *over. Episkiazo* means "*over-*shadowing." *Episkopos* means "*over-*seer." *Epignosis* means "*over-*knowledge"; it is a specific kind of knowledge that comes from the overshadowing Spirit of revelation.

Paul only used *epignosis* 16 times in the body of his epistles and it is a fascinating study to note exactly where he used this technical word. One of my favourite places is in Ephesians 1:17, where Paul discusses the revelation of the knowledge of the Father of glory. This is the knowledge of the glory. Another favourite is in Colossians 1:9, where Paul prays that "you may be filled with the knowledge [*epignosis*] of His will in all wisdom and spiritual understanding."

This relates specifically to the will of God being done on earth as it is in heaven. God wants us to be filled with a revelatory knowledge of the nature of His will concerning supernatural healing and the higher purposes of the realm of God being released on earth. My third favourite use of epignosis is in 2 Timothy 3:7, where Paul laments the tragic reality in the church of those who are "always learning and never able to come to the knowledge [*epignosis*] of the truth." The never-ending accumulation of religious knowledge has the potential to eclipse the true revelatory epignosis that unlocks heaven on earth and ushers us into a face to face encounter with the Father of glory!

When Jesus was on earth He was happily releasing the *scientia gloriam* to His disciples. This was not an esoteric knowledge. It was freely given to those who had eyes to see and ears to hear. "To you it has been given to know the mysteries of the kingdom of God, but to the rest it is given in parables, that 'Seeing they may not see and hearing they may not understand.'" (Luke 8:10) The knowledge of the glory is freely given, but those who reject the key of the revelatory knowledge of God end up with an empty religion that uses the same vocabulary minus the encounter!

In order to release the glory of God on earth as it is in heaven, it was essential for the disciples to be comprehensibly equipped with the "prophet's reward" of seeing everything the prophet could see in order to release the glory in the same way Jesus released it on earth. "A multitude gathered from the surrounding cities to Jerusalem, bringing sick people and those who were tormented by unclean spirits, ***and they were all healed***." Where is this verse in the Bible? Matthew? Mark? Luke? No! It comes from the book of Acts! It was the *scientia gloriam* poured out through the overshadowing Spirit of revelation that resulted in the phenomena of Acts 5:16. The knowledge of the glory, poured out upon good receptive hearts, always results in the release of a supernatural lifestyle that facilitates the release of the glory on earth. The apostles embraced this Christlike lifestyle and they brought forth 100% Kingdom fruitfulness in the early days of the church.

We are now living in the most privileged time in human history. Whilst it could be argued that the disciples of the first century, who witnessed first-hand the miracles of Christ and who were trained directly by Christ to do the same works of the Kingdom and even greater, were the most privileged people in human history; a case could also be made that we are potentially positioned in the 21st century to enter into an even greater place of privilege and blessing. We have access to the same revelatory knowledge of the glory that is being restored to the church in this present apostolic move of God and, in addition, we have the added blessing of 20/20 hindsight to look back over 20 centuries of church history to study the ways of God in order to know how, why and when God moved in extraordinary revival power upon the earth.

If only we can break through the strongholds of the self life through the power of the Spirit to adopt the apostolic lifestyle of prayer and fasting and learning how to pull on the unlimited resources of heaven, we can potentially become part of a global glory awakening and participate in a massive, unprecedented end time glory outpouring where we get to witness the glory of the Lord literally covering the entire earth as the waters cover the sea. The prelude to this global glory awakening is the release of the prophetic knowledge of the glory that is currently being poured out upon the church. The light of the knowledge of the glory of God in the face of Christ is now being poured out all over the earth. The glory which tragically departed has now been restored, and God has a remnant of faithful believers all over the earth who are accessing the glory of the Holy of Holies in worship and intercession. Through relentlessly encountering the King of Glory in a posture of worship they are accessing the *epignosis* realm and are receiving the keys of the Kingdom of Heaven.

Jesus said, "I will give you the keys of the Kingdom of Heaven; whatever you forbid on earth will be what is forbidden in Heaven, and whatever you permit on earth will be what is permitted in Heaven!" (Matthew 16:19 J.B. Phillips)[1] Heaven sets the tone for ministry here on earth. Once we receive the vision of God's will on earth (revealed in the perfect ministry of Jesus) we must corporately and individually wrestle with whatever stands in the way of us doing the very same works that Jesus Himself did. If our lifestyle is not consonant with the lifestyle of Jesus, we will not see the same results. But conversely, if we can get free of the lifestyle issues that hinder us from emulating the very lifestyle of Christ and the apostles, we can be certain of a phenomenal outcome. It is a certainty!

If we want to talk about *the science of the glory,* we can say that if the people of God submit to the Lordship and prophetic training of Christ in the fullness of what that means, according to Jesus we can predict the outcome!

Now, that is good science! Every disciple of Christ who has purposed in his or her heart that they will embrace the calling to become a healing revivalist, and who have personally wrestled with the obstacles to fulfilling their prophetic destiny, have begun to see Kingdom breakthrough. For those who have pressed on to demolish the remaining subtle strongholds that hinder even greater fruitfulness, they have testified that even greater works have accompanied their ministry. It's not rocket science; it's a simple result of the law of cause and effect or sowing and reaping.

Jesus is the cause, and the release of the glory is the effect. The greatest obstacles, as everyone knows who is pressing in for a greater release of the glory of God on earth, are the subtle residual issues of the self life that have not yet been demolished by the power of the cross. All of us, if we are honest, still contribute significantly to blocking the fullness of the will of God being done on earth through our personal lives. The spotlight shines upon the church in this hour to stand and deliver! Every disciple who genuinely wants to replicate the ministry of Jesus must be completely willing to come into full alignment with their heavenly assignment and be willing to do whatever is necessary to fulfil their destiny.

God is raising up supernatural communities all over the earth that are pressing into a greater release of the supernatural. Acts 5:16 is the benchmark and heaven is prophesying that this is an attainable goal. Many have proven this to be true throughout church history and these forerunners have left a glorious paper trail so that the rest of the church can follow in their footsteps. There are some excellent paper trails out there if we will source them and apply them to our own lives! The science of the glory is not so mysterious. The *lack of will* to go after a replication of Acts 5:16 in our day is the greater mystery. This lack of resolve can only be understood through the lens of spiritual warfare!

Jesus ever lives to intercede for His church. He is praying: "Father, I desire that they also whom You gave Me may be with Me where I am, that they may behold My glory which You have given Me; for You loved Me before the foundation of the world." (John 17:24) Jesus is praying for every veil to be removed so that the light of the glory of God in the face of Christ can shine brightly into our hearts. He is praying for intense glory encounters that will rock our world and ruin us for life! This prayer was powerfully answered in the life of Paul and his faithful followers. "But we all, with unveiled face, beholding as in a mirror the glory of the Lord, are being transformed into the same image from glory to glory, just as by the Spirit of the Lord." (2 Corinthians 3:18)

But just a few verses later Paul introduces the spiritual warfare factor, where he exposes the work of the evil one who blinds or veils people's eyes, "lest the light of the gospel of the glory of Christ, who is the image of God, should shine on them." (2 Corinthians 4:4) The battle lines are drawn and we cannot change them. There is an intense spiritual battle being waged over the life of every single believer in Christ. Will the prayer of Jesus prevail, resulting in the veil being completely removed, or will the work of the evil one prevail so that the veil remains? Or will Christians live in the twilight zone of occasionally encountering the glory of Christ, only to have the evil one snatch away the revelation because of a lack of intentionality to continue to press into the realm of heaven? Jesus warned that "the wicked one comes and snatches away what was sown in his heart." (Matthew 13:19)

I don't want to oversimplify what is in fact a complicated situation. There are a number of factors that contribute both on a personal and on a collective level to the present culture of the church that actually work against the ultimate purpose of God in revealing the fullness of the glory of Christ through His church. More often than not it is a case of the good standing in the way of the best. There are a lot of "good" things that the church engages in that sideline the best of heaven being released on earth. The church in every generation is confronted by the same challenge of Acts 5:16. Will we go after God's highest and best, or will we settle for second best and forfeit the possibility of participating in the greatest revival in history? There are billions of people who do not know Christ, and the most successful method in church history to reach the multitudes has always been the outpouring of signs and wonders and miracles of resurrection and healing. Entire towns came to Christ in the book of Acts in response to one significant miracle when the glory was revealed!

GLORY EXPLOSIONS

Part of the art of the science of the glory is in discovering the keys to releasing glory explosions. I am the spiritual director of a community, New Earth Tribe on the East Coast of Australia, and together we are pursuing the lost art of releasing glory explosions. Although we are still in training in this area, we have seen almost a hundred people healed at one time in a large New Age festival in Melbourne, Australia, in 2009. We were ministering from the main performance stage before a large audience, and God led me to walk around the audience and open up a portal of healing over the people. Some were healed without anyone even touching them. Then we released a healing tunnel and well over a hundred people passed through. Almost everyone who passed through that tunnel was healed! This has now been repeated in subsequent festivals with identical results!

In Chapter Twelve we talked about *mega dunamis* versus *micro dunamis*. It takes mega dunamis to release a glory explosion. The English word *dynamite* comes from *dunamis*. Church history is full of stories of explosions of God's glory, beginning with the day of Pentecost. A glory explosion is the explosive release of the atmosphere of heaven falling suddenly upon the earth and resulting in a surge of spiritual power, accompanied by healings and conversions to Christ. One of the most famous glory explosions in the Old Testament occurred at the inauguration of Solomon's Temple. "The house of the Lord was filled with a cloud so that the priests could not continue ministering because of the cloud; for the glory of the Lord filled the house of God." (2 Chronicles 5:13-14)

Dynamite is a "high explosive," meaning that it is detonated through an electric signal. A stick of dynamite contains nitro-glycerine. When it is detonated it releases an explosive shock front that exceeds the speed of sound. High explosives can release an explosive velocity up to 9,000 metres per second! One stick of dynamite releases a massive 2.1 mega joules of energy in a split second, resulting in extreme explosive force. Dynamite is most commonly used in mining and is capable of blowing up mountains! We should not underestimate the power of God's glory. Jesus promised power to His church to reach the multitudes with mighty signs and wonders. When God's glory fell for the first time on the church, it released a glory zone over the city of Jerusalem. The effect of the explosion in Acts 2 was so great that men were "pricked in their heart" (Acts 2:37) and "fear came upon every soul." (Acts 2:43) Three thousand men were swept supernaturally into the kingdom. Only days later, additional miracles caused 2,000 more men to come to Christ.

THE DIVINE RADIATION ZONE

Sometimes the glory realm of heaven falls in such a way that it literally creates a divine "radiation zone." Everyone coming within that expanding portal of tangible power is brought under intense conviction. This is true revival! During the First Awakening in the United States, Jonathan Edwards and David Brainerd experienced numerous glory explosions. Edwards was so impressed with the life and ministry of David Brainerd that he published, *The Life and Diary of David Brainerd.* In that book Brainerd described one event that echoed Pentecost.

> The power of God seemed to descend on the assembly like a rushing mighty wind and with an astonishing energy bore all down before it. I stood amazed at the influence that seized the audience almost universally and could compare it to nothing more aptly than the irresistible force of a mighty torrent... Almost all persons of all ages were bowed down with concern together and scarce one was able to withstand the shock of the astonishing operation.[2]

Similar explosions occurred during the Third Awakening under Charles Finney. Some of these explosions have attained legendary status in the annals of church history! Finney in his autobiography recorded a number of these events. "The winter of 1857-58 will be remembered as the time when a great revival prevailed throughout all the Northern states. It swept over the land with such power, that for a time it was estimated that not less than fifty thousand conversions occurred in a single week."[3] In one account of the revivals under Finney we read:

> The moving of God in the village [of Rome, New York] was such that no one could enter the place without feeling that the presence of God was there in a peculiar and wonderful way. For example, there was a sheriff who resided in Utica [New York] who found it necessary on occasions to come to Rome. He had been told of the revival and with others had done a great deal of laughing at the things that he had heard. One day it was necessary for him to make a trip to conduct some business there. He drove his coach, having no particular impression on his mind, until he crossed an old canal which was about a mile outside the city. As soon as he crossed the canal an impression came upon him that he could not

shake off. This feeling continued to increase as he entered the village. Reaching the hotel he noticed that everyone seemed in such a state of mind that they could scarcely attend to business. The sheriff himself found it was necessary for him to divert his attention from time to time to keep from weeping. He hastened through with his business and returned to Utica, where a short time later he was soundly converted.[4]

In the 1859 revival there were reports of ships entering a literal glory zone as they drew near to certain ports on the East Coast of the United States that were experiencing revival. "Ship after ship arrived with the same talk of sudden conviction and conversion. A captain and an entire crew of thirty men found Christ at sea and arrived at port rejoicing."[5] Finney was himself astonished at the intensity of the manifestations of the glory falling upon the people:

> I had not spoken to them, I should think, more than a quarter of an hour, when all at once an awful solemnity seemed to settle down upon them; the congregation began to fall from their seats in every direction, and cried for mercy. If I had had a sword in each hand, I could not have cut them off their seats as fast as they fell. Indeed nearly the whole congregation were either on their knees or prostrate, I should think, in less than two minutes from this first shock that fell upon them. Every one prayed for himself, who was able to speak at all. Of course I was obliged to stop preaching; for they no longer paid any attention. I saw the old man who had invited me there to preach, sitting about in the middle of the house, and looking around with utter amazement. I raised my voice almost to a scream, to make him hear, and pointing to him I said, "Can't you pray?" He instantly fell upon his knees, and with a stentorian voice poured himself out to God; but he did not at all get the attention of the people. I then spoke as loud as I could, and tried to make them attend to me. I said to them, "You are not in hell yet; and now let me direct you to Christ." For a few moments I tried to hold forth the gospel to them; but scarcely any of them paid any attention. My heart was so overflowing with joy at such a scene that I could hardly contain myself. It was with much difficulty that I refrained from shouting, and giving glory to God.[6]

The glory of heaven became so tangible on earth that on occasions Finney witnessed mass conversions to Christ without even opening his mouth to preach!

A circumstance occurred in this neighbourhood, which I must not fail to notice. There was a cotton factory, a place now called New York Mills. It was owned by a Mr. W, an unconverted man, but a gentleman of high standing and good morals. My brother-in-law was at that time superintendent of the factory. I was invited to go and preach at that place, and went up one evening, and preached in the village schoolhouse, which was large, and was crowded with hearers. The Word, I could see, took powerful effect among the people, especially among the young people who were at work in the factory. The next morning, after breakfast, I went into the factory, to look through it. As I went through, I observed there was a good deal of agitation among those who were busy at their looms, and their mules, and other implements of work. On passing through one of the apartments, where a great number of young women were attending to their weaving, I observed a couple of them eyeing me, and speaking very earnestly to each other; and I could see that they were a good deal agitated, although they both laughed. I went slowly toward them. They saw me coming, and were evidently much excited. One of them was trying to mend a broken thread, and I observed that her hands trembled so that she could not mend it. I approached slowly, looking on each side at the machinery, as I passed; but observed that this girl grew more and more agitated, and could not proceed with her work. When I came within eight or ten feet of her, I looked solemnly at her. She observed it, and was quite overcome, and sunk down, and burst into tears. The impression caught almost like gunpowder, and in a few moments nearly all in the room were in tears. This feeling spread through the factory. Mr. W, the owner of the establishment, was present, and seeing the state of things, he said to the superintendent, "Stop the mill, and let the people attend to religion; for it is more important that our souls should be saved than that this factory run." The gate was immediately shut down, and the factory stopped; but where should we assemble? The superintendent suggested that the mule room was large; and, the mules being run up, we could assemble there. We did so, and a more powerful meeting I scarcely ever attended.

It went on with great power. The building was large, and had many people in it, from the garret to the cellar. The revival went through the mill with astonishing power, and in the course of a few days nearly all in the mill were hopefully converted.[7]

These kinds of events, though not common, occur through the lives of exceptionally anointed ministers who were literally possessed by the Holy Spirit. Finney's experience in the cotton factory bears a striking resemblance to an experience of Smith Wigglesworth when he was travelling on a train. He tells the story about what began as a normal train trip but ended in extraordinary revival.

I was travelling to Cardiff in South Wales. I had been much in prayer on the journey. The carriage was full of people whom I knew to be unsaved, but as there was so much talking and joking I could not get in a word for my Master. As the train was nearing the station, I thought I would wash my hands... and as I returned to the carriage, a man jumped up and said, "Sir, you convince me of sin," and fell on his knees there and then. Soon the whole carriage of people were crying out the same way. They said, "Who are you? What are you? You convince us all of sin."[8]

David Hogan is an extraordinary contemporary revivalist who has led over 100,000 Mexican hill tribe people to Christ through his ministry. He and his team have also seen well over 500 people raised from the dead. His reports of the revival in Mexico are as thrilling as anything in the book of Acts. At a healing conference in 2007 he told the story of the glory of God falling upon two villages with such intensity that everyone within the divine radiation zone came to Christ and experienced complete physical healing!

It was 1995 at 7:45 in the morning and I was standing in front of 500 of our pastors and without warning God decided to take over! I and our leadership had just got through making a covenant to give our lives for the souls of Mexico to the last man. As soon as we said "Amen" the Shekinah glory fell out of the sky! And I have to tell you that before the Shekinah glory fell in 1995 we were already raising the dead by multiples! We were already running at full speed! Hundreds of churches! We were getting 500 to 1,000 new converts a month! We were seeing the glory of God and miracles; it was amazing! And we really thought we understood what God wanted us to do! But that was kindergarten....*He* fell down and you should have seen *Him*! He went out into the villages: He went two villages wide! Unbelievers were knocked out in their homes! Believers, witchdoctors, God haters; everybody went down under the presence of God! We were all knocked out. My last remembrance was I looked up to heaven to ask Him what it was. He wasn't interested in my question! He hit me! I woke up and I was a long way away, not quite a hundred feet from where I was. I looked at my clock and it was 12:15 PM! We had 100% healing of everybody that was there![9]

THE GLOBAL GLORY REVIVAL

These kinds of extreme occurrences are now happening all over the world as the glory of the Lord is being poured out. God wants to grip His people with the reality of heaven and the unlimited power that can be unleashed through a radically set apart life. He wants to draw us into a conscious lifestyle of co-labouring with Him in unlocking heaven and releasing the glory realm. The knowledge of the glory is not released through a formula that can be emulated by unregenerate men and women. It is released through a lifestyle of worship and extreme faith as God's beloved sons and daughters learn how to unlock heaven and behold the glory of the Lord in such a way that they are supernaturally transformed and begin to glow with the glory.

The knowledge of the glory is a knowledge that only comes through direct encounter. There is no other way to access this kind of prophetic knowledge. There is a supernatural "crossing over" into an experiential dimension of the glory realm that awaits those humble saints who are willing to give up their entire life in order to be overtaken by the life of Jesus. Smith Wigglesworth, who by many accounts is regarded as one of the most anointed men of the 20th century, was literally possessed by the Holy Spirit.

Wigglesworth noted that there is a vast difference between possessing the gift of the Holy Spirit and being possessed by the Holy Spirit. He lived in a realm where he didn't exercise the gifts of the Spirit; the gifts controlled him! He was overtaken by the Spirit so that the Spirit could demonstrate what He wanted to do through any believer who is yielded to such an extent that they become a lightning rod to release the glory. Wigglesworth raised 23 people from the dead and lived a life of apostolic signs and wonders. And he didn't really get going in full tilt supernatural ministry until his fifties!

Once a believer is marked by the knowledge of the glory, there is no going back. The physical world begins to shake around believers who are glowing in the glory. Glory explosions take place spontaneously even without words! If you think about Jesus and the impact that this one man, anointed by the overshadowing glory cloud of heaven, had upon the physical realm everywhere He went, you are suddenly gazing into the reality of the heavenly calling of every man and woman in Christ. You are staring into your own personal destiny! One person anointed by the Spirit of Glory can begin to release a physical quake of the presence of another world. The apostles gathered to pray together for a greater release of the glory that resulted in supernatural miracles. "And when they had prayed, the place where they were assembled together was shaken; and they were all filled with the Holy Spirit, and they spoke the word of God with boldness." (Acts 4:31)

On another occasion Paul and Silas had been cast into prison for releasing the supernatural ministry of Jesus. "But at midnight Paul and Silas were praying and singing hymns to God, and the prisoners were listening to them. Suddenly there was a great earthquake, so that the foundations of the prison were shaken; and immediately all the doors were opened and everyone's chains were loosed." (Acts 16:25-26) On both of these occasions in the book of Acts the prayers of the saints, moved by the Spirit of faith, caused a physical shaking to take place around them. This reminds me of the lyrics of a song called "History Maker."

Is it true today that when people pray, Cloudless skies will break,
Kings and queens will shake? Yes it's true and I believe it;
I'm living for you![10]

The glory waves of heaven have the power to shake the earth, to shake the heavens, to shake kings and queens and to move mountains. David said, "In my distress I called upon the Lord and cried out to my God; He heard my voice from His temple and my cry came before Him, even to His ears. Then the earth shook and trembled; the foundations of the hills also quaked and were shaken.... The Lord thundered from heaven and the Most High uttered His voice!" (Psalm 18:6-7,13) The knowledge of the glory restores a vision of a God who shakes heaven and earth with the sound of His voice, who releases waves of heaven's glory that reverberate through the physical universe, releasing a shift in the very fabric of the universe, releasing creative miracles that astonish the recipients, gripping their hearts with a revelation of God.

Paul had a vision for the manifestation of the sons of God on earth. "For the earnest expectation of the creation eagerly waits for the revealing of the sons of God." (Romans 8:19) The sons of God are coming into the days of their full manifestation upon the earth as they enter into the intimacy of true sonship. Out of that explosion of intimacy with the Father comes a manifestation of the glory of the Lord. He is "bringing many sons to glory!" (Hebrews 2:10)

Just as the glory of the Lord was revealed through His one and only Son, so now, those who are in the Beloved Son (Ephesians 1:6) are destined to reveal His glory as they enter into the experiential essence of true sonship. Part of that destiny is to shake and restructure the very fabric of the cosmos! The knowledge of the glory of our Father is the pathway to moving in creative miracles. This is a prize worth laying aside every distraction to pursue. Paul said, "I press toward the goal for the prize of the upward call of God in Christ Jesus." (Philippians 3:14) He tasted the realm of "extraordinary miracles" and was ruined. And he calls us to imitate him in his pursuit of Christ so that the glory of the Lord covers the earth as the waters cover the sea.

Chapter Fifteen

TAKING BACK THE HIGH PLACES

We have reached the last chapter of this book and now I want to tie together some of the themes that have been raised throughout the course of Part One and Part Two of this study. In coming to a conclusion I want to sharply contrast the biblical model of transforming reality at a quantum level with the New Age concept of creating reality. These are the only two models in the history of metaphysical thought that offer any hope of affecting a shift in the nature of reality at a physical or material level.

QUANTUM PHYSICS AND NEW AGE POSITIVISM

Jesus clearly leads the way in presenting a vision for the participation of redeemed humanity in the creative works of God, but New Age ideology now also seeks to offer humanity the speculative potential to change the nature of reality through the power of focused human consciousness. And gauging by the popularity of New Age literature with the "quantum" buzzword in the title it is safe to assume that there are many New Age adherents who are feverishly seeking to create their own reality through the power of the mind. Financial prosperity and physical and emotional wellbeing are the two main areas that people seek personal empowerment in.

As we have seen in the second part of this book, there is compelling evidence both from the historical records of the life and ministry of Christ and also from contemporary experience that the supernatural ministry of healing and the demonstration of power over nature is both real and super-naturally powerful. Christ does indeed heal the sick and He is looking for people to train in His supernatural healing modality!

But there is a new kid on the block! The spiritual science of applied New Age spirituality contends that through the power of positive affirmations and conscious intention there is a realistic promise of attaining the occult power to create your own reality. These two approaches to transforming nature at a quantum level now compete in the spiritual marketplace. It is the competition between an intimacy based relational model and a model built upon formula and pseudo-scientific technique. So as we draw this book to a conclusion, I would like to compare these approaches.

People tend to love spiritual formulas. Like Simon the magician in the book of Acts, many people are willing even to pay for the capacity to work great signs and wonders without the cost of being in right relationship with the Creator. The same could be said of the seven sons of Sceva who attempted to cast out demons from the village demoniac. They tried to speak the words of God over the demonised man like some kind of magical incantation. "In the name of Jesus whom Paul preaches…" Do you remember the demon's reply? "Jesus I know and Paul I know but who are you?"[1] A person who is not filled with the Holy Spirit and who is not in right relationship with God can try to speak the word of God over someone and it will still be of no effect. It is not just a matter of the words that are spoken but it is a matter of *who* speaks the words.

Many people who embrace New Age occult philosophy and practices attempt to affect miracles and healings through the power of the spoken word. Within the New Age community it is confidently taught and believed that people have the capacity to "create their own reality" through the power of the human mind and through positive affirmations. Frequently, advocates of this healing modality will quote the words of Jesus about the "Kingdom of Heaven being within you" and about the power of your words to speak to the mountains and to see them crumble.

New Age practitioners teach these techniques as though they were some scientific formula that can be mastered and exercised to create your own reality, whatever you want it to be. The words of Christ are freely quoted in many New Age books and seminars. But whenever that which was taught by Jesus is reduced to a mere "word formula" the glorious third heaven healing model demonstrated by Jesus and His disciples descends into a "second heaven" healing modality that inevitably taps into the demonic realm as its source of spiritual energy. The demonic realm is extremely happy to work with anyone's magical formulas.

As we have seen throughout this book, one of the defining characteristics of the New Age healing modality is the appeal to quantum physics to lend scientific credibility to the idea that human consciousness has the capacity to create reality. Both the *What the Bleep* movie and *The Secret* seek to marshal evidence for this assertion by pointing to the fact that the "observer" has the ability to collapse the wave function when seeking to observe the behaviour of a sub-atomic particle.

Is an electron a wave or a particle? Well, it all depends upon the conscious observer who is seeking to observe the particle. The lesson of quantum physics is that conscious observation exercises a direct influence upon reality in the quantum world. We have seen how this has become the primary argument to support the assertion that human consciousness has the capacity to alter reality on any scale. The *What the Bleep* movie took this argument to new heights of sophistication with dazzling computer animations and special effects to capture the imagination of their audience.

In New Age metaphysics the argument is extended to assert that the entire quantum field is really the result of the existence of the observer and that the quantum world is in reality the product of consciousness. If, (and of course this is a huge hypothetical "if"), the quantum world is the product of consciousness, then perhaps human beings actually have an untapped potential to create reality to such an extent that they can miraculously heal their own body and attract unlimited wealth and personal success. While this is indeed a "quantum" leap in logic, it is nevertheless asserts that you, the observer, can create your own reality by imagining and thinking it into being. This belief must be followed up with endless positive affirmations and declarations that you will have a spectacular day because you have willed it into being.

Of course, the truth is that only God can create in this way. The Creator is the only true "Observer" who can directly alter the very structure of the quantum world through supernatural intervention. But New Agers would actually agree with this assertion! They would respond by affirming that "you are God." As God, you have the capacity to reconstruct reality at a quantum level and thus create your day by creating your own reality. They assert that the human mind is really the mind of God and that we potentially have complete mastery over nature at a quantum level if we will sit at the feet of the New Age masters to learn how to create our own reality. This becomes the ultimate New Age power trip: a parallel universe where every human being has the as-yet-un-tapped capacity to control the universe at a quantum level.

But this is a "second heaven" modality at its best. Whoever takes the bait and embraces the New Age idea that you can create your own reality descends into the abyss of New Age witchcraft, endlessly seeking to attract positive energy to reinforce their conscious attempts to re-engineer their own reality through the power of positive thoughts and affirmations. "Witchcraft" by definition is the attempt to procure spiritual power to establish your own will. Whenever someone attempts to manipulate the spirit realm to achieve certain goals, no matter how noble and well intentioned those goals may be, that person has crossed over into New Age witchcraft.

Anybody who seeks to attract positive energy into their life through their thoughts or their words is immediately dabbling in witchcraft, whether consciously or unconsciously. This modality has nothing to do with what Jesus taught His disciples. It is a perversion of the third heaven model of ministry prescribed by Jesus and it invites people into fellowship with the powers of darkness in order to achieve the power to create their own reality.

The two popular documentaries, *What the Bleep* and *The Secret*, both invoke quantum physics as the key to creating your own reality. The "law of attraction" teaches people how to harness this universal principle to change the circumstances of their life. It all sounds very scientific and it is highly appealing to those who are searching for a Western scientific rationale for New Age teachings. But let's take a moment to consider to what extent human beings can harness the power of positivity to create their day.

Quantum physics does indeed reveal that the observer has a significant impact on that which is observed within the quantum field. This is no longer in dispute. But this single scientific phenomenon has been elevated to dizzying heights amongst cutting edge New Age teachers who seek to empower human beings to change their world. The power to affect significant personal change has become the holy grail of New Age spirituality.

Some quantum physicists have theorised that the observer actually creates an entirely new reality through the process of observation. The property of "particle" only comes into existence when it is forced into this state by an observer, in other words, when a measurement forces quantum realities to identify themselves in a single state. When they are not being observed, they are nothing more than a mere "potentiality" or "probability." This has led to speculation that there are no established "realities" out there unless the observer interrupts the quantum world by forcing a measurement upon it. According to this line of reasoning, there are no objective "it's" out there until they are observed. There are only tendencies and probabilities, but no objective realities.

New Agers speculate that if this is true, human beings are actually always creating reality rather than merely observing reality. The downside of this is that if you are having a bad life, guess what: you created it! Critics of these teachings highlight the fact that the teaching inadvertently apportions blame to the true creator of your personal nightmare: You! This can become quite a heavy guilt trip that leaves people living under crippling condemnation if their life begins to fall apart. This implication is actually unavoidable. There is no way around it!

Nevertheless, New Age teachers soldier on and try to downplay the darker implications of their own belief system. Because they seek to remain positive and upbeat, they deliberately side step the unavoidable flipside of this teaching. Life has a way of throwing curve balls at us, so there must be many believers in the "law of attraction" wondering what they have done wrong to attract so many problems in their life. In order to maintain faith in the teaching, they have to tell themselves that eventually, through trial and error, they will get it right.

DON'T YOU REMEMBER CREATING THE UNIVERSE?

Amit Goswami, the New Age quantum physicist who appears in *What the Bleep*, published a book in 2008 called *God is not Dead* in which he argues for an impersonal New Age concept of God who is expressed *exclusively* through human consciousness. In Goswami's philosophy there are two central players in the universe: the conscious observer and the non-local quantum field.

Each measurement causes a change in the state of matter from a wave of possibility to a particle of actuality. This change is known as the collapse of the wave function. An understanding of collapse requires consciousness. If we follow this thinking, it means that without consciousness there is no collapse, no material particle, no materiality.[2]

Goswami asserts that this consciousness is "God" and that "God" can create new realities through conscious interaction with nature. Goswami is accompanied in this belief by Fred Alan Wolf who also appears prominently in *What the Bleep*. In 2005 Wolf released a 4-CD set titled *Meet the Real Creator – You!* in which he unashamedly joins Goswami in asserting that if there is a "God" then you alone are God! These two teachers are unafraid to co-opt explicitly Christian language to market their ideas amongst a culture that still has a Christian memory. And they are unafraid to offer the "true interpretation" of the teachings of Jesus to wrestle them out of the hands of an oftentimes powerless Christian church.

This radical new proposal has led to endless metaphysical speculations about the role of conscious beings in creating new realities. It is this fertile field of philosophical speculation that has become the source of great inspiration to New Age thinkers. This single idea has taken metaphysical thinkers into all kinds of speculative theories about the very nature of reality itself and about whether reality even exists without an observer.

This has brought about a shift from a belief in the independent existence of the material universe to a belief in the subjective observer who, through their conscious observation of the universe, gives reality to the material world around them. In this process, there has been a shift from the supremacy of materialism to the supremacy of consciousness over matter. Goswami asserts that consciousness is the ground of all being. In 1995 he published a book titled *The Self Aware Universe: How Consciousness Creates the Material World*. He writes, "The centrepiece of this new paradigm is the recognition that modern science validates an ancient idea – the idea that consciousness, not matter, is the ground of all being."[3]

This shift in paradigms reflects a movement away from the rigid objectivity of the modernist worldview to the subjectivity of the postmodern mindset. It is well known that Einstein struggled with the unfolding revelation of the new physics because he held tenaciously to the modernist mindset. He resisted the emerging concept of non-locality and what he called "spooky action at a distance." It is interesting that these developments in quantum theory reflected a wider shift that was taking place in Western thinking.

Postmodernism rejects the notion of objective reality that is "out there" waiting to be discovered. The postmodern mindset asserts that human beings create their own sense of reality based upon their own subjective interpretation of what is true and real to them. Something is real only if we determine it to be real. In line with postmodern philosophy, the "new physics," as it is often called, lends support to the notion of the subjective observer as the key player who gives shape and definition to the material world at a quantum scale.

Even though the act of observation does create new quantum realities, this doesn't necessarily extrapolate to the macroscopic universe as a whole and to our role in the universe as subjective observers. The universe and everything in it does have an independent objective existence apart from conscious observation. But this is where the New Age philosopher takes issue.

New Age metaphysicists now take the view that consciousness is the only thing that creates reality and that without conscious beings observing the universe there would be no universe, just the probability of a universe. This is the launch pad for the New Age assertion that we create our own reality on a grand scale. Why? Because, according to New Age beliefs, if there is any legitimacy at all to the term "God," it is that you alone are God.

Einstein famously said, "I like to think that the moon is there even if I am not looking at it." But New Age metaphysicists boldly assert that it is only there because you, the observer, have observed it to be there. In an interview, Goswami explains that there is no actual material existence without the primacy and "downward causation" of consciousness.

> Now in the new view, consciousness is the ground of being. So who converts possibility into actuality? Consciousness does, because consciousness does not obey quantum physics. Consciousness is not made of material. Consciousness is transcendent. Do you see the paradigm-changing view right here – how consciousness can be said to create the material world? The material world of quantum physics is just possibility. It is consciousness, through the conversion of possibility into actuality, that creates what we see manifest. In other words, *consciousness creates the manifest world.*[4]

Goswami does not shrink back from the assertion that divine consciousness expressed through self-conscious human beings is the cause of the material universe. This is the price tag for rejecting the concept of a personal Creator.

The question always arises, "The universe is supposed to have existed for fifteen billion years, so if it takes consciousness to convert possibility into actuality, then how could the universe be around for so long?" Because there was no consciousness, no sentient being, in that primordial fireball which is supposed to have created the universe, the big bang. But this *other* way of looking at things says that the universe remained in possibility until there was self-referential quantum measurement – so that is the new concept. An observer's *looking* is essential in order to manifest possibility into actuality, and so only when the observer looks, only then does the entire thing become manifest – including time. So all of past time, in that respect, becomes manifest right at that moment when the first sentient being *looks*.[5]

This is the logical conclusion amongst those who reject the biblical concept of a personal God who created the heavens and the earth! From this philosophical springboard flows endless New Age speculation about the power of human consciousness to re-engineer reality. This philosophy places the subjective observer in the driver's seat of the universe as the exclusive creator of reality. Everything necessarily flows out of the individual's conscious awareness that they are the creator of reality.

In fact, the New Age worldview proclaims that you are always creating either success or failure through the creative power of your words. If you are a negative person you project that negativity onto the world around you and you bring negativity back upon yourself. If you are a positive person you will attract positive energy. The "law of attraction" expounded in *The Secret* DVD sends its adherents into an endless spiral of projecting positive energy out into the universe in order to hopefully attract a positive response from the universe.

Do we create reality through intentional observation or does reality already exist independently of our observation? The biblical view is that reality exists independently of the observer because God created the world and brought it into being before there were any human observers. The world can and does exist quite comfortably without conscious human observation. Einstein was right: the moon does exist even when it is not being observed!

From a biblical perspective there is not a shred of evidence that we have been endowed with God-like attributes to **create** ultimate reality in the physical universe. That attribute is the sole prerogative of God alone. God somewhat facetiously asked Job if he had any recollection of creating the universe. "I will question you, and you shall answer Me: 'Where were you when I laid the earth's foundation? Tell me, if you understand. Who marked off its dimensions? Surely you know! Who stretched a measuring line across it? To what were its foundations fastened? Or who laid its cornerstone when the morning stars sang together and all the angels shouted for joy?'" (Job 38:3-7 NIV)

The Lord delights in His creative power. He "throws down the gauntlet" by asking who rivals Him in His creative power. "To whom will you compare Me? Who is My equal?" asks the Holy One. Look up into the heavens. Who created all the stars? He brings them out one after another, calling each by its name. And He counts them to see that none are lost or have strayed away." (Isaiah 40:25-26 NLT) "I am the One who made the earth and created people to live on it. With My hands I stretched out the heavens. All the millions of stars are at My command." (Isaiah 45:12 NLT)

Believing that you are God doesn't alter the equation. This belief serves only to place someone on the ultimate treadmill of mental gymnastics to try to create their own perfect reality which is doomed to end in deep frustration. Enormous energy is expended in trying to "create your day," and if your day turns into a bummer there is always the accompanying condemnation over what you did wrong or didn't do right that resulted in you creating a less than perfect day. Tomorrow always represents a new opportunity to get it right as long as you concentrate a little bit harder than the day before!

The greatest danger in drawing people into this lifestyle of intense mind control is that it will draw someone into an engagement with second heaven realities in an attempt to invoke spiritual power to create your day. The "law of attraction" as it is presented in *The Secret* focuses upon the attraction of positive energy through being a supremely positive person. This particular branch of New Age positivity emphasises the attraction of the "positive energy of the universe" through being super positive.

As is typical with all forms of occult practice, there is an attempt to harness spiritual power. The key to harnessing this spiritual power is the use of the mind and the spoken word. A person's *confession* becomes fundamental to attaining health, wealth, success and personal wellbeing. This seductive idea even infiltrated the church through certain misguided teachers in the "Word of Faith" movement in the 20th century, alluring followers of Christ into re-heated New Thought metaphysics.

It is a fundamental New Age belief that energy follows thought. Whichever way a person directs their thoughts will determine what kind of energy they will attract. Positive thoughts attract positive energy. All New Age practices ultimately focus upon the power of the mind to create reality. This is the logical outworking of the belief that "you are God" and that your thoughts have the potential to create new realities. New Age positivism always leads the practitioner into witchcraft.

Positive thoughts must be reinforced by positive confessions and positive affirmations. New Agers borrow heavily from the language and concepts of Christ, but they seek to outwork many of the concepts in the teachings of Christ through the power of the flesh. It is not at all uncommon to find New Age teachers quoting Jesus in His teaching on the power of the spoken word. In fact, Jesus is one of the greatest sources of spiritual inspiration when it comes to the whole area of the power of words.

A really big part of New Age practice is the use of words, invocations, affirmations and mantras which are repeated with great focus and concentration in order to achieve healing, transformation, prosperity, wellbeing and happiness. Instead of attracting the power of God they end up attracting the power that flows from the second heavens. This is the very essence of witchcraft: the invocation of spiritual power or spiritual energies to achieve certain life goals. Words reflect the intent to create reality; they are the vehicle through which a person allegedly creates their own reality.

If the trends in New Age metaphysics are to be believed, then there is literally no limit to the endless possibilities of our God-like power to create a better life and a better world. It all comes down to the way you think and the way you speak. This is the promise of 21st century New Age metaphysics that has captured the popular imagination and is being spread throughout the world to a society that is eager to affect quantum change, both personally and collectively. People are desperately seeking personal empowerment!

THE QUANTUM ENIGMA AND DIVINE REVELATION

Quantum physicists appear to have reached an impasse in their ability to adequately explain the mysteries of the quantum world. Operating within a strictly naturalistic paradigm, it would appear that secular scientists have hit a brick wall in their attempts to provide an explanation of the reality of the quantum universe. This is where the New Age Quantum Mystics have stepped in with their metaphysical speculations and their attempts to impose a New Age, Eastern worldview upon the quantum world. But as we have seen, their ability to give a broader explanation of the origin of the material world in the absence of human consciousness leaves many unanswered questions.

I believe the only way humanity can arrive at an intellectually satisfying answer to the quantum enigma is to view the realities of the quantum world through the lens of biblical revelation. Nothing else on the planet makes a lot of sense without understanding reality through the lens of that which God has revealed through His Word, so why should we expect to correctly understand the quantum world without the assistance of divine revelation?

There are too many parallels between the new discoveries of the quantum world and the revelation of the Bible to merely dismiss these things as coincidence. Let me illustrate what I mean. The main features of quantum mechanics that we would consider weird or counter-intuitive just happen to parallel the very same expressions of supernatural interaction between heaven and earth as revealed in the pages of Scripture. The greatest unsolved mysteries of quantum mechanics are the observer effect (which is revealed in the mystery of the double-slit experiment), non-locality and quantum entanglement, and each of these three peculiar features of the quantum world are analogous to aspects of divine revelation as it touches the theme of heaven invading earth.

Could it be that the answer to the problem of the double-slit experiment could actually be theological? Similarly, could biblical theology hold the key to an accurate interpretation of quantum non-locality and entanglement as unique features of our universe? If so many of the parables that Jesus told 2,000 years ago use imagery and concepts from nature to illustrate spiritual truths, could the mysteries of nature embedded within the quantum world actually be divinely revealed parables of deeper spiritual truths? As we draw this book to a conclusion we would like to explore some of these questions.

Both God and His eternal kingdom exist in a dimension outside of space and time. God is an infinitely transcendent Being! His kingdom exists in an eternal, extra-dimensional realm that is not subject in any way to the constraints and limitations of either space or time. God inhabits eternity.[6] He created time because He is the Alpha and the Omega, the Beginning and the End![7] He is the "Eternal God,"[8] the great "I AM," and His kingdom is described as an "Eternal Kingdom."[9] God infinitely transcends all concepts of "beginning" and "ending" because He was before the beginning and will exist after the end. John spoke of "The One who existed from the beginning." (1 John 1:1 NLT) God is revealed as the "Father of eternity."[10] The truth is, He even transcends eternity!

Whenever the eternal Kingdom of Heaven breaks into the time-space continuum, it carries attributes that are not in any way constrained by time. One of these attributes is "infinity." God is infinite in that He is not constrained by concepts of "finiteness." Something which is "finite" is bound by certain constraints. That which is finite has both a beginning and an end, whereas infinity is an attribute of God. "Great is our Lord, and mighty in power; His understanding is infinite!" (Psalm 147:5) "Known to God from eternity are all His works." (Acts 15:18) In the same way, the eternal Kingdom of Heaven is an infinite kingdom because it is a manifestation or extension of God Himself. "For Yours is the kingdom and the power and the glory forever." (Matthew 6:13) "The kingdom, the power and the glory" are a manifestation of the Eternal God. The kingdom constitutes everything that is "in Him!"

It is extremely hard to fathom what Paul calls a "world without end!"[11] Such concepts of infinity and eternity completely boggle the mind, but those who embrace the biblical revelation of these mind-expanding concepts are in a much better position to attempt to conceptualise the kind of realities that are encountered in the quantum world. We were created to comprehend eternity. Solomon said, "He has also set eternity in the hearts of men; yet they cannot fathom what God has done from beginning to end." (Ecclesiastes 3:11 NIV)

As image-bearers, we are hard-wired for eternity even though we cannot intellectually comprehend it. But such is the nature of biblical revelation: we are confronted with concepts that transcend rational comprehension, yet these things are nourishment for the human spirit. We welcome these thoughts as we meditate and feed upon the revelation of an infinite and eternal God who is uncreated and who exists outside of space and time.

The recipients of biblical revelation who have made these concepts their "daily bread" are not challenged in the ultimate sense by the counter-intuitive realities of the quantum world. As the "buffer zone" between heaven and earth, the strange and enigmatic attributes of the quantum realm make perfect sense. The seeming irrationality of the double-slit experiment represents an insurmountable stumbling block to the rationalist mindset, but it merely confirms that which biblically enlightened men and women already know: there is a supernatural realm which impinges upon and which undergirds the natural realm. The double-slit experiment messes with our concept of time because multi-dimensional, non-local Hilbert space is not subject to the arrow of time. It contradicts our classical notion of "before" and "after."

The mysteries of the quantum world cannot be accurately comprehended apart from biblical revelation. This is true not only of the world of the quantum but also of the macroscopic or classical world of nature. Divine revelation ties everything together into a comprehensible whole which has regard for the attributes of the natural order as they interface with the attributes of the transcendent supernatural order. The unfolding revelation of the quantum mechanical world points inexorably to these greater metaphysical realities.[12]

QUANTUM PARABLES

If Jesus came to earth in the 21st century, we might wonder if some of the parables He told would encompass the world of quantum mechanics. Jesus reached into many areas of nature to find parabolic metaphors to communicate deep spiritual truths. Perhaps we could propose some deep quantum parables to explain the infinite and eternal Kingdom of Heaven breaking into the earthly realm. Jesus said, "To what shall we liken the Kingdom of Heaven? Or with what parable shall we picture it?" (Mark 4:30)

Even in the first century, Jesus touched upon the concept of non-locality when He described the supernatural presence of the Kingdom in the midst of the world. The Kingdom cannot be physically observed because it exists in another dimension. "The kingdom of God does not come with your careful observation, nor will people say, "Here it is," or "There it is," because the kingdom of God is among you."[13] (Luke 17:20-21) So, based upon this biblical precedent, let's consider some 21st century quantum parables.

1. To what shall we liken the Kingdom of Heaven? Or with what parable shall we picture it?" The Kingdom of Heaven can be likened to a quantum particle that exists in a non-local dimension outside of space and time. But when God, who inhabits this transcendent heavenly dimension deems to bring non-local heavenly realities into existence in the material universe, behold, entirely new realities spontaneously materialise at His command!

The kingdom coming on earth as it is in heaven can be likened to the appearance of the Son of Man. The living Word of God, who *was* in the beginning, became localised in space and time through the incarnation. He who existed from the beginning and who framed the worlds became flesh and blood and dwelt amongst us so that we who exist in the material world might have the privilege of beholding the One who eternally existed outside of space and time, the very One who created the heavens and the earth through His powerful Word. God is a non-local eternal Spirit, but He chose to become localised in the physical world in order to manifest His glory.

The presence of the non-local Kingdom of Heaven is revealed on earth through "signs" that point to the presence of the Kingdom. When God chooses to perform a supernatural miracle of healing or a resurrection within time and space, He intentionally localises previously non-local heavenly realities by calling those things that are not as though they are. The eternal realm breaks in with exquisite mathematical order and heaven comes to earth!

The eternal kingdom of infinite power and glory breaks into the finite space-time continuum. With a word, God collapses the quantum field and materialises new body parts that previously did not exist. In like manner, He also dematerialises tumours, growths and cancer cells by taking them out of existence at a quantum level through the word of His power. He is unquestionably the Lord of the quantum field.

2. To what shall we liken the Kingdom of Heaven? Or with what parable shall we picture it? The Kingdom of Heaven is like a quantum particle that exists in two places at one time. In the double-slit experiment, physicists see the evidence that a single quantum particle passes through two slits at once but cannot explain why. All the scientific evidence reveals that this non-local particle has actually been in two places at once. So is everyone born of the Spirit.

Jesus said, "No one has ascended to heaven but He who came down from heaven, that is, the Son of Man who is in heaven." (John 3:13) So too, everyone who has been born of the Spirit is now also simultaneously on earth and in heaven at the same time. Whilst on earth Jesus spiritually bi-located, and now His disciples experience this same bi-location miracle!

Jesus is the firstborn from the dead, the firstborn among many brothers. The entire spiritual family now lives in two realms at the same time!

3. To what shall we liken the Kingdom of Heaven? The Kingdom of Heaven is an eternal realm. It is a "world without end" because it has no beginning and no end. The kingdom is eternal because God is eternal. The realm of heaven can be likened to the non-local quantum field because it is not in any way bound by the constraints of time. On earth, humans are bound by concepts of past, present and future and they live within an ever changing continuum as they continually observe the passage of time. But the realm of God is not bound by time. On the other side of the quantum looking glass, a non-local quantum wave knows prophetically the choices that people will make even before they are made. For a quantum wave there is no such thing as past or future. In the same way, God, who inhabits eternity, knows from the perspective of eternity every choice before it is made.

4. To what shall we liken the Kingdom of Heaven? Or with what parable shall we picture it? The Kingdom of Heaven is like quantum entangled particles that are supernaturally linked together beyond space and time. Jesus is the light of the world yet He said to His disciples that they also were the light of the world. Because Christ, who is the light, lives inside His people, they actually become light. "For you were once darkness, but now you *are light* in the Lord." (Ephesians 5:8) Both Jesus and His brethren are like entangled partners in the Kingdom of Light. The cross acted as a divine beam splitter. One glorious particle of light passed through the inglorious experience of the cross and through the atonement Jesus became over a billion refracted particles of light, who now flood the entire earth with the light of the glory of God! Paul said that Christ is now a "many-membered body." "For as the body is one and has many members, but all the members of that one body, being many, are one body, so also is Christ!" (1 Corinthians 12:12)

Like entangled photons, their destinies are now intertwined as "sons of light." We are now gloriously "pre-destined to be conformed to the image of the Son." (Romans 8:29) Because Christ shines the light of the glory of God, we also "shine like stars in the universe." (Philippians 2:15 NIV) Daniel prophesied that, "Those who have insight will shine brightly like the brightness of the expanse of heaven, and those who lead many to righteousness, like the stars forever and ever." (Daniel 12:3 NASB) It is the nature of light to shine. The Greek word for light is *phos* and when this light radiates the glory of God, Paul used the word *photizo*.[14]

As light bearers, we are living photons! Whatever happens to one living "photon" affects every other entangled photon of light. The manifestation of the light of the glory of God attracts hostility and opposition. When one photon of light suffers persecution, they fill up the sufferings of Christ and Christ suffers afresh through the rejection and persecution of His followers.[15] But conversely, because "One Photon" is destined to glory, it follows that every other entangled "photon" will automatically experience this glorification. "Whom He predestined...these He also glorified." (Romans 8:30)

This is the glory of a heavenly quantum entanglement! Our destiny is not only intertwined with Christ but also with our brothers and sisters in the light. Just as Paul said that "we should live together with Him" (1 Thessalonians 5:10), so Paul said to His brethren, "You are in our hearts to die together and to live together." (2 Corinthians 7:3) God is light and we are now sons and daughters of light who are called to "Arise and shine, for your light has come, [because] the glory of the Lord is risen upon you." (Isaiah 60:1)

TAKING BACK THE HIGH PLACES

As a theologian and teacher, I am personally fascinated by the theological implications of quantum physics and the intersection between these two disciplines. Throughout this book I have intentionally set my own investigation of quantum mysteries in the light of biblical revelation against the backdrop of the New Age hijacking of quantum physics. I have repeatedly sought to interact with current New Age thought on this topic, because the New Age community has sought to claim the high ground of interpreting the discoveries of quantum physics to the wider community as evidenced in the plethora of books on this subject and movies such as *What the Bleep Do We Know?*

The tone of the New Age community's authoritative pronouncements would suggest that they believe they have the sole prerogative to interpret the mysteries of the quantum world because of the *apparent* convergence between Eastern spiritual concepts and the mysteries of the quantum mechanical world. The suggestion is that they have something of a manifest destiny to explain quantum mysteries.

In ancient Israel the people of God found themselves in an intense spiritual battle to possess the Promised Land. Part of this protracted battle included the conquest of the high places. The "high places" held great prophetic significance in the Promised Land. "Happy are you, O Israel! Who is like you, a people saved by the Lord; the shield of your help and the sword of your majesty! Your enemies shall submit to you, and *you shall tread down their high places.*" (Deuteronomy 33:29)

The "high places" were always deemed to be the supreme place to occupy and the ultimate geographical location to commune with the gods. Like the ancient ziggurats of Mesopotamia, these towers, such as the "Tower of Babel," were designed to bring their builders closer to the heavens and hence closer to their deities. The architects of "Babel," which incidentally means the "gate of God" said, "Come, let us build ourselves a city, with a tower that reaches to the heavens." (Genesis 11:4 NIV)

The "high places" were a place of elevation and vision. "So it was the next day that Balak took Balaam and brought him up to the high places of Baal, that from there he might observe the extent of the people." (Numbers 22:41) The high places were always centres of religious devotion. "They also built for themselves *high places*, sacred pillars, and wooden images on every high hill and under every green tree." (1 Kings 14:23) The children of Israel were instructed by the Lord to occupy the high places and to tear down the altars and images associated with pagan idolatry. The Kings of Israel were individually evaluated by whether or not they cut down the high places.

> Asa did what was good and right in the eyes of the Lord his God, for he removed the altars of the foreign gods and the *high places*, and broke down the sacred pillars and cut down the wooden images. He commanded Judah to seek the Lord God of their fathers, and to observe the law and the commandment. He also removed the high places and the incense altars from all the cities of Judah, and the kingdom was quiet under him. (2 Chronicles 14:2-5)

> Jehoshaphat was thirty-five years old when he became king, and he reigned twenty-five years in Jerusalem. And he walked in all the ways of his father Asa. He did not turn aside from them, doing what was right in the eyes of the Lord. *Nevertheless the high places were not taken away*, for the people offered sacrifices and burned incense on the high places. (1 Kings 22:42-43)

Hezekiah was twenty-five years old when he became king, and he reigned twenty-nine years in Jerusalem. And he did what was right in the sight of the Lord, according to all that his father David had done. He *removed the high places* and broke the sacred pillars, cut down the wooden images. (2 Kings 18:2-4)

Now Josiah also *took away all the shrines of the high places* that were in the cities of Samaria, which the kings of Israel had made to provoke the Lord to anger; and he did to them according to all the deeds he had done in Bethel. (2 Kings 23:19)

In the Promised Land the idolatry of the high places was always intended to be replaced with devotion to Yahweh. God promised to give the children of Israel the high places so that they would prevail militarily and spiritually. Mountains are the place of prophetic promise. Great military battles always surrounded the mountains of Israel because they held strategic significance. They symbolised a place of elevated prophetic vision and intimacy with God. "And he carried me away in the Spirit to *a great and high mountain*, and showed me the great city, the holy Jerusalem, descending out of heaven from God." (Revelation 21:10) God Himself promised that it was the destiny of His people to occupy a strategic place in the top of the mountains.

Now it shall come to pass in the latter days that the mountain of the Lord's house shall be established *on the top of the mountains*, and shall be exalted above the hills; and all nations shall flow to it. Many people shall come and say, "Come, and let us go up to the mountain of the Lord, to the house of the God of Jacob; He will teach us His ways and we shall walk in His paths." (Isaiah 2:2-3)

Whenever the church steps back from its prophetic calling to occupy the high places of the earth, there will be others who willingly step into the void left by the church. The people of God have been given a stewardship by the Lord Himself and they have become the custodians of the very revelation of God in the earth. We have a clear mandate to make disciples of all the nations and to teach them everything the Lord has taught us in His Word. (Matthew 28:19-20) Part of this body of revelation includes the accurate interpretation of nature in the light of biblical revelation. The followers of Christ are "the church of the living God, the pillar and foundation of the truth." (1 Timothy 3:15 NIV) We have an intimate relationship to the truth because we are followers of He who is the Truth.

The great mountains that the church must repossess are the mountains of divine revelation, supernatural power and divine love. Whenever the church abdicates its role as the custodian of divine truth in the earth, these mountains are automatically occupied in our culture by those who claim to be able to interpret spiritual reality to the multitudes. In our 21st century Western culture, the New Age community has stepped into the void left by a church that has abdicated its kingly and priestly role.

The New Age movement has largely occupied the high places of revelation, power and love in our 21st century Western culture. They have held the high ground in offering revelation concerning the invisible realm. They have held the high ground in offering spiritual power in the arena of healing. They have held the high ground in promising love and community to the world [peace, love, brotherhood, harmony, unity, oneness, etc.].

One of the primary areas where the New Age has sought to occupy the high ground in the arena of the revelation of the invisible world has been in their agenda to interpret quantum physics to a world that is hungry for spiritual revelation and spiritual power. A mystical interpretation of the mysteries of the quantum world accompanied by a bold promise of achieving health, wealth and personal success has found a huge market in our postmodern culture.

The spiritual marketplace has been flooded with a mountain of books promising prophetic insight into the dynamics of the quantum world coupled with promised insights that will release the spiritual power to create your own reality. New Age quantum mystics powerfully exploit this renewed spiritual hunger that is a feature of radicalized postmodern culture. New Age spirituality is the spirituality of choice for postmodern people who have given up the hope of finding absolute truth and who have settled for anything that will help them create their own sense of truth and reality.

My prayer is that this book, *Quantum Glory,* will represent one small step closer to the goal of the church laying hold of its prophetic destiny to be the head and not the tail in the earth. Quantum physics is unequivocally God's quantum physics! The unveiling of the quantum world that has occurred in the past century, as scientists have continually probed matter to its fundamental core, ought to have been interpreted by a loud chorus of prophetic voices who could have assisted the wider culture to accurately interpret the discoveries of the quantum world in the clear light of biblical revelation. Regrettably this did not happen!

While the church was all but silent in explaining the prophetic significance of these scientific discoveries, the New Age quantum mystics stepped boldly into the arena and placed a contrived eastern mystical interpretation on something which in actuality reflects the glory and majesty of God and which gives us a scientific basis for understanding the very mechanics of the supernatural invasion of heaven to earth.

NON-LOCAL SUPERNATURAL INTERVENTION

Interpreted in the light of sacred Scripture, the revelations of the wave/particle duality, of extra-dimensionality, of non-locality, of quantum entanglement and of quantum realities that transcend time and space, lead us toward a scientific explanation of an "other-worldly" dimension to our universe that permits non-local interventions from outside of time and space! While the non-local quantum universe does not constitute a revelation of the supernatural in and of itself, it nevertheless paves the way for a scientifically workable hypothesis for non-local intervention into what was once regarded as an inviolable material system that did not allow for the possibility of non-local influences.

Like so many in my generation, I was raised with a typical Western rationalistic mindset that precluded supernatural intervention and causation. It was not until I began to personally experience the supernatural (over 30 years ago) in a way that I could not deny that I opened my mind to the possibility of divine supernatural intervention in the physical realm. I have witnessed a resurrection from the dead! I have seen and heard with my own eyes and ears a broken bone "pop" back suddenly into its correct position. I have watched legs and arms grow centimetres right before my very eyes on numerous occasions. I have seen God remove a chunk of glass from a woman's foot and watched the shock on the woman's face as she unwrapped the bandage and realised that the glass had been supernaturally removed! The chunk of glass appeared on the ground alongside her shoe! I totally love that miracle!

I have been used by the Lord in so many healings that I have truly lost count. I have had words of knowledge that have resulted in instant healings of severe and chronic pain. I have laid hands on deaf ears and seen them instantly opened! I have smelled the supernatural fragrance of the Lord. I have seen the visible glory cloud descend on a building that was experiencing a glory explosion. I have seen the temple of the Lord filled with the smoke of His glory and, along with others, have simultaneously smelt smoke in the room during a time of intense intimate worship.

I have watched as people have been covered in a fine gold dust right before my eyes. I have seen oil flowing supernaturally from people's hands and have experienced this myself. I have handled gemstones that have supernaturally appeared in glory-filled meetings! I have seen a gold tooth inside a man's mouth that supernaturally appeared. I have heard words of knowledge spoken by prophets that have literally astonished me. I have seen a prophet get a person's name and telephone number in a public meeting and then proceed to ring the number and talk to the person he had just identified prophetically! I have seen prophets accurately tell people their first and last name and their exact address!

I have been hit so hard by the raw power of God that I have been knocked to the ground in ecstasy. This has happened far too many times to count. I am the director of a spiritual community that has been experiencing an outpouring of the Holy Spirit ever since 2006, where we experience supernatural healings on a regular basis. Not a week goes by without reports of amazing healings in our healing rooms, in our meetings or on the streets. We experienced more than one and a half thousand healings in our outreaches into New Age festivals in 2009.

In addition I have cast out so many demons that I have lost count. I have had demonised people scratch me with their fingernails; I have been violently assaulted and had one person spit in my face during a deliverance session. I have watched demons contort people's faces and bodies and heard them speak things that were absolutely disgusting. These experiences with demonised people were all significant encounters with the supernatural realm. I have seen a man who has never walked before get up out of his wheelchair unaided and walk across the room for the first time in his life! I have heard angelic choirs and supernatural musical instruments being played during times of intense glory-filled worship. I have experienced significant visions and dreams from God.

I have met people who have been physically transported instantaneously over great distances, just like Philip in the book of Acts. I have other friends who have watched milky white eyes turn brown right before their eyes as God instantly healed blindness. I have met a man who has raised numerous people from the dead in Africa, including a woman who had been dead for up to three days! This same man, Supresa Sithole, has been given the ability to speak more than ten languages supernaturally.

I have talked to people who have literally been taken into heaven and to others who have had astonishing open visions and who have seen angels. I have personally seen many supernatural things over a period of 30 years, and I continue to see the supernatural on a regular basis! In short, I have been so dislocated out of traditional rationalistic unbelief through countless supernatural experiences that I am now 100% convinced that Jesus is real and that the Bible is true.

There is no doubt that we bring our experiences to our research. Even biblical research conducted by someone with a full blown spirit of unbelief can result in the development of a theology that denies the very words of the Bible. The same is true of research into the mysteries of the quantum world. Seen through the lens of 30 years of supernatural encounters, it is plain to me that the physical universe is crafted by a super-intelligent Being who has designed it in such a way that it permits non-local supernatural intervention.

However, the same features of the quantum world, when studied by a complete unbeliever without firsthand experience of the supernatural power of God, can cause them to deny the possibility of any supernatural intervention. Such is the position of arch-atheist Victor Stenger, who is so violently opposed to any relationship between quantum physics and the supernatural that he has written a series of books slamming any suggestion of a link between the two. Stenger is a professor of physics but he sees no evidence whatsoever in the science of quantum physics to support the idea that the strange world of the quantum provides a link between the supernatural and the natural realms.

But I have come to an entirely different conclusion. As a servant of Christ with a wealth of experience in the supernatural, I have concluded that the non-local world of quantum mechanics represents a divinely created "buffer zone" between heaven and earth. The strange world of the quantum exhibits attributes that form a bridge between the supernatural world and the natural world. I have come to the study of the quantum world with an unwavering conviction of the reality of a supernatural God. I do not believe that the quantum world is itself supernatural, but it has definite features and qualities that permit supernatural intervention and spontaneous acts of creation.

In addition, the quantum world exhibits "mind-like" attributes that support the thesis of intelligent design, most notably the mathematical properties of the Golden Ratio which appear to be something of a divine signature throughout nature. The exquisite mathematical fine tuning within the quantum field strongly suggests that the building blocks of matter are in fact the product of the mind of God and not the product of pure random chance.

The quantum world specifically reveals the glory of a Creator who is the supreme Mathematician and Physicist, who intricately designed the atom (the fundamental building block of matter) as a miracle of precision golden mathematics. The ultra-fine tuning of the mathematical constants discovered within the atomic and sub-atomic world and throughout the entire universe are as much a revelation of the mind of Christ as the Scriptures themselves, if we concede that mathematics is an informational language and a legitimate expression of the "Word of God."

Just as God spoke the heavens and the earth into existence through His glorious Word, so He continues to interrupt the ordinary downward spiral of our physical existence with miracles that reveal the glory of His supernatural power over nature. The thing that staggers my mind is the fact that Christ came to earth and demonstrated His glory through an outpouring of the supernatural, but then He went on to enlist ordinary men and women to do the very same miracles through their faith in Him as an unfolding expression of their developing intimacy with God. I have had the privilege of being swept up in this unfolding drama of heaven invading earth and I have become an eyewitness of His glory and His majesty! And all I can say is thank you, God!

Appendix:

QUANTUM GOLDEN FIELD THEORY

I n this appendix we will endeavour to describe how Professor El Naschie discovered the significance of the Golden Section within the quantum field. His astonishingly accurate mathematical predictions were based upon the creative marriage between the mathematics of the "Golden Mean" and the "Cantor Set." The Cantor Set was discovered by the mathematician Georg Cantor [1845–1918]. If we want to understand the relationship between the quantum world and the Golden Mean, we need to put some building blocks in place so that we can grasp the concepts that played a key role in the development of El Naschie's theory of fractal space-time. The first concept we need to grasp is the "Cantor Set."

A "Cantor Set" is an infinite set constructed using only the numbers between 0 and 1. A Cantor Set is constructed by starting with a line of length 1, and removing the middle 1/3. Next, the middle 1/3 of each of the pieces that are left are removed, and then the middle 1/3 of the pieces that remain after that are removed. The set that remains after continuing this process forever is called the Cantor Set. The Cantor Set contains an uncountable number of points.[1]

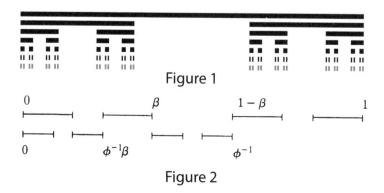

Figure 1

Figure 2

The Cantor Set is a unique geometric topological space. It is also an infinite fractal because each diminution exhibits the attributes of self-similarity as Figure 1 indicates. A special mathematical relationship has been discovered between the Cantor Set and the Golden Mean which is also an infinite fractal. Roger L. Kraft, in a paper titled *A Golden Cantor Set*, explains that "the Golden Ratio solves a simple but interesting geometric problem involving Cantor Sets." According to Kraft, "Before we marry the Golden Ratio to a Cantor Set, we should find out what these two have in common. We see that what they both bring to this relationship... is the notion of self-similarity."[2] It turns out that the Golden Ratio and the Fibonacci numbers are an important element of the Cantor Set. In Figure 3 below, Kraft points out that in a two dimensional Cantor Set the 8 lines all have Golden angles. "Any rectangle with a diagonal along one of these lines is a Golden rectangle, i.e., a rectangle where the lengths of its sides is φ. Thus figure [3] is full of golden rectangles."[3]

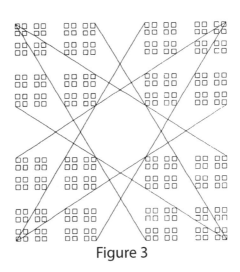

Figure 3

Every metric space has what is called its "Hausdorff Dimension." In mathematics the Hausdorff Dimension is always a real number, either rational or irrational, which is attributed to any metric space. El Naschie's mathematical breakthrough came when he discovered that the Hausdorff Dimension of the Cantor Set was actually φ = (√5 – 1)/2. Subsequently, both Cantor Sets and the Golden Ratio were found to fractalise infinitely. In other words, they generate fractal-like self similar patterns over multiple scales. El Naschie hypothesised that space-time in a quantum topology was infinite dimensional based upon the Cantor Set and its Golden Mean value of the Hausdorff Dimension. El Naschie's "Quantum Golden Field Theory" is based entirely upon this mathematical fact. This discovery gave rise to a unique theory of "Cantorian space-time" which El Naschie called "E-infinity," where "E" = energy; hence "E-infinity" describes a unique model of quantum space-time that exhibits infinite energy at every resolution. E-infinity is therefore an infinite fractal space that continues to fractalise at every successive scale. El Naschie explains this breakthrough in the development of an entirely new conception of space-time.

> In our work which began about two decades ago, we started exploring the possibility of a geometry which in a sense reconciles the irreconcilable, namely, having points which are no points in the ordinary sense. In other words, we could have our cake and eat it by using geometry with points which upon close examination reveal themselves not as a point but as a cluster of points. Every point in this cluster, when re-examined, reveals itself again as another cluster of points and so on ad infinitum. Not surprisingly, this type of geometry has been well-known for a long time to mathematicians and seems to have been discovered first by the German mathematician Georg Cantor, the inventor of Set-Theory. The famous Triadic Cantor Set is probably the simplest and definitely the best known example of such geometry. Cantor Sets are at the heart of modern mathematics and a particular form of non-metric spaces and geometry, known in modern parlance as fractals. However, Cantor Sets have never been used explicitly to model space-time in physics. Material scientists, mechanical engineers, chemists, and biologists, all a part of the hard-core non-linear dynamicists, apply Cantor Sets across the fields. By contrast it seems indeed that our group is the first to take the idea of a Cantorian fractal space-time seriously and give it a viable mathematical formulation with the help of which specific and precise computations can be made.[4]

Some background is necessary to understand the role of the Golden Mean and the random Cantor Set in its relation to space-time. The original concept of "space-time" integrates the four dimensions of space and time into a coherent whole in which time interacts with three dimensional space to create a unique reality called "space-time." Space-time is distinct from three dimensional space which has traditionally been understood to be separate from time. Einstein, in his general theory of relativity, demonstrated that time is relative to space and time can actually be warped or distorted by the force of gravity. Einstein's scientific breakthrough gave birth to an entirely new reality called "space-time" that is distinct from our everyday experience of time and space as separate realities.

The traditional scientific conception of space-time has classically been that of a smooth and flat 3 + 1 Euclidean geometric space-time. Actual quantum space-time, according to Mohamed El Naschie, is a fractal structure inherent throughout the entire fabric of the cosmos. The concept of fractal space-time is a relatively new approach to understanding the fabric of space at a quantum level. Benoit Mandelbrot first coined the term "fractal" in 1975. The term "fractal space-time" was first coined in 1983 by Garnet Ord, an English-Canadian physicist.[5] In this tradition El Naschie began to argue in 1990 that actual space-time at the quantum scale was a non-classical Cantorian space-time with an entirely different geometry based upon the Cantor Set and the Golden Mean. Within this framework El Naschie asserted that the force of gravity is actually caused by the fractal fluctuations of time at a quantum level.[6] The Italian physicist, Professor Gerardo Iovane, explains El Naschie's unique Cantorian space-time:

> Reading El Naschie's papers and other previous contributions it clearly appears that the E-infinity theory is more than a new framework for understanding and describing nature and not only a set of equations. Probably the main point of the theory is the fact that everything we see or measure is resolution dependent. As reported by El Naschie, in the Cantorian E-infinity view, space-time is an infinite dimensional fractal that happens to have D = 4 as the expectation value for the topological dimension. In particular, the topological dimension 3 + 1 = 4 means that in our low energy resolution, the world appears to us as if it were four-dimensional. In particular, if we also add the time dimension, we can obtain a manifold dimension, that can be approximated by $4 + \phi^3$ where ϕ is the Golden Mean. This means that the dimension becomes resolution dependent; consequently it all depends on the energy scale with which we are making our observation.[7]

It is now universally accepted that quantum space-time is radically different from three dimensional Euclidean space. *Hilbert space*, named after the German mathematician, David Hilbert, is the term used to describe any structure of finite or infinite dimensional space that is distinguished from classical Euclidean space. Hilbert space is not an abstract theory. It is determined mathematically with stunning precision. According to Amir Aczel,

> We must let go of all our preconceptions about the world derived from our experience and our senses, and instead let mathematics lead the way. The electron lives in a different space from the one in which we live. It lives in what mathematicians call a *Hilbert space*, and so do the other tiny particles and photons. This Hilbert space, developed by mathematicians independently of physics, seems to describe well the mysterious rules of the quantum world – rules that make no sense when viewed with an eye trained by our everyday experiences. So the physicist working with quantum systems relies on the mathematics to produce predictions of the outcomes of experiments or phenomena, since this same physicist has no natural intuition about what goes on inside an atom or a ray of light or a stream of particles. Quantum theory taxes our very idea of what constitutes reality. What does "reality" mean in the context of the existence of entangled entities that act in concert even while vast distances apart? The beautiful mathematical theory of Hilbert space, abstract algebra, and probability theory – our mathematical tools for handling quantum phenomena – allow us to *predict* the results of experiments to a stunning level of accuracy; but they do not bring us an *understanding* of the underlying processes.[8]

It is the mathematical equations themselves that point toward the existence of Hilbert space. Roger Penrose, in his book, *The Emperor's New Mind*, explains how the existence of Hilbert space allows an explanation of quantum superposition. Scientists have been perplexed by the unquestionable fact that in quantum superposition a single particle shows all the evidence of being in two places at one time. Penrose argues that the answer lies in the mathematical, multi-dimensional Hilbert space, but this is difficult to conceptualise because we are so trained to think in terms of three dimensional space.

"A single point of Hilbert space now represents the quantum state of an entire system. The most fundamental property of a Hilbert space is that it is called a vector space – in fact, a complex vector space. This means that we are allowed to add together any two elements of the space and obtain another such element. We must be able to do this because these are the operations of quantum linear superposition."[9] In Hilbert space an electron or a photon really can be in two places at the same time.

El Naschie tells us that "the golden mean is indeed the crucial link between Hilbert space and E-infinity theory."[10] According to El Naschie, "It is essential to have a resolution-dependent geometry which changes its structure and topology as the resolution of the observation is changed. Such geometry is essentially a fractal. More specifically it is a Cantorian geometry identical to that of E-infinity theory."[11] At "low resolution," fractal space-time is not apparent but when we zoom in at "high resolution," the distinction between *actual* quantum space-time and *apparent* space-time becomes evident.

The quantum world, of course, is so small that it is powerfully affected by the dimensional fluctuations of space-time, giving rise to the force of gravity which is one of the four fundamental forces of physics and the most mysterious and difficult of the four forces to explain. The quest to explain the nature of gravity at a quantum scale is the holy grail of physics and it is this quest that has given rise to string theory which also posits additional hidden dimensions. Physicists use the term "quantum gravity" because the force of gravity is clearly generated at a quantum level, and the idea that this mysterious force is generated within an infinite dimensional fractal space-time is certainly an intelligent and appealing proposition. Physicists are deeply aware of the fundamental incompatibility between general relativity and quantum mechanics, as Brian Green explains:

> By probing to even smaller distance scales...we see that the random quantum mechanical undulations in the gravitational field correspond to such severe warpings of space that it no longer resembles a gently curving geometric object. Rather it takes on [a] frothing, turbulent, twisted form. John Wheeler coined the term *quantum foam* to describe the frenzy revealed by such an ultramicroscopic examination of space (and time) – it describes an unfamiliar arena of the universe in which the conventional notions of left and right, back and forth, up and down (and even of before and after) lose their meaning. It is on such short distance scales that we encounter the fundamental incompatibility between general relativity and quantum mechanics. The notion of a smooth spatial geometry, the central principle of general relativity, is destroyed by the violent fluctuations of the quantum world on short distance scales. On ultramicroscopic scales, the central feature of quantum mechanics – the uncertainty principle – is in direct conflict with the

central feature of general relativity – the smooth geometrical model of space (and space-time).[12]

E-infinity theory has been proven to be successful because of its relationship to the Golden Mean based number system and its subsequent power to predict the actual mass of high energy sub-atomic particles. Cantorian space-time geometry is readily reconciled to the fixed Golden Mean and is now becoming accepted amongst some physicists as the "real geometry" of space-time at a quantum scale. The emergence of these insights, built solidly on golden mathematical proofs, is giving rise to what El Naschie calls "Quantum Golden Field Theory,"[13] where the term "Golden" refers to the primary role of the Golden Ratio as it relates to the fabric of the space-time manifold. According to this theory, a unique feature of the quantum field is the appearance of fractal-like structures in hidden dimensions. Fractal cosmology is both an observational reality and a theoretical concept where fractal properties have been discovered all the way from the shape of galaxies right down to the Planck scale. Both Cantor Sets and the Golden Mean share these unique fractal properties.

The fractal structure of El Naschie's Cantorian space-time manifold is posited as the actual nature of the fabric of space-time at the quantum scale. References are made to the Russian doll as a comparison to these hidden dimensions. Readers would be familiar with the Russian doll that contains another doll inside, with yet another doll inside. This is the fractal principle of self-similarity. According to El Naschie,

> That is why in this manifold there is no clash between internal dimensions and classical dimensions. Looked at from very far it looks like a four dimensional manifold exactly as the space-time of relativity. On closer examination, however, it is a four dimensional manifold surrounding another four dimensional manifold which is again enclosing a further four dimensional manifold and so on ad infinitum. This Russian doll picture is substantiated mathematically by the continuous fraction expansion of the Hausdorff dimension.[14]

Remember that according to El Naschie, Cantorian space-time is a discrete fractal space-time with infinite dimensions. It is identified as "Cantorian" because it has the property of "infinite" dimensions expressed through a fractal. As we might expect, El Naschie arrives at a description of this Cantorian space-time manifold through some rather complex mathematical equations.

As we have seen, the "miracle" of this new model is that it provides an accurate prediction of the mass of elementary high energy particles based upon the Golden Mean. El Naschie claims that his analysis, in cooperation with the insights of other theoretical physicists, "constitutes the first mathematical derivation of the exact dimensions of space-time starting from basic principles. In this derivation our Golden Mean Hausdorff dimension Cantor Set played the role of the elementary particle of space-time."[15]

There appears to be compelling evidence that El Naschie has actually broken through into a fresh scientific paradigm for understanding the true nature of the quantum space-time manifold. His description of E-infinity theory has been hailed as an extraordinary breakthrough by many other physicists who see tremendous merit in the concept of the fractal nature of space as the source of the force of gravity.

According to Susie Vrobel, director of the Institute for Fractal Research, "El Naschie's Cantorian space-time is a fractal structure inherent in space-time itself. It is based on a Cantorian geometry. Among many other physical phenomena, Young's double-slit experiment may be re-interpreted by the Cantorian space-time model by assuming that the wave interference is a result of the geodesic waves of space-time itself." Vrobel explains that "El Naschie's E-infinity – a discrete hierarchical fractal space-time with infinite dimensions – allows for the description of both relativity and quantum particle physics."[16] According to El Naschie the interference pattern of quantum particles in the famous double-slit experiment can be resolved through this new understanding of Cantorian space-time with its unique geometry. El Naschie explains:

> Through my work on E-infinity theory, I realized that, in a space-time manifold which is infinite-dimensional, a dimensional fractal is possible in "fractal land." The extra dimensions are the logical loop holes. For instance, in two dimensions, by putting both our hands on a table, it is impossible, no matter how hard we try, to bring our left and right hands to be congruent. However, by turning one hand in the extra third dimension, we can rotate it and bring it to exactly cover the other hand on the table. This magic can be continued in E-infinity, in a manner of speaking, indefinitely, so that in E-infinity space-time, we can do infinitely many more

things that we cannot do in the 3 + 1 Euclidean space-time of our daily experience.

Thus, I started constructing a space based on the two-slit experiment, which is infinite-dimensional in the fractal self-similar hierarchal sense, when observed with quantum mechanical high resolution. However, at our low resolution, low-energy scale of classical mechanics, the very same space-time manifold looks like an ordinary 3 + 1 = 4 dimensional space-time. Proceeding in this way, we found that the space of E-infinity theory which is an infinite dimensional but hierarchal fractal called a Cantor Set, may be modelled by a classical geometrical structure called "K3 manifold," provided this manifold is made fuzzy. The mathematical theory of fuzzy sets is highly developed and used extensively in many practical and engineering problems. Fractal geometry is, by its very nature, fuzzy, and that is how we were able to give K3 – which is used in string theory for other purposes – a fuzzy outlook. Proceeding in this way, we did not only give a geometrical topological rational explanation for the two-slit experiment, but were also able to determine the particle content of this space-time manifold.[17]

Professor Gerardo Iovane agrees that El Naschie's E-infinity theory solves the wave/particle duality problem presented in the double-slit experiment:

We are going to show the link between the E-infinity Cantorian space and the Hilbert spaces. In particular, El Naschie's E-infinity is a physical space-time, i.e., an infinite dimensional fractal space, where time is spacialized and the transfinite nature manifests itself. El Naschie's Cantorian space-time is an arena where the physics laws appear at each scale in a self-similar way linked to the resolution of the act of observation. By contrast the Hilbert space is a mathematical support, which describes the interaction between the observer and the dynamical system under measurement. The present formulation, which is based on the non-classical Cantorian geometry and topology of space-time, automatically solves the paradoxical outcome of the two-slit experiment and the so-called particle-wave duality. In particular, measurement (i.e., the observation) is equivalent to a projection of E-infinity in the Hilbert space built on 3 + 1 Euclidean space-time. Consequently, the wave-particle duality becomes a mere natural consequence of conducting an experiment in a space-time with non-classical topological and geometrical structures, while observing and taking measurements in a classical smooth $3 + 1$ Euclidean space-time. In other words, the experimental fact that a wave-particle duality exists is an indirect confirmation of the existence of E-infinity and a property of the quantum-classical interface.[18]

Carlos E. Castro, Ph.D., is a colleague of El Naschie's and is also an advocate of E-infinity theory. Castro agrees that E-infinity theory solves the mystery of the wave/particle duality. "A straightforward explanation of Young's two-slit experiment of a quantum particle is obtained within the framework of the Noncommutative Geometric associated with El Naschie's Cantorian-Fractal transfinite space-time continuum."[19] The mystery of a single quantum particle traversing the two slits at once and creating its own interference pattern has perplexed quantum physicists because it implies "the coexistence of a point particle at two separate spatial locations."[20] This was the initial discovery that defied classical Newtonian physics and set in motion the development of the emerging science of quantum physics.

Following the lead of string theorists, E-infinity theorists invoke the existence of other dimensions enfolded within the customary four dimensions of space and time. The invocation of these other dimensions means "a 'point' within E-infinity can in a sense occupy two different locations at the same time."[21] El Naschie's golden mathematics delivers mathematical proofs that vindicate his formula and they are all solidly based on the Golden Mean. According to Castro, "El Naschie considered from the start the backbone random Cantor Set, whose dimensionality with probability one equals the Golden Mean: $\phi = (\sqrt{5} - 1)/2$."[22] Because the mathematical formulas deliver accurate outcomes, it raises the obvious question: "Is this all nothing but a numerical coincidence or design that we live in $4 + \phi^3$? And that $4 + \phi^3$ is also the average dimension of the Cantorian-Fractal space-time E-infinity!"[23]

El Naschie is an extremely progressive thinker who exhibits an ability to think outside traditional scientific paradigms to achieve new scientific breakthroughs. For the purpose of our study the most important thing to note is the innovation of El Naschie's use of the Golden Mean to pioneer new insights into the fabric of the cosmos. The Golden Mean appears to fractalise all the way through nature from the structure of spiral galaxies down to the smallest possible Planck scale. In a groundbreaking scientific paper titled "A

Universal Scaling Law for all Organised Matter" we read, "It is both appropriate and significant that the so-called 'golden ratio' is reflected in our scaling law (which maps energy dynamics at all scales), since it is prominently found everywhere in nature."[24]

It would appear that we live in a golden universe where nature's numbers exhibit a fractal pattern everywhere we care to look. El Naschie appreciates this fact and he has adventurously postulated a new and innovative theory based upon the certainty of the Golden Mean as a universal mathematical constant. His adventures seem to be paying off in many ways, as he is able to prove mathematically that the use of the Golden ratio is indeed a powerful new tool for interpreting the amazing world that we live in, especially at a quantum scale.

What does all of this imply for the construction of the fabric of the cosmos at the quantum scale? It would suggest that the mind of God has crafted the quantum building blocks of matter on an explicit Golden Mean based number system where this extraordinary mathematical signature progresses from the unfathomably ultramicroscopic scale all the way up to whatever scale we choose to consider. In addition to this, the mass of elementary high energy particles and their coupling constants are further derivations of Golden Mean mathematics.

All of this really does suggest that the sub-atomic quantum world is a glorious symphony of Golden Mean numbers and equations and El Naschie is indeed justified in calling it a "Quantum Golden Field Theory!" When all of the attributes of the Golden Mean within the quantum field are pieced together, it builds a composite picture of an intricately fine-tuned model of the atom that exists in an alternative space-time with attributes and qualities that explain the fundamental mystery of the double-slit experiment.

As with all scientific theories, time will tell whether El Naschie's innovative fractal space-time theory will be widely accepted in the scientific community. However the ubiquity of the Golden Mean throughout the whole of nature strengthens the probability that once again this curious mathematical number could in fact play a strategic role in the mathematical description of the very fabric of the cosmos. From all of these new scientific discoveries we conclude that ϕ really is the divine number!

Bibliography

Aczel, Amir (2002) *Entanglement: The Greatest Mystery in Physics* New York, John Wiley & Sons

Al Khalili, Jim (2004) *Quantum: A Guide for the Perplexed* WN Publishers

Arntz, William, Chasse, Betsy and Vincente, Mark (2005) *What the Bleep Do We Know?* HCI Publishers

Barrow, John D. (2002) *The Constants of Nature: From Alpha to Omega – The Numbers That Encode the Deepest Secrets of the Universe* Vintage Books

Bohm, David (1980) *Wholeness and the Implicate Order* London, Routledge & Kegan Paul Books

Bohr, Niels (1958) *Atomic Physics and Human Knowledge* New York (Edited by John Wiley and Sons)

Braden, Gregg (2009) *The Spontaneous Healing of Belief* Carlsbad, California Hay House

Capra, Fritjof (1975) *The Tao of Physics: An Exploration of the Parallels Between Modern Physics and Eastern Mysticism* Berkeley, California, Shambhala Publications

Chester, Marvin (1987) *Primer on Quantum Mechanics* New York, John Wiley & Sons

Clarke, John James (1997) *Oriental Enlightenment: The Encounter between Asian and Western Thought* London, Routledge & Kegan Paul Books

Clegg, Brian (2006) *The God Effect: Quantum Entanglement, Science's Strangest Phenomenon* New York, St. Martins Press

Davies, Paul (1984) *God and the New Physics* New York, Simon and Schuster

Davies, Paul (1984) *Superforce* New York, Simon & Schuster

Davies, Paul (1988) *The Cosmic Blueprint* New York, HarperCollins Publishers

Davies, Paul (1995) *About Time: Einstein's Unfinished Revolution* New York, Simon & Schuster

Davies, Paul and Gribbin, John (2007) *The Matter Myth: Dramatic Discoveries that Challenge Our Understanding of Physical Reality* New York, Simon & Schuster

Davis, John Jefferson (2002) *The Frontiers of Science and Faith* Downers Grove, Illinois, InterVarsity Press

Denton, Michael (1986) *Evolution; A Theory in Crisis* Adler & Adler Publishers

Dubay, Thomas (1999) *The Evidential Power of Beauty* San Francisco, Ignatius Press

Edwards, Jonathan (2000) *The Life and Diary of David Brainerd* Sovereign Grace Publishers

Ferguson, Marilyn (1987) *The Aquarian Conspiracy* Los Angeles, J.P. Tarcher

Feynman, Richard (1985) *QED: The Strange Theory of Light and Matter* Princeton University Press

Feynman, Richard (2005) *Six Easy Pieces: The Fundamentals of Physics Explained* New York, Basic Books

Feynman, Richard P. (2001) *The Character of Physical Law* Cambridge Massachusetts, MIT Press

Finney, Charles (1977) *The Autobiography of Charles Finney* Minnesota, Bethany House

Frodsham, Stanley (1948) *Smith Wigglesworth: Apostle of Faith* Gospel Publishing

Gitt, Werner (2000) *In the Beginning Was Information* Christliche Literatur-Verbreitung, Germany

Gordon, Jon W (2003) *The Science and Ethics of Engineering the Human Germ Line: Mendel's Maze* New York, Wiley – Liss/John Wiley & Sons

Goswami, Amit (1993) *The Self-Aware Universe: How Consciousness Creates the Material World* Los Angeles, J.P. Tarcher

Goswami, Amit (2008) *God is not Dead: What Quantum Physics Tells Us About Our Origins and How We Should Live* Charlottesville, Virginia, Hampton Roads Publishing Company

Greene, Brian (1999) *The Elegant Universe* New York, W.W. Norton & Co.

Greene, Brian (2005 *The Fabric of the Cosmos* Vintage Books

Gribbin, John (1996) *Schrodinger's Kittens: In Search of Reality* Phoenix Books/Orion Publishing

Hawking, Stephen (2007) *God Created the Integers* New York, Running Press

Heil, John Paul (2001) *The Transfiguration of Jesus* Biblical Institute Press

Heisenberg, Werner (1958) *The Physicist's Conception of Nature* Hutchinson Press

Heisenberg, Werner (1959) *Physics and Philosophy: The Revolution in Modern Science* New York, Harper and Brothers Publishers

Heisenberg, Werner (1971) *Physics and Beyond* New York, HarperCollins Publishers

Herbert, Nick (1987) *Quantum Reality: Beyond the New Physics* New York, Anchor Books

Herrick, J.A. (2003) *The Making of the New Spirituality* Downers Grove II InterVarsity Press

Jastrow, Robert (1978) *God and the Astronomers* New York, W.W. Norton

Johnson, Bill (2005) *When Heaven Invades Earth* Destiny Image

Lewis, C.S (1977) *The Magician's Nephew* New York, Collier Books

Lindsay, Gordon (1972) *Charles Finney: Prince of Evangelists* Christ for the Nations Publishers

Livio, Mario (2003) *The Golden Ratio: The Story of PHI, the World's Most Astonishing Number* New York, Broadway Books/Random House

Lloyd, Seth (2007) *Programming the Universe* Vintage Books

Lucas, Ernest (1996) *Science and the New Age Challenge* Leicester England IVP

McAlister, Del Marie *Activating the Anointing* (unpublished manuscript)

Nadeau, Robert and Kafatos, Menas (2001) *The Non-Local Universe: The New Physics and Matters of the Mind* New York, Oxford University Press

Olsen, Scott (2006) *The Golden Section: Nature's Greatest Secret* Wooden Books, Walker and Co.

Oppenheimer, J.R. (1954) *Science and the Common Understanding* New York, Simon and Schuster

Peacocke, Arthur (1993) *Theology for a Scientific Age* Minneapolis Minnesota, Augsburg Fortress Publishers

Penrose, Roger (1990) *The Emperor's New Mind: Concerning Computers, Minds, and the Laws of Physics* Oxford University Press

Polkinghorne, John (1987) *One World: The Interaction of Science and Theology* West Conshohocken PA, SPCK/Princeton University Press

Polkinghorne, John (2002) *Quantum Theory: A Very Short Introduction*. London, Oxford University Press

Pratney, Winkie (1994) *Revival: Its Principles and Personalities* Huntington House Publishers

Prentice Hall Science Explorer (2002) Upper Saddle River, New Jersey, Prentice-Hall

R.J. Russell, Nancy Murphy and Arthur Peacocke (Editors) (1995) *Chaos and Complexity* Vatican Observatory Press

Restak, Richard M. *(1996) Brainscapes: An Introduction to What Neuroscience Has Learned About the Structure, Function, and Abilities of the Brain* Hyperion Books

Ross, Hugh: (2001) *The Creator and the Cosmos* (3rd Edition) NavPress

Russell, Bertrand (1918) "The Study of Mathematics," in *Mysticism and Logic, and Other Essays*, London: Longmans, Green

Schafer, Lothar (1997) *In Search of Divine Reality* University of Arkansas Press

Schrödinger, Erwin: (1983) *My View of the World*. Woodbridge CT, Ox Bow Press

Schroeder, Gerald (2001) *The Hidden Face of God* New York, Free Press

Seife, Charles (2007) *Decoding the Universe: How the New Science of Information Is Explaining Everything in the Cosmos* London, Penguin Books

Sithole, Surprise: *Rush Hour* (2008) Columbia, North Carolina MOW Books

Sorge, Bob Glory (2000) *When Heaven Invades Earth* Oasis House

Stenger, Victor "The Pseudophysics of Therapeutic Touch." In *Therapeutic Touch* (2000) Edited by Bela Scheiber and Carla Selby Amherst, New York, Prometheus Books

Stewart, Ian (1995) *Nature's Numbers: The Unreal Reality of Mathematics* New York, Basic Books

Storms, Sam (2004) *One Thing: Developing a Passion for the Beauty of God* Christian Focus Publications

Talbot, Michael (1981) *Mysticism and the New Physics* London, Routledge & Kegan Paul

Tipler, Frank J. (2007) *The Physics of Christianity* New York, Doubleday

Welchel, Tommy (2006) *They Told Me Their Stories* Dare2Dream Books, Oklahoma

Wheeler, J. A. (1998) *Geons, Black Holes, and Quantum Foam: A Life in Physics* New York: W.W. Norton & Co.

Wilbur, Ken (2001) *Quantum Questions: Mystical Writings of the World's Greatest Physicists* 2nd Edition, Boston MA Shambhala Publications

Wolf, Fred Alan (1996) *The Spiritual Universe: One Physicist's Vision of Spirit, Soul, Matter, and Self* New York, Simon and Schuster

Zukav, Gary (1979) *The Dancing Wu Li Masters: An Overview of the New Physics* New York, HarperCollins

SCIENTIFIC PAPERS

Carlos Castro: *Noncommutative Geometry, Negative Probabilities and Cantorian-Fractal Space-Time* July 2000 See: Chaos Solitons Fractals Vol. 12 p. 101-104

El Naschie, M.S: *A Review of E Infinity Theory and the Mass Spectrum of High Energy Particle Physics* Chaos, Solitons and Fractals. Vol. 19

El Naschie, M.S: *An Outline for a Quantum Golden Field Theory* Chaos, Solitons and Fractals. Vol. 37

El Naschie, M.S: *Asymptotic Freedom and Unification in a Golden Quantum Field Theory* Chaos, Solitons and Fractals Vol. 36

El Naschie, M.S: *Dimensional Symmetry Breaking and Gravity in Cantorian Space* Chaos, Solitons and Fractals, Vol. 8 p. 753-759.

El Naschie, M.S: *Hilbert Space, Poincare´ Dodecahedron and Golden Mean Transfiniteness* Chaos, Solitons and Fractals Vol. 31 p. 789

El Naschie, M.S: *The Idealized Quantum Two-Slit Experiment Revisited* Chaos, Solitons and Fractals Vol. 27 843–849

El Naschie, M.S: *The Theory of Cantorian Space-time and High Energy Particle Physics* Chaos, Solitons and Fractals Vol. 41

El Naschie, M.S: *The Theory of Cantorian Space-Time and High Energy Particle Physics* Chaos, Solitons and Fractals Vol. 41 p. 2635–2646

El Naschie, M.S: *Towards a Quantum Golden Field Theory* in International Journal of Non-linear Sciences and Numerical Simulation' 2007, Vol. 8; Number 4, p. 477-482

Feynman, Richard P. *Simulating Physics with Computers* in The International Journal of Theoretical Physics Vol. 21

Haramein, Nassim; Hyson, Michael; Rauscher, E. A: *Scale Unification – A Universal Scaling Law for Organised Matter*

Iovane, G Cantorian *Space-Time and Hilbert Space: Part I – Foundations* Chaos, Solitons and Fractals Vol. 28 p. 858

Kraft, Roger L. *A Golden Cantor Set* The American Mathematical Monthly, Vol. 105, No. 8 (Oct., 1998), p. 718-725.

Marek-Crnjac, L. *A Short History of Fractal-Cantorian Space-Time* Chaos, Solitons and Fractals Vol. 41 p. 2697–2705

Rakočević, Miloje M. *The Genetic Code as a Golden Mean Determined System* In Biosystems Vol. 46, p. 283-291.

Stakhov, Alexey *Fundamentals of a New Kind of Mathematics* Chaos, Solitons and Fractals.' Vol. 27

Vrobel, Susie *Fractal Time, Observer Perspectives and Levels of Description in Nature* In: Electronic Journal of Theoretical Physics (EJTP) Special Issue 2007.

Weiss, Harald and Weiss, Wolkmar *The Golden Mean as Clock Cycle of Brain Waves* Chaos, Solitons & Fractals Vol. 18

Yang, Chi Ming *On the 28-Gon Symmetry Inherent in the Genetic Code Intertwined with Aminoacyl-tRNA Synthetases – The Lucas Series* in Bulletin of Mathematical Biology (2004) Vol. 66, p. 1241–1257

Yang, Chi Ming *Towards Understanding How the Genetic Code Is Intertwined with Aminoacyl-tRNA Synthetases*

Endnotes

CHAPTER ONE – THE HIJACKING OF QUANTUM PHYSICS

[1] Robert Nadeau and Menas Kafatos: "The Non-Local Universe: The New Physics and Matters of the Mind." p.viii

[2] Paul Davies: "God and the New Physics." Preface

[3] Ibid

[4] Hermann Bondi quoted in "God and the New Physics."

[5] http://richarddawkins.net/article,804,Snake-Oil-and-Holy-Water,Richard-Dawkins-FORBES-ASAP--October-4-1999

[6] "One World: The Interaction of Science and Theology." p. 115-116

[7] "The Physics of Christianity" Frank J. Tipler p.130-131

[8] Ken Wilbur: Quantum Questions: Mystical Writings of the World's Greatest Physicists. p. ix

[9] Einstein quoted in Wilbur. p.105

[10] Ibid. p. 104

[11] Niels Bohr: Atomic Physics and Human Knowledge p. 20

[12] Werner Heisenberg: Physics and Philosophy 1959 p. 173

[13] Ibid

[14] Quantum Questions op.cit. p. 32

[15] http://en.wikipedia.org/wiki/Buddhism_and_science

[16] Erwin Schrodinger: "My View of the World"

[17] Quoted in Quantum Questions op.cit. p.77

[18] John James Clarke: Oriental Enlightenment: The Encounter Between Asian and Western Thought. p. 168

[19] Ibid

[20] David Bohm: Wholeness and the Implicate Order 1980 quoted in: http://www.spaceandmotion.com/Physics-David-Bohm-Holographic-Universe.htm

[21] Ibid

[22] Ibid p. 19

[23] Ibid.

[24] Oppenheimer quoted in "The Tao of Physics" by Fritjof Capra. p.18

[25] J. R. Oppenheimer; "Science and the Common Understanding" (Oxford University Press, 1954) pp 8-9

[26] Fritjof Capra: Tao of Physics: An Explanation of the Parallels Between Modern Physics and Eastern Mysticism 1975

[27] http://en.wikipedia.org/wiki/The_Tao_of_Physics

[28] Gary Zukav: "The Dancing Wu Li Masters: An Overview of the New Physics" 1979 p.7

[29] Ibid. p.8

[30] Ibid

[31] http://www.seatofthesoul.com/sp_workshops.html

[32] Wu-Li Masters op.cit. p.331

[33] Shirley Maclaine quoted in J.A. Herrick: "The Making of the New Spirituality." p.96

[34] http://www2.cruzio.com/~quanta/qtantra1.html

[35] http://www.ramtha.com

[36] Marilyn Ferguson: "The Aquarian Conspiracy." p. 146

[37] Pantheism is an Eastern spiritual concept which teaches that "all is God."

[38] Fred Alan Wolf: "The Spiritual Universe." p.95

[39] Ibid. p. 86

[40] Amit Goswami: "The Self-Aware Universe: How Consciousness Creates the Material World." p.11

[41] http://en.wikipedia.org/wiki/Amit_Goswami

[42] www.dalailamafilm.com

[43] http://richarddawkins.net/article,804,Snake-Oil-and-Holy-Water,Richard-Dawkins-FORBES-ASAP--October-4-1999

[44] Victor Stenger: "The Pseudophysics of Therapeutic Touch." In "Therapeutic Touch" Edited by Bela Scheiber and Carla Selby (Prometheus Books 2000)

[45] http://csicop.org/si/9701/quantum-quackery.html

[46] Wilbur: Quantum Questions p.xi

[47] Ernest Lucas: Science and the New Age Challenge. p. 33

[48] Capra, op. cit. p.227

[49] Ibid. p. 226

[50] Zukav, op. cit. p.177

[51] Lucas, op. cit. p.42

[52] Zukav, op. cit. p. 315

[53] Lucas, op. cit. p.47

[54] Michael Talbot: Mysticism and the New Physics. p.42

Chapter Two – Entering the World of the Quantum

[1] Richard Feynman: "Six Easy Pieces: The Fundamentals of Physics Explained." p. 5

[2] Prentice Hall Science Explorer. Upper Saddle River, New Jersey USA: Prentice-Hall, (2002) (Science Textbook), p. 32

[3] http://en.wikipedia.org/wiki/Atom#Size_comparisons

[4] Richard P. Feynman: "Six Easy Pieces: The Fundamentals of Physics Explained." p. 34

[5] Gerald Schroeder: "The Hidden Face of God." p.4

[6] Brian Greene: "The Elegant Universe." p.141

[7] http://www.pbs.org/wgbh/nova/elegant/scale.html

[8] Greene op. cit. p.419

[9] Ibid. p.424

[10] Feynman. op. cit. p.34

[11] For a fascinating discussion of absolute hot see: http://www.pbs.org/wgbh/nova/zero/hot.html

[12] Sam Storms: "One Thing: Developing a Passion for the Beauty of God." p.92

[13] Arthur Peacocke: "God's Interaction with the World" in "Chaos and Complexity" Edited by R.J. Russell, Nancey Murphy and Arthur Peacocke. 1995 p.280

[14] Arthur Peacocke: "Theology for a Scientific Age." 1993 p.121-124

[15] John Jefferson Davis: "The Frontiers of Science and Faith." 2002 p.49

[16] Ibid. p.50

[17] Niels Bohr quoted in Werner Heisenberg: "Physics and Beyond." p.206

[18] Marvin Chester: "Primer on Quantum Mechanics."

[19] Richard P. Feynman: "The Character of Physical Law."

[20] Richard P. Feynman: "Simulating Physics with Computers," in The International Journal of Theoretical Physics. Vol. 21 p.471

[21] Paul Davies and John Gribbin: "The Matter Myth: Dramatic Discoveries that Challenge Our Understanding of Physical Reality." p.14 Simon & Schuster, 2007

[22] Ibid.

[23] John Archibald Wheeler: "The Physicist's Conception of Nature."

[24] Jim Al Khalili: "Quantum: A Guide for the Perplexed." p.12

[25] Ibid p.18-21

[26] "Progress in Religion." A Talk by Freeman Dyson. http://www.edge.org/documents/archive/edge68.html

CHAPTER THREE – TIME AND THE QUANTUM

[1] Brian Greene: The Fabric of the Cosmos. p.206

[2] David Bohm; Wholeness and the Implicate Order 1980 p. xv

[3] http://en.wikipedia.org/wiki/Wheeler's_delayed_choice_experiment

[4] John A. Wheeler quoted in Nadeau and Kafatos: "The Non-Local Universe." p.50

[5] http://www.bottomlayer.com/bottom/basic_delayed_choice.htm

[6] Ibid. p.188-9

[7] Op. Cit. The Non-Local Universe p.50

[8] ibid

[9] John Wheeler quoted in Paul Davies: "About Time: Einstein's Unfinished Revolution." p.178

[10] Ibid p. 178-9

[11] http://thinkexist.com/quotation/the_distinction_between_past-present-and_future/184152.html

[12] Daniel Greenberger quoted in Davies: "About Time." p.163

[13] http://www.bottomlayer.com/bottom/basic_delayed_choice.htm

[14] Ibid

[15] John Gribbin: "Schrodinger's Kittens: In Search of Reality." p.142

[16] http://cosmos.asu.edu/publications/reviews/sci_am_1.pdf

[17] Paul Davies: "About Time: Einstein's Unfinished Revolution" [1995] p.

[18] Ibid

[19] Ibid

[20] http://cosmos.asu.edu/publications/reviews/sci_am_1.pdf

[21] Paul Davies: About Time. p.25

[22] Ibid. p.180-181

23 Op. cit. The Fabric of the Cosmos. p.193

24 Ibid.

25 The "Delayed Choice Quantum Eraser" is an actual experiment that combines aspects of Wheeler's delayed choice experiment with aspects of the quantum eraser experiment. For further details see Greene. p.194-199

26 Fabric of the Cosmos. p.199

27 Quoted in Amir Aczel: "Entanglement: The Greatest Mystery in Physics." p.55

28 Jeane Staune: "On the Edge of Physics." http://www.science-spirit.org/article_detail. php?article_id=14

29 Ibid

30 Amir Aczel: "Entanglement: The Greatest Mystery in Physics." p.250

31 Brian Clegg: "The God Effect: Quantum Entanglement, Science's Strangest Phenomenon." p.1-2

32 Paul Davies: "About Time." p.181

33 http://www.altair.org/Qtunnel.html

34 Jeane Staune op. cit.

35 Paul Davies: "About Time." p.165-166

36 Ibid. p.164

37 http://news.nationalgeographic.com/news/2004/08/0818_040818_teleportation.html

38 http://en.wikipedia.org/wiki/Quantum_teleportation

39 Ibid.

40 Richard Feynman quoted in Robert Nadeau and Menas Kafatos: "The Non-Local Universe." p.41

Chapter Four – Quantum Non-Locality and the Spiritual Realm

1 Robert Nadeau & Menas Kafatos: "The Non Local Universe: The New Physics and Matters of the Mind." p.1

2 From issue 2148 of New Scientist magazine, 22 August 1998, page 27 http://www.newscientist.com/article/mg15921485.300-why-god-plays-dice.html

3 Feynman is quoted in Frank J. Tipler: "The Physics of Christianity." p.6

4 http://www.hedweb.com/manworld.htm#believes

5 http://www.bleepstore.com/store/pc/viewPrd.asp?idcategory=0&idproduct=1764

6 http://www.berkeley.edu/news/media/releases/2001/02/20_physic.html

7 Timothy Ferris: Weirdness Makes Sense. New York Times September 29, 1996 http://query.nytimes.com/gst/fullpage.html?res=9E07E3D9173CF93AA1575AC 0A960958260

8 Op. cit. See http://www.science-spirit.org/article_detail.php?article_id=14

9 Ibid

10 Nick Herbert: Quantum Reality: Beyond the New Physics. p.51-52

11 Raymond Chiao. The Quantum Wave of Faith. http://www.science-spirit.org/article_ detail.php?article_id=15

12 On the Edge of Physics. http://www.science-spirit.org/article_detail.php?article_id=14

13 http://www.plim.org/nonlocal.htm

14 Patricia A. Williams: "Of Mind and Matter." http://www.science-spirit.org/article_detail. php?article_id=436

[15] "The Non-Local Universe: The New Physics and Matters of the Mind." Robert Nadeau and Menas Kafatos. p. viii

[16] Henry Stapp Ph.D. was a colleague of Werner Heisenberg and Wolfgang Pauli.

CHAPTER FIVE – GOD: THE ULTIMATE OBSERVER

[1] Gribbin op. cit. P.142-143

[2] http://www.wie.org/j11/goswami.asp

[3] http://www.wie.org/j11/goswami.asp?page=3

CHAPTER SIX – SUPERNATURAL SOUND WAVES

[1] 21 degrees Celcius.

[2] 1230 kilometres per hour or 344 metres per second.

[3] Or 101.325 Kilopascals in metric measurement.

[4] These patterns can be observed on the Internet by searching for images under the title of "cymatics" or by googling the word "cymatics" or by searching YouTube for "cymatics."

[5] To see this experiment on the Internet search for "Faraday Waves" on YouTube.

[6] There is an extraordinary film clip of a wine glass shattering in extreme slow motion on YouTube.

[7] See "Tacoma Narrows Bridge" on Wikipedia for a film clip of the collapse.

[8] http://www.frank.germano.com/earthquake.htm

[9] Ibid

[10] William Arntz, Betsy Chasse and Mark Vincente: *What the Bleep Do We Know?* p.93

[11] http://web.archive.org/web/20060202105450/www.newageretailer.com/for-retailers/emasaruemoto_web.pdf

[12] http://en.wikipedia.org/wiki/Masaru_Emoto. See also: http://www.altmeduniversity.net/courses3.htm

[13] http://web.archive.org/web/20060202105450/www.newageretailer.com/for-retailers/emasaruemoto_web.pdf

[14] http://www.randi.org/jr/052303.html

[15] http://web.archive.org/web/20060202105450/www.newageretailer.com/for-retailers/emasaruemoto_web.pdf

[16] http://www.life-enthusiast.com/twilight/research_emoto.htm. Emoto has his own eclectic philosophy of life after death, arguing that people come back in the form of water. "In Buddhism, we talk about attaining sattori, or reaching enlightenment. People who attain sattori do not become ghosts. They are able to achieve a certain stage of development at the soul level and return to God for a while before they move on to their next assignment. We travelled here to earth on the water crystals of spheres of ice. Earth is not our native home. So these souls can return to their native homes for awhile. That is sattori, or enlightenment. However, most people on the planet are not able to attain enlightenment. Few souls have been able to go "home" and I believe they have remained on earth in the form of water. This connects into the concept of reincarnation, where these spirits keep falling back to earth and need to redo their lives here." Ibid.

[17] 344 metres per second.

[18] NASB 1995 Version

[19] There is a certain irony in this passage because the next verse in Isaiah 30 says, "Topheth has long been prepared; it has been made ready for the king. Its fire pit has

been made deep and wide, with an abundance of fire and wood; the breath of the Lord, like a stream of burning sulfur, sets it ablaze." (Isaiah 30:33 NIV) The term "Topheth" is a derivation of the Hebrew word "toph" which means "drum." It was a high place outside Jerusalem where the ancient Canaanites sacrificed their children to Molech by burning them alive to the sound of loud drumming to drown out their anguished cries.

CHAPTER SEVEN – STRING THEORY AND THE VOICE OF GOD

[1] www.sns.ias.edu/~witten/papers/string.pdf

[2] Brian Greene: The Elegant Universe. p.143-146

[3] C.S. Lewis: "The Magician's Nephew." Chapter Eight

[4] Ibid. Edited extracts from Chapter Nine

[5] Brian Greene op.cit. p.143

[6] Ibid p.146-147

[7] Molecular Chords: November 16, 2007. http://www.physorg.com/news114440170.html

[8] http://msowww.anu.edu.au/~pfrancis/Music/library/index.html

[9] http://www.nasa.gov/vision/universe/features/halloween_sounds.html

[10] http://www.space.com/scienceastronomy/planetearth/space_symphony_000323.html

[11] http://www.space.com/scienceastronomy/blackhole_note_030909.html

[12] NLT except for the last verse (v.13) which is NKJV.

CHAPTER EIGHT – QUANTUM INFORMATION AND THE MIND OF GOD

[1] http://www.geocities.com/gregorianstudycircle/cosmic_code.html

[2] John Polkinghorne: "Quantum Theory: A Very Short Introduction." p. xi. (Oxford University Press 2002)

[3] http://goldennumber.net/life.htm

[4] Werner Gitt: "In the Beginning Was Information." p.178

[5] Jon W. Gordon: "The Science and Ethics of Engineering the Human Germ Line: Mendel's Maze." p.22

[6] Ibid.

[7] Michael Denton. Evolution: A Theory in Crisis. p.330

[8] Brainscapes. p.41

[9] Evolution: A Theory in Crisis. p. 330-331

[10] Gregg Braden: "The Spontaneous Healing of Belief." p.17

[11] Zuse quoted in Braden. Ibid

[12] John Archibald Wheeler [in Braden. p.21]

[13] J.A. Wheeler: "Geons, Black Holes, and Quantum Foam: A Life in Physics" (1998). p.340. New York: W.W. Norton & Co.

[14] Braden. op.cit. p. 20

[15] Ibid. p.24

[16] http://www.wired.com/wired/archive/14.03/play.html?pg=4

[17] Seth Lloyd: "Programming the Universe" chapter 1 http://www.randomhouse.com/kvpa/lloyd/excerpts.html

[18] Seth Lloyd: "Programming the Universe."

19 http://goldennumber.net/life.htm

20 Stephen Hawking: "God Created the Integers."

21 http://www.halexandria.org/dward010.htm

22 Michael Denton: "Evolution: A Theory in Crisis." p.328-329

23 Max Planck: "The Nature of Matter." From a speech given at Florence, Italy in 1944

24 http://comp.uark.edu/~schafer/epilogue.html

25 Lothar Schafer quoted in "Sacred Mathematics."

26 Ibid

27 Ibid

28 Lothar Schafer: "In Search of Divine Reality." p.28

29 Charles Seife: "Decoding the Universe: How the New Science of Information is Explaining Everything in the Cosmos." p.242

30 Ibid. Eddington [1882-1944] quoted in the preface of Schafer: "In Search of Divine Reality."

31 Lothar Schafer: "In Search of Divine Reality." p.112 See also http://comp.uark.edu/~schafer/epilogue.html

32 Lothar Schafer: "The Emergence of Consciousness in Biological Evolution and Quantum Reality." http://www.paseoart.com/skipsilver/ziusudra/lothar/essay.html

33 http://en.wikipedia.org/wiki/Mathematical_beauty#cite_note-0

34 Albert Einstein Quotes on Spirituality. http://www.simpletoremember.com/vitals/einstein.htm

35 Roger Penrose: "The Emperor's New Mind: Concerning Computers, Minds, and the Laws of Physics." p.112

36 Quoted in "The Evidential Power of Beauty." p.131

37 Fred Hoyle: "The Universe." p.16

38 Paul Davies: "The Cosmic Blueprint." 1988 p.203

39 Ian Stewart: "Nature's Numbers: The Unreal Reality of Mathematics." p.3,6

40 John D. Barrow: "The Constants of Nature: From Alpha to Omega – The Numbers That Encode the Deepest Secrets of the Universe." p.3

41 Hugh Ross: The Creator and the Cosmos. p.153

42 Paul Davies: "Superforce." p.243

43 Richard Feynman: "QED: The Strange Theory of Light and Matter," Princeton University Press 1985, p.129.

44 Professor Hugh Ross: "The Creator and the Cosmos." (3rd Edition 2001) p.146

45 Ibid. p.146-147

46 The Creator and the Cosmos. p.151

47 Ibid. p.160

48 Ibid. p.157

49 Paul Davies: "Superforce." (1984) p.243

50 Robert Jastrow; "God and the Astronomers" (New York: W. W. Norton, 1978), p.116.

51 The Creator and the Cosmos. p.160

52 Quoted in Livio. p.243

53 http://en.wikipedia.org/wiki/Paul_Erdos

54 The first digit, "1" occurs 2,694 times. "2" occurs 859 times. "3" occurs 495 times. "4" occurs 322 times.

[55] Basic fractions are commonly referred to throughout the Bible, in particular halves, thirds, quarters, fifths and tenths [which is usually called the "tithe." Ma'aser in Hebrew = one tenth].

[56] This will be more clearly explained in the next chapter.

[57] Quoted in Ross: "The Creator and the Cosmos." p.159

[58] Gerald Schroeder: "The Hidden Face of God" p. 4

[59] Ibid. p.8

[60] Nick Herbert: "Quantum Reality." p.159

[61] Schroeder. op. cit. p.7

CHAPTER NINE – GOLDEN PHYSICS AND QUANTUM GEOMETRY

[1] Bertrand Russell: The Study of Mathematics, in Mysticism and Logic, and Other Essays, Chapter 4, London: Longmans, Green, 1918.

[2] Mario Livio: "The Golden Ratio." p.241

[3] Ibid. p.246

[4] Scott Olsen: "The Golden Section: Nature's Greatest Secret." p.10

[5] There are 66 books in the Bible, 39 in the O.T. and 27 in the N.T. This is a 3:5 golden ratio.

[6] 1 stadia = 185 metres

[7] Olsen op.cit. p. 34

[8] Gematria is the Greek word for "geometry" and is the science of deriving numbers from the Hebrew alphabet. Isopsephy is the adoption of the principle of Gematria for the Greek language.

[9] Jesus = Ιησους = 10 + 8 + 200 + 70 + 400 + 200 = 888.

[10] Christ = Χριστός = 600 + 100 + 10 + 200 + 300 + 70 + 200 = 1,480.

[11] Olsen, op. cit. p.34

[12] Ibid. p. 26

[13] Quoted in Olsen. p.56

[14] http://goldennumber.net/life.htm

[15] http://www.mi.sanu.ac.yu/vismath/stakhov2008a/index.html

[16] Feynman quoted in: Alexey Stakhov and Boris Rozin: "The Golden Section, Fibonacci Series and New Hyperbolic Models of Nature." http://www.mi.sanu.ac.yu/vismath/stakhov/index.html

[17] Ibid.

[18] Ibid.

[19] http://www.geocities.com/gregorianstudycircle/cosmic_code.html

[20] Greene. Op.cit. p. 419

[21] http://dgleahy.com/dgl/p.30.html S. B. Hoath does the same thing with Planck time and Planck mass. "Planck length $l_P = \varphi \times 10\text{-}35$, Planck time $t_P = \varphi 3.5 \times 10\text{-}44$, and Planck mass $m_P = \varphi\varphi \times 10\text{-}8$."

[22] Olsen. Op. cit. p.57

[23] Ibid

[24] Professor M.S. El Naschie: "A Review of E Infinity Theory and the Mass Spectrum of High Energy Particle Physics" in Chaos, Solitons and Fractals. Vol. 19. p.220

[25] See also D.G. Leahy: *The Physical Constants: Functions of the Golden Bowl Arrangements on the φ-Level of Existence Itself*. See: http://dgleahy.com/dgl/p13.html

[26] Ibid. p.234-235

[27] El Naschie quoted in Olsen: Ibid.

[28] Ibid.

[29] El Naschie: "An Outline for a Quantum Golden Field Theory." In "Chaos, Solitons and Fractals." Vol. 37 (2008) p.317

[30] Ibid.

[31] Ibid. p.321

[32] Ibid. p.322

[33] Ibid.

[34] Ibid.

[35] Ibid. p.318

[36] Ibid. p.319

[37] M.S. El Naschie: "Asymptotic Freedom and Unification in a Golden Quantum Field Theory." Chaos, Solitons and Fractals." Volume 36 (2008) p.522-523

[38] Alexey Stakhov: "Fundamentals of a New Kind of Mathematics." Chaos, Solitons and Fractals. Volume 27 (2006) p.1137

[39] http://www.jstor.org/pss/3029218

[40] http://www.mi.sanu.ac.yu/vismath/stakhov2008a/index.html

[41] Ibid. p.18

[42] Ibid.

[43] Ibid. p.44

[44] http://www.mcs.surrey.ac.uk/Personal/R.Knott/Fibonacci/phi3DGeom.html

[45] Ibid. p.10

[46] Ibid.

[47] http://goldennumber.net/dna.htm

[48] Professor Miloje M. Rakočević: titled "The Genetic Code as a Golden Mean Determined System." In Biosystems. 46, pp.283-291. The "Farey Tree" is a mathematical algorithm based on a Fibonacci sequence.

[49] Chi Ming Yang: "On the 28-Gon Symmetry Inherent in the Genetic Code Intertwined with Aminoacyl-tRNA Synthetases – TheLucas Series" Bulletin of Mathematical Biology (2004) 66, 1241–1257

[50] Chi Ming Yang, Ph.D. "Towards Understanding how the Genetic Code is Intertwined with Aminoacyl-tRNA Synthetases." Scott Olsen explains the Lucas number series: "In addition to the Fibonacci numbers, nature occasionally uses another series... Lucas numbers (2, 1, 3, 4, 7, 11, 18, 29, 47, 76, 123, 199...) are similar to Fibonacci numbers in that they are additive (each new number is the sum of the previous two numbers) and multiplicative (each new number approximates the previous number multiplied by the modular ϕ. What is fascinating about the Lucas numbers is that they are formed by alternately adding and subtracting the golden powers of ϕ and its reciprocal $1/\phi$. These are not approximations but absolutely exact!" Olsen op.cit. p.16

[51] http://www.blobs.org/science/article.php?article=2#3

[52] Scott Olsen op. cit. p.20

[53] Ibid

[54] See www.goldenmeangauge.co.uk

55 http://goldennumber.net/body.htm

56 Olsen op. cit.

57 Seth Lloyd: "Programming the Universe" p.3 See also: http://www.randomhouse.com/kvpa/lloyd/excerpts.html

58 Chaos, Solitons & Fractals 18 (2003), Harald Weiss and Wolkmar Weiss http://www.volkmar-weiss.de/chaos.html

59 http://eperdidas.wordpress.com/2007/11/19/the-golden-mean-as-a-clock-cycle-for-brainwaves/

60 http://www.cs4fn.org/programming/shelovesme.php

61 http://www.geocities.com/gregorianstudycircle/cosmic_code.html

62 Ibid. Eddington [1882-1944] quoted in the preface of Schafer: "In Search of Divine Reality."

63 Ibid. p.109

64 Ibid. p.111 Shafer's entire Epilogue can be read online at http://comp.uark.edu/~schafer/epilogue.html

65 Ibid. p.109

66 Ibid. p.112

CHAPTER TEN – QUANTUM PHYSICS AND THE SUPERNATURAL

1 NIV and NLT. We have already seen how Ezekiel 28 reveals the fall of Lucifer. Combined with Isaiah 14, these two passages of Scripture are describing the King of Tyre and the King of Babylon, respectively, but they function on two levels. On both occasions the prophet likens these two proud and ungodly kings to Satan who fell from a lofty and exalted position. The language and imagery exceeds that of earthly kings. It is as though the Lord is saying to these two earthly kings that their pride and arrogance reminds him of the fall of Lucifer in the beginning.

2 Thomas Dubay: "The Evidential Power of Beauty." p.83-84

3 Verse 18 quoted from NKJV. Verse 19 quoted from the NIV.

CHAPTER ELEVEN – JESUS' KEY TO QUANTUM MIRACLES

1 James Moffatt. 1926

2 Rolland Baker wrote the foreword to Surprise Sithole's book *Rush Hour*, which catalogues the many visions and trips to heaven that characterise the life of this extraordinary man. Surprise Sithole: *Rush Hour* p.v, vi

CHAPTER TWELVE – QUANTUM PHYSICS AND THE GLORY OF GOD

1 Tommy Welchel: *They Told Me Their Stories* p. 49-50 (2006) Dare2Dream Books, Oklahoma

2 Ibid. p.66

3 Ibid. p.37-38

4 Ibid. p.50

5 http://en.wikipedia.org/wiki/Lux

6 0° C

7 100° C

[8] -210° C

[9] -195.79° C

[10] Bob Sorge: *Glory: When Heaven Invades Earth*. P.56-58

[11] Ibid. p.58

[12] Ibid. p.68-69

CHAPTER THIRTEEN – MINISTERING OUT OF THE GLORY CLOUD

[1] Luke 4:18 quoted from NKJV. Luke 4:19 quoted from NIV.

[2] Bill Johnson: *When Heaven Invades Earth* p.134

[3] Del Marie McAlister: *Activating the Anointing* p.23

[4] "Dove" in ISBE Vol. 1 p.988 [emphasis added]

[5] John Paul Heil: *The Transfiguration of Jesus*. p.130-131 Google Books

[6] http://eternalword.wordpress.com/2006/11/20/living-under-an-open-heaven-patricia-king-2/

CHAPTER FOURTEEN – SCIENTIA GLORIAM: THE KNOWLEDGE OF THE GLORY

[1] The reason I have quoted from the J. B. Phillips Translation for this verse is because of the curious Greek sentence structure which Phillips uniquely captures in his translation. Phillips makes only five notes on the entire New Testament and one of them concerns this passage. He says, "There is a very curious Greek construction here, viz, a simple future followed by a perfect participle passive. The force of these sayings is that Jesus' true disciples will be so led by the Spirit that they will be following the heavenly pattern. In other words, what they 'forbid' or 'permit' on earth will be consonant with the divine rules." [In other words: on earth as it is in heaven!] J. B. Phillips: *The New Testament in Modern English* p. 552. The only other translation of the New Testament that I have personally found that includes the correct syntax is Dr. Kenneth Wuest's *New Testament: An Expanded Translation*. Wuest was a Professor of New Testament and a noted Greek scholar. He translates this passage as follows: "I shall give to you the keys of the kingdom of heaven; and whatever you bind on earth [forbid to be done], shall have been already bound [forbidden to be done] in heaven; and whatever you loose on earth [permit to be done] shall have already been loosed in heaven [permitted to be done]." The clumsy Greek syntax may have contributed to the shabby renderings of almost all other translations of this passage which imply that we bind and loose and heaven merely ratifies our determinations. The strength of the correct translation is that heaven makes the decree and we echo the decree here on earth: in other words: we perform the will of God on earth just as it is done in heaven!

[2] Jonathan Edwards: *The Life and Diary of David Brainerd* pp. 142-143

[3] Finney's Autobiography p.149

[4] "Charles Finney" by Gordon Lindsay p.15-16

[5] Winkie Pratney: *Revival: Its Principles and Personalities*, Huntington House Publishers, 1994 p.25

[6] Finney's Autobiography p.38

[7] Finney's Autobiography p.64-65

[8] Stanley Frodsham, *Smith Wigglesworth, Apostle of Faith*, p.80

[9] Transcript from David Hogan's message at *Growing in the Supernatural 2* conference at Scottsdale, Arizona, August 8, 2007

[10] "History Maker" performed by Delirious, written by Martin Smith ©1996 Curious? Music UK

Chapter Fifteen – Taking Back the High Places

[1] "Some Jews who went around driving out evil spirits tried to invoke the name of the Lord Jesus over those who were demon-possessed. They would say, 'In the name of Jesus, whom Paul preaches, I command you to come out.' Seven sons of Sceva, a Jewish chief priest, were doing this. One day the evil spirit answered them, 'Jesus I know, and I know about Paul, but who are you?' Then the man who had the evil spirit jumped on them and overpowered them all. He gave them such a beating that they ran out of the house naked and bleeding." (Acts 19:13-16 NIV)

[2] Amit Goswami: *God is not Dead,* p.20

[3] Amit Goswami: *The Self Aware Universe: How Consciousness Creates the Material World.* p.2

[4] "Scientific Proof of the Existence of God" http://www.enlightennext.org/magazine/j11/goswami.asp

[5] Ibid

[6] "For thus says the High and Lofty One Who inhabits eternity, whose name is Holy: 'I dwell in the high and holy place with him who has a contrite and humble spirit, to revive the spirit of the humble and to revive the heart of the contrite ones.'" (Isaiah 57:15)

[7] "I am the Alpha and the Omega, the Beginning and the End," says the Lord, "who is and who was and who is to come, the Almighty." (Revelation 1:8)

[8] "Abraham planted a tamarisk tree in Beersheba, and there he called upon the name of the Lord, the Eternal God." (Genesis 21:33 NIV) Paul spoke of "the prophetic writings" that were written "by the command of the Eternal God." (Romans 16:26 NIV)

[9] "You will receive a rich welcome into the eternal kingdom of our Lord Jesus Christ." (2 Peter 1:11 NIV)

[10] "For a child will be born to us, a Son will be given to us; and the government will rest on His shoulders; and His name will be called Wonderful Counsellor, Mighty God, Eternal Father, Prince of Peace." (Isaiah 9:6 NASB) A better rendering of this phrase is *Father of eternity* where the Hebrew word for "father" [*ab*] means "originator." This rendering avoids the
confusion of the "Son" with the Father. It also reveals Jesus as the very "source of eternity!" This resonates with another Messianic prophecy which describes the Eternal Son: "But as for you, Bethlehem Ephrathah, too little to be among the clans of Judah, from you One will go forth for Me to be ruler in Israel. His goings forth are from long ago, from the days of eternity." (Micah 5:2 NASB)

[11] "To Him be glory in the church by Christ Jesus throughout all ages, *world without end.*" (Ephesians 3:21 KJV)

[12] This is where David Bohm was going with his concepts of Implicate and Explicate Order. The explicit order of quantum mechanics points to the implicit order of a deeper platonic dualism; as above, so below!

[13] NIV/NLT. This word "among" has generated considerable debate. The Greek word is "entos." Some Bibles translate it as "The Kingdom of God is within you" whilst others translate it as "The Kingdom of God is among you." Because Jesus is describing the *presence* of the Kingdom, the Greek word "entos," which can be translated as either "within" or "among" is better translated as "among" because that word denotes *presence* which is the obvious theme. It is also highly unlikely that Jesus would say to the Pharisees that the Kingdom of God was "within" them because they were definitely not born again.

[14] "The god of this age has blinded the minds of unbelievers, so that they cannot see the light [*photizo*] of the gospel of the glory of Christ, who is the image of God." (2 Corinthians 4:4) "For it is the God who commanded light [*phos*] to shine out of darkness, who has shone in our hearts to give the light [*photizo*] of the knowledge of the glory of God in the face of Jesus Christ." (2 Corinthians 4:6)

[15] I now rejoice in my sufferings for you, and fill up in my flesh what is lacking in the afflictions of Christ, for the sake of His body, which is the church, (Colossians 1:24)

APPENDIX

[1] See: http://www.mathematicianspictures.com/Mathematicians/Cantor.htm

[2] Roger L. Kraft: *A Golden Cantor Set*. The American Mathematical Monthly, Vol. 105, No. 8 (Oct., 1998), pp. 718-725. See: http://www.jstor.org/pss/2588988

[3] Ibid p. 724

[4] M. S. El Naschie: "The Theory of Cantorian Space-time and High Energy Particle Physics." Chaos, Solitons and Fractals 41 (2009) p. 2636

[5] L. Marek-Crnjac: "A Short History of Fractal-Cantorian Space-Time." Chaos, Solitons and Fractals 41 (2009) 2697–2705

[6] M. S. El Naschie, "Dimensional Symmetry Breaking and Gravity in Cantorian Space." Chaos, Solitons and Fractals, 1997, 8, 753-759.

[7] G. Iovane: "Cantorian Space-time and Hilbert Space: Part I – Foundations." Chaos, Solitons and Fractals 28 (2006) p. 858

[8] Amir Aczel: "Entanglement: The Greatest Mystery in Physics" p. xi-xii

[9] Roger Penrose: "The Emperor's New Mind" p.332

[10] M. S. Naschie: "Hilbert Space, Poincaré Dodecahedron and Golden Mean Transfiniteness" Chaos, Solitons and Fractals 31 (2007) p. 789

[11] M. S. El Naschie: "The Idealized Quantum Two-Slit Experiment Revisited." Chaos, Solitons and Fractals 27 (2006) 843–849

[12] Brian Greene: "The Elegant Universe." p.127-129

[13] M. S. El Naschie: "Towards a Quantum Golden Field Theory" in International Journal of Nonlinear Sciences and Numerical Simulation 2007, Vol. 8; Number 4, pages 477-482

[14] M. S. El Naschie: "The Theory of Cantorian Space-time and High Energy Particle Physics." Chaos, Solitons and Fractals 41 (2009) 2635–2646 p. 2638

[15] Ibid. p. 2640

[16] Susie Vrobel: "Fractal Time, Observer Perspectives and Levels of Description in Nature."

[17] http://esi-topics.com/nhp/2006/september-06-MohamedElNaschie.html

[18] G. Iovane: "Cantorian Space-time and Hilbert Space: Part I – Foundations." Chaos, Solitons and Fractals 28 (2006) p. 857

[19] Carlos Castro: "Noncommutative Geometry, Negative Probabilities and Cantorian-Fractal Space-Time." July 2000 See: http://arxiv.org/abs/hep-th/0007224

[20] Ibid

[21] ibid

[22] Ibid

[23] Ibid. Emphasis mine.

[24] Nassim Haramein, Michael Hyson, E. A. Rauscher: "Scale Unification – A Universal Scaling Law for Organised Matter." http://www.theresonanceproject.org/pdf/scalinglaw_paper.pdf

ADDITIONAL INFORMATION

Additional copies of this book can be purchased from Phil Mason's personal website: www.philmason.org, and from the sites mentioned on page 400. Phil's website also contains a large selection of his unique teaching materials with downloadable MP3s, individual CDs, CD sets and DVDs. PayPal, Master Card and Visa Card facilities are available for safe online transactions. We ship books worldwide. Additional postage and shipping charges apply.

If this book has interested you, you may also be interested in obtaining a two-part DVD series titled, *Quantum Physics and the Glory of God*. These DVDs are a multi-media rich lecture presentation from the Deep End School of the Supernatural. These DVDs distill many of the themes in this book into a visual presentation.

There is also a DVD available on *Sacred Geometry*. This is a multimedia rich presentation from the Deep End School. It is rare to find an exclusively biblical presentation on this subject, because Sacred Geometry has almost exclusively been the domain of the New Age community. The Bible is the only book that provides the interpretive key to unlocking the meaning of the design that New Agers behold in nature. Sacred Geometry as a scientific and spiritual discipline powerfully supports the intelligent design thesis.

NEW EARTH TRIBE

Phil and Maria Mason are the spiritual directors of *New Earth Tribe*: a spiritual community located in Byron Bay, New South Wales, Australia. In November 2010, the "Tribe," as it is affectionately known, celebrated its 12th birthday. Ever since 2006 this community has experienced a sustained outpouring of supernatural ministry that is continually increasing. Byron Bay is world renowned as a centre of New Age spirituality. Finding themselves in the midst of the New Age marketplace, they have developed a passion to penetrate this culture with the supernatural healing power of Christ. As they have pressed into this goal, they have experienced a significant outpouring of healing which has released an ecstatic atmosphere over the community.

Jesus said that, "God's kingdom is like a treasure hidden in a field and then accidentally found." Most people stumble into this treasure and when they truly find it the result is always profoundly life changing. "The finder is *ecstatic* – what a find!" (Matthew 13:44 MSG) The more we live in the atmosphere of the supernatural, the more we are elevated into a state of spiritual ecstasy. And we were made for ecstasy! Whenever Jesus healed the sick, those who witnessed the miracles were astonished and amazed. Jesus called the miracles "signs and wonders." They were tangible signs of the invasion of the Kingdom of Heaven which induced a sense of astonishment, joy and wonder. Revival culture is sustained by a continued outpouring of these signs and wonders much like the community of believers in the book of Acts. The outpouring of the Spirit is always accompanied by an outpouring of authentic joy and ecstasy.

The greatest core values of the Tribe are community and intimacy. We are twelve years into a journey into spiritual community and we are finding more and more that true fulfilment in God is only enjoyed in the context of committed relationships. Any good fruit that has come out of our community is a result of an unswerving commitment to real, accountable friendships that are both loving and truthful. We truly love the power of community and we wholeheartedly preach it as the foundation for lasting revival. Our journey has also seen an explosion of wild worship and unique creativity that has accompanied the outpouring of the supernatural. We are committed to the journey of becoming an authentic "book of Acts" community in the 21st century that turns the world upside down! To find out more about this community please visit our website at: www.newearthtribe.com

DEEP END SCHOOL OF THE SUPERNATURAL

Phil and Maria are also the directors and founders of the *Deep End School of the Supernatural*. The 9-month part-time school founded in 2003 trains people of all ages in the Kingdom ministry of Jesus Christ. One of the unique features of this ministry is the importance placed upon contextualisation. Students are trained to understand New Age/postmodern culture and to develop an intelligent response to the explosion of this culture by developing a model of ministry that takes into account the unique challenges created by the emergence of radical postmodernism with its categorical rejection of absolute truth. Oftentimes Christian ministry in the 21st century lacks this contextualisation of the gospel.

The Deep End School is empowered by a specific ministry philosophy. The shift from the modernist era to the postmodernist era represents a transition away from mere words that describe reality to the subjective experience of reality. We are now living in a "show me" generation rather than a "tell me" generation. As a result, people are fatigued by a "word only" approach to marketing spirituality. They want to see tangible demonstrations of the world we are attempting to describe. We have found that the kingdom ministry of Christ is the key to penetrating the hearts of postmodern seekers. Postmodernists have been awakened to the reality of supernatural power and spiritual experience.

Subsequently the Deep End School trains students to heal the sick, break demonic bondages, heal broken hearts and flow in the prophetic. As an extension of this approach to ministry the school trains its students to release the glory realm of heaven through true supernatural encounters with God that usher people into the ecstasy realm. Postmodern seekers are hungry for authentic spiritual encounters that open up the realm of ecstasy and bliss. That is why they are flocking to New Age practitioners who offer their adherents an experience of supernatural power. New Age/postmodern seekers intentionally bypass expressions of spirituality that cannot deliver an encounter. It is time to give this generation an encounter with the living God that will raise up a generation of ecstatic lovers of Christ.

To find out more about this nine-month school, please visit our website at: www.deependschool.com

THE SUPERNATURAL TRANSFORMATION SERIES

If you have enjoyed reading this book, Phil Mason has also written a four-volume series on the theme of the supernatural transformation of the heart. This series, due for release in late 2011, outlines a Kingdom ministry-based model of personal transformation. God seeks to transform our hearts from the inside out as we embrace the call to a deep heart journey of intimacy with God and with one another in spiritual community. This profound theology of the heart puts in place all the conceptual building blocks for deep personal transformation. It begins with the miracle of the new creation and it unfolds the process of transformation from one degree of glory to another as we allow God to demolish every stronghold of the mind, the will and the emotions so that we can be gloriously transformed into the very image of Christ. The context of this transformation is spiritual community that values genuine supernatural encounter with Christ.

Volume 1: The Knowledge of the Heart

Volume 2: The New Creation Miracle

Volume 3: The Prophetic Ministry of Christ to the Heart

Volume 4: Kingdom Ministry and Personal Transformation

Please visit Phil's website at www.philmason.org for additional information on how to obtain a copy of this series.

Additional copies of this book may be purchased at bookstores and at XPmedia.com

BULK ORDERS

We offer special wholesale discounts to churches, ministries, schools and bookstores. For US wholesale discounts, contact: usaresource@xpmedia.com. For Canadian bulk orders, contact: resource@xpmedia.com.

This book and other books published by XP Publishing are also available to bookstores through Anchor Distributors.

For purchase in Australia and New Zealand, contact: www.philmason.org

www.XPpublishing.com
XP MINISTRIES